SHARING
YERBA MATE

Sharing Yerba Mate

HOW SOUTH AMERICA'S MOST POPULAR DRINK DEFINED A REGION

Rebekah E. Pite

THE UNIVERSITY OF NORTH CAROLINA PRESS

Chapel Hill

Designed by Jamison Cockerham
Set in Arno, Scala, Kilroy, and Archive Roundface Script
by Jamie McKee, MacKey Composition

Cover art: Carlos Enrique Pellegrini (1800–1875),
Cielito, cielo que sí! Ou le guitariste, ca. 1831.

Manufactured in the United States of America

LIBRARY OF CONGRESS CATALOGING-IN-PUBLICATION DATA
Names: Pite, Rebekah E., author.
Title: Sharing yerba mate : how South America's most
popular drink defined a region / Rebekah E. Pite.
Description: Chapel Hill : University of North Carolina Press,
2023. | Includes bibliographical references and index.
Identifiers: LCCN 2023008525 | ISBN 9781469674520 (cloth ; alk. paper) |
ISBN 9781469674537 (paperback ; alk. paper) | ISBN 9781469674544 (ebook)
Subjects: LCSH: Mate (Tea)—South America—History. | Mate (Tea)—Social
aspects—South America. | Mate (Tea) industry—South America—History. |
South America—History. | South America—Social life and customs.
Classification: LCC GT2920.M3 P58 2023 | DDC 394.1/5098—dc23/eng/20230329
LC record available at https://lccn.loc.gov/2023008525

FOR MOM, NANNY, POPPY,
CHRIS, SOFIA, AND ELIJAH

CONTENTS

ILLUSTRATIONS

FIGURES

SHARING
YERBA MATE

CONTEMPORARY SOUTH AMERICA

Source: Created by John H. Clark, Geospatial Services librarian, Lafayette College, Easton, PA, following "Free vector and raster map data [1:10m]: Land, Ocean, Admin–0 Countries, Gray Earth," Natural Earth, 2021, https://www .naturalearthdata.com.

INTRODUCTION

Sharing the South American Drink

I sat in the reading room of Argentina's Archivo General de la Nación—the national archive—scouring finding aids and riffling through dusty boxes of documents. It was June 2001, my first time in Argentina, and I had learned how helpful talking to archivists could be. Toward the end of the week, one of the archivists, Gabriel, asked if I would like to join him and the other archivists for a break. "Claro," of course, I replied.

Gabriel led me back to a small room crammed with desks covered with towering stacks of paper. Three of his colleagues were already there. One held a thermos in his hand. He poured some steamy hot water into a gourd filled with what appeared to be chopped-up, dusky green tea leaves and slurped the liquid through a silver *bombilla* (filtered tube or straw). Then, he refilled the gourd with water and passed it to one of his colleagues. In a few sips, she drained the *mate* (pronounced MAH-teh with an emphasis on the first syllable and spelled in an entertaining variety of ways to convey the pronunciation of the second syllable in English: e.g., maté, matè, matte, matee, matté).[1] It was my turn. Someone explained, "This is a mate. You drink it out of the bombilla, but don't touch it. The water is hot. Be careful."

I cupped the mate in my hands. It was warm to the touch. I brought the bombilla carefully to my lips and took a timid sip, afraid to burn my lips. The liquid was scorching, the flavor intense. Bitter and grassy. I started to hand it back. Gabriel stopped me, "You're supposed to finish it all, and don't be afraid to slurp. That's a compliment to the mate server." I took a few more sips with added gusto and handed it back to the archivist holding the thermos. The round continued as everyone chatted boisterously.

When I returned to the reading room, I felt warm inside, and not just from the hot drink and the buzzy effect of the caffeine. I felt that I had been welcomed into a special club.

Looking back, I can't remember whether I knew about the Indigenous infusion called *yerba mate* (literally, herbs in a cup) before this moment in the archive. But like so many newcomers before me, I started paying more attention to this deeply communal ritual. I had no intention of writing about it yet but began to say "yes" when invited to join a mate circle and to take note of all the places I saw this ritualized drink.

For more than two decades now, I have seen people drinking mate and a chilled version of this infusion, called *tereré*, across much of southeastern South America. In Buenos Aires, the urban metropole, construction workers on break share mate in the nook of a digger, friends sitting on picnic blankets in the park pass around a gourd, and loved ones share a mate around the kitchen table in the morning or after work. In Uruguay's capital, Montevideo, businesspeople in suits cross the city with thermoses tucked under their arms to infuse their mates at work or on a break, and young people sprawled along the long stretch of *rambla* that skirts the River Plate pass a mate back and forth. In rural areas across Argentina and Uruguay, people sit outside their homes drinking mate. In Asunción, Paraguay, folks at outdoor markets enjoy a *mate cocido* made by brewing yerba in hot water, straining it, and adding caramelized sugar and sometimes milk. In the plazas of this capital city, and in the countryside surrounding it, women sell pitchers of ice water and prescribe a combination of *yuyos* (wild medicinal herbs) to make tereré. In taking in all of these tableaus, I came to appreciate that drinking mate, and in warmer climates tereré, is a regular, valued, and visible part of everyday life. Yerba drinkers abound in the southern part of South America that includes but extends beyond Argentina, Uruguay, and Paraguay to parts of southern Brazil, Chile, and Bolivia.

The earliest Spaniards who encountered the ground-up mixture called *ka'a*, prepared and consumed by the Guaraní people, mistakenly assumed it was yerba, or an herb. The term stuck and continues to be used to refer to the dried and ground leaves of a native holly plant that grows in the humid forests where eastern Paraguay, southern Brazil, and northeastern Argentina now meet. In turn, the Quechua term for cup, or mate, became associated not only with the vessel in which the yerba is placed but also with the ritual that surrounds consumption.

Since the colonial era, the drinking of yerba mate has been an intimate, convivial ritual in which locals regularly welcome newcomers to join the mate circle. Even if they resist at first, most long-term travelers and immigrants eventually take up mate drinking as a way of participating and belonging in a new land. Sometimes people drink it alone while working or studying, but given the opportunity, most seem to prefer to share it with others. "It is difficult to transmit to those who do not enjoy mate, the deeply felt sense of shared ritual experienced by passing the mate from hand to hand, a feeling accentuated by always using the same bombilla," Argentine historian Juan Carlos Garavaglia explains.[2]

Despite efforts by those involved in South American yerba production since the colonial era to promote yerba mate in Europe and, eventually, the United States, it has become relatively popular in the Global North only in the twenty-first century in a manner that disconnects the stimulating effects of yerba from the traditional ritual of drinking mate. Today, consumers in the United States can find loose-leaf yerba and bottled iced yerba mate drinks in cafés or the health food aisle of their local market. Tech workers and partyers in Europe chug bottles of cold yerba mate to fuel their all-night endeavors in what is marketed as a healthier way. Since the mid-twentieth century, long before many in Europe or the United States started consuming yerba drinks, return migrants to Syria and neighboring nations regularly drank yerba mate through a bombilla.[3] Save for this important exception, the South American ritual of sharing a mate with a bombilla has not traveled well, and many outside this region mistakenly but understandably assume yerba mate to be just another form of tea.

As in the past, the vast majority of yerba mate is still consumed within southern South America rather than outside it. In striking contrast to other global hot drinks, including coffee, tea, and hot cocoa, which people across the globe enjoy daily, yerba mate has generally remained a South American drink for the past five centuries. Similarly, while coffee, tea, and chocolate are grown in tropical and subtropical zones across the globe, yerba mate remains a decidedly South American agricultural commodity, produced at a significant scale only in Argentina, Brazil, and Paraguay.[4] Despite being introduced to Europe around the same time as coffee and tea, yerba mate did not become popular there. According to anthropologist Christine Folch, this failure stemmed from many factors. During the colonial era, these included the Spanish Empire's tribute-oriented economic structures and the difficulty of transplanting the crop. In the nineteenth century, Paraguayan leaders' mismanagement and the devastation of the War of the Triple Alliance stymied yerba exports. From the colonial era to today, outsiders' ideas about the body and promoters' inability to distinguish mate from other more familiar stimulating drinks made the shared bombilla less appealing than an individual cup of tea or coffee.[5] The generous amount of time dedicated to partaking in this deliberately slow-paced ritual likely also contributed to its lack of popularity in fast-paced societies.

Like yerba mate, other more global drinkable plants began in specific contexts: tea in China; cacao in Mesoamerica; and coffee in northern Africa. People sought out each of these plants not only for their taste but also for the energizing effects of what we now know to be caffeine and theobromine (yerba mate and cacao laying claim to both). Locals valued them so highly that they created mythical origin stories about their discovery and used them as a form of currency. While tea, cacao, and coffee were once for the exclusive enjoyment of the elite, yerba mate uniquely sated non-elites before elites caught wind of it. But the popularization of all of these stimulating drinks came at a major cost. Since the colonial era, a growing number of workers have toiled to grow, harvest, and process each of these stimulating plants for little to no recompense.

At the other end of the commodity chain, modern mate drinkers stand apart from other contemporary caffeine enthusiasts in preserving the communal and noncommercial tradition common to early food and drink.[6] Cafés in southern South America, for example, have typically not served mate but rather coffee, tea, hot chocolate, soda, and sometimes a cup of *mate cocido*, brewed as if it were a cup of tea. Starting in the late nineteenth century, some members of the upper and middle sectors of society, especially in cosmopolitan Buenos Aires, began to publicly shift away from the native drink toward what they considered more modern caffeinated alternatives. Even so, as has long been the case, most people in southern South America continue to drink mate or tereré through a bombilla at home, while traveling, at work, in the park, or in the plaza.

We know relatively little about the transnational history of yerba mate, most likely because of its lack of popularity beyond South America. English-language scholars have published dozens of books about the history of coffee and tea and more than a handful about cacao but, as of 2020, only one on the economic history of yerba mate. Very recently, US-based scholars have finally begun to enliven our understanding of the complex histories of yerba mate in Argentina.[7]

Sharing Yerba Mate builds on an exciting recent corpus of Latin American food histories, such as Jeffrey Pilcher's *Planet Taco* (2012), John Soluri's *Banana Cultures* (2005), and Heidi Tinsman's *Buying into the Regime* (2014), which focus, respectively, on the historical, transnational trajectories of tacos from Mexico, bananas from Honduras, and grapes from Chile to the United States. These books reveal that a focus on a particular food (or dish) has much to tell us about the agency of plants, Latin American people, and imperial actors in the transnational processes of agricultural production, environmental change, labor relations, globalization, culinary practices, and capitalism. Focusing on yerba mate adds to this corpus by shifting our attention away from histories of consumption in the United States toward the little-known stories of consumption and circulation within Latin America. In other words, it encourages us to see Latin Americans not only as producers of major commodities but also as consumers of them.[8]

While many transnational studies focus on US and European imperialism in the region, this study highlights the agency of Latin Americans in the establishment of a major commodity chain in which neither the people of the United States nor Europeans were particularly interested or active. This stands in contrast to the more familiar histories of other coveted labor-intensive "drug foods" like sugar, coffee, and tea desired abroad. In 1985, anthropologist Sidney Mintz's pathbreaking book *Sweetness and Power* linked enslaved laborers' production of sugar in the Caribbean with industrial workers' consumption of sweet tea in Great Britain, launching a wave of food and commodity histories.[9] Historians ever since have traced the consumption of foods like sugar or coffee in Europe and the United States but have generally overlooked their consumption in (post)colonial zones, obscuring our understanding of how people in productive regions experience and understand themselves vis-à-vis such local commodities.[10] Due to the long history of extracting wealth from Latin America, scholars have concentrated on the stories behind commodities that benefited those in the Global North.[11]

By focusing on yerba mate, we enrich our understanding of the difference it made (and did not make) when the commodity largely stayed within South America, primarily serving local interests and consumers. The "open veins of Latin America"—a poignant phrase that Uruguayan scholar Eduardo Galeano coined to characterize the long history of extracting resources from this region—carried goods that flowed not only out of Latin America but also within it.[12]

The large and diverse region often referred to as the "Southern Cone" has sometimes been studied as a unit. Environmental historians, in particular, stress the importance of going beyond borders.[13] Still, most modern histories of southern South America focus on individual nations. In turn, research that adopts a transnational approach tends to emphasize the shared history of military conquests, political movements, dictatorships, and economic strife.[14] Scholars have focused on conflict rather than connection. And yet, as Will Durant and Ariel Durant would have it, "Civilization is a stream with banks. The stream is sometimes filled with blood from people killing, stealing, shouting, and doing the things that historians usually record; while on the banks, unnoticed, people build homes, make love, raise children, sing songs, write poetry, and even whittle statues. The story of civilization is the story of what happens on the banks."[15] In southern South America, what happened "on the banks" included daily pauses to share some rounds of mate—a ritual that persisted in the face of many a "stream . . . filled with blood."

The pages that follow trace the *longue durée* of southern South America's most popular caffeinated commodity and communal ritual. By shifting our attention to what Michel de Certeau has called "the practice of everyday life," this history highlights the humanity of South Americans.[16] Participating in a mate circle is about much more than the consumption of a caffeinated drink; it is also about taking time to be with other people. Centering the history of mate drinking, therefore, highlights the priority that generation after generation of South Americans have put on forging and maintaining social connections on a daily basis. By exploring the history of this communal ritual and local commodity together, new perspectives emerge, not only about the history of daily life but also about community formation, identity construction, commerce, politics, and nation building in southern South America.

Tracing yerba mate across a shifting array of political borders emphasizes that this story does not map onto a national historiography. Since the late nineteenth century, the discipline of history has been concerned with the constitution of nations and national modes of thinking that created the "modern world." Indeed, many of the popular studies of yerba mate produced in Argentina and, to a lesser extent, in neighboring nations proudly depict this iconic infusion as a national accomplishment. In 1913, Argentine scholar León Denis expressed his hope that one day historians "will decide to study the Argentine industries of the past," including yerba mate, rather than "the bloody events that already have such a big place in our national history."[17] Many have heeded his call. For example, in 1989, Francisco Scutella published a book titled *El mate: Bebida nacional Argentina* (Mate: Argentina's national drink).[18] Other Spanish-language writers, most notably Juan Carlos Garavaglia, Pau Navajas, and Javier Ricca, have taken a more regional approach to their histories. They point out that yerba mate, or rather what the Guaraní called ka'a, not only preceded national borders but also continued to cross them.[19]

As in this case, food and drink are not nearly as national or apolitical as often presumed. A shared taste for yerba mate as a beverage, ritual, narrative, and commodity produced in a specific, labor-intensive manner developed during the colonial era and persisted beyond it.[20] But that does not mean that the emergence of new republics did not matter. As we shall see, republican governments fought, negotiated, and signed treaties, while transnational entrepreneurial elites competed for yerba profits in specific national contexts and made (sometimes deliberately misleading) claims about their yerba's national origin. Meanwhile, during and especially after the wars of independence of the 1810s and 1820s, mate served as a powerful symbol of local culture and new nations. Therefore, tracing the symbolic and quotidian place of yerba mate in the region emphasizes the daily and embodied manner in which people constructed ideas about national and cultural identities, as well as the influential role of food and drink in the process of creating what Benedict Anderson famously referred to as an "imagined community."[21]

This book is a story about the ways in which yerba mate materially and symbolically brought people together and divided them over the course of five centuries in South America. The focus on a commodity so central to many southern South Americans' everyday experiences allows us to appreciate the benefits of tracing what anthropologist Arjun Appadurai refers to as the "social life of things." As Appadurai explains, "Even though from a theoretical point of view human actors encode things with significance, from a methodological point of view it is the things in motion that illuminate their human and social context."[22] In a similar vein, as historian Rebecca Earle found in her book on the global history of the potato, a focus on one foodstuff "transforms the messiness of lived experience" into a narrative with a clear and revealing focal point.[23]

On the pages that follow, our focus on yerba mate will introduce us to yerba workers and promoters, mate drinkers and servers, as well as labor activists and politicians. We also will meet and learn from the many people who studied, wrote about, and visually represented yerba mate since the colonial era. While foreigners dominated the production of colonial and early national sources about what they considered to be an exciting, "exotic" ritualized drink, local people and governments became more involved in producing sources about yerba mate with the growth of national industries and surging expressions of nationalism in the twentieth century.

One of the joys of writing (and reading, I hope) a social and cultural history of yerba mate is the wide range of sources from which to draw. Among the many voices we hear are those of travelers. Their writings reflect their European and, later, American backgrounds, profit-making aspirations, and particular local experiences, as well as their own literary conventions. Most were imperial actors who also entered the business of storytelling, regaling faraway readers with exciting tales about places they would never experience. While I have consistently thought about these dynamics in approaching the evidence that travelers left behind, we will pause together, at times, to consider how travelers' biases and intentions might have distorted how they understood and wrote about this unique ritualized drink. Together with locals' memoirs, travelers' accounts provide us with richly textured descriptions of the practices of drinking mate and tereré in specific historical contexts, whether at a swanky colonial party, around a campfire, or in one's own kitchen.

In turn, qualitative sources and quantitative statistics produced by government and industry groups support our understanding of larger trends in the production, distribution, promotion, and consumption of this popular local commodity. Like travelers' and locals' written accounts, qualitative and quantitative reports produced by governmental and corporate entities can also mislead or fail to accurately capture the dynamics of the yerba mate business. As we shall see, there were frequent cries of deliberate miscounting, yerba surreptitiously crossing borders, and falsification. Reading various countries' reports alongside those provided by contemporaries in the yerba business and scholars who studied it helps enhance our understanding of the yerba market. To orient the reader, overarching trends in production, trade, and consumption are depicted in graphs and maps that appear in the chapters that follow.[24]

Visual depictions of yerba mate from the early eighteenth century until today also allow us to see this history in new ways. As cultural historian Johan Huizinga signaled at the dawn of the twentieth century, history is a "mode of forming images." But historians have too often used visuals as "window dressing" to illustrate their points rather than to construct them, as visual historian Peter Burke attests.[25] Here, a close study of the composition and circulation of a wide corpus of paintings, prints, photographs, postcards, and advertisements reveals not only how people lived and drank mate but also how ideas about mate drinkers and servers were formed by powerful image makers with subjectivities and agendas of their own. Drawing on my visual database of nearly 1,500 digital files with origins in South American libraries, archives, markets, media outlets, and art and mate books, as well as digitized collections, we will explore how yerba mate has served as a visual symbol that helped define South American culture since the colonial era.[26]

As images traveled, they not only marked South Americans as different from Europeans but also influenced local practices and expectations. As we shall see, in the late nineteenth century, the most iconic mate drinker transitioned from the figure of the elite woman of Spanish descent attended by the non-White server to the figure of the rural, male gaucho served by his female counterpart. These figures, along with the mate itself, operated as powerful regional and national icons, and their predominance reflected and shaped hegemonic understandings of power and local culture along gender, race, and class-specific lines.

In recognition of the tensions between how observers and locals deployed racial terms and how we might describe people today, I preserve original Spanish or Portuguese terms to signal understandings of race and uses of racial terminology in South America that are different from those in the Anglophone world. Following the lead of recent activists and scholars, I capitalize racial terms in English such as Black, White, and Indian to highlight their nature as historical constructions rather than natural identity categories.[27]

Latin American scholars have shown that the construction of race-based identities in this region was shaped not only by appearance but also by notions of public honor, wealth, and levels of education. Here, we can also appreciate the impact of quotidian acts like mate drinking on identity formation. As we shall see, this daily ritual helped create and reflect boundaries between, for example, creole elites who regularly drained silver mates and European visitors who refrained (at least, at first), as well as between Black servants, who prepared and tested the first sip of the mate, and their White patrons and guests whose mates they were required to serve.

Sharing Yerba Mate proceeds chronologically to reveal dynamic shifts in yerba production, patterns of consumption, and, in particular, the meanings attached to mate drinking and mate drinkers over time and place. It argues that yerba mate profoundly shaped the formation of social and national identities in the Río de la Plata region because it served as both a local commodity and a highly visible, embodied ritual. While the first chapter provides an overview of yerba as a commodity and mate as a ritual in the colonial era, subsequent chapters delve more deeply into specific periods during the national era and alternate between a focus on mate (chapters 2, 4, 6) and a focus on yerba (chapters 3, 5). Rather than devoting equal attention to every country, the focus on specific nations and transnational regions shifts with the source base and the most dramatic trends.

Following the extensive travels of yerba mate, we will traverse a vast and disparate geography. Most of the book focuses on the region of southeastern South America surrounding the Río de la Plata estuary (River Plate), comprising parts of Argentina, Paraguay, Uruguay, and southern Brazil, where all yerba has been produced and most of it has been consumed. We start in the colonial era, long before any of these nations, or even the idea of them, existed. Some readers will be surprised to learn that the west coast story of mate drinking in the Viceroyalty of Peru (today Peru, Ecuador, Chile, and parts of Bolivia) was the most important one to Europeans and those in the yerba business during the colonial era. As new nations emerged, the principal story of yerba mate consumption shifted eastward to the Río de la Plata region, along with contemporary commercial interests.

From a geographical perspective, the lens will be broadest when production, trade, and promotion are a key part of the story, and more tightly focused on the capital cities of Argentina and Uruguay when discussing urban practices and representations of rural mate drinking. This approach follows my sources, the places where I was able to conduct research, and the historical trajectory of yerba mate. During the national period, Buenos Aires and Montevideo dominated not only as consumer markets but also as image producers, while first Paraguay, then Brazil, and eventually Argentina dominated as producers. While we will learn a little about the history of mate consumption in Chile and southern Brazil and a bit more about Paraguay, future studies, I hope, will push our understandings in these contexts further.[28]

In some ways, this is a story about how yerba mate became most strongly associated with Argentina by the twentieth century. There was, however, no indication in the eighteenth century that it would be that way. At that time, the focus was on production in Paraguay and consumption in the Viceroyalty of Peru. In the nineteenth century, Brazil dominated the harvesting and exportation of yerba. But by the 1930s, Argentina had established itself as the largest producer of yerba, a position it has maintained to this day. How did Argentina, which prior to the war grew only negligible amounts of yerba, surpass Brazil and become the world's largest yerba producer and claim the most visible modern mate drinkers? And what happened to the consumption and symbolic place of yerba mate as new nations emerged, cooperated, and competed over, among many other things, the colonial product known as the "herb of Paraguay"?

To understand these and other historically revealing dynamics, we will need to broaden our lens, starting long before any South American nations existed. In the pages that follow, we will explore how the place of yerba mate not only survived but thrived during the disruptive processes of colonialism and nation making. We also will learn how this local drink helped to shape the experiences and identities of so many people who called southern South America home. By focusing on a ritualized beverage, we can see the ways in which people in this region forged connections and distinctions on an everyday basis for more than five centuries.

FIGURE 1.1. Detail of Amédée François Frézier, *The Tincture or Decoction of the Herb of Paraguay*, in *A Voyage to the South-Sea and along the Coasts of Chili and Peru in the Years 1712, 1713, and 1714* (London: Jonah Bowyer, 1717), 236, plate 36. Courtesy of Colección Biblioteca Nacional de Chile, Santiago, available at Memoria Chilena, www.memoriachilena.cl/602/w3-article-71933.html.

CHAPTER ONE

Making Ka'a South American, 1520s–1810s

Three wealthy women of Spanish descent dressed in long gowns and capes gather in a sunlit parlor in Lima, the viceregal capital of Peru, in the early 1700s. One kneels in front of a low table, where a giant silver mate gleams.[1] Likely the hostess, she holds between her lips the long silver tube that emanates from the bowl, preparing to drink what contemporaries referred to as the "herb of Paraguay." She fills the room with the gurgling whoosh made from slurping the infusion through the silver tube, its bitter taste mellowed by the sweetness of the sugar that the servant added before offering the mate service to her and her companions (fig. 1.1).

This vision of South American mate drinking was created by French engineer and artist Amédée François Frézier in the early 1700s based on his three-year stay in the region. Frézier's official mission was to map ports, towns, and routes to inform the French king's ministers about trade possibilities in Peru and Chile. He also became intrigued by local customs. Shortly after returning home, in 1717, he released this illustration of the mate ritual—apparently the first of its kind—in his lively 300-page illustrated report. Readers in Europe gobbled up his book, published first in French and shortly thereafter in English and Spanish.[2]

Just like a scientific drawing, Frézier included a key to his copper engraving for readers unfamiliar with South America. Here, the seated woman (item C) purses her lips to "suck through" a long "silver pipe" the "tincture or decoction" made with the "herb of Paraguay," he explained. The large bowl from which she drinks (item D), Frézier continued, is "a gourd adorned with silver," locally referred to as a "mate" (the Quechua word for cup). In front of the women stands a steaming "silver pot to heat the water, in the midst of which is the fire" (items E and G),[3] and next to them, an unlabeled *caldero* (or large copper pot) to hold the heated water. Frézier also inserted an *apartador* (separator) on the right side of the mate cup, a technology sometimes used in eighteenth-century Peru to separate the yerba from the infused water.[4]

Like other colonial observers, Frézier pictured the act of drinking mate as a primarily female and leisurely pursuit. But the fair-skinned ladies in his composition were not alone. Above them, Frézier included heroic portraits of Spanish conquistadors. Their inclusion facilitated a double male gaze by the artist and the men he painted. In this way, Frézier suggested that the conquistadors' bravery made possible the leisurely lifestyles, comfortable surroundings, and fine dress of women of Spanish descent.

Frézier's written account suggests that he witnessed many people— women and men, elites and commoners—imbibing mate across the Vice- royalty of Peru. A fan himself, he declared the herb's flavor "agreeable" and even better than tea. Since he had seen only the ground-up powder, he could not reveal how the so-called herb of Paraguay was made but provided a full description of how it was brewed:

> Instead of drinking the Tincture, or Infusion, apart, as we drink Tea, they put the Herb into a Cup, or Bowl, made of a Calabash, or Gourd, tipp'd with Silver, which they call *Mate*; they add Sugar, and pour on it the hot Water, which they drink immediately, without giving it Time to infuse, because it turns as black as Ink. To avoid drinking the Herb which swims at the Top, they make use of a Silver Pipe, at the End where of is a Bowl, full of little Holes; so that the Liquor suck'd in at the other End is clear from the Herb. They drink round with same Pipe, pouring hot water over the same Herb, as it is drank off.[5]

Frézier, like so many who followed him, sought to make legible to outsiders a local ritual involving a stimulating substance with properties like tea that was consumed in a radically different, communal fashion.

During the colonial era, many people in South America regularly drank mate and invited foreigners such as Frézier to join the mate circle, impressing upon them the importance and intimacy of a ritual in which partakers share the same mate cup and filtering tube (or straw). Locals left few clues about their mate-drinking practices, in part because this custom, a regular part of everyday life, seemed unremarkable to other residents of the region. But Europeans who came to what they considered the New World in search of adventure, material wealth, and scientific knowledge became fascinated with mate drinking. Intending to entertain folks back home, they produced a wealth of textual and visual sources about this unique and, in their minds, exotic ritual. Their depictions require a careful reading that keeps their European biases in mind but allow us to glean vivid details about daily life in South America that are difficult to find elsewhere.[6] Male travelers (like Frézier) focused their attention on local urban elites, with whom they socialized and wished to do business. More peripatetic travel writers also provided information about the many people across the region who drank mate.[7]

Unlike chocolate from Mesoamerica and tea from Asia, which were primarily enjoyed by the upper strata in those regions of origin for a long time, what became known as the "herb of Paraguay" transcended social classes from the outset. During the colonial era, it not only found its way into the mouths of rich and poor but also helped bridge the gap between locals and newcomers.

This chapter tells the story of how a native plant from Paraguay became a high-status commodity that European artists associated with elites of European heritage born in the New World but was enjoyed by men and women of all socioeconomic backgrounds within colonial South America. The Paraguayan herb made its way across most Spanish-held territory in the region, at first under the bureaucratic authority of the Viceroyalty of Peru, founded in 1542, and much later the Viceroyalty of the Río de La Plata, established in 1776.

Given this book's focus on how the emergence of nations shaped yerba as a commodity and mate as a ritual, this chapter spans a much longer period than subsequent chapters. It allows us to see how the colonial era initiated a new phase in the exploitative production and massive consumption of a stimulating plant native to the upper Río de la Plata region that endures to this day.

Colonial subjects' growing access to yerba (or herb) delighted them but came with steep repercussions. During the colonial era, more Indigenous and eventually other poor indentured laborers found themselves drawn into

COLONIAL SOUTH AMERICA, CA. 1780

Source: Created by John H. Clark, Geospatial Services librarian, Lafayette College, Eaton, PA, following "Free vector and raster map data [1:10m]: Land, Ocean, Admin-0 Countries, Gray Earth," Natural Earth, 2021, https://www.naturalearthdata.com; and Werner Stangl, *HGIS de las Indias*, "Raw Data: tables and geopackages," Harvard Dataverse, V1, 2020, https://doi.org/10.7910/DVN/29XTPY (accessed April 9, 2021).

the hellish process of gathering and making yerba (described a bit later). At the same time, the poor majority enjoyed this stimulant for sociability and to gather the energy required to perform all kinds of labor. Despite its initial discovery and production by Indigenous peoples, the plant used to make this infusion became associated with its region of origin (Paraguay) rather than with the Guaraní-speaking people who made it edible in the first place. Throughout the colonial era, the commodity of yerba and the ritual of drinking mate forged profound economic and social connections across much of Spanish South America and even parts of southern Brazil.

MAKING KA'A INTO A COLONIAL COMMODITY

Long before a single European mouth touched a silver mate tube, an Indigenous people called the Kaingang consumed the stimulating leaves they found in the humid native forests of the semitropical river region of central South America called Mbaracayú. Like their better-known coca-chewing counterparts in the Andes, the Kaingang masticated the stimulating—but in this case, not intoxicating—leaves for energy. They weaved them into belts, plucking and chewing on them one or two at a time while on the move.[8]

The semi-sedentary Guaraní-speaking peoples migrated from the north in search of their "land without evil," a mythical place they imagined to be free from violence or strife. They settled alongside the Kaingang and other Indigenous groups in the large semitropical basin fed by the Paraguay, Uruguay, and Paraná Rivers. The Guaraní brought with them an awareness of how to plant crops and how to read the forest to understand the potential uses of different trees and plants.[9] The Guaraní called the energizing leaf chewed by the Kaingang—and likely other groups that lived in the region—ka'a. In Guaraní, the meaning of this word extended beyond this leaf to all life-giving plants found in the forest, including weeds and foliage.[10]

Guaraní mythology holds that Tupã, one of the most important deities, introduced the people to this type of ka'a and encouraged scorching the leaves to preserve them.[11] The Guaraní followed this quick blast of heat with a longer process of slowly drying the leaves over a domed structure called *barbacuá* (barbecue) (see fig. 3.2). Once prepared in this manner, the leaves preserved their stimulating and nutritious properties for up to two years and became tastier. Through the Guaraní's new and enduring production process, the leaf, as yerba mate expert Pau Navajas explains, "is transformed, its bright green color becomes a light olive green, at the same time that its simple bitter vegetal flavor turns complex and herbaceous, with a slightly sweet finish."[12]

For the Guaraní, this complex leaf represented a divine gift to be enjoyed communally, like other highly valued things. Guaraní people often shared ka'a as a form of greeting, employed it as a cure (especially as an emetic), and used it in special religious ceremonies. In the town of Concepción, for example, the *karaí* (the local prophet or spiritual leader) used ka'a to make divinations, seal a marriage, and welcome illustrious guests.[13] The Guaraní ingested the dried leaves by chewing on them or infusing them with cold or hot water, which they strained through their teeth or perhaps a natural reed straw.[14]

The Guaraní apparently engaged in some precolonial trade of ka'a, since it has been found in Incan tombs, suggesting its cachet.[15] But the Guaraní did not make the trade of ka'a or other goods a point of emphasis. In fact, there was no word for trade in Guaraní.[16] Living in a semisedentary and subsistence society, Guaraní-speaking peoples did the work necessary to survive by acquiring foodstuffs and medicines like ka'a but placed a higher value on leisure than on accumulation and on communal sharing rather than on individual possessions.[17]

Europeans in the New World lived by a markedly different ethos. While proclaiming their mission as bringing glory to God and the Spanish king by converting polytheistic heathens to Christianity, most conquistadors focused their attention on bettering their own lot in life by obtaining material wealth rather than on saving the souls of Indigenous people. With the help of diseases such as smallpox that they unwittingly brought with them, and with fortuitous timing, the Spanish—with considerable aid from their numerous Indigenous and African allies—declared that they had subsumed the (still-rebellious) Incan empire by the 1520s.[18] On the Atlantic coast, their Portuguese contemporaries established a few trading posts on the coast of Brazil. Iberians from both coasts went off in search of other empires to plunder. Many were drawn to the land in the center of South America, which they dreamily called "El Dorado" (The Golden Land). For the ethnically diverse groups of Guaraní-speaking people who lived there, this was Paraguai, or the place veined with waterways.[19]

The conquistadors did not find gold, but not for a lack of trying. They did, however, encounter the Guaraní and their dietary staple, the cassava root, and consumption of wide variety of local plants, including ka'a. As historian Rebecca Earle has shown, early Iberian arrivals across Spanish America relied upon humoral theory, or the idea that the body was inherently porous and could be changed by climate and food, to understand why their appearance differed from the diverse peoples they lumped together as Indians. Spaniards initially eschewed certain local foods, especially staple crops such as cassava or maize, out of fear that consuming them might turn them into the native peoples they sought to civilize. They also went to extravagant lengths to import and grow cherished foods from the Old World, including the holy trinity of wheat, olives for oil, and grapes for wine. They made exceptions for Indigenous foods they found delightful, like the frothy, flowery, and spicy cacao drink popular in Mesoamerica.[20]

Early Iberian arrivals to South America had no experience yet with stimulating hot beverages.[21] Colonial storytellers became fond of the notion that early Spaniards resisted consuming ka'a and tried to persuade the Guaraní to end the practice because of their desire to be seen as a people more interested in saving Indian souls than in edifying themselves. In one well-traveled story, Hernando Arias de Saavedra, governor of Asunción and the Spanish district of the Río de la Plata in the 1590s, became the first person of Spanish descent to encounter this local stimulant. Hernandarias (as he was known) supposedly searched the bags of the Guaraní and found ground powder (or ka'a) within them. Burning this booty in the central plaza, he was said to have remarked, "Do not be misled by this demonstration, because I am moved by all the love I have for you, because listen, what my sage heart tells me is that this herb will be the ruin of your nation."[22] Saavedra's often-repeated anecdote points to the considerable efforts the Spanish undertook not only to subdue the Guaraní but also to tell stories in which they celebrated the execution of their self-proclaimed role as noble civilizers eager to improve, among other things, locals' diets.[23]

Yet like many later immigrants, conquistadors and early settlers took up a new habit of mate drinking.[24] As early as 1541, four years after the Spanish founding of the city of Asunción, Spaniard Pedro Montañez's list of possessions included "a big gourd (or mate) and milled yerba."[25] By the late sixteenth century, Iberian alarmists were concerned not only about Indigenous consumption of ka'a but also about yerba's popularity among Spanish immigrants. In 1596, a member of the town council of Asunción wrote to Hernandarias, "The vice and bad habit of drinking yerba has spread so much among the Spaniards, their women and children, that unlike the Indians who are content to drink it once a day they drink it continuously and those who do not drink it are very rare."[26]

The question of how such Spaniards (and others) came to prefer drinking their mate through a bombilla (the straw-like tube with a filter on the end used to strain the infusion) remains a hotly debated topic. Scholars disagree about whether the Guaraní or the Spanish deserve credit. In the 1950s, historian Raul A. Molina confidently stated that Spaniards invented the bombilla and suggested (almost certainly inaccurately) that gauchos might have conceived of the non-metal version.[27] In his magisterial study of the economic history of yerba during the colonial era, historian Juan Carlos Garavaglia notes that none of the early colonial sources referenced any native use of what the Spanish called the "bombilla" and concludes that Europeans must have invented it.[28] In contrast, Navajas points out that Spaniards did not use this filtering tube in Europe and, therefore, were unlikely to have introduced it to the New World.[29] Folklorists Federico Oberti and Amaro Villanueva concur that native artisans likely created mate tubes, using palm trees or vines as well as their artisanal weaving skills to make the filter at the end.[30]

Primary evidence from the Jesuits in the eighteenth century—some two centuries after the encounter—points to both Spanish and native uses of the bombilla. Still, these sources suggest the endurance among the Guaraní, and other non-elites, of the use of unfiltered tubes called *caños*. Some native (and poor) peoples also continued to use their teeth as a filter. For example, Jesuit father Martin Dobrizhoffer, who spent 1749 to 1767 in Guaraní territory, claimed, "The Spanish sip it through a *cañito de plata* [silver tube with a filter on the end, more often referred to as a bombilla] .... Others use wood or cane *cañito*, with a filter on the end. The Indians who do not use [this type of filtered tube] involuntarily consume a quantity of the yerba leaf."[31] Given the paucity of archeological or textual evidence from pre- and early colonial native peoples in this region, the inventors of the bombilla remain something of a mystery.

What we do know is that Spaniards initiated the fabrication of the silver bombilla in the seventeenth century. They most likely drew inspiration from the bombilla made by Indigenous artisans with natural materials, adding to its perceived value by making it with the precious metal that served as the engine of the Spanish colonial economy.[32] We can also affirm that the Guaraní introduced the Spanish not only to the process of picking and preserving the ka'a but also to the communal ethos at its core.

In this fertile region fed by numerous rivers and blessed with a pleasant climate and abundant natural resources, Spanish conquistadors lamented the apparent lack of precious metals or hierarchical Indigenous empires, and most left. Those who stayed dreamed of gaining the rarefied title of *encomendero*, a status that entitled the beneficiaries to grants of Indigenous laborers from the crown as a result of proving their bravery in conquest or colonization. Early *encomenderos* in Guaraní territory forced Indigenous laborers to do agricultural work, producing sugar, tobacco, wine, and ka'a for export. By the late sixteenth century, they had settled on ka'a as their primary moneymaker.

For the rest of the colonial era, this Indigenous stimulant would serve as the region's most valuable commodity, even if tobacco sometimes brought a larger windfall.[33]

To make this so, the Spanish forced the Guaraní to change their harvesting practices. Instead of picking only what was needed for local consumption and a small amount for trade, Indigenous laborers were now ordered to "mine" yerba from wild stands of bush-like trees, a practice that was intensified in the 1620s and 1630s.[34] Tellingly, the Spanish referred to the crop as "oro verde," or green gold, and treated yerba as a "mineral," positing that like gold or silver, it emerged from the ground without human intervention.[35]

Despite possessing little value in Europe, yerba's relatively low local price but consistently high demand provided a steady source of wealth for Spanish American *encomenderos* and the Spanish crown. Free and indebted labor proved cheap for the Spanish. And yet, because barter was at the center of the colonial economy in this region, profits were hard to come by, even for large Paraguayan landowners.[36] With no gold or silver coin in circulation, yerba served as the main form of exchange.[37]

Poor yerba workers suffered in the dangerous environment of yerba picking, preliminary processing, and porting. Starting in the late seventeenth century, conscripted Indigenous laborers were joined by some non-Indigenous laborers who, while technically free, nevertheless found themselves in the trap of debt peonage.[38] Yerba *mineros* (or mine workers) were marched across swampy land and fast-moving rivers on their way to and from labor camps in distant humid forests in the *montes* (hills), where they would be forced to work from sunup to sundown for months with little food to sustain them and the nagging fear of snakes and jaguars on the prowl.[39] Gathering yerba was "hard and painful, requiring extraordinary human fortitude and leaving behind a trail of victims," as Paraguayan historian Efraím Cardozo writes.[40]

Spanish methods took a tremendous toll on the bodies of laborers, as well as on those of the oxen and mules that they brought as beasts of burden. The foreigners' methods changed the forest. Dobrizhoffer, who came to South America in 1749 as a Jesuit missionary, decried how Spaniards lazily cut down entire trees rather than pluck the most useful branches like the Indigenous people did, a result of Spanish greed for quick but unsustainable material wealth.[41]

The lack of precious minerals or empires in eastern South America led the Spanish crown to focus its attention on the western portion of the Viceroyalty of Peru. Jesuit missionaries seized the opportunity to fill what Europeans perceived as a vacuum in the eastern region of the upper Río de la Plata. Members of this brotherhood came from across Europe to central South America, where they founded and worked on missions that sought to educate, feed, and clothe Indigenous peoples while introducing them to Christianity. As committed administrators, the Jesuits decided to use Guaraní labor to make profits to grow their missionary work. Many Guaraní, in turn, judged the Jesuits' protections as superior to the dangers of other more rapacious Europeans seeking to exploit them and agreed to live on the missions. First established in the early 1600s, the Jesuit order had by the 1740s established thirty Guaraní missions with some 40,000 inhabitants between the Paraná and Uruguay Rivers.[42]

Jesuit priests understood that to be successful they needed to meet their would-be converts halfway by learning their language and selectively respecting locals' customs and desires but initially maligned yerba consumption as a vice in need of suppression. In 1610, Jesuit father Diego de Torres sent a letter to the Inquisition board in Lima decrying what he labeled a "diabolical" ritual. He complained that in both Tucumán and Paraguay, locals consumed massive quantities of yerba, often with the intention of inducing vomiting. "The Indians," he warned, had initiated the consumption of yerba "born from a pact with and by clear suggestion of the devil."[43] He continued that Spaniards—and even some priests—had become so addicted to this "vice" that they consumed yerba every day and refused to stop doing so, even during the religious mass.[44] The Inquisition board did not prohibit the production and consumption of yerba as Torres requested. And so, Jesuit priests continued to complain. In 1639, Jesuit priest Ruiz de Montoya, who worked in the missions in the northeastern region of Paranapanema (now in southern Brazil), decried this "sinful beverage" as damaging and even deathly to undernourished workers forced to pick it in the faraway hills. He lamented that these laborers consumed so much yerba that it "swells their feet, legs and bellies, while their faces display nothing but bone and death's-head pallor."[45] Such denunciations, however, did not last much longer.

Finding bans ineffectual and yerba not so bad after all—especially as it seemed to energize rather than inebriate workers—Montoya and his fellow

Jesuits reversed their policy in the 1640s.[46] The Guaraní likely persuaded the Jesuit fathers to change their minds not by emphasizing spiritual beliefs but rather by pointing out that ka'a made their work easier, sustained them when there was no food, purged their stomachs of phlegm, made their senses alert, and keep them from getting too drowsy.[47] (Twentieth- and twenty-first-century scientists would largely confirm the Guaraní's understanding of yerba's stimulating, satiating, and diuretic properties.)[48] Later European arrivals, accustomed to the buzz generated by other tantalizing stimulants available in Europe, such as chocolate, tea, coffee, and tobacco, helped ease various prohibitions on the local herb that earlier governors introduced or ignored.[49]

The Jesuits were not the first to reverse course. Earlier in the century, from 1603 to 1634, Hernandarias attempted to outlaw the production and consumption of yerba, a move rejected by the crown and early colonial subjects who had become committed to the local drink.[50] For the Spaniards, yerba offered a good, cheap stimulant and ritual of belonging in a new land, while for some natives, yerba, like tobacco, also maintained a spiritual mythology and purpose.[51]

Over the course of the seventeenth century, the production and trade of yerba significantly expanded, and the price dropped across South America.[52] As of 1620, the small city of Asunción (with some 500 inhabitants) received 250,000 pounds of yerba per year, while the trading ports of Santa Fe and Corrientes received 1 million pounds each.[53] The presence of local waterways was crucial to making this expansion possible. As historian Jerry Cooney explains, "Without the tributaries of the Río Paraguay, it would have been more difficult to tap the *yerbales* [yerba forests]. Without the Paraguay-Paraná system, it would have been impractical to ship yerba."[54] It was not just people and animals, especially oxen and mules, but also the environment, specifically the native forests and navigable rivers in the Río de la Plata region, that enabled the scaling-up of the yerba trade across seventeenth-century South America. The Jesuit-Guaraní missions played a significant role in this expansion, but as we shall see, they remained outpaced by other yerba producers to the north.

The Jesuit-Guaraní missions' first major innovation dramatically changed the market by creating two types of yerba with different price points. While the missions produced the standard yerba known as *de palos* (or with little branches), like their competitors, they introduced a higher-quality product known as *caaminí* that garnered twice the profit.[55] To make *caaminí*, Guaraní laborers removed branches as well as debris that might have gotten mixed in, such as dirt or rocks, leaving only the tender leaves, which they ground up for high-end consumers to enjoy.

In the early 1700s, the Jesuit-Guaraní missions offered their second major innovation in the form of the yerba plantation. Having figured out that they could replicate the germination process that birds undertook in the *yerbales silvestres* (wild yerba forests) by bathing the wild seeds in water before planting, Jesuit priests tasked Guaraní laborers with setting new trees in evenly spaced plots and caring for them within the mission.[56] Guaraní artisans also made engraved mates and, likely, the filtered tubes used to drink out of them.[57] For the Jesuit missions in the north, yerba plantations promised the dual benefits of keeping Guaraní labor within the missions and allowing the Jesuit fathers to more actively control production and trade, thereby turning a greater profit.[58] The Jesuits publicly celebrated the plantation model as a technological advance as well as a moral one, proclaiming that their plantations would end the exploitative conditions yerba workers endured in the remote native yerba forests, linking such exploitation not with themselves, of course, but with other less-conscientious colonial producers. Nevertheless, most Indigenous people living in their own settlements (called *pueblos de Indios*) possessed few wild yerbales nearby. And even when they did, the Spanish crown prevented Indigenous groups from harvesting the yerba groves unless they were in debt, preferring to grant licenses for profit to people of Spanish descent.[59]

During the seventeenth and eighteenth centuries, yerba flowed from the northern missions down the Paraná and Paraguay Rivers to the southern missions and especially the city of Santa Fe, where it was moved over land all the way up to the Andes, or where it continued downriver to Buenos Aires and Montevideo and to smaller markets.[60] The Spanish crown declared in 1662 that ships from Paraguay sailing down the Paraná stop at the city of Santa Fe, a rule called the Puerto Preciso (Precise Port) that increased revenues in Santa Fe and made yerba more expensive elsewhere until its 1780 repeal.[61] Despite this requirement, the Jesuits focused on trading yerba and other goods such as textiles with Buenos Aires and Santa Fe rather than with Asunción, since the products sold at significantly higher rates to the south.

In Asunción, frustrated local yerba interests decried their disadvantage due to the significantly higher tax burden they faced than that enjoyed by the religious order.[62] "The settlers envied the Jesuits their political links, resented their dominance in yerba, and most of all, coveted their access to Indian labor," historian Thomas Whigham explains. In 1664, Jesuit and non-Jesuit yerba producers agreed to a political compromise brokered by the Spanish crown, in which the religious order agreed to cap its production of yerba

COLONIAL YERBA PRODUCTION AND TRADE ROUTES

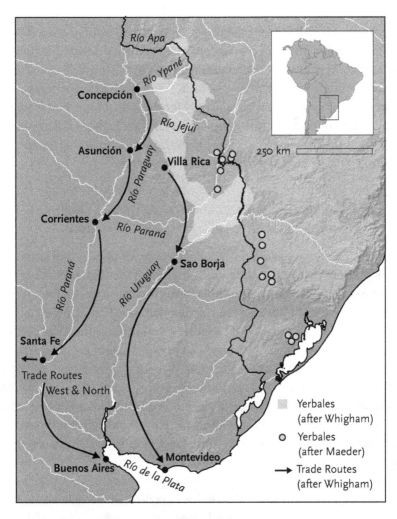

Source: Created by John H. Clark, Geospatial Services librarian, Lafayette College, Eaton, PA, following "Free vector and raster map data [1:10m]: Land, Ocean, Admin-0 Countries, Gray Earth," Natural Earth, 2021, www.naturalearthdata.com; Thomas Whigham, *The Politics of River Trade: Tradition and Development in the Upper Plata, 1780–1870* (Albuquerque: University of New Mexico Press, 1991); and Ernesto J. A. Maeder and Ramón Gutiérrez, "Pueblos y estancias de Misiones (1750)," in *Atlas histórico y urbano de la región del nordeste argentino* (Resistencia, Chaco, Arg.: Instituto de Investigaciones Geohistóricas, 1994), 66–67.

at 12,000 arrobas (or 300,000 pounds)—a limit that lasted until the early 1700s.[63]

Despite protests by other speculators that the Jesuits exceeded their limits, other non-Jesuit enterprises remained extremely active in supplying the market.[64] For example, Garavaglia estimates that in the early 1700s, some 85 percent of the total volume of yerba in Santa Fe and Buenos Aires came from Asunción and Corrientes and only the remaining 15 percent from the Jesuit missions. Yet because the Jesuits produced the higher-valued *caaminí*-style yerba, they still brought in some 30 percent of profits during this period, down from 40 percent in the late seventeenth century.[65]

CONSUMING THE HERB OF PARAGUAY ACROSS EIGHTEENTH-CENTURY SOUTH AMERICA

During the early eighteenth century, Indigenous knowledge and labor and Jesuit innovations expanded the consumption of the Guaraní's ka'a across South America. French adventurer and artist Amédée François Frézier, discussed at the start of this chapter, clarified that "the Trade for the Herb of *Paraguay* is carry'd on at *Santa Fe*, whither it is brought up the River of *Plate*, and in Carts." He distinguished between the two grades of yerba, associating the finer quality with Jesuit production. Well-off residents from La Paz to Cuzco purchased the pricier, more refined version "worth half as much more as the other," while folks living near the mines of Potosí to La Paz consumed the more economical and rustic variety.[66] He estimated that some 50,000 arrobas (or 1.25 million pounds) of both types of yerba made their way from Paraguay to Peru in the course of a year.[67]

As these numbers suggest, across the region, locals would "make much Use of, The Herb of Paraguay," as Frézier detailed. Some called it "*S. Bartholomew's* Herb, who they pretend came into those Provinces, where he made it wholsome [*sic*] and beneficial, whereas before it was venomous," he wrote.[68] Jesuit fathers and other Europeans were fond of creating new origin stories to legitimize a supposedly venomous Indigenous product by linking it with Christian saints. Priest Florian Pauke, for example, claimed that Saint Thomas (rather than Tupã) had first introduced the Guaraní to yerba.[69] In a similar vein, this infusion, when drunk as a tea, became known as *té Jesuita* (Jesuit tea), though this way of drinking yerba happened primarily on the missions and in Europe.[70] Within South America, attempts at changing the primary association to the Jesuits proved far less successful than the herb's longer-standing connection to Paraguay.

Frézier explained that the Spanish living in Peru (such as the ladies he illustrated) had adopted the custom of drinking the "herb of Paraguay" but noted that his French compatriots in Lima were far less comfortable with its communal nature "in a Country where many are pox'd." Since the worried French visitors could not resist the local stimulant, they apparently "invent[ed] the Use of little Glass-Pipes" to use individually.[71] Locals appeared generally unconcerned about disease transmission through the shared bombilla, though perhaps some (as today) refrained from sharing mate if they were visibly sick.

This would not be the last time newcomers tried to find a workaround to partake in this local custom and share mate with others while seeking to protect themselves from contagion. And yet this fear of contagion in the early eighteenth century emerged when people across the world regularly shared common cups and bowls (germ theory was still some two centuries in the future). Outsiders' principal discomfort stemmed from the intimacy of sharing of the bombilla. Most did not, as some Jesuit fathers, drink individual cups of brewed yerba. Locals succeeded in convincing the majority of newcomers that passing around a shared cup and straw played a defining role in what it meant to drink mate properly. But the French who insisted on using their own glass tube suggested that for some outsiders, the sharing of the bombilla represented a level of intimacy, and even equality, that they were unwilling to endorse.

Frézier mostly drank mate with wealthy South Americans who could afford sugar and silver-tipped mates, but he understood the mate ritual's predominance among others in this Pacific region. He followed his explanation of how mate was drunk, adding that "even the Poorest use it once a Day, when they rise in the Morning." He also pointed to a racialized pattern of consumption in silver mining regions like Potosí. "The Use of this Herb is necessary where there are Mines, and on the Mountains of *Peru*," he observed, continuing, "Where the Whites think the Use of Wine [made with the Paraguayan herb] pernicious; they rather choose to drink Brandy, and leave the Wine to the *Indians* and Blacks, which they like very well."[72] In the cities, everyone but newcomers drank mate, but in mining regions, it seems that consuming Indigenous stimulants, both yerba and the Andean leaf known as coca, was a racialized class marker. While White supervisors in the Potosí mines could select brandy over native plants, laborers depended on Indigenous stimulants like mate and coca to fuel their grueling work in high-altitude locales.[73]

Consuming mate also defined gradations of assimilation in the colonial era. In 1758, Spanish navy captain Antonio de Ulloa shared that all kinds of people across Peru and Chile drank the local infusion every morning before eating any food and often enjoyed it as their "evening regale." He continued, "I have nothing to object against the salubrity and use of this liquor; but the manner of drinking it is certainly very indelicate, the whole company drinking successively through the same pipe."[74] Some newcomers shared his judgment, and Ulloa claimed that drinking mate helped divide recent arrivals to the Pacific coast from Spain (whom he called "Chapitones") from locally born or identified people of Spanish descent (or Creoles). "The Chapitones make very little use of it; but among the Creoles it is *the highest enjoyment*; so that even when they travel, they never fail to carry with them a sufficient quantity of it."[75] Enjoying mate or refusing it provided a tangible way of showing one's appreciation (or lack thereof) for local customs.

The Spaniard noted that people in this Pacific coast region of South America had little access to chocolate, and most engaged in the elaborate mate ritual twice a day.[76] Locals prepared their mates in an enticing manner by macerating the herb and sugar together, infusing it with "boiling water . . . and squeez[ing] into the liquor a few drops of the juice of lemons or Seville oranges, mixed with some perfumes from odiferous flowers."[77] Spaniards' taste for citrus, sugar, and rose water had already been established by the Arab presence in Iberia, and the addition of other floral notes—as well as the yerba itself—hailed from Indigenous plants and preferences.[78] Prepared in this manner, mate became a quintessentially Spanish American drink.

Throughout the colonial era, the Guaraní and other Indigenous groups in the region remained committed to drinking ka'a, which the Spanish and Portuguese crowns both recognized. For example, since at least the early 1700s, colonial authorities frequently offered yerba, along with tobacco, sugar, weapons, or cloth, and sometimes cattle, to the caciques (native leaders) of the Charrúas and Minuanes in the Río de la Plata region in an effort to secure positive relations with them.[79]

YERBA PRODUCTION AND CONSUMPTION IN THE POST-JESUIT ERA

In the mid-eighteenth century, mate drinkers included a diverse Native population, Black and Brown miners, mixed-race commoners, and White colonial elites in both urban and rural settings.[80] As a result, yerba enjoyed massive demand and promised great profits. Ulloa claimed that while the temperate region of the Jesuit missions also produced tobacco and cotton, "these articles are far less advantageous [in terms of profit] to the inhabitants than the herb called Paraguay." He continued that this herb "alone would be sufficient to form a flourishing commerce in this province, it being the only one which produces it."[81]

Around this time, as European Bourbon rulers sought to tighten their political and economic control over the colonies, they began to see the wealthy, landholding Jesuit order as a competing authority in need of removal. Beginning in 1758, the Portuguese, and then some five years later the French, expelled the Jesuits from their colonies. In 1767, the Spanish crown followed suit and ordered the removal of the Jesuits from Spanish America, an act completed the following year when the Jesuits sailed to Europe with their mates, bombillas, and yerba in tow.[82] The Guaraní offered little protest.[83]

Frenchman Louis-Antoine de Bougainville witnessed this historic moment. Bougainville dreamed of creating a colony of his own on the islands off the east coast of South America, and like others who possessed commercial interests in the region, he not only decried but also overstated the Jesuits' domination of the yerba mate trade. He blamed the Jesuits for controlling the exclusive commerce in this commodity and calculated that "five million of piastres were the clear yearly profit of the pious fathers." He even accused the Jesuits of actively destroying wild stands of trees and jealously guarding the secrets of germination, neither of which was true.[84]

What would happen to the production and trade of yerba with the Jesuits gone? According to many popular histories of yerba mate, this was a devastating blow. With the demise of the yerba plantation and the decline of Jesuit trade networks, some reported that the supply simply dried up.[85]

Since the Jesuits never supplied much more than a quarter of the total quantity of yerba mate, however, production never collapsed. Historian Julia Sarreal shows that the volume of yerba mate trade actually increased for a couple of decades after the Spanish crown replaced the Jesuits with priests from other orders and government-appointed officials charged with overseeing the missions. The Guaraní, who took on a larger role in decision-making than they had under the Jesuits, shifted from producing higher-quality and more labor-intensive yerba made with just the tender leaves (*caaminí*) to lower-quality and less labor-intensive yerba that included the branches (*de palos*). The variety with the branches, of course, commanded a lower price. This meant that despite doubling their production, yerba producers made roughly the same profits as before.[86]

As conditions in the missions deteriorated under new Spanish-appointed officials, the Guaraní abandoned the domesticated yerbales. From the late eighteenth century through the late nineteenth century, Guaraní laborers, like most South Americans involved in yerba production, harvested and traded *yerba de palos* from native forests.[87] The exploitation of wild yerbales proceeded with little concern for conservation. Based on the premise that yerba was a natural resource without limits, and in light of still growing demand, yerba-picking camps advanced closer to the northern frontiers along the Apa, Ypané, and Jejuí Rivers.[88] Once again, yerba mate became the only major caffeinated crop not produced on plantations.[89]

What did the demise of Jesuit trade networks and the production of high-quality *caaminí* mean for locals who had developed a taste for the Paraguayan herb? Commoners across the region who had tried only the lower-grade *yerba de palos* continued to consume it without hesitation as long as they could. What about elites who primarily consumed the more refined product? Historian Ross Jamieson contends that around the turn of the eighteenth century, South American elites in Chile and Argentina started to replace what he characterized as "the colonial habit of *yerba maté*" with coffee, which they considered a more cosmopolitan beverage.[90]

The late eighteenth century did not represent the first time that yerba had to compete with other stimulating drinks. In the mid-seventeenth century, Jesuit father José Cardiel worried that the introduction of chocolate into Chile and Peru might decrease demand for yerba there.[91] But just as in the mid-colonial era, even as the demise of Jesuit trade networks hiked up the price and decreased the availability of yerba across the Andes in Peru and Chile, South American elites continued to covet and even show off their access to the Paraguayan herb. In a sign of things to come, they also began to incorporate other stimulating drinks, like coffee enjoyed at new cafés, into their repertoire.[92]

WHEN PERUVIAN ELITES WERE THE
MATE'S MOST VISIBLE DRINKERS

For estimates of the size and scale of the mate trade, historians can consult statistics kept by Jesuits and different representatives of the Spanish colonial government that enforced quotas and collected taxes.[93] To understand labor practices and religious ideas, we can again turn to the Jesuits, who kept detailed records. Uncovering historical patterns of consumption and symbolic associations with mate beyond the Jesuits, though, is a trickier task. Fortunately, European travelers and artists (who in some cases, such as Frézier's, were both) left behind their highly mediated but revealing impressions. While travelers' written accounts emphasized the scale of the yerba trade, the ritual, and the wide range of people who partook in it across the region, artists' visual depictions focused on the very privileged demographic of fair-skinned criollos (people of Spanish descent born in the New World). In particular, artists trained their viewers' eyes on criollo women—criollas—who drank mate in the Viceroyalty of Peru.

Most colonial artwork did not highlight mate drinking but rather emphasized ecclesiastical themes for the church and formal portraits of colonial authorities and elites. As formally trained artists from Europe and members of Indigenous art guilds in the Andes took the lead in producing such artwork, we are left to wonder whether more popular artists depicted the mate ritual in their communities, and if so, how.[94] Taken together, the dozen or so surviving colonial compositions that include a mate suggest that this South American ritualized drink provided a visible marker of the differences in European-descended elites' lives in the so-called New World versus the Old World.

In the 1770s and 1780s, three artists painted criollas, associating their identity and respectability with their propensity to drink mate. These paintings belonged to the contemporary genre of types, made most recognizable in contemporary *casta* (or caste) paintings. Artists who produced such paintings in New Spain and Peru engaged in the quixotic mission of representing supposedly discrete ethnic and racial identities of those born in the New World. The Peruvian *casta* series featured mostly Spanish men with their female partners and children with varying levels of African, Indigenous, and European ancestry; there were no Spanish or criolla mothers (or mates) present.[95] In contrast, in the contemporary paintings of criolla types, women of Spanish descent stood on their own. Each was accompanied by a mate, not a man. The silver mate served as a potent symbol of how these fair-skinned, well-dressed elite women had become locals, or criollas, rather than Spanish women.

Let us take a closer look at how the presence of the mate defined the criolla identity of these female subjects. In 1774, an artist named Pedro M. composed a portrait of an ornately dressed married woman, generically described as "Sra. Criolla de Lima" (Mrs. Criolla of Lima), for a Chilean viceregal official. He painted a fair woman in an elaborate dress standing next to a table with a claw-footed silver mate and bombilla, a steaming kettle at her feet. The woman holds a rose to her lips, perhaps perfuming them before drinking her mate to enhance the taste or in reference to the patron saint referred to as the "Rose of Lima."[96]

Future artists depicted a similar tableau. Three years after Pedro M., Spanish cartographer and artist Juan de la Cruz Cano y Olmedilla painted *Española criolla de Lima* (Spanish creole woman from Lima), featuring a woman in a

FIGURE 1.2. Juan de la Cruz Cano y Olmedilla, *Española criolla de Lima*, 1777. Courtesy of Biblioteca Nacional de España digital platform.

frilly dress, cupping a silver mate in her hand, as part of his 1777 series on sartorial customs across the Spanish Empire (fig. 1.2).[97] This female subject holds the bombilla to her lips, showing viewers in Europe how she consumes the local drink. Eleven years later, in 1788, Venetian engraver Theodorum Viero offered another illustration: *Dama criolla de Lima* (Creole lady of Lima). He too pictured this criolla representative of Lima holding a mate in her hands with a long silver bombilla between her lips. Curiously, she appears outside on an ornate staircase, seemingly a reference to Venice, Viero's home city. Despite her surroundings, the mate she holds emphasizes her belonging in the city of Lima instead.

Like the three Spanish women in Frézier's composition a half decade earlier, these elite women's association with drinking mates covered in silver—extracted by exploited workers fueled by yerba and coca in the mines of Potosí—symbolized wealth, time for leisure, the ability to dispense patronage to the lower classes, and their status as criollas who participated in local traditions. By the late eighteenth century, criollas in the Viceroyalty of Peru had become *the* emblematic mate drinkers in the eyes of the transatlantic elite. The new generation of European artists who helped make them so no longer deemed it necessary to include conquistadors in their compositions to highlight the success of the colonial project in creating criollos' tony lifestyles in the New World. Sumptuous clothing and silver mates conveyed the message on their own.

In contrast to the flurry of artistic compositions linking mate drinking to elite women in the capital of the Viceroyalty of Peru, none have made their way to us from the colonial region of the Río de la Plata. This colonial backwater, a region that would encompass the future nations of Argentina, Paraguay, and Uruguay, was filled primarily with campesinos (or rural dwellers) and inspired far fewer travelers' and artists' depictions of everyday life in general, and mate in particular.[98] And yet locals in Buenos Aires had been drinking mate since at least 1580. Across the Río de la Plata region, in places where the Spanish had established control during the colonial era, yerba served as a staple of everyday life.[99]

The rare artist who focused on this region, mid-seventeenth-century Jesuit father Florian Paucke, did not include mate in his artwork depicting customs and types in the Río de la Plata region, but he emphasized the importance of yerba in his written account.[100] Pauke served with Indigenous peoples he referred to as *mocovíes* on the missions of San Javier (1751–64) and San Pedro (1765–67), both outside the city of Santa Fe. Too far south to grow yerba, they exchanged cattle for yerba with Guaraní missions farther north. In his memoir, he shared that he drank mate every day, following the local custom of taking it early in the morning, in the afternoon, and at dusk. Pauke claimed to have introduced yerba to the *mocovíes*. Whether or not this is true, it is clear that he used yerba to incentivize their conversion, sobriety, and labor.[101] In recounting his negotiations over a work strike with Cithaalin, one of two caciques on his mission, he recalled telling him, "The yerba has been given to you all so that you work and [yet] sometimes you drink [alcohol] too; if you only want to drink and not work, then you will not receive more yerba."[102] Pauke told his European readers that this pronouncement helped, but we do not have the words of Cithaalin or other *mocovíes,* who apparently sought to resist the Jesuits' work imperatives, to verify it.

Other Jesuit fathers who worked to the north on missions where ka'a was cultivated expressed greater interest in this plant, though none seems to have illustrated the Guaraní or local Spaniards consuming it. Fellow Jesuits Pedro Montenegro and José Sánchez Labrador, both with botanical inclinations, sketched the tree they referred to in Guaraní as "caá" and "caà," respectively, and in Spanish as "Arbol de la yerba" (tree of the herb) in their respective works. In 1710, Montenegro drew a sketch of a single yerba branch covered with leaves and berries that attracted local birds, which played a key role in the germination process, as was later confirmed. Some sixty years later, Sánchez Labrador drew a more recognizable version of this tree, not only associating it with the production of "Caà" and the "herb of Paraguay" but also referring to the product it created as "té del Sud" (or Southern tea).[103]

A new generation of European chroniclers and artists shifted their attention to depicting the mate ritual in the Viceroyalty of Peru from the northern city of Lima to the southern region of Chile. In his mid-nineteenth-century history of Chile, Claudio Gay depicted a mixed-sex *tertulia* (an elite intellectual or social gathering that served as a forum for sharing news, ideas, and gossip) in 1790 Santiago fueled by mate and chocolate (fig. 1.3).[104] In a grand room under a massive crystal chandelier, a trio of female musicians playing stringed instruments enlivens the party. A small group of gentlemen in powdered wigs on the left side of the room share mate. In the center of the picture, two servants scoop hot cups of chocolate to offer the guests. Due to its distant Mesoamerican origins and desirability in Europe, chocolate was a more expensive and luxurious offering than mate. Still, both were available, with only mate consumed in the illustration.

Despite the grandeur of elites pictured drinking here, it was not only wealthy Peruvians and Chileans who were able to partake in the mate-drinking ritual in the mid- and late eighteenth century in this region. While elite

FIGURE 1.3. Claudio Gay, *Una tertulia en Santiago*, 1790, 1854,
Colección Biblioteca Nacional de Chile, Santiago, available at
Memoria Chilena, www.memoriachilena.cl/602/w3-article-98715
.html. Originally published in Claudio Gay, *Atlas de la historia física
y política de Chile*, vol. 1 (Paris: E. Thunot, 1854), no. 30.

artwork provides few clues about non-elite consumption, written accounts
by Jesuits who ventured beyond their missions and colonial travelers who
went beyond major cities reveal mate's geographic and socioeconomic reach.
In 1747, Jesuit father Francisco Xarque explained that yerba from Paraguay
made its way all across the Viceroyalty of Peru. "There are no Spanish homes,
nor Indian ranchos [humble homes made with natural materials like adobe
and straw] in which it is not the drink, the daily bread."[105]

A few years prior, British commodore John Byron's expedition around
the world included an unintended stop on an island he called Chaco off the
coast of Chile in the early 1740s.[106] There, locals eagerly awaited the annual
ship with supplies from Lima and experienced "distress," as he put it, when
the yerba to make mate did not appear alongside crucial supplies of maize,
cloth, hats, and wine (for the church), as well as luxuries such as sugar, brandy,
tobacco, linen, and ribbon. "Matte, an herb from Paraguay, used all over South
America instead of tea, is also a necessary article," Byron concluded.[107] While
yerba, unlike other foodstuffs such as maize, did not prove biologically necessary for survival, by the mid-eighteenth century, it had become a social

necessity rather than a luxury. The consumption of the Paraguayan herb stimulated many colonial South Americans' everyday lives and, in this isolated island off the Pacific coast, linked residents to the mainland.

Similarly, British adventurer George Vancouver explained in 1795 that poor rural dwellers outside the Chilean port city of Valparaíso regularly drank mate. Horrified by the conditions of the humble homes there, he explained to readers back home that they "contained the most common necessaries to the existence of human life; a dirty table, a stool, a wretched bed in one corner, and five or six crosses." He expressed his surprise that despite these conditions, residents allowed themselves what he called the "luxury" of drinking the Paraguayan herb and often possessed bombillas and a small number of other utensils made of silver. Silver was more affordable than Vancouver realized—or we might imagine today—due to the proximity of the silver mine at Potosí and the Spanish mercantilist policy of barring the export of precious metals.[108] Once obtained, silver was illegal to sell per Spanish colonial law, and people passed it down through the generations.

Locals also expected and consumed yerba in regions far from the sea. In 1773, circuit judge Alonso Carrió de la Vandera highlighted the prevalence of female-dominated consumption in the Andean highlands: "In Cuzco, Huamanga, Huancavélica . . . and above all Arequipa, the señoritas make all visitors drink three mates in the morning and another three in the afternoon."[109] As elsewhere, colonial women in the highlands took the lead in hosting guests, drinking mate, and initiating newcomers to this ritual.

Over the course of the seventeenth and early eighteenth centuries, patterns of daily life and consumption shifted significantly for elites but also for the poor majority. Common folks joined the well-to-do in consuming tobacco, yerba, and alcohol and in their access to a few luxuries, such as a silver bombilla to drink their mates.[110]

LOOKING EASTWARD TOWARD THE VICEROYALTY OF THE RÍO DE LA PLATA AND SOUTHERN BRAZIL

In the late eighteenth century, as Spanish debt mounted and more silver leaked through Buenos Aires, the Spanish crown sought greater political control over and economic profit from its colonies. About a decade after the Jesuits' expulsion, in 1776, the Spanish established the Viceroyalty of the Río de la Plata with the aim of benefiting from trade and contraband moving through the region. Buenos Aires served as the viceregal capital after establishing itself as a center of (often illegal) trade and replaced Lima as the dreaded local tax collector for the region. This Atlantic port city now held bureaucratic authority over the region that would become the nations of Argentina, Bolivia, Paraguay, and Uruguay, a future no one saw coming at the time.[111]

In the late eighteenth century, cities in the Viceroyalty of the Río de la Plata remained centers of colonial wealth and power, with Buenos Aires soon rising to the top. Montevideo had the superior natural port, but Buenos Aires's greater distance from Portuguese control made it a safer choice for the Spanish crown. Colonial authorities considered much of the region outside the principal cities of Asunción, Buenos Aires, Montevideo, Potosí, and Santa Fe to be "frontier regions," sparsely populated, controlled by Indigenous groups, subject to border disputes with Portugal, or some combination thereof. In the late eighteenth century, in an attempt to solidify its borders against Portuguese and native populations, the Spanish throne supported a policy of frontier settlement, offering town charters to settlers who claimed lands for themselves on behalf of the Spanish crown. Several regions that these settlers claimed would become the most important centers of yerba mate production and transport.[112]

Yerba mate would remain essential to the economy of South America in the late colonial era, as local officials and entrepreneurs realized. The new viceroy of the Río de la Plata, Pedro Antonio de Ceballos, declared that workers be given mate both before and after work, as well as every couple of hours.[113] Merchants in Buenos Aires financed more yerba ventures to the north, which helped enrich the region, alongside exports of salted meat and cowhide, and expanded the production and trade of yerba.[114]

Paraguay's exports of yerba sank the year the Jesuits were ordered out, but then skyrocketed. In the four decades following Jesuit removal, export volume increased more than tenfold, reaching some 327,150 arrobas (or over 8 million pounds) by 1808.[115] The late colonial expansion of the yerba trade more deeply integrated Paraguay into the economic zone of the greater Río de la Plata.[116] At the same time, yerba producers in Paraguay began to face new competition, as their neighbors in southern (and still Portuguese) Brazil began to export unprocessed yerba to the lower Platine region in the early nineteenth century.[117]

European profiteers, travelers, and observers followed the money. In the late colonial era, many shifted their attention from South America's Pacific coast to the Atlantic coast, chasing profits in various commodities that included but went beyond yerba. Transferring their regional focus, these Europeans also began to associate mate drinking with the new Viceroyalty of the Río de la Plata and even with the frontier region of Paraná recently claimed by the Portuguese crown.[118] Like those who preceded them, this new generation of European travelers often turned their own and, in turn, their readers' attention to the unique sociality of the mate ritual.

In 1808, a self-proclaimed British gentleman dedicated a whole chapter of his *Notes on the Viceroyalty of La Plata* to the local custom of drinking mate. While the author did not provide an illustration, he painted one with his words. In a typical courtyard in Montevideo during the summer, below grapevines, "men spend their hours in conversation and smoking. The women [pass their time] at their needles, thrumming the guitar, or taking their favourite *maté*." [119] Like many before him, the British gentleman feminized the act of mate drinking, while elaborating that pretty much everyone drank mate. He explained, "To the use of this herb, the inhabitants are universally and immoderately addicted. It is not entirely confined to the natives of the country, but strangers, and those from Old Spain, after living some time among them, become equally fond of it. It serves them for breakfast, the use of tea, coffee, and chocolate, being uncommon in families."[120] Like earlier European observers, this gentleman author shared with his anticipated European readers the popularity of this unique beverage and the way that South Americans consumed it. While he admitted that he liked the taste of this local infusion when prepared like a tea, he found sharing of the same tube particularly objectionable and apparently never tried it. "They suck, one after the other, as it is passed from hand to hand, far from considering it a breach of decorum, and without any of those sentiments of repugnance with which an European is usually infected."[121]

In the Viceroyalty of the Río de la Plata, the practice of sharing the same cup and bombilla crossed boundaries, including those between slave owners and the people they held as slaves. The British gentleman shared his astonishment that in Montevideo, "the slave drinks it as well as his master, and usually out of the same vessel too."[122] Similarly, Pauke, who spent the mid-eighteenth century on Jesuit missions just north of the city of Santa Fe, detailed that distinguished Spaniards did not drink the first mate but rather "made their slave, *la mulatilla*"—a daughter of White and Black parents—drink it before them. "The reason," he explained, "is that the yerba is frequently mixed with dust and sand."[123] In both cases, the enslaved domestic servants whom these foreigners observed likely not only took the first sip but also prepared mates for their masters by heating the water and later replacing the yerba when it lost its flavor, all important domestic labor that will be discussed at greater length in the next chapter.

It is not clear why the intimacy of this act between unequal parties caught foreigners' attention in the colonial Viceroyalty of the Río de La Plata and not in Peru. Perhaps it points to different roles for servants in this region, a greater desire for the newly wealthy to show off their status, or the lower quality of yerba in the east. For slave owners in the Viceroyalty of the Río de La Plata, their enslaved servants' initiation of the mate service ensured the quality of their infusion and likely helped to allay fears of poisoning. Sharing the same mate and bombilla also fostered unequal and yet intimate, quotidian connections between masters and human beings legally bound to serve. It was not different in a mechanical sense for people of different stations to drink from the same mate as it was for social peers, but this form of everyday intimacy (like wet nursing) preserved racial hierarchies. Servants were expected to take the first sip for their patrons (and their guests) in an obligatory act of service, while European visitors were invited to participate in the entire round in a show of the patron's hospitality.

Mate consumption predominated not only across nearly all sectors of society in Spanish America but also in missionary regions under Portuguese control. British businessman John Luccock, in Brazil from 1808 to 1818, was captivated by the popularity of what he called "matté" in the newly acquired Brazilian region known as Paraná. Given that the territory of Paraná previously hosted several Jesuit missions, locals had long harvested and consumed this stimulant now referred to in Brazil as *cangunha* or *congonha*. There, as in other regions of Spanish America, locals shared the drink made with flash-dried, ground-up leaves, which Luccock observed were more yellow than green (the preference for a green variety in Brazil emerged only in the late twentieth century). People in Paraná took their mate in a "half a cocoa-nut." Despite this local twist, the social norm of partaking persisted. Luccock warned that even for a foreigner, for whom "disgust may arise from the sight of some of the mouths, receiving the pipe in their turn, it would be deemed the height of ill-breeding to decline a share of Matté."[124]

Luccock found a similar ethos but a different caffeinated drink elsewhere in Brazil. Describing his travels through the countryside to the north, he praised the generous hospitality of locals and shared their expectation of presumably male guests: "He is expected to take breakfast where he passes the night; coffee and milk are early prepared." Honoring this early morning ritual was important; "to suffer a guest depart without it would be considered as a want of hospitality on the part of the host, [and] to decline partaking of it would be construed as incivility on that of the guests."[125] As with the sharing of the mate cup, the ritual of drinking coffee and milk together strengthened even a temporary relation. This proved true not just in the Brazilian countryside but also in the city. Luccock described how elite families in Rio de Janeiro would share a cup of coffee after lunch before their siestas.[126]

For European outsiders, participating in coffee-drinking customs likely felt more comfortable but also less intimate than the actual sharing of the cup and tube that the mate ritual required. In Paraná and much of Spanish South America, coffee drinking was rare. More often, locals offered and expected foreigners to share mate with them and considered it rude if they refused.[127]

~~~~~~

The consumption of yerba powerfully linked most of Spanish South America and parts of Portuguese South America during the colonial era. By the seventeenth century, a local plant used for ceremonial and medicinal purposes by the Guaraní in the precolonial era had become a commodity. As it traveled across Spanish America, reaching into the heart of the Viceroyalty of Peru, the Guaraní's ka'a became associated with the place of origin called Paraguay. The Jesuits, together with the Guaraní who earlier discovered and now worked to pick and process it, played a major role in introducing this stimulating herb from Paraguay to fellow South Americans. Even so, the Jesuits' expulsion did not rupture the economic and social connections that yerba producers and consumers helped forge across the region. Instead, even more yerba flowed across South America after the departure of the Jesuits.

By the eighteenth century, most people living in South America considered yerba a necessity rather than a luxury, even as the top echelons of society infused the ritual with materials that distinguished it from that of their supposed inferiors. Starting in the seventeenth century, elites in the Viceroyalty of Peru drained their high-grade yerba *caaminí* through elaborate silver-gilded mates perfumed with citrus fruits and flowers and sweetened with expensive sugar.[128] In turn, poorer people drank their less-refined and generally unsweetened *yerba de palos* from gourds, coconuts, or cow-horns (called *guampas*), with some draining their yerba through a silver bombilla.

The type of mate and bombilla and the quality of yerba differentiated the wealthy from the poor, and the Guaraní tradition of sharing a mate communally persisted throughout the region during the colonial era. This intimate form of commensalism straddled the socioeconomic hierarchy and provided a way to participate in local culture. With the notable exceptions of some newly arrived Spaniards and mine managers, nearly everyone across colonial Spanish South America participated. From the top echelons to the bottom, mate facilitated leisure and sociability. As a stimulant, it energized elites for social events and enabled workers to socialize and endure intensive labor.

By the eighteenth century, mate appeared as an important but unremarkable part of daily life for residents and as a captivating ritual for newcomers, in both Spanish-controlled South America and Portuguese-controlled Paraná. Most new arrivals found it hard to resist. While some needed time to accept the use of a common bombilla, and a few invented proto-hygienic alternatives, nearly all who left behind a record joined the mate circle. This decision allowed them to participate more intimately in local culture and to show off their understanding of what they depicted as an exotic South American ritual for their readers on the other side of the Atlantic. Travelers' descriptions of the mate ritual in detail supplied contemporary readers with precious information about the ubiquity and dynamics of this local drink during the colonial era.

Europeans told readers about a diverse range of peoples who drank mate in settings as disparate as a humble home in rural Chile or a courtyard trellised by grapevines in Montevideo, but artists focused their visual depictions on elite women—and to a lesser extent, men—in the Viceroyalty of Peru. This geographic focus reflected their commercial interest in South America's wealthiest colony during much of the colonial era. The choice of subjects conveyed a powerful vision of a colonial project so successful that women—and at evening parties, also men—from Old World families enjoyed the leisurely and exotic local pleasure of sipping from silver mates in beautiful South American surroundings. That they showed only Spanish criollo elites drinking mate, even as they wrote about how almost everyone drank mate, reflects just how important this marker became in distinguishing people of European descent in the New World from those in the Old, and among the Spanish elite, recent arrivals from the already acculturated.

The late colonial association of mate drinking with criollo elites presented a particularly cruel irony given that the precolonial Guaraní prized leisure over accumulation but became ensnared in European schemes for the very profits that now made leisure and luxury more possible for elite European descendants than for them. The Guaraní took the lead in picking and processing ka'a before *and* after the Europeans arrived. Jesuit sources lamented the exploitation of Indigenous peoples at the hands of the Spanish, even as the Jesuit fathers demanded hard work from Guaraní laborers in the hilly yerba forests and on their missions. In turn, local competitors condemned the Jesuits' unfair advantage. For their part, European observers frequently lambasted the Jesuits, mentioned the trade, and focused their attention and illustrations on the practice of drinking mate in urban locales. As a result, the backbreaking labor carried out first by Guaraní and eventually by other indentured laborers to produce yerba for a thirsty and growing South American market remained underrepresented in contemporary artwork.

At a more intimate scale, the work performed by domestic servants or slaves to heat water and infuse mates in elite homes is absent in most of the surviving artwork.[129] One rare artistic exception has made its way to us. The inside lid of a painted wooden box made to hold yerba, most likely crafted for an elite family in Cuzco in the 1740s, shows a pale, elegantly dressed couple sitting outdoors awaiting the mate that a kneeling Indigenous girl infused for them from an embellished silver container. The artist positioned this server at the margin of the composition, suggesting that service to her patrons is the most important thing about her. When this painted box is snapped open, it provides a rare vision of the racialized hierarchies of domestic service in the colonial era. It promotes the supposed naturalness of Indigenous servitude to European colonists, a particularly cruel irony when serving a distinctly Indigenous infusion. When the lid is closed, however, the scene features Spanish soldiers fighting without a native person in sight. The flags these soldiers planted in the ground suggest Spanish dominance within the region had been secured.

The early nineteenth-century wars of independence shattered the seeming impermeability of three centuries of Spanish colonialism. How would South America's break from Spain and Portugal, and the messy process of nation making that followed, affect the colonial commodity of yerba and its symbolic association within new republics? And what would become of the intimate colonial hierarchies linked to the mate ceremony? Because yerba mate was both a ritual and a commodity, new political associations and economic conflicts mattered, enabling the local drink to become an even stronger marker of social connection *and* differentiation.

CHAPTER TWO

Establishing Mate Hierarchies in Would-Be Nations, 1810s–1860s

A light-skinned couple sits nestled at the base of an enormous ombú tree (fig. 2.1). The man plays guitar. The woman awaits the mate about to be handed to her by a brown-skinned man who squats on the ground. This second man's skin color, long braided hair, and sandals suggest Indigenous ancestry; the red Phrygian cap on his head, his politics. This cap, associated with the French Revolution, now symbolized independence from Spain.[1]

Around 1831, Charles Henri Pellegrini painted this revolutionary watercolor in his new hometown of Buenos Aires. Born to Italian parents but raised in France, Pellegrini titled this painting *Cielito, cielo que sí* (Little piece of heaven, heaven, yes) in homage to a popular poem penned by writer Bartolomé Hidalgo a decade earlier.[2] In that work, written in response to the Spanish king Fernando VII's pronouncement that the region should remain loyal to him, a patriotic gaucho holding guard in the hills scoffed:

Cielito, cielito que sí [Little piece of heaven, little piece of heaven, yes,]
guardensé su chocolate, [you keep your chocolate,]

aquí somos puros indios [here we are pure Indians]
y sólo tomamos mate [and we drink only mate].[3]

In Hidalgo's view, the wars of independence that erupted in the capital of the former Viceroyalty of the Río de La Plata in 1810 had clearly divided locals into "pure Indians" who drank mate and Spanish outsiders who preferred chocolate. This was, on some level, a pragmatic distinction, since chocolate was scarce and yerba plentiful in the independence-era Río de la Plata region. The opposite held true in Spain. But this culinary distinction also reflected contemporary thinking. Despite the Indigenous origins of cacao in Meso-america, where Spaniards first encountered it, people in the Río de la Plata came to associate chocolate with the Spanish rather than with their more distant counterparts to the north.[4]

Across Spanish America, revolutionaries shared antipathy for Spanish rule while royalists remained loyal to it, but neither group, nor those who abstained from the political drama, possessed the notion of a pan–Latin American identity during the independence era (1810–25).[5] Even the ambitious revolutionary Simón Bolívar hoped to form four or five countries that would loosely follow former viceregal boundaries rather than one united region.[6] Within these viceregal units, revolutionary leaders sought to drum up popular support against the Spanish by stressing the common goals brought about by shared birthplace and native cultural roots that preceded Spanish oppression. Hidalgo, a *mulato* (a person of mixed African and European ancestry) who hailed from the eastern bank of the Río de la Plata, enthusiastically gestured toward the indigenous nature of the local drink to express locals' patriotism and difference from Spain.[7]

In the La Plata region, the free spirit of the rural figure of the gaucho, rather than the bravery of earlier Indigenous peoples, would eventually be celebrated as representing a distinct national spirit in Argentina, Uruguay, and parts of southern Brazil. Hidalgo also participated in early efforts to redeem the gaucho, whom writers had villainized as a vagabond or bandit. As in the aforementioned poem, Hidalgo published many literary works in which he positioned the gaucho as a noble rural figure worthy of respect.[8] In his subsequent visual homage, Pellegrini offered a patriotic guitar-playing gaucho who not only sings about independence but also wears a black cap emblazoned with the word *Federación* (Federation) in red. Behind him, another gaucho draped in a red poncho swirls his lasso. These sartorial gestures signal both men's allegiance to a new kind of political leader, the caudillo, a provincial strongman who built a personalistic base of loyal supporters who accepted

FIGURE 2.1. Carlos Enrique (in French, Charles Henri) Pellegrini, *Cielito, cielo que sí! Ou le guitariste*, ca. 1831, as reproduced in C. E. Pellegrini, *Tableau pittoresque de Buenos Ayres* (Buenos Aires: Librería L'Amateur, 1958), no. 17.

his rule in return for military protection and other favors. In this case, the reference was to Juan Manuel de Rosas, the governor of the province of Buenos Aires, who dominated local politics from 1829 to 1852. In 1832, Rosas made wearing the Federalist red *divisa* obligatory, but even before, wearing red became a visible statement of political support of, or protection from the wrath of, the Federalist Party.[9]

In the post-Rosas era the gaucho would eventually become the most visible symbol of local culture and, as such, the premier mate drinker, but this was still off in the future in the early nineteenth century. Indeed, colonial observers would not have been surprised to see that the mate-drinking figure in Pellegrini's 1831 composition was both White and female. Neither would contemporaries. The mythical White woman served as a potent symbol of new republics emerging across the Western world. Pellegrini's "lady liberty" held a mate but also wore a blue head covering and shawl. Blue was the color of the liberal Unitarian Party, which originally recruited Pellegrini across the Atlantic to serve as a hydraulic engineer in Buenos Aires. By the time he arrived in 1828, after an unanticipated ten-month stay in Montevideo, Pellegrini's job offer had disappeared due to Rosas's takeover.[10] So, too, would many of the Unitarians, who fled into exile. Pellegrini remained but dedicated himself to art rather than engineering. Throughout the nineteenth century, the worlds of politics and art—both dominated by highly educated and relatively well-off men of European descent—remained tightly intertwined.

~~~~~~

This chapter tells the story of how the South American viceroyalties' breakup with Spain and its contentious aftermath shaped the markets and meanings for the local ritualized beverage, infusing it with new politics. With the disruption of the colonial bureaucracy and marketplace, new economies emerged and competed with one another. Southern Brazil became a major producer and exporter of the so-called herb from Paraguay. Across the Andes, people in what would become Peru and Ecuador lost access to the Paraguayan herb, while others in Chile maintained the local tradition, even as access to yerba became more irregular. In the former Viceroyalty of the Río de La Plata, folks across the social scale continued to fill their mates with yerba from Paraguay and, increasingly, Brazil.

Like their colonial predecessors, some travelers drawn to the region for commercial and military reasons penned entertaining accounts meant for fellow Europeans. Their continental upbringing, elite standing, and commercial motives shaped their presentation of the mate ritual as an exotic and Indigenous marker of South American culture that they could translate in entertaining ways for folks back home. Despite their obvious biases, European chroniclers' written accounts give us access to specific, sensorial descriptions of the mate ritual. They also allow us to appreciate that the nearly universal practice of drinking mate changed little with independence in regions that preserved their access to yerba.

In contrast, if we turn our attention to the intensifying flurry of visual representations of the mate ritual, we can see a dramatic shift in the symbolic meanings associated with the local drink. In the 1830s, a new category of artists known as costumbristas, who hailed from France, England, and South America, began to depict the daily customs, including mate drinking, of a wider variety of non-elite people for European and South American audiences.[11] Like Pellegrini, many portrayed mate drinking as political and hierarchal, making the case for their creole allies' rights to rule over and be served by their supposed racial inferiors. Despite political discourse that proclaimed racial difference did not matter in the new republics, racial hierarchies persisted in everyday life and accelerated on the canvas.

This chapter focuses on costumbrista artwork, which circulated more widely via the new technology of lithography, because it is the primary genre that both influenced and highlighted the mate ritual's changing symbolism in the immediate postcolonial world. In continuity with the colonial era, elite White women preserved their status as the most symbolically important mate drinkers in new nations. As we learned in the previous chapter, colonial illustrations of elite women in the Viceroyalty of Peru regularly included a heated pot of water at their feet, which was almost certainly provided by a servant of Indigenous, African, or mixed descent. Neither the artists nor the elites who commissioned these works decided to include the servant in the picture. In this postcolonial moment, though, a new generation of artists replaced the pot with a person, usually a non-White mate server.

The visual culture surrounding the mate ceremony reveals the way in which racialized hierarchies—alongside the overlapping hierarchies of gender and class—assumed greater visibility and symbolic power in representations of elite domestic life in the early national era. Such quotidian inequalities persisted alongside dramatic attempts by creole men to exercise and consolidate their political power in would-be nations.

BREAKING APART

What would happen to the production and consumption of the Paraguayan herb as this region splintered apart during and after its declarations of independence from Spain? The intra-regional political and military drama matters here because yerba served as the most lucrative of goods produced in what became the Viceroyalty of the Río de la Plata during the colonial era.[12] Therefore, understanding yerba's history requires a basic understanding of how the South American nations that dominated its postcolonial production and consumption began to emerge.

Since at least 1810, political elites in Buenos Aires held aspirations to declare this region's independence from Spain and to govern a new republic that would preserve the borders of the Viceroyalty of the Río de La Plata. Just one year later, Paraguay declared its independence, rejecting claims from not only Buenos Aires but also Spain and Portugal. As local wars with and against the Spanish reached a climax, in 1825, a new nation now referred to as Bolivia, in Simón Bolívar's honor, broke off. Despite this supposed end to the Spanish American wars of independence, the region continued to fracture. In 1828, the Estado Oriental de Uruguay (Eastern State of Uruguay), which had been one among several provinces in the United Provinces of the River Plate, became a republic of its own in 1828. Uruguay was formed after Britain, eager to profit off of free trade in the region, pointed its cannons at the Argentine and Brazilian armies to convince them to renounce their respective claims to this area, at least for the moment.[13] As historian Karen Racine explains, Great Britain offered military support, financial resources, commercial opportunities to Spanish American independence leaders, and, just as important, a liberal model that allowed them to believe that "they could retain a privileged place for themselves" in new nations.[14]

Before the late nineteenth century, all the former regions included in the Viceroyalty of the Río de La Plata as well as Brazil, which became an empire of its own in 1822 and a republic in 1889, had yet to claim their current form. In the La Plata region, liberal Unitarians and their Federalist enemies fought one another for political control in violent clashes across what would become the Republic of Argentina, while their counterparts, referred to as the (liberal) Colorados and (Federalist) Blancos, waged war in the Republic of Uruguay.[15] The principal geographical borders of current-day Argentina were not established until the 1880s in the wake of its genocidal "Conquest of the Desert" against Indigenous nations and the Triple Alliance War against Paraguay, which enabled Argentina to seize the province of Misiones and eventually enter the yerba-growing industry.[16]

In the decades following independence, South American republics existed on paper but could hardly claim any definitive expression of sovereignty. Within the former Viceroyalty of the Río de la Plata, Paraguay stood out for its early political consolidation and the ideological coherence provided by its widely recognized, long-standing name.[17] By 1814, Dr. José Gaspar Rodríguez de Francia had taken over, declaring himself the "Supreme and Perpetual Leader of Paraguay," or "El Supremo" (The Supreme one), a title that lasted until his death in 1840. Like others seeking to establish authority in the political vacuum left by the Spanish crown's removal, Francia devoted more attention to consolidating his own power than to developing the Paraguayan economy and its main colonial export, yerba, or its sidekick, tobacco.[18] Francia was eager to meet the demand for these products within Paraguay but showed little interest in doing so in the politically unstable lower Platine region. He flirted with the European market, sending a shipment of

Paraguayan yerba (along with tobacco, spirits, sugar, and lace embroidery) with the British brothers J. P. and W. P. Robertson to England.[19] However, the Atlantic trade of Paraguayan products with Europe never took off.[20] Francia's approach, combined with the unreliable nature of all river trade in the region in the 1820s and 1830s, meant that while folks in Paraguay enjoyed plentiful access to yerba, other South Americans could not count on the regular importation of yerba from Paraguay during "El Supremo's" long rule.[21]

The rupture of the colonial marketplace, together with Francia's decisions, complicated Paraguay's trade within the former Viceroyalty of Río de La Plata and decimated it within the still-convulsing Viceroyalty of Peru by 1820, where the Royalist army deliberately sealed off trade routes during the fighting.[22] As historian Juan Carlos Garavaglia emphasizes, "The very old river route that from 1580 to 1820 had bound Paraguay with the space organized around its most dynamic poles, Potosí and Buenos Aires, was definitively broken."[23] The overland road to Alto Perú was also obstructed. Residents of what would become Peru and Ecuador quickly lost their access to and eventually their memory of the Paraguayan herb, but pockets of Bolivia and especially Chile held on.[24]

Within the lower Platine region, greater distance from native yerba forests meant higher prices for Paraguayan yerba. By the late 1820s, an arroba (roughly 11.5 kilograms) of Paraguayan yerba sold for seven pesos in nearby Corrientes and some fifty pesos, more than seven times as much, in Buenos Aires.[25] Given Francia's apparent disinterest in meeting demand in the lower Platine region in a more affordable manner, yerba speculators in Brazil began to more aggressively employ indentured laborers to harvest the native forests in the provinces of Paraná and Rio Grande do Sul. "There workers extracted a poor grade of yerba, rendered still poorer by the admixture of grasses and base materials when prepared for shipment," according to Thomas Whigham. Often called "yerba de Paranaguá," after the port from which it embarked, Brazilian yerba flowed downriver to Santa Fe, Buenos Aires, and Montevideo, where it sold in greater quantities and for substantially lower prices than the higher-quality product shipped and often smuggled out of Paraguay.[26] Paraguay's postcolonial approach to yerba allowed Brazil into the game.[27]

Echoing Jesuit times, by the end of the independence era there were once again two qualities of yerba. Elites distinguished themselves not only by their more expensive, silver-gilded mates and the sugar they used to sweeten them but also by the superior grade and provenance of their yerba. While the wealthy could afford to pay for higher-priced Paraguayan yerba, when available, commoners made do with the inferior and reputedly impure Brazilian variety, appreciating its lower price point and some even seeming to prefer its familiar taste.[28]

Despite declining revenues and mounting competition from Brazil, Paraguay not only maintained its legendary reputation for the best yerba in the region but also gained the enduring power of official scientific recognition. In 1822, French botanist Auguste de Saint-Hilaire, who spent some five years conducting research, mostly in Brazil, formally declared the scientific name of what most colonial subjects had called the "herb of Paraguay" to be *Ilex paraguariensis* (or Paraguayan holly).[29] In his report to France, he clarified that despite labeling this plant as Paraguayan, he encountered it in both the former Jesuit regions of Paraguay and the forests of Curitiba, Brazil. On behalf of his beloved host country of Brazil, he pointed out that even as Spanish Americans liked to point to the "big difference between the herb prepared in Paraguay and that of Brazil, pretending that they are different plants," botanically, they were "perfectly similar." The superiority of the ilex from Paraguay, Saint-Hilaire conceded, stemmed not from the plant itself but rather from the manner in which Paraguayans produced it.[30]

Saint-Hilaire's scientific designation became controversial, especially for future Brazilians and Argentines, who had obvious reasons to prefer that the botanical name for yerba not be linked to Paraguay. Argentine author Pau Navajas––who not only wrote a rich history of yerba mate but whose family now owns Argentina's largest yerba company, Las Marías––explains that fellow French botanist Aimé Bonpland first described and scientifically cataloged this plant in 1818 after seeing it on the island of Martín García, located at the mouth of the Uruguay River, well beyond the semitropical region where yerba typically grows. Navajas laments that Bonpland did not get documentation back to France in time, and as a result, Saint-Hilaire's designation and the official scientific association with Paraguay stuck. Bonpland apparently wished to name it *Ilex theezans mihi*, or "Holly for my tea."[31]

Some have since suggested that Saint-Hilaire made a mistake in his association with Paraguay, pointing out that he first found the plant in Brazil. Others mention that Saint-Hilaire later sought to change the name to *Ilex mate* (Holly in a cup) but was unsuccessful.[32] Enduring debate around the naming of the species points to the weight of formal names assigned by early nineteenth-century European scientists to native South American plants in the formation of national economies and identities.

The emergence of new republics with unclear boundaries and little sense of shared national identity did not immediately shift locals' understandings of their relations to one another. And despite the new scientific link between yerba and Paraguay, the practice of making and drinking mate mostly remained the same during the independence era as it had been under the Spanish. During the revolutionary period, people across the La Plata region, and even elites in Chile, were rarely without yerba for their mates and offered them to insiders and outsiders alike.

Emeric E. Vidal, a member of the British military and an artist, spent the heady years of 1816 to 1818 in the former Viceroyalty of Río de La Plata and reported that mate drinking spanned the social hierarchy, from urban elites to poor rural dwellers.[33] Vidal pointed out that elites continued to cultivate distinctive mate consumption practices. They drank from elaborate silver vessels and added more ingredients than just hot water, just as their well-to-do colonial predecessors had done: "Sugar and spices, particularly cinnamon, are added by the higher classes to the *matté*, which is thus rendered a very pleasant drink."[34] In more humble rural settings, the offering of a simpler mate was to be expected and appreciated. "Throughout the provinces, the weary traveler, let him stop at what hovel soever he may, is sure to be presented with the hospitable *matté*-cup, which, unless his prejudices are very strong indeed, will be found a great refreshment," wrote Vidal.[35]

While Vidal's popular written account emphasized that mate drinking spanned the social hierarchy, he created and published only one image of this ritual, in which two soldiers shared a mate (fig. 2.2). In contrast to earlier depictions of elite female or mixed-sex groups drinking mate at a leisurely pace in a salon, Vidal portrayed common men on the move. Specifically, the soldiers Vidal painted in this watercolor engaged in a goodbye ritual that would become known as the *mate del estribo* (stirrup mate or goodbye mate), in which a man on a horse trotted off after one final energizing sip of mate offered by a person staying behind.[36]

Why did Vidal portray this ritual in a dramatically new way? As a member of the British military eager to remove the Spanish presence in the Río de la Plata region, Vidal interacted primarily with other male soldiers, many of whom drank mate. He also seemed aware that this local infusion provided a visible and symbolic way of distinguishing men fighting for their homeland from those fighting for Spain. Vidal clarified that the soldiers he painted were

FIGURE 2.2. Emeric E. Vidal, *Miliciens de la Bande Orientale*, ca. 1820. Courtesy of Biblioteca Nacional de Uruguay, Montevideo, Sala de Materiales Especiales.

lingering in the doorway of a *pulpería* (country store) on the eastern bank of the River Plate.[37]

In striking contrast to revolutionary soldiers' enthusiasm for mate, some Spaniards apparently refused, at least in theory, to drink this uniquely South American infusion. According to British major Alexander Gillespie, the Spaniards' rejection was generated "more from pride, than real dislike."[38] His observation seems plausible. For Spaniards still present in the Río de la Plata region, *not* drinking mate in public offered a visible way to distinguish themselves in a land where nearly everyone enjoyed this local infusion. Spurning mate could also serve as a political statement, given the separatist spirit that Vidal, then Hidalgo, and eventually Pellegrini linked to mate. And yet, as Gillespie pointed out, because chocolate and tea were difficult to come by in this region, he and his British troops drank mate for breakfast. The Spanish, too, probably had less access to alternatives than they would have preferred.[39]

Vidal's watercolor was unique for this era, both as a rare illustration of mate and because very little artwork on any topic was produced in the tense 1810s and 1820s. Even so, the generosity of common folk sharing mate inside and outside the militias was something travelers to the countryside of the Viceroyalty of the Río de la Plata continued to remark upon. Take for example British engineer and botanist John Miers, who in 1819 embarked with his pregnant wife on an overland journey from Buenos Aires to Chile in search of copper and other mineral resources. Heeding warnings from Buenos Aires residents (frequently called *porteños*) that bands of rebels called *montoneros* might attack their party, they selected what promised to be a safer southerly route through the Pampas region. After sleeping outside in the village of Mercedes near what he referred to as the postmaster's family's "small miserable mud hut," Miers awoke in the morning to "a curious and picturesque scene": members of the postmaster's extensive family were seated on "small blocks of wood" around a roaring fire, conversing and sharing a mate.[40]

Miers wrote about this mate-drinking scene in a way that played up the exotic nature of this ritual and racialized its participants. He told his European readers that upon seeing this group drinking mate outside, he was overtaken by the sensation that he was "bivouacking among the Indians, or among some savage outcasts of society." Miers had a taste for this kind of exotic adventure. He quickly joined the mate-drinking circle after being invited, as he explained in a lengthy diary entry on Sunday, April 11, 1819:

> I got up and joined the party, all of whom bustled to make room for me. A fresh matecito [small mate] was made for me, without a word being said respecting it. An old man threw out the leaves they were using and pulled from under on which he sat a small kid's skin, with the feet and tail tied into knots, so as to form a bag; in this he kept his store of yerba. He took out a small handful of the yerba, put it into the calabash ... and filled it up with boiling water from a copper pot, which forms an essential part of the household goods of every gaucho. Then putting in the bombillo or tin tube (they are generally of silver), he stirred it round, took a sip himself to ascertain its goodness, and then presented it to me, touching his hat the moment I received it.[41]

Miers justified this long description to his readers because drinking mate was a "habit which, without variation ... will be found, among high and low, universal[ly] in these parts of South America."[42] He accompanied his description with a simple drawing of the mate, straw, and pot (used by this servant-less family) for hot water.

Despite Miers's literary flourish and simple illustration, which made it seem like it was the first time he had observed locals drinking mate, he was no neophyte. Indeed, Miers also mentioned that he carried yerba with him on his journey across South America and used it, along with sugar and tobacco, as a bargaining chip and token of his appreciation for residents of the countryside, as colonial authorities had done before him and as new republican authorities would continue to do.[43] Rosas's government, for instance, provided privates in the army, Indigenous leaders, shepherds, and herdsmen with yerba as part of their monthly rations, along with meat and salt.[44] For his part, Miers reported that he gave the postmaster "a stock of tobacco and paper to make segars; and to his old wife a quantity of yerba and sugar." He noted their appreciation, given that "all these articles were extremely scarce and dear here."[45]

This scarcity of such goods was even greater across the Andes in Chile, although the upper strata of society still appeared to have regular access. In 1822, the rare early female travel writer Maria Graham, an Englishwoman, described her experience with the infusion made from "the herb of Paraguay, commonly called matte, so universally drank or rather sucked here."[46] As the daughter of a British naval officer, she enjoyed the unique opportunity as a European woman to travel to South America. Graham did not observe any mate in the coffee-drinking imperial city of Rio de Janeiro, where she spent considerable time, but described mate as "the great luxury of the Chilenos," both male and female, who enjoyed it first thing in the morning and after the afternoon siesta.[47] (Nineteenth-century Brazil stood apart because mate drinking did not occur in the city but rather in the countryside.)[48] Graham told unfamiliar European readers how the local infusion was prepared in Chile. "The herb appears like dried senna; a small quantity of it is put into the little vase with a proportion of sugar, and sometimes a bit of lemon peel, the water is poured boiling on it, and it is instantly sucked up through a tube about six inches long."[49]

Like some colonial travelers who preceded her, Graham expressed her discomfort about sharing the same tube with others. She described to her readers that she refrained from partaking in this communal practice during the first three weeks of her stay in the Chilean port city of Valparaíso.[50] On a visit to the home of some well-to-do shopkeepers in early June 1822 she relented. She explained that her hosts invited her to take a seat on a covered bench that ran the length of a room, and soon thereafter a "matee maker, who, after putting in the proper ingredients, poured the boiling water over them, applied the bombilla to her lips, and then handed it to me." Graham found it surprisingly good, "harsher than tea, but still very pleasant."[51]

Thereafter, drinking mate became a regular part of Graham's life. Due to her wealthy English background, well-connected father, and strong intellectual and social skills, elite Chileans regularly invited her to drink mate with them at their homes and in the countryside.[52] Graham was even paid a visit by local military heroes Generals San Martín and Zenteno. On this occasion, she recalled that she apologized "for having no matee to offer." She claimed the generals responded that they preferred "tea without milk" to accompany their cigars.[53] Did they say this to flatter her or to be polite? Or was Graham editorializing about their supposed preference for British tea over the local mate for her readers? We will likely never know. What we do know is that even if chocolate and tea were sometimes available, Graham had come to prefer mate on certain occasions. Escaping the rain after a long day's ride, she delighted in "having the comfort of a huge brasero of coals, and sheepskins laid under our feet while we took matee, more refreshing still than tea after a day's journey."[54]

The infusion served in silver cups was made by servants who laid blankets under the mate drinkers' feet.[55] Although in her account, Graham paid these mate servers little attention, they consistently provided her and her hosts with such comforts. On one occasion, she specified that these mate servers were "some pretty little Indian girls, very nicely dressed."[56] Young children of Indigenous, African, and mixed descent were often required to do a wide range of generally unpaid domestic tasks, including mate serving, for White families across South America.[57]

Even as Graham gave the impression that mate drinking was everywhere in Chile, the wars of independence disrupted trade within the region, hiking up the price of yerba in Chile and pushing it out of reach for those even slightly lower on the social scale.[58] Contemporary mining expert Peter Schmidt-meyer, who was born in Switzerland and raised in England, suggested in his account of his two-year stint in Chile in 1820–21 that the ubiquity of mate in Chile diminished bit by bit. By 1821, the price had risen to approximately seven shillings sterling a pound in Chile, and as a result, Schmidtmeyer noted, "a palatable infusion cannot be produced, without using far more of it than is required for making good China tea." He continued that "the poorer classes are nearly deprived of an enjoyment, which, particularly among women, extended also to social pleasure."[59] As in the colonial era, women in the early national period still hoped to place mate drinking at the social center of their lives, in this traveler's view.

A rarefied few could afford to partake. The rich still breakfasted on either chocolate or yerba and sometimes offered it at the social gatherings called *tertulias*. Schmidtmeyer included two of his illustrations of these evening parties in his account. The first, held in Santiago, featured music and dancing but no mate or refreshments. "It is very justly expected that society should

FIGURE 2.3. Peter Schmidtmeyer, *Tertulia and Mate Party*, ca. 1820–21.
Courtesy of Colección Biblioteca Nacional de Chile, Santiago, available
at Memoria Chilena, www.memoriachilena.cl/602/w3-article-78513
.html. This image later inspired a postcard. It was originally published
in Peter Schmidtmeyer, *Travels into Chile over the Andes in the Years
1820 and 1821: With Some Sketches of the Productions and Agriculture*
(London: Longman, Hurst, Orme, Brown, and Green, 1824), 1:266.

be frequented for the sake and pleasure of it, and not for eating or drinking,"
he wrote.[60] In contrast, the other party, hosted at a rural estate in the Valle
de Guasco, included mate as part of the revelry. In his note, Schmidtmeyer
clarified that "this tertulia is shown . . . with the addition of maté drinking,
although now seldom introduced to parties, owing to the scarcity of hierba,
and to a change in fashion, which also gradually tends to raise women from
their carpets and to place them on chairs or sofas."[61] In figure 2.3, portraying a
contemporary gathering much humbler than the colonial version later imagined by Claudio Gay (see fig. 1.3), women sit on such "carpets" in the center
of the room, and one drains a mate. In contrast, none of the men sit on the
floor. A female servant peeks her head into the relatively simple room, likely
to see whether more hot water or anything else is needed, but also perhaps to
satisfy her own curiosity about what the partygoers are doing or discussing.

For poor families farther east, who made up the majority of the Río de la
Plata region, mate served not as an occasional luxury but instead as a form
of sustenance.[62] In 1828, French surveyor Narciso Parchappe explained that
among the poor people he met in the Pampas, "mate is the only thing that
is drunk in the morning and for this the kettle is on the fire from daybreak."

Chapter Two

As Parchappe suggested, mate helped fill poor people's stomachs and energized their work, but it also provided a communal ceremony that included people of markedly different statuses. He continued, "The poor wake up and gather around the kitchen range in the kitchen and father, mother, children, workers, and slaves all together pass amongst them the bitter beverage."[63] Parchappe, like the gentleman chronicler we met in the last chapter in Montevideo, pointed his readers to the fact that families (in this case, unlikely to be very poor since they owned slaves) shared mates not only with guests but also with those who worked for them.

What did the intimacy of sharing a mate among people with markedly different statuses such as these look like? To consider this question, we can shift our attention to artwork of the era. As in Schmidtmeyer's case, a growing number of compositions featured the figure of the mate server in an important material and symbolic role.

THE SERVERS AND THE SERVED

A new generation of artists captivated by the postcolonial mate ritual included a new element not frequently seen in colonial representations: the servant. Writings from both the colonial and early national eras sometimes mention servants preparing mate, but their presence was usually elided in earlier paintings and drawings.[64] This was not, of course, because colonial elites lacked the labor of (often enslaved) servants to heat the water in the kitchen, port it to the salon, and replenish the yerba when it had lost its flavor. Rather, the absence of servants in artwork reflected the apparent lack of interest on the part of colonial elites who commissioned artists to make this domestic work visible. This was a context-specific choice. Colonial illustrations regularly showed elite White women being attended to by Black domestic slaves, especially when out in public. The presence of slaves visibly protected these White women's honor in a patriarchal society with a clear race-based hierarchy in which White women were not supposed to be out on the street alone, and elites erroneously assumed that non-White women had no honor to protect.[65] In contrast, neither colonial elites nor the artists who painted them seemed motivated to include a servant to protect White women's honor within the intimacy of the home.

After the break from Spain, a new group of artists working in the Río de la Plata region brought the servant into their compositions in a growing market for lithographs and illustrated books. Pellegrini, as we saw earlier, depicted the symbolic mate server as an Indigenous man in his 1831 vision of

FIGURE 2.4. Carlos Enrique Pellegrini, *Bailando el minuet en casa de Escalada*,
1831. Scan of lithograph courtesy of Museo del Grabado Facebook page,
original held by Museo Histórico Nacional, Buenos Aires, Argentina.

independence. In the next couple of years, he would include a female mate
server (*cebadora*) of African descent in a series of three lithographs that featured three different elite *tertulias* in the city of Buenos Aires.[66] Pellegrini
regularly attended such parties and depicted them in vivid detail. He painted
women in elaborate gowns and dramatic *peinetones* (hair combs) that represented female standards of beauty and the newfound wealth of this region.[67]
The men he illustrated appeared in suits with tails, some with red vests that
signaled their allegiance to the Federalist Party. In contrast, Pellegrini showed
the mate-serving maid wearing a simple blue dress with a white collar.

By focusing on one of Pellegrini's compositions, we can appreciate how
the mate ceremony allowed for a particular, and potentially tension-filled,
choreography of public intimacy between the servers and the served at a
party, a choreography now visible to many viewers of the artwork, not only
to those in attendance. In the painting *Bailando el minuet en casa de Escalada*
(Dancing the minuet in the Escaladas' house), Pellegrini placed the servant
in an interior doorway just outside the room (fig. 2.4).

This servant peeks out onto the party scene while holding a silver mate
to her lips. As the mate server for the party, she might be taking the first sip
out of a newly prepared mate to make sure the temperature of the water is
hot and the straw unclogged and that the yerba tastes fresh before handing it

to a guest. At the same time, the servant's positioning in the doorway allows for the possibility that she is taking a moment to herself to enjoy the mate. Or perhaps, she is observing, or even spying, on partygoers (as might have also been the case in Schmidtmeyer's composition a decade earlier). Under Rosas, liberal elites worried that their Black servants would be more loyal to the Federalist governor, who actively sought support from people of African descent.[68] So perhaps Pellegrini was hinting at this anxiety. In any case, at an actual *tertulia*, the mate server would not be permitted to stand in the doorway for long, as she would be expected to run to and from the kitchen to fetch more hot water, which another servant was likely heating in the kitchen.[69]

Pellegrini put the mate-drinking guests (himself and two of the women) at the center of his composition. Local and foreign writers also noted the importance of mate at elite social gatherings in the city of Buenos Aires. In his memoirs, Argentine writer and doctor José Antonio Wilde described the parties of his youth as affairs fueled by mate; "they usually danced until about midnight or a little longer, when earlier, they only served mate, and when the party lasted until daylight, they added chocolate."[70] For his part, French naturalist Arsène Isabelle remarked in his book on his travels to Argentina, Uruguay, and Brazil that if other male foreigners were invited to such parties, they should "master their senses" to protect themselves from the local elite "seductive women" who would offer them mate. The visitor was likely a source of amusement for these women, because, he explained, "it is very difficult to drink mate for the first time without burning your tongue, without clogging up the *bombilla* by sucking it too forcefully." He continued: "Observe those ladies, how they try to repress their laughter behind the pretty fan behind which they pretend to hide their faces."[71] A local woman's familiarity with mate put her in an insider position and, at least in this foreigner's eyes, made her more "seductive." Local women already knew the language of the mate ritual, and while they might laugh at beginners' missteps, they could also help newcomers like Isabelle to learn from them how to speak it.

While Isabelle and other writers highlighted the lead role that elite women played in offering and drinking mate, they also sometimes mentioned that the work of Black servants made this possible. "Mate is drunk at any time," Isabelle explained. "When a visitor arrives, *una negrita* [a little Black girl] brings it right away to her mistress who offers it to the people present one after the other."[72]

As Isabelle's comment suggests, the abolition of race-based slavery did not accompany independence in the Viceroyalty of Río de La Plata, leaving many people of African descent in positions of servitude. After declaring independence from Spain, abolition dragged on for the better part of a half century in most of the region.[73] This trend was particularly pronounced in the city of Buenos Aires, where the slave trade picked up in the late seventeenth and early eighteenth centuries, and census takers estimated that *negros* (Blacks) and *mulatos* (people of mixed African and European ancestry) made up a third of the city's population by 1810.[74] The presence of young servants of at least partial African descent in elite homes was further guaranteed by an 1813 law in Buenos Aires that promised the future freedom of children born to enslaved mothers, but obligated these children, who were legally referred to as *libertos*, to serve their masters until they were no longer minors.[75]

Swiss artist and pathbreaking lithographer César Hipólito Bacle, who immigrated to Buenos Aires in 1828 and printed many of Pellegrini's lithographs, portrayed the *liberto* as a mate server in his early 1830s artwork. Intended for a series of six notebooks of local "customs and types," Bacle included a couple of iterations of a composition in which two White ladies (likely sisters) share an early morning mate served by a diminutive Black male servant in an ornate sitting room in Buenos Aires.[76] Bacle released these lithographs in 1835 as part of a six-notebook series containing forty-six illustrated plates that sold for 100 pesos in color and for 40 pesos without color.[77] Purchasing these notebooks proved much less expensive than commissioning a painting, allowing the upwardly mobile an opportunity to obtain an image of a beloved local ritual and an enduring postcolonial racial hierarchy.

A closer look reveals how Bacle developed the racial choreography of mate service. In his lithograph called *Señorita Porteña por la mañana* (A Buenos Aires young lady in the morning), a young woman drains a small mate while her sister awaits her turn, and the Black servant stands with his arms crossed on the margin of the composition (fig. 2.5).[78] While the standing sister towers above the server, even the seated sister is noticeably taller than he is. He is half their size and barefoot. In another version of this composition, Bacle pictured this same young Black servant with his back to the viewer as he waits for the seated woman to drain her mate. With one arm slightly bent, he appears ready to take the mate from her to go back and forth to the kitchen to retrieve the hot water.[79]

In both compositions, Bacle's placement of the servant suggests that the boy's servile role is more important than his identity or appearance. The viewer sees his back or side but not his face. While this young servant's legal status was likely that of a *liberto*, the family he served and their elite peers more likely referred to him as a *criado*—a softer and more ambiguous term for supposedly free children raised by families who took them in and expected

FIGURE 2.5. César Hipólito Bacle, *Señora Porteña por la mañana*, 1833.
Original lithograph appeared in *Trages y costumbres de Buenos Aires*,
no. 1. (Buenos Aires: Bacle y Cía, Impresores litográficos del Estado,
ca. 1833–35). Digital file courtesy of Museo Marc Facebook page.

them to work as domestic servants in return for their keep, training, and sometimes a scant wage that barely set them apart from the enslaved. The condition of servitude was often passed down from one generation to the next.[80]

The presence of young Black domestic servants elevated the status of the families they served in early to mid-nineteenth-century Buenos Aires. As historian María de Lourdes Ghidoli explains, "The *criado* of African descent comes to symbolize the accumulation of objects that decorated *porteño* homes, and that emphasized the economic and social status of those who lived in them."[81] In addition to their symbolic value, such servants performed a wide range of materially important work. Their presence and labor allowed the families they worked for to mark their high status, enjoy moments of leisure, and entertain without doing much work themselves.

While the figure of the Black servant *cebador* or *cebadora* was most visible in contemporary artwork produced in and around Buenos Aires, the labor of servants was not limited to the region. For instance, revolutionary leader José Artigas, who hailed from the eastern bank of the River Plate and, like Hidalgo, dreamed of preserving a united Río de la Plata region, was famously attended to by a Black soldier, referred to as "Ansina," who made his mates.[82] Since Hidalgo, somewhat ironically, later became known as the father of Uruguayan independence, he appeared as a frequent subject of nationalist artwork intended to glorify national heroes. While earlier portraits of him during his lifetime did not show him with a mate, late nineteenth-century patriotic artist Pedro Blanes Viale painted *Artigas dictando a su secretario D. José G. Monterroso* (Artigas dictating to his secretary D. José G. Monterroso), a composition in which the figure of "Ansina" is shown infusing a mate for General Artigas and his companions. Unlike Vidal's common soldiers pictured with similar complexions and standing, this Black soldier is placed crouching by the fire to retrieve the kettle, well below the men he is to serve the newly revolutionary drink. The "faithful Ansina," as he was referred to, became Uruguay's best-known mate server (and a potent symbol of Afro-Uruguayan contributions to independence) as Hidalgo's painting recirculated on stamps and in other formats.[83]

General Justo José de Urquiza, a caudillo from Entre Ríos who broke with Rosas in 1850 and led the Argentine Confederation from 1854 to 1860, also breakfasted on mate served by a Black man. In his capacity as an official representative of the US government, naval officer Thomas Jefferson Page observed that the leader of the Argentine Confederation was given mate "at an early hour by a negro servant." Page clarified in a footnote that this man was much more than a mate server. He had worked for a long time as "the body-servant of Urquiza" and at the battle of Monte Caseros apparently "came well-nigh to capturing Rosas."[84]

Early to mid-nineteenth-century travelers regularly pointed to the presence of young Black servants throughout the Río de la Plata region, serving political leaders and other members of high society. For example, describing their journey from Buenos Aires to Paraguay, the enterprising Robertson brothers from Scotland remarked on the ubiquity of enslaved young Black servants at every point along their route.[85] In the intermediary port city of Santa Fe, they observed that "at the feet of each lady (not, however, including the young unmarried ones), sat a *mulatilla*, a female mulatto slave [of African and European ancestry], nine or ten years of age," who rolled the lady's tobacco and served her mate.[86] Farther north in the Guaraní-speaking province of Corrientes, the Robertsons noted that after a post-meal siesta in a hammock, they would awake to a mate and a cigar brought by an attractive "female mulatto slave."[87]

The Robertsons' ultimate goal was to make it to the famously elusive nation of Paraguay and do business there. After returning to Britain, they sought to profit off sales of their entertaining account of their four-year stay in Paraguay. Describing their first meeting with Francia, who had yet to become the "Supreme and Perpetual Leader of Paraguay," the Robertsons noted that he "had a maté-cup in one hand, a cigar in the other; and a little urchin of a negro, with his arms crossed . . . in attendance."[88] Francia, who spoke French and read European philosophers like Voltaire, also routinely drank mate first thing in the morning and after his afternoon siesta.[89] In keeping with "the primitive and simple hospitality common in the country," the Robertsons remarked that Francia invited the brothers to share a cigar and mate with him.[90] The young Black and likely enslaved servant or the "elderly negress," who, according to the authors, "were the only servants Francia had," most certainly did the work needed to facilitate such "simple hospitality."[91]

Neither of these servants appeared with Francia in the official portrait of the man who had reigned as the "Supreme Leader of Paraguay" for over two decades by the time the Robertsons published the first of their three volumes about their time in Paraguay in 1838. Instead, Francia appeared alone under a veranda outside his residence holding a silver mate while smoking tobacco, with his signature visible below the lithograph (fig. 2.6).[92] While the specific identity of the creator of this portrait has been lost, it is remarkable that it was created and circulated in the first place, especially since Francia neither recruited nor supported artists.[93] Perhaps the Robertson brothers commissioned this portrait after returning to England, as they made far more money

FIGURE 2.6. Portrait of Paraguayan president José Gaspar Rodríguez de Francia, as published in John Parish Robertson and William Parish Robertson's books on Paraguay, ca. 1838, held by Museo del Barro, Asunción, and reproduced in Pau Navajas, *Caá Porã: El espíiritu de la yerba mate, una historia de plata* (Corrientes, Arg.: Las Marías, 2013), 179.

writing these memoirs for British and American readers who subscribed to their series than they did in trade from Paraguay.[94]

In step with British readers' interest in South American Indians and the Paraguayan economy under Francia, the other illustration included in the Robertsons' account featured Guaraní laborers preparing yerba high up in the Paraguayan hills. In this illustration, four Indigenous laborers in loin-cloths attend to the drying and chopping of yerba in a forest clearing, an arduous process that the Robertsons described in detail in their memoir.[95] The unknown artist is far less interested in the laborers who do the work than in the stages of work they perform. The Guaraní's trellis-like system for slowly drying the leaves, called *barbacuá*, occupies the center of the drawing.[96]

While a small number of illustrations in the late 1850s and 1860s would more accurately represent the work done to gather, produce, and transport yerba, the artists who created them dedicated their attention to the different stages of work rather than to the people actually doing this labor.[97] Indigenous and mixed-race laborers in the hills served as the first in a chain of people who made the consumption of mate possible for a broad and racially diverse society dominated by people of European descent. Most "peons," as the Robertsons referred to them, found themselves caught in a cycle of debt that forced them to continue to return again and again to the hard work of picking, transporting, curing, chopping, and packing yerba in Paraguayan forests for little to no personal gain.[98]

DISAPPEARING NATIVE MATE DRINKERS
AND HIGHLIGHTING COMMONERS

In contrast to the small number of visual sources depicting yerba production in Paraguay, visual sources produced in the lower Platine region (the emerging Republics of Argentina and Uruguay) during the 1830s and 1840s rarely focused on the production of yerba. (This is hardly surprising given that only a small slice of this region, specifically, the future Argentine province of Corrientes, contained native yerba forests.) Even as artists in the lower Platine region produced a growing number of illustrations featuring common people drinking mate, they typically ignored those who preserved an Indigenous identity. This represented an ideological decision about whom to feature rather than an accurate reflection of who was actually drinking mate. In the countryside, foreign travelers reported that Indigenous groups across the region, including the Pampas, Mapuches, and Guaraní, regularly drank mate.

Indiens Charruas

Senaqué.　　　Vaimaca-Pérû.　　Guyunusa.　　　Tacuabé.

FIGURE 2.7. François de Curel, *Indiens Charruas*, ca. 1833, Colección Octavio Assunção, Montevideo. Courtesy of Biblioteca Nacional de Uruguay, Montevideo, Sala de Materiales Especiales.

They also noted that caciques from a variety of Indigenous nations continued to receive yerba from the government.[99]

The one well-known illustration of an Indigenous person with a mate from the 1830s conveyed not native continuity but rather extinction. In *Indiens Charruas* (Charruan Indians), a seated man named Senaqué holds an empty mate in his hand, looking skyward (fig. 2.7). Next to him, his nation's chief, Vaimaca, stands, and a couple, Guyunusa and Tacuabé, sit empty-handed. While the details remain murky, some two years prior, leaders of the Eastern Republic of Uruguay set an ambush on this native tribe, asking them to join their troops in a fight against Brazil but killing them instead.[100] Two years later, this group of four became known as the "last Charrúas," after being forcibly taken across the Atlantic to be put on exhibit in France.[101] Initially directed to a French audience, this lithograph of the "last Charrúas" was eventually reproduced and circulated by Uruguayans (more commonly referred to as Orientales, or Easterners, in reference to their location on the eastern banks of the River Plate). In the twentieth century, it would inspire everything from a sculpture in Montevideo to a national stamp.[102] In the 1830s and after,

Chapter Two

the presence of the mate in Senaqué's hand suggested that he and his fellow Charrúas had bequeathed this Indigenous infusion to the would-be White nation. This echoed Pellegrini's representation of the native mate server on the other side of the River Plate who had even more directly handed the mate to the White "lady liberty" figure beneath the tree.

Some five years after the original lithograph of the Charrúas, General Fructuoso Rivera appeared in a lithograph called *Mi General, un mate* (My general, a mate) (fig. 2.8). In 1838, Basque immigrant Juan Manuel Besnes e Irigoyen, who served as the primary chronicler of the emerging Eastern Republic of Uruguay, created a composition in which a humble man, flanked by his wife and child, gratefully hands the first president of Uruguay and former general in the independence struggles a mate. Rivera, who appears to have been responsible for the slaughter of the Charrúas, does not disappear but becomes more powerful on the canvas.[103] The artist represents the symbolic power of mate as something a leader should be offered by those under him. Here, a political hierarchy dictates who should serve whom.

In contrast, the main political leader in the province of Buenos Aires, Governor Rosas, did not appear with a mate in his hand in any of his numerous official portraits. Rosas regularly drank mate without sugar and even had a preferred mate server, Eugenia Castro, a young woman who lived with and cared for his family and with whom he had six illegitimate children.[104] Deeply concerned about his public image, Rosas commissioned portraits that emphasized his military might and political power but did not, as in other contemporary visual depictions of the mate ritual, highlight the subordination of Blacks and country people to White elites. While his political rival, Unitarian liberal and future Argentine president Domingo Sarmiento, accused Rosas of being a ruthless mate-drinking gaucho-caudillo, the Federalist governor made a deliberate choice not to represent himself in this manner.[105]

At the same time, several artists and their benefactors now visibly linked Rosas's followers with their mate consumption. In 1842, a local baron commissioned the visiting French painter Auguste Raymond Quinsac de Monvoisin to complete a large oil painting titled *Soldado de Rosas* (Rosas's soldier), which shows an olive-skinned guard, who protected Rosas's residence in San Benito de Palermo in Buenos Aires, leaning against a brick wall and drinking a mate.[106] Some three years later, Italian artist Cayetano Descalzi offered his interpretation in *Boudoir Federal*, in which a pale woman braids her hair in front of a mirror, a silver mate by her side, and a portrait of Rosas hangs on the wall.[107] As this new generation of oil paintings attests, some elites commissioned paintings that took longer and cost more to produce than watercolors,

FIGURE 2.8. Juan Manuel Besnes e Irigoyen, *Mi General, un mate. . . . Muy bien, mi amigo el excelentísimo Fructuoso Rivera*, 1838, lithograph on paper. Courtesy of Museo Histórico, Montevideo, Uruguay, folder 1278.

in an effort to make visible the profound commitment to Rosas's authoritarian and patriarchal government. Entranced by exotic markers like mate, these foreign painters and their patrons portrayed the caudillos' supporters in a way that Rosas himself did not wish to highlight.

Under Rosas, it was not just those who celebrated the Federalist government who had to show their unwavering, red-colored loyalty. In 1838, the Federalist government accused Bacle, the official state lithographer who depicted the two young ladies served their morning mate by a young Black servant, of being a Unitarian sympathizer. Rosas's feared police force took Bacle to prison, and he fell ill and died shortly thereafter.[108]

Originally a supporter of Rosas's Federalist Party, Carlos Morel became one of the first locally born and formally trained artists to earn recognition as a fine arts painter. In the late 1830s and early 1840s, Morel offered his compatriots not only a portrait of General Rosas (without a mate, of course) but also paintings that celebrated the customs of the popular classes and prominently featured mate. He showed men in red liberty caps drinking mate in the Plaza Montserrat, at a rural party with dancing, and while preparing an asado (beef barbecue) during a stop at night. In *Una hora antes de partir* (An hour before leaving), an extended family drinks a mate before setting out while a man in a Federalist cap looks on. A Federalist soldier also appears in Morel's 1841 illustration *La familia del gaucho* (The gaucho's family). This soldier literally prods the child in the woman's arms, perhaps symbolically pushing this family toward a Federalist future.

Morel was becoming increasingly disenchanted with the Federalist regime. In 1842, he moved to Rio de Janeiro after Rosas's forces assassinated his brother-in-law, José María Dupuy. Upon returning to Buenos Aires, his last publicly facing effort was to publish a series of his lithographs in an album called *Usos y costumbres del Río de la Plata* (Traditions and customs of the Río de la Plata) in 1845.[109] Art historians have suggested that in his remaining years, Morel suffered from mental illness brought on by Rosas's political oppression.[110]

During Rosas's governorship, political hierarchies influenced who could make art and what it looked like. If we shift our attention to the figure of the common mate server, we can also appreciate that gender and race were at work in determining the hierarchy of service. Beginning in the late 1830s, when artists included women in a mixed-sex group of rural commoners or soldiers, these women increasingly were shown serving the mate. For example, while Morel failed to show the gaucho's wife serving him a mate—she was holding their child, after all—he included fair-skinned women serving troops both in his depiction of Plaza Montserrat and in *Una hora antes de partir*.[111]

But we should not conclude that women always did the serving in mixed-sex groups. Recall, for example, how in the countryside, British copper speculator Miers and the circle of mate drinkers he joined were served by an older man. Instead, these images spoke to the consolidation of the idea that within a popular, servant-less group, a common woman, if present, was there to serve.

As we shall see in chapter 4, in the late nineteenth century, a racially indeterminate rural woman with some Indigenous ancestry known as *la china* (pronounced CHEE-nah) would become the most visible of all mate servers. In an early manifestation of this trend, German immigrant artist Johann Moritz Rugendas featured a racially indeterminate woman with braids serving mate to Federalist troops in the central plaza of Buenos Aires in front of the town hall and Independence Pyramid.[112] Then, in 1852, Juan Camaña presented a woman of Indigenous descent with braids falling down her back serving a group of Rosas's soldiers a mate. Eight years later, W. Baldino painted *La tarde en el campo* (Afternoon in the countryside), in which a tall man drinks a mate provided by a diminutive female half his height.[113] Their height differential recalled urban compositions from the 1830s that featured tall elite families and short Black slaves.

Even as women with some Indigenous ancestry began to appear in mid-nineteenth-century artwork as rural mate servers, those with clearer Indigenous identities remained conspicuously absent.[114] And while Indigenous consumption of yerba was similarly erased in colonial-era artwork, its absence was even more pronounced as a wider range of mate drinkers proliferated in paintings and lithographs. The portfolio of artist Jean León Pallière, who was born in Rio de Janeiro, trained in Paris, and produced perhaps the largest number of visual representations of mate in southern South America during the late 1850s and 1860s, is illustrative.[115] Typically, Pallière featured common folks of European or mixed descent, rather than people who preserved a distinct Indigenous identity, drinking mate during their journeys in wagons, in the interiors of ranchos, near a country store, or outside post houses.

In 1861, Pallière offered another rare and less familiar illustration titled *Indians of the Land of Fire*, in which an Indigenous woman drinks from a mate. Because the mate drinker, the two women accompanying her, and the baby nursing from the seated woman's breast are in the southernmost region of Tierra del Fuego, these Indigenous mate drinkers were not yet incorporated into the territory claimed by the Argentine republic. This location outside the national territory is likely what led Pallière to make this painting. Even when Indigenous mate drinkers appeared in visual sources, they were typically depicted in marginal spaces or as historical relics, as in the case of the Charrúas.[116] In this way, the symbolically charged local drink enjoyed by White elites or racially indeterminate folks could be visibly disassociated from its Indigenous present.

Pallière also released another painting around this time focused not on common people, like most of his work, but rather on the elite. In *Damas Porteñas* (Buenos Aires ladies) (1861), two elite White women seated outside in elaborate gowns share a mate served by a diminutive brown-skinned servant. Maintaining the visual stereotype produced some three decades prior, the servant stands barefoot with his arms crossed. The abolition of slavery was finally achieved in the Argentine Confederation in 1853 and Buenos Aires in 1861 and with it intermediate statuses such as the *liberto*; nevertheless, elite White patrons' nostalgia for the service of darker-skinned people persisted.[117]

Not all compositions included a mate server. In 1861, Argentine artist Prilidiano Pueyrredón, who returned to Buenos Aires from exile in 1854 after the fall of Rosas, painted *Un alto en el campo* (A stop in the country), the most celebrated piece of artwork of the nineteenth century that features a mate (fig. 2.9).[118] In this tableau, an extended family makes a stop near a post

FIGURE 2.9. Prilidiano Pueyrredón, *Un alto en el campo*, 1861. Note the woman at center holding a mate and bombilla. Courtesy of Museo Nacional de Bellas Artes, Buenos Aires, Argentina.

house on the outskirts of Buenos Aires.[119] At the focal point of the painting, a White lady sits in the nook of a large ombu (later declared the national tree), cradling a mate. Some three decades after Pellegrini placed "lady liberty" in his illustration of independence, it is noteworthy that a woman, not a man, preserved the symbolically significant place of the most important mate drinker, once more seated at the base of a tree.

Soon after the painting's public exhibition, a contemporary journalist opined that the subjects Pueyrredón painted were "legitimate porteños born and raised in Lomas de Morón, in proximity to Buenos Aires," who enjoyed the same racial and family background.[120] The journalist contrasted the deep roots and racial coherence of this family with the contamination he associated with growing numbers of immigrants moving to the countryside. Such xenophobic concerns would become much more widespread among criollo elites as immigration rates soared in the 1870s and on, as we shall see in chapter 4. For now, it is striking that some four decades after Hidalgo suggested there was a clear division between local mate-drinking Indians and chocolate-drinking Spaniards, a locally born family of Spanish descent that drank mate had already become idealized members of an emerging Argentine nation.

A few years prior to this painting, a song often regarded as one of the first tangos, "Tomá mate, ché" (Drink mate, hey), debuted in 1857 in a comedic play called *The Gaucho of Buenos Aires*. Santiago Ramos performed the lead role, singing lyrics that echoed Hildalgo's in the aptly named Teatro Victoria (Victory Theater) in Argentina's capital city.

> *¡Tomá mate, tomá mate, tomá mate, ché, tomá mate!* [Drink mate, drink mate, drink mate, hey, drink mate!]
> *que en el Río de la Plata* [because in the Río de la Plata]
> *no se estila el chocolate* [chocolate is not in style]*!*[121]

The difference lay in who articulated this distinction, as Ramos had emigrated from Spain and sang in the Andalusian style. By the mid-nineteenth century, mate served as a potent symbol of belonging in the River Plate region that even a man of Spanish origin could perform as his own.

~~~~~~

From the 1810s through the 1860s, people living in the former Viceroyalty of Río de La Plata participated in and experienced dramatic attempts to establish political authority in rivalrous would-be nations. In this context, mate acquired new political meanings that were especially visible in the artwork of the time. Soldiers and revelers drank it in their fight for independence from Spain. Rosas's troops and mixed-sex parties traveling in the countryside enjoyed mate during their breaks. Elites consumed it conspicuously in their portraits and served it at parties, even as they also began to frequent cafés that popped up in cities like Buenos Aires and Montevideo.[122] At home and at parties, these elites were now visibly attended by young Black and Brown servants who not only infused their mates but also routinely drank the first sip from the same mate cup and bombilla in a moment of intimacy between unequal parties.

As previous generations had done, these locals invited travelers in their midst to join them in the mate ritual. European writers told unfamiliar readers that the custom provided locals in this region with refreshment and stimulation but also with the means to nurture social connections, keep their parties energized, and integrate visiting guests. In his self-described *Two Thousand Miles' Ride through the Argentine Provinces* from the early 1840s, British merchant William MacCann wrote that everyone—from well-off hosts in elaborate ranches to gauchos working under the open skies—shared their mates with him, always first thing in the morning and often while making supper or before bed. At a small-town celebration in the Pampas in honor of the Declaration of the Independence of the Argentine Provinces on May 25, MacCann recounted that "all the influential and respectable people" gathered to drink mate, eat "sweetmeats, and other sundry refreshments," and play music and dance. They of course invited MacCann to join them. Entranced by this celebration that lasted until the next morning, he concluded his account, "The manners and bearing of the guests at this little festivity, although in one of the most secluded villages in the province, were marked by the courteous grace and etiquette . . . with a universal gaiety and air of enjoyment rarely seen in the select assemblies of European capitals, and more resembling the genial cheerfulness and freedom of a family party."[123] Elaborate parties like this one, as well as more simple rounds of mate around an open fire, provided an opportunity for someone like MacCann, who brought his British prejudices with him, to appreciate and even feel a part of local culture. "Mate is as necessary for these people as tea is to the English," MacCann maintained.[124]

Like most outsiders who spent considerable time in the region, Mac-Cann became a fan of this ritualized infusion. So too did British chemist and author Charles Blachford Mansfield, who rather uniquely traveled to the region purely for pleasure rather than for commercial gain, becoming enamored. In a poem at the end of his book, he characterized yerba as the "heart-enchanting lotus of South America."[125]

For his part, French ship lieutenant and artist Adolphe d'Hastrel, who served in the Río de la Plata region from 1839 to 1841, became obsessed with drinking mate and painting it. Several decades after returning to France, he created a retrospective self-portrait of himself in Montevideo in which he placed a silver mate and a book on his side table; he likewise painted a portrait of his wife there holding a simple mate in her hand.[126] These mates visibly signaled his and his wife's adoption of and affection for Rioplatense culture.

Similarly, d'Hastrel's illustrations of common "types" from the region linked locals' identities with their mate drinking, invoking earlier portraits by European artists in the colonial era, who represented the criolla from Lima with a mate. D'Hastrel offered his European contemporaries a mate-drinking common woman from the province of Buenos Aires and another from Asunción, Paraguay, as well as a pale, rosy-cheeked *cebadora* in a courtyard. He also introduced two mate-drinking male types: the provincial gaucho and the Federalist rancher, figures who were associated more with their professional standing than with their place of origin, as were his female subjects. In 1850, the Parisian Musée de Costumes displayed d'Hastrel's types as part of an exhibit on women's and men's "typical" dress around the world.[127]

Even as most foreigner visitors like d'Hastrel positively associated mate with South American culture and localized identities there, some holdouts remained. Thomas Woodbine Hinchliff, who delighted in local hospitality in the city of Buenos Aires and on the country estates he visited in the early 1860s, preserved a strong dislike of the local infusion, which he described as a staple, along with beef, throughout the region.[128] Detailing his time visiting some caretakers who lived on the outskirts of a large ranch, he explained that when the "dark lady" of the house emerged with a mate for the men in his party, he suffered inside: "I have to bend in the saddle and take the matè -pot with every appearance of gratification." But since he never liked mate, he was not very good at drinking it. "I burn my lips with the bombilla, and then suck so awkwardly that I fill my mouth with the chips, inwardly execrating the good woman for her politeness, while she doubtless looks upon me as an unfortunate creature unacquainted in the ways of the world."[129]

By now we are well aware of the hierarchies of service that would have governed such an interaction considered so central to the "ways of the world" in the Río de la Plata region. The gender and racial identity of the "dark lady" mate server, to which Hinchliff referred, along with her family's status as ranch caretakers rather than as ranch owners, dictated that she would be the one to serve the mate to the ranch owner and his British guest.

Colonial hierarchies of patriarchy and racism intensified in mate-related artwork and persisted in everyday life in the early national era. Tracing this history helps us to see how even as colonial caste hierarchies began to officially disappear in new, supposedly race-blind republics, these hierarchies became more visible in other realms, particularly elite homes. The growing number of paintings and lithographs helped to naturalize persisting race-based inequalities and the place of White people to benefit from them in the postcolonial era. In artwork and everyday life, fair-skinned local elites and visitors were attended to by *cebadores* who were not only darker but also younger than those they served. In servant-less homes of commoners, like the setting to which Hinchliff referred, the woman of the house (or her daughter) took charge of serving the mate. Still, an important exception remained where racial hierarchies continued to trump gendered ones. As we have seen, both in artwork and everyday life, Black or Brown men and women frequently served White women—as well as, of course, White men. White or racially indeterminate men served one another only when no one else was present.

What were the dynamics at the other end of the commodity chain? In yerba forests, the less visible colonial exploitation of laborers persisted. Colonial profiteers made access to the yerba needed for this ritual into a capitalist commodity that relied on unpaid, or virtually unpaid, labor. In the postcolonial era, the exploitation of indentured yerba pickers, many of whom were of Indigenous or mixed descent, continued. This pattern, common to all major commodities—especially stimulants such as tea, coffee, and sugar—is at once deeply disturbing and far from unique. As in the colonial era, during the early national period, most people outside the yerba-producing region drank mate with little exposure to the exploitation of yerba producers in the faraway hills. There, indentured laborers, Indigenous and non-Indigenous, toiled for little or no gain for the benefit of others. Most worked in Paraguay and southern Brazil and a much smaller number in the Argentine province of Corrientes.[130] In Paraguay, their labor helped fill the government's coffers.

Carlos Antonio López, who took over as Paraguay's president after Francia's 1840 death, made yerba into a state monopoly. In 1848, he issued a decree that granted members of the *pueblos de indios* (Indigenous nations) citizenship, stating that by 1852, these new citizens would lose their access to communal lands and be obligated to serve in the military and pay their taxes in yerba mate.[131] Following colonial precedent, López warned that anyone who abandoned their work in the yerbales would be treated as a "deserter," legally subject to the death penalty but in practice most likely fined and flogged.[132] López's policies roped more poor young men in rural communities (including former Indigenous nations) into working in the yerbales. After the 1852 fall of Rosas (who fled into exile with a good supply of yerba), the reopening of river trade and forced expansion of the workforce enabled Paraguay to regain its pre-independence levels of yerba exports.[133] Like Francia before him, López kept the price of yerba low for Paraguayans but set a high fixed price for others. Meanwhile, during the previous three decades, Brazilian yerba had changed the market. Thus, despite a significant increase in the export of Paraguayan yerba and Brazil's lower quality, Brazilian producers continued to meet more of the demand in the lower Platine market through the 1860s.[134] (See graph 3.1.)

Would Paraguay be able to recapture the market? How would the war that raged between this nation and its increasingly powerful neighbors Brazil and Argentina shape that possibility? As we shall see in the next chapter, the war and its aftermath would usher in major changes for both Paraguay and the herb that had long been at the center of this region's economy.

CHAPTER THREE

~~~~~~

Taking the Herb of Paraguay, 1860s–1910s

~~~~~~

In 1868, an unknown photographer created a black-and-white image of a young Paraguayan prisoner of war serving a mate to the cavalry captain of the Rio Grande do Sul division of the Brazilian army (fig. 3.1). The prisoner was a boy who appeared to be of at least partial Indigenous descent and stood with a kettle in one hand and a mate in the other.[1] In the image, he hands the mate to the fair Brazilian captain, whose bushy beard attests to his age and whose uniform reflects his authority.[2] The seated man wears boots that distinguish his superior class position from that of the shoeless boy who serves him.[3] The captain does not even bother to look at the boy, whom he clearly regards as his inferior. Like the enslaved mate servers who preceded him, this young boy's presence is a visible testament to the officer's status.

Since the colonial era, mate played an important symbolic role distinguishing South Americans from Europeans and servers from the served. But as national competition became more visible and violent within South America, nation-based hierarchies became more pronounced. This photograph was taken during the War of the Triple Alliance (1864–70), a brutal and bloody conflict that pitted the Republics of Brazil, Argentina, and Uruguay against Paraguay. The photographer probably created the image as part of a series of photographs showcasing Brazilian officers with Paraguayan prisoners of

FIGURE 3.1. Photograph of a Paraguayan prisoner of war serving a mate to a Brazilian cavalry captain in January 1868. Courtesy of Biblioteca Nacional do Brazil, Rio de Janeiro, *Álbum escursao ao Paraguay*, photo 23.

war.[4] Given the slow and careful process of taking a photograph in this era, these were not random snapshots but rather carefully crafted compositions meant to visually express Brazil's superiority over Paraguay.[5] This superiority was not only about the protagonists' relative power but also about Brazil's and Paraguay's comparative military might. Like other Paraguayan captives pictured with Brazilian military men, this mate server was portrayed as part of a conquered people. Making an even finer point, here the boy hands an infusion made with the plant the Guaraní originally discovered, and which the Paraguayan government made a state monopoly, into Brazil's hands. How had Brazil come to assert superiority over Paraguay, with a Brazilian captain even claiming the right to be served the "herb of Paraguay" by a Paraguayan prisoner of war?

In the lead-up to the war, Paraguay's mercantilist, state-led economy seemed poised to persist, but postwar Paraguay was another story. In his post as US minister to Paraguay from 1861 to 1868, Charles Ames Washburn had a front-row seat to the war. He juxtaposed prewar Paraguay, when "the land was always represented as of surpassing beauty and fertility, and the people of exceeding gentleness and hospitality," with the horrors of war that made him come to see Paraguay as a "secluded region . . . [and] the scene of the darkest tragedy of modern times."[6]

From 1864 to 1870, war raged in southeastern South America. It started as a conflict between the Paraguayan republic and the Brazilian empire, later joined by Argentina and Uruguay. Known as the War of the Triple Alliance, the Paraguayan War, or the Guerra Guasu (or "Great War"), it holds the unfortunate distinction of being the bloodiest and most destructive war fought in South America's history. Since independence, different factions within the Río de la Plata region continued to engage in a series of civil wars. Armed struggle was not new; instead, the Great War represented its bloody pinnacle.[7] Paraguay not only suffered defeat but also lost more than half of its population as well as control over its economy.

The Great War was not fought over access to yerba per se, and yet it radically remade the regional balance of power within the yerba industry, the historic backbone of the Paraguayan economy. Brazil had surpassed Paraguay as the largest exporter of yerba prior to the war, but Paraguay remained a significant producer of what was widely considered to be a higher-quality product. After the war, Brazil and Argentina seized additional land from the vanquished nation, including land on which they could grow yerba. Faced with a demographic and economic catastrophe, a new generation of Paraguayan leaders would sell most of the state's remaining land, including yerbales, to international entrepreneurs in the 1880s.

This chapter tells the story of how South America's Great War dramatically shifted the dynamics of yerba production and consumption. It helps us understand the impact of the privatization of the Paraguayan yerba industry after the war and leftist writers' increased attention to the exploitation of yerba workers. It also examines why Paraguay acquired national symbols that differed from those of its neighbors in the late nineteenth and early twentieth centuries. While prewar visual culture emphasized Paraguayan locals' regular consumption of yerba, in the postwar era, another picture emerged. In postcards purporting to represent national customs, Paraguay was depicted as a land of women and agricultural production rather than a site of consumption or gauchos. It was portrayed, like the young Paraguayan mate server, as a country meant to serve others in the region whatever they desired.

THE BUILDUP TO THE CONFLICT

In the 1850s, US naval officer Thomas Jefferson Page published an account of his four-year stay in Paraguay. He told his English-language readers (in a way locals might have found condescending) that most Paraguayans seemed content: "Give the Paraguayans maté, beef, and mandioca [manioc root], and they are satisfied. . . . Shut out, first by the policy of Spain, and again by the tyranny of Francia, from all communication with other lands, they neither know nor desire their luxuries. The climate is deliciously soft; and with the festivals of the Church and an occasional 'dance,' to break the monotony of existence, they dream it away, imagining that the true and only Elysium is Paraguay."[8] Like others before and after him, Page envisioned Paraguay as an isolated paradise full of contentment and little upward striving.[9]

"Next to smoking," quipped British physician and author George Frederick Masterman, who spent the better part of the 1860s in Paraguay, "sipping the infusion of the yerba matè was the great excuse for idling the time away." He continued that early in the morning and after the siesta "were the legitimate hours for indulging in it . . . but those who had plenty of yerba, and, as usual, little to do, passed half their waking hours *matè* in hand." Like other outsiders, Masterman faulted the Paraguayans for their purported tendency toward idleness, which simultaneously overlooked how hard many Paraguayans worked and denigrated the relaxed sociability that many locals valued.

Paraguayans' commitment to mate drinking helped define what he characterized as "national customs."[10]

Outsiders appear to have been the first to publicly make nation-specific claims about mate. Even more directly than Masterman, Page stated in the 1850s that mate was the "national beverage" of Paraguay. He wrote, "This *national beverage* is served in a gourd. . . . In all well-regulated houses the servant [whom he described elsewhere as the "little negro"] continues to serve the *national beverage*, regardless of quantity, until this word [*Gracias*], which means both 'Thanks' and 'Enough,' is uttered."[11] This hierarchical choreography of mate service was one that Masterman also recognized. "As soon as the gourd is emptied," he observed, "a servant who has been standing, with the arms formally crossed, before you, refills it with water from a little kettle and again hands it to you" and other members of the group.[12] In nineteenth-century Paraguay, locals referred to such servants, as well as others in a dependent position—whether a slave, a yerba worker, or even a wife—in Guaraní as *tembiguái.*[13]

In the early 1860s, a fellow traveler from London, Thomas Woodbine Hinchliff, made a similar claim about the "national drink," which, as we saw previously, was served to him by a "dark lady," who along with her husband worked for a wealthy rancher. Surprisingly, Hinchliff was not in Paraguay but rather on a large ranch to the east of the River Plate. In other words, he was in the Eastern Republic of Uruguay. Is this the nation to which Hinchliff referred? More likely, he referred to the lower Platine region, including both Argentina and Uruguay.[14]

During the early 1860s, major political changes were afoot in the Río de la Plata region as would-be nations inched closer to securing their modern form. The Argentine republic did not emerge until 1862 with the official unification of the governments representing the capital city of Buenos Aires and the Argentine Confederation. For its part, the Eastern Republic of Uruguay retained its autonomy from its domineering larger neighbors Argentina and Brazil, at least in theory. The new Paraguayan president, Francisco Solano López, who took over for his father, Carlos Antonio López, in 1862, convinced himself that the endurance of Uruguay's sovereignty proved crucial to maintaining the regional balance of power and Paraguay's place within it. While López kept his eye on Brazil's expansionist desires and Argentina's contentious politics, at home, the definitive transfer of power from father to son allowed for a profoundly autocratic state to endure in Paraguay.[15]

From an economic vantage point, the yerba industry played the leading role in Paraguay's well-being, providing the state with around half of its revenue.[16]

This nationally run industry seemed poised to recapture some of its former glory during Solano López's presidency (1862–70). Even as the younger López's 1853 trip to Europe to promote yerba proved unsuccessful, Paraguay's position in the South American yerba market appeared to be improving. His father's opening of river trade, together with the recent conscription of an Indigenous and mestizo labor force in the yerbales, enabled Paraguay to finally restore pre-independence levels of production by the early 1860s.[17]

At the same time, demand downriver had shifted toward Brazil, its finest variety of yerba directed to the lower Platine region and a coarser variety to Chile.[18] The supply of Brazilian yerba proved more reliable and less expensive than its Paraguayan counterpart, and Brazilian production levels continued to outpace Paraguayan output in the 1860s.[19]

The Paraguayans nevertheless maintained a superior reputation and higher price point for their yerba. Those in a position to do so willingly paid more for the original "herb of Paraguay," which most considered far superior to the reputedly impure Brazilian variety, as well as to the small amount of product coming out of what would become northeastern Argentina. In 1860, French explorer and scholar Alfred Demersay, who had previously traveled throughout the Río de la Plata region, explained, "The Paraguayan variety is more bitter and aromatic than that of Misiones [Argentina] or Paranaguá [Brazil], and gives four time more infusions."[20]

Demersay was not the first (or last) to offer this opinion. The frequent association between this product and the region called Paraguay, both before and after it became a colony and then a nation, possessed deep roots. This plant's official scientific name of *Ilex paraguariensis* (since 1822) linked the holly tree used to produce yerba with the nation of Paraguay, despite its presence elsewhere in the region. Like Auguste de Saint-Hilaire, Demersay recognized that yerba from Paraguay and Brazil were botanically identical. Nevertheless, he associated the local infusion most closely with Paraguay, titling his 1867 study of the industry *Étude économique sur le maté ou thé du Paraguay (Ilex paraguariensis)* (Economic study on mate or Paraguayan tea).[21]

Demersay's account offered not only a glimpse into the enduring association of yerba with Paraguay but also the most detailed illustration of its production to date (fig. 3.2).[22] In this composition set along the Paraná River, shirtless Indigenous laborers remove branches from the trees, port them into the clearing, dry them on the tentlike *barbacuá*, and grind them into smaller pieces. Like previous illustrations, this metal engraving highlights the types of labor these men performed, but the artist made some of these laborers' faces visible and the physical strain of their work evident. For example, on the

FIGURE 3.2. Metal engraving drawn by Dessin de Fuchs, *Cosecha del mate en la ribera de Paraná, en el Paraguay*, 1865. Originally published in Alfred Demersay, "Fragments d'un voyage au Paraguay," in *Le Tour du monde*, vol. 11 (Paris: Hachette, 1865).

lower left part of the drawing, a man is literally weighed down by the yerba on his back, an image that future social critics and eventually photographers would highlight. This illustration has endured the test of time and now graces a popular Paraguayan yerba brand called Kurupí.[23]

In the early 1860s, artists also depicted people in Paraguay drinking mate, not just harvesting yerba.[24] In 1864, French mate enthusiast Adolphe d'Hastrel, discussed in the previous chapter, created a metal engraving that featured two women and one man sharing a mate, titled *L'habitants du Paraguay* (The inhabitants of Paraguay), which he published in a French and then British illustrated magazine (fig. 3.3). In this composition, a woman balancing a water jug on her head offers a mate to a man while another woman touches his arm. In keeping with local practices, both peasant women stand barefoot and wear low-cut tops and lace-embroidered skirts with a sash across the waist.[25] As we shall see in the next chapter, rural women offering a man a mate would become a popular motif in the visual culture of late nineteenth-century

FIGURE 3.3. Adolphe d'Hastrel, *L'habitants du Paraguay*, metal
engraving, 1864. Originally published in *L'illustration* (Paris),
Nov. 5, 1864, reproduced in *Illustrated Times*, Dec. 24, 1864.

Argentina and Uruguay. Still, d'Hastrel's composition suggested something more than a heterosexual romance between one man and one woman in this illustration of Paraguayan types. Like others did, he associated Paraguayan culture with polygamy, or at very least, a looser sexual morality than that of the country's neighbors.[26] For their part, Paraguayans maintained a long-standing practice of sexual relationships outside marriage and less commitment to lifelong monogamy than that held by others in the region who lived under a stronger Catholic Church.[27]

Guaraní ideas about sexuality and the gendered division of labor survived the colonial epoch into the national era, even as they shifted with the increasing commodification of this labor and its products. According to historian Barbara Potthast, Guaraní women took the lead in harvesting crops and raising their families, while men hunted, fished, and fought. This gendered division of labor persisted into the late nineteenth century as women continued to provide for their families and men were frequently called away to work in export industries, including the yerbales, and to serve as soldiers.[28] Closer to home, Paraguayan women raised crops, prepared food, and did domestic work for their family members but also for male customers who paid them. Some of these men became their lovers, as d'Hastrel's painting seems to suggest.[29]

In 1865, another artist offered a homier and less sexualized composition of daily life in Paraguay for a British audience, which like the previous illustration included two women and one man. In *Un rancho en Araguay, Paraguay* (A ranch in Araguay [likely Aregua], Paraguay), a seated man drinks from a mate while one woman looks on with a kettle in her hand and another woman grinds corn. This composition reflected foreigners' common view that Paraguayan women worked harder than supposedly lazy Paraguayan men.[30] The man sits and drinks his mate, while the woman standing to his left presumably performs the work of heating water and infusing his mate and the woman to the right grinds the maize for future meals. Meanwhile, chickens peck under the thatched awning, suggesting a stable, well-provisioned home. This scene of rural tranquility, mate drinking, and male leisure in the Paraguayan countryside soon became unimaginable.

THE WAR AND ITS FALLOUT

Just months before this illustration was published abroad, war broke out between Paraguay and Brazil. The war was triggered when in 1864 the Brazilian army invaded Uruguay and helped install a Colorado Party government favorable to its own interests. López feared that left unchecked, the expansionist Brazilian empire would eventually take over Paraguay. Preferring that his well-trained army initiate war rather than wait for it, he declared war on Brazil.[31] When the Paraguayan leader's request to cross through Argentine territory to defend his Uruguayan allies was rejected on the basis of neutrality laws, Paraguay declared war on Argentina. López counted on external support that never came from his Federalist allies in Argentina and Blanco allies in Uruguay.[32] In May 1865, Brazil, Argentina, and (the pro-Brazilian government in) Uruguay signed a secret document called the "Treaty of the Triple Alliance," stating their intention to join forces to overthrow López and seize some Paraguayan territory, including prime land on which to grow yerba, but also to preserve an independent Paraguayan state between them.[33] The following year, the allied forces entered Paraguayan territory, where both sides became entrenched in a grinding war of attrition for the next four years.

Despite their far superior resources, the armies of the Triple Alliance faced a Paraguayan army under López that refused to give up, convinced as it was that the very survival of Paraguay was at stake.[34] "Paraguay was the only 'nation' or 'near-nation' in the region," Thomas Whigham explains, united by "narrow traditions of paternalism and community solidarity within a unique cultural environment."[35] This did not mean that all Paraguayans, especially rural campesinos, had an unwavering commitment to the nation-state. As Michael Huner argues, common people in Paraguay shared a profound linguistic and cultural bond, which revolved around speaking Guaraní and feeling reverence for the Paraguayan soil, church, and nation, which surpassed their commitment to any specific Paraguayan government.[36] López's government sought to bridge this gap during the war by embracing the Guaraní language, which most Paraguayans spoke, and sponsoring propaganda in this native tongue that emphasized the Guerra Guasu as national self-defense against the enslaving empire of Brazil. This propaganda also suggested that Paraguayan troops were involved in a racial struggle between White Paraguayans and Black Brazilians, the latter pejoratively referred to in Guaraní as "*kamba*" (or "darkies") and further dehumanized as "monkeys."[37]

In contrast to the difficulties of conscription to this increasingly unpopular war in Brazil and Argentina, Paraguayan men, women, and children felt they had to fight in and for their homeland. As the war took more Paraguayan men's lives, boys, like the one pictured serving the Brazilian captain a mate in figure 3.1, famously wore fake beards to appear older in battle. For their part, Paraguayan women continued to do most of the agricultural work at home, not only sustaining their families but also helping to provision the army.[38] Many women harvested tobacco, and some apparently even went to the hills to harvest yerba, which had previously been a male undertaking.[39] As the war dragged on, women moved to the front lines to serve as crucial camp followers who cooked and cared for the troops, including their male partners and sons, and served as their dance partners in times of both victory and defeat.[40] On a daily basis, the women at the camps offered the soldiers mates, regularly taken first thing in the morning around the campfire.[41]

During the war, drinking mate served an important role connecting and sustaining troops on both sides of the conflict. Dionísio Cerqueira, a Brazilian student who enlisted as a volunteer, wrote in his detailed postwar account that the men of the Brazilian army were divided on their preferred hot drink. While those from northern regions like Bahia preferred coffee, men from the south (like the captain from Rio Grande do Sul pictured at the start of the chapter) were accustomed to drinking mate. In good times, Brazilian soldiers had access to both beverages and sugar to sweeten them. In bad periods, mate had to suffice. "There were many months in which we did not drink anything but mate," Cerqueira lamented.[42]

On the Paraguayan side, troops expected to be provisioned with yerba. Paraguayan colonel Juan Crisóstomo Centurión shared in his memoir that he regularly drank mate with other higher-ups in the army and that yerba continued to serve as a means of trade and currency.[43] On Paraguayan ships, sailors drank so much yerba that the navy banned the practice to prevent soldiers from dumping their leftovers overboard and staining the ships green.[44]

The supply of yerba in particular and food more broadly began to fall precipitously as the war wore on. Despite being cut off from any imports, in the early years of fighting, local provisioning from state-owned cattle ranches and farms ensured a steady food supply for the troops and most other Paraguayans.[45] But as more cows were slaughtered for the army, more men and boys were drawn into the fighting, and a growing number of women moved to the front to cook and care for them rather than farm, cook, and market at home, the food supply began to run short. Paraguayan yerba production, which had met local need and helped finance the first two years of the war, declined steeply, and Brazilian exporters met yerba demand elsewhere.[46] In 1867 Paraguay, the lack of salt, wood, and yerba haunted locals, as did the scarcity of staple crops of corn, manioc, and tobacco that women had long taken the lead in producing.[47] As Potthast puts it, "Even though the government argued the opposite, civilians and soldiers, alike, experienced greater hunger all the time and missed yerba mate and tobacco."[48]

Six years of fending off Brazilian and Argentine troops left Paraguay severely depleted. Historians have estimated that a staggering 60 percent of its total population and up to 90 percent of its adult men perished during the war due to the combined ravages of military battles, disease, and hunger.[49] In the 1870s, the gender ratio of Paraguay shifted dramatically, with approximately four times more women surviving the war than their male counterparts.[50]

Paraguayan women played a major role in sustaining their nation during the war and reviving it after. And yet women did not gain political power after the war despite their heroism and the praise they received during the conflict. As Potthast explains, "Paraguay won worldwide fame for becoming 'the country of women,' but it did not become a country for women."[51]

Brazilian troops occupied the vanquished, predominantly female nation for the next six years. After their 1876 departure, surviving male Paraguayan political elites, who allied with members of the Triple Alliance against López, split into two factions of the liberal party that wrestled each other to fill the postwar political vacuum. Paraguay now experienced the radical political instability at the top that Argentine and Uruguayan republican governments had previously suffered in the wake of independence from Spain. The liberal free-market ethos eclipsing mercantilism in much of South America in the late nineteenth century proved particularly complicated in a nation whose economy had been all but destroyed. As two leading political scholars of Paraguay explain, the 1870s to the 1930s were "marked by a tumultuous series of coups, countercoups, palace 'revolutions,' and two-day presidencies, as rival groups within each party fought over the rich pickings to be gained from association with the foreign economic interests that soon came to dominate the country."[52]

Among the "rich pickings," yerba was high on the list. Brazil seized land for a new yerba-growing region it called Mato Grosso, expanding its production beyond Paraná and Rio Grande do Sul. The Republic of Argentina formally claimed a slice of the long-disputed Misiones—home to many of the former Jesuit missions—as part of its national territory in 1881, gaining access to land that would allow this nation to eventually become the largest yerba producer.[53]

But in the 1880s, Argentina's outpacing of its rivals in yerba production was still some five decades off. In the decades following the war, Brazil not only maintained but even expanded its role as the region's largest yerba producer and exporter.[54] Even so, because its yerbales had been little damaged in the war, Paraguay regained prewar levels by the 1880s, largely based on the production of small and medium-sized ventures.[55]

PARAGUAY: LAND LOST AFTER THE
WAR OF THE TRIPLE ALLIANCE

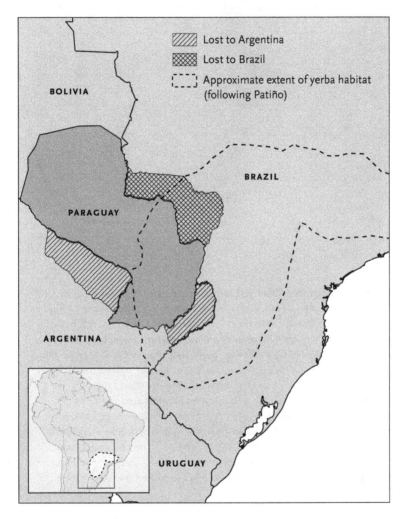

Source: Created by John H. Clark, Geospatial Services librarian, Lafayette
College, Eaton, PA, following "Free vector and raster map data [1:10m]: Land,
Ocean, Admin-0 Countries, Gray Earth," Natural Earth, 2021, https://www
.naturalearthdata.com; Victor Manuel Patiño, *Plantas cultivadas y animales
domésticos en América equinoccial,* vol. 3., *Fibras, medicinas, misceláneas* (Cali, Col.:
Imprenta Departamental, 1967), 24; Maximilian Dörrbecker, *Karte Tripel-Allianz-
Krieg–vor dem Krieg,* Wikimedia Commons, 2015, https://commons.wikimedia.org
/wiki/File:Karte_Tripel-Allianz-Krieg_-_vor_dem_Krieg.png (accessed August 30,
2021); and Maximilian Dörrbecker, *Karte_Tripel-Allianz-Krieg_-_nach_dem_Krieg,*
Wikimedia Commons, 2015, https://commons.wikimedia.org/wiki/File:Karte
Tripel-Allianz-Krieg-_nach_dem_Krieg.png (accessed August 30, 2021).

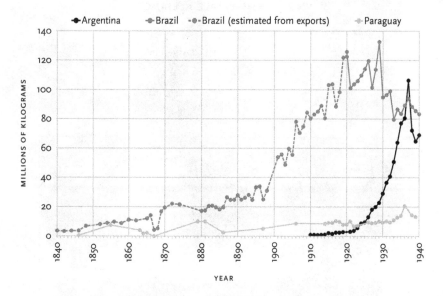

Source: Created by Paul Miller, visual resources curator at Lafayette College, Eaton, PA, from statistics published in the sources indicated in note 54. Figures were aggregated, converted to kilograms as required, and compared. In cases of disparity, any instances of major deviation, lesser precision, or obvious error were discarded. Reasonably differing figures were then averaged together per annum to arrive at the data points rendered. For Brazil, no direct production data were discovered prior to 1920; however, there are export statistics going back to the 1840–41 fiscal year. In those years in which both sets of figures overlap (1920–41 and 1961), analysis reveals that Brazil exported between 56 percent and 90 percent of its harvest per year, with all but three years falling into a narrow 65–83 percent range. By applying the 74 percent mean export percentage to the available export statistics, reasonably likely approximations of Brazilian production levels represented by the dashed line were derived.

Despite this recovery, the cash-strapped and heavily indebted Paraguayan state was playing with a weak hand and sold off nearly 80 percent of its land to larger commercial interests in the 1880s.[56] This included native yerba forests that it held in the eastern region, cattle ranches that spanned the country, and the quebracho forests in the western Chaco region.[57] La Industrial Paraguaya (LIPSA) dominated the Paraguayan yerba industry. Established in Asunción in August 1886 shortly before the Paraguayan government began selling off state-owned land, by 1889 LIPSA bought up more than half of all the yerbales in Paraguay, becoming the largest private landowner in all of eastern

Chapter Three

Paraguay.[58] Wealthy locals, prominent politicians—including President General Bernardino Caballero (1880–86)—and a small number of foreigners from Great Britain were the first investors.[59] LIPSA took possession of some 2.65 million hectares of land, or the geographic area of half of Switzerland. It also set up yerba mills in Asunción, Corrientes, and Buenos Aires and diversified its business by selling timber, rubber, and foodstuffs produced on its five large estancias (ranches).[60] As the company's profits soared during the 1890s, LIPSA became a potent symbol for some Paraguayans (including politicians who had invested in it) of their nation's ability to recover and modernize in the postwar era.[61]

LIPSA was joined by a Brazilian and a French investor, who likewise made a fortune during this era—not only on yerba harvesting and processing but also on lumber and shipping.[62] Brazilian entrepreneur Tomas Larangeira, who named his firm Matte Larangeira after himself, became a major player in the quickly privatized postwar production of yerba. Indeed, Larangeira's story helps reveal how the tide shifted. In the 1870s, this Brazilian businessman, who had supported the government commission that set the demarcation of the border between Paraguay and Brazil (tellingly, by supplying commissioners with food), spent time studying the Paraguayan yerba industry while waiting for permission to start his own business in Brazil.[63] In 1882, he used his tight links with provincial officials in Mato Grosso to secure the first legal concession to exploit the native forests in this region just across the new border with Paraguay.[64] In the next decades, he dominated the production of yerba in Mato Grosso and established it as a competitor with the earlier yerba-producing Brazilian provinces of Paraná and Rio Grande do Sul. Together, these Brazilian provinces would continue to outpace Paraguayan production, even as Larangeira also still profited from Paraguayan yerba production.[65]

French investor and shipping magnate Domingo Barthe also played an outsized role in the postwar Paraguayan yerba industry. He created a shipping line that facilitated travel between Argentina and Paraguay and a new brand of yerba called Yerba Asunción. He was later accused and found guilty of passing off his yerba in Argentina as that of LIPSA's. Apparently, he never went to jail or paid the fine assessed to him.[66]

Meanwhile, in Argentina, European immigrants lured by funding and land concessions moved to the red-dirt region of Misiones to try their hand at growing yerba and other local crops. These immigrants and the locals they employed laid the seed for new yerba mate plantations that eventually enabled Argentina to become a significant player in the marketplace. "In returning to a system of yerba plantations, Misiones came full circle to the Jesuit example.

The same phenomenon occurred in Rio Grande do Sul and Paraguay, though on a more limited scale," Whigham explains.[67]

But even as Paraguay ceded much of its yerba industry to foreigners and faced increasing competition from its neighbors, Paraguayan yerba survived the war with its superior reputation intact. In 1871, Washburn, the US ambassador, noted, "An article of an inferior quality grows in some parts of Brazil and in the Argentine district of Misiones; but though it passes under the same generic name as that of Paraguay, and has some of its peculiar qualities, it has little of the flavor or aroma of the Paraguayan article, and is never used when the other can be had."[68] As had long been the case, Paraguayans and elites elsewhere tended to prefer Paraguayan yerba.

Even as this preference persisted after the war, the industry that produced it was radically restructured. Brazil and Argentina's land seizures took valuable regions for yerba production away from Paraguay. International capitalists hailing from England, France, Brazil, Argentina, and even some capitalists from Paraguay itself took over for the Paraguayan state as owners and profiteers of the remaining Paraguayan yerbales. Furthermore, in the 1880s, an Argentine company called La Platense asserted a virtual monopoly over the riverways that transported the yerba downstream.[69] The industry that had been at the center of the colonial and postcolonial Paraguayan economy was now in private and often foreign hands.

What difference did this make? The most obvious change was the transfer of profits from the Paraguayan state and yerba traders to a small cadre of international entrepreneurs who had the capital to profit off of the land. The new profiteers continued to exploit yerba workers (previously called *mineros*, or miners, and now more commonly *mensúes*, or monthly laborers) in an expanded system of debt peonage.[70] In the meantime, the liberal Paraguayan state's laws and media outlets provided critics opportunities to lambast the state's codification of laws that condoned traditional forms of labor exploitation in this new era. While some of those who profited most were from abroad, Paraguayans made up the labor force.

HIGHLIGHTING YERBA LABORERS' OPPRESSION

In the early 1880s, local critics began to use Paraguay's press to critique the treatment of local yerba workers. An editorial published in the Paraguayan newspaper *La reforma*, for example, decried the system of debt peonage so common in the yerba mate industry. "It seems that many peons do not get a salary or other compensation from their employer," the author explained. "Before they were enslaved with rum, now with forcibly contracted debts."[71]

In 1908, Rafael Barrett, a Spanish anarchist, journalist, and social critic who spent four years in Paraguay, sought to reveal "Lo que son los yerbales" (What the yerba forests really are). What they were, he argued, were state-approved "slave camps."[72] Barrett's indictment appeared first in the Paraguayan newspaper *El diario* in June 1908 and the following years in Argentina and Uruguay, after being forced into exile.[73] He observed that the postwar Paraguayan government's policies and legal codes had allowed the transnational liberal elite who dominated the industry and oppressed workers to profit. While Barrett attributed this phenomenon to modern liberal capitalism, he must have known that the exploitation of yerba workers went back centuries. During the colonial era, the Jesuits offered impassioned critiques that the Spanish worked their Indigenous laborers into poor health and even death. Anticipating that contemporary readers might doubt his words, he clarified that he was not being dramatic but rather pointing to the most common trends.

Barrett told his readers how the trap for these poor agricultural workers was typically set. Recruiters for major yerba interests offered a young man (legally referred to as "peon") an advance, requiring him to sign a contract that stipulated that he would pay off this sum via his own labor. The cash-strapped laborer typically left this advance behind with his family or quickly spent it before commencing his servitude. The contracted peon then found himself legally obligated to work for his employer until he could repay his advance, which proved impossible. Barrett wrote, "He has sold himself into slavery. Nothing can save him. The advance has been cleverly calculated in relation to his rate of pay and the price of food and clothing in the plantations, such that even if he works himself to death he will always be in debt to the owners. If he attempts to flee, he is hunted down. If they are unable to bring him back alive, they kill him."[74] Once the peon signed the contract, he became the owner's property and had no viable means of changing that status. "If we were to imagine that a peon could summon up just an ounce of independent spirit and the necessary strength from his aching body to cross the immense forest in search of a magistrate," posed Barrett, "he would still only find a judge who is in the pay of Industrial Paraguaya, Matte Larangeira or the *latifundistas* [large estate owners] of Alto Paraná."[75] Judges on the payrolls of private yerba companies provided little recourse for workers if they overcame the obstacles to reaching them in the first place.

Since the Triple Alliance War, Barrett claimed that some 30,000 to 40,000 Paraguayans had been "annihilated in this manner."[76] For its part, the Paraguayan state claimed some 25,000 Paraguayan laborers worked in their yerbales, but whether they were all working in Paraguay and whether Barrett's numbers should be added to this figure remain unclear.[77] What we know is that tens of thousands of people from Paraguayan villages were legally trapped, laboring and perishing in extremely poor conditions in the yerbales in Paraguay and also in Brazil and eventually Argentina. And yet some yerba workers managed to escape. They fled, like others to the *monte* (or wilderness), in search of liminal space where neither the government nor its international capitalist allies had control.[78] The practice of running away endured throughout the nineteenth century, which is made evident by the January 1871 law criminalizing those who escaped the yerbales and by the armed squads employed by LIPSA to chase down deserters.[79] The Paraguayan government did nothing to protect workers or stop LIPSA, due to the company's unrivaled power as well as local authorities' interests in or bribes received from it.[80]

Lacking both unions and legal protections, other oppressed laborers joined workers in the yerbales in this dangerous form of resistance. Workers in *obrajes* (workshops) and private homes also continued to run away. As Milda Rivarola points out, the mostly female domestic workforce faced conditions similar to those of yerba workers: small or nonexistent salaries, physical mistreatment by their patrons, and a lack of fixed work hours.[81] Physical violence, including whipping, served as a regular tool to seek to maintain the servitude of *tembiguái*, whether in the forest, the workshop, or the home.[82]

Barrett's series focused on making people see the oppression of male yerba workers. Although his publications originally appeared without illustrations or photographs, he used words to paint a picture of the humanity of yerba workers for his readers. "Look closely into the forest," Barrett warned. "You will see a huge bundle walking. Look below the bundle and you will find an oppressed creature in whom all trace of humanity is gradually being erased." Barrett concluded, "This is no longer a man, but a peon of the yerba plantations."[83]

Who were these indebted yerba workers toting bundles of branches that often weighed over 200 pounds?[84] Barrett implied in 1908 that recent recruits were younger because so many adult men had previously died toiling in the forests. He also suggested they were White: "With regards to those who are still suffering this yoke—many of them are minors, as I have explained—one fact will suffice to illustrate their state. They are much lower than Indians in intelligence, energy, dignity—in fact, in any aspect that one may wish to consider. This is what the Industrial Paraguaya has done to the white man."[85] Was Barrett's racial categorization of White male victims a move to evoke sympathy in Western audiences? If so, his characterization would have resonated with contemporary lamentations of the so-called white slavery of European immigrants who found themselves victims to unfair contracts.[86] Or, did Barrett and his contemporaries understand these laborers to be White? This also seems plausible given that Barrett had spent so much time in Paraguay and that many late nineteenth-century Paraguayans wished to be considered part of this esteemed category regardless of their heritage—because the association with Whiteness granted them respect, not the denigration associated with those who preserved Black (*kamba*) or Indian identities.

In contrast to mainstream Paraguayan notions about race, and Barrett's words, contemporary foreign chroniclers with less awareness of local dynamics suggested that a profoundly racialized labor hierarchy persisted in the yerbales and beyond. E. J. M. Clemens, a female travel writer from the United States who traveled across Argentina, Paraguay, and Uruguay, as well as the Platine regions of Bolivia and southern Brazil, told readers at home that in this region, the laborer who is referred to as a peon "is the descendant of the conquered, amalgamated, or *reduced* Indians." She continued that the "labor line" in South America divided the social classes "as distinctly as the color line separates the freedman and white citizen of the United States." In the yerbales, peons did all the work—a point she made citing Washburn.[87]

Washburn explained that laborers, whom he condescendingly labeled "swarthy native[s]," did the work of producing yerba at their "comfortless camp." He also included an illustration of the processes he described in detail. In the illustration, Indigenous laborers in loincloths perform the work while two White overseers look on under a tentlike structure.[88] In the eyes of Washburn and other US observers, a clear racial hierarchy governed who oversaw the work and who did it in the yerbales.[89]

Clemens focused her attention not on the hills but on the home, where a family's respectability within the category of *gente decente* (literally, decent people) depended on employing servants of the other class and not getting one's hands dirty.[90] In keeping with what we learned in the previous chapter, Clemens detailed in her section on Paraguay that servants typically served yerba mate in upper-class homes while a family member did so among the laboring class. She specified that in an elite home, this servant was often the family's godchild. "The relationship of the godparent is recognized by law, and it is very customary for the *gente decente* to sustain this relation to children of the *peon* class." She continued, "It is often a godchild who brings in the *maté* and otherwise serves about one's person and is the attendant while travelling."[91] While no longer legally enslaved by the early 1880s, this child, often referred to as a *criado* or *criada*, was still expected to serve his or her godparents, their family, and their guests.

A racialized labor hierarchy persisted in the servile dynamics of the home but also in the yerba forests. In "respectable" homes, darker-skinned domestic servants often attended to lighter-skinned patrons. In the yerbales, men, many of whom were of Indigenous and mixed descent, labored for little or no recompense to enrich their White overseers and, even more so, business owners and bankers who were from Europe or locals of European descent. In 1915, Barrett's critiques inspired a movement to end the "slave-like" conditions in the yerbales called "Movimiento Promoteo" (Promise Movement) in the capital city of Asunción. It was an energetic but short-lived effort, which died with its leader, Leopoldo Ramos Giménez, who was murdered in July 1916, as threats were issued to other participants.[92]

CONSUMING FOOD AND YERBA IN THE POSTWAR ERA

A growing number of foreign travelers who published accounts on Paraguay in the postwar era depicted the consumption of yerba, along with a few other locally grown staples, as another enduring part of daily life. Writing in 1890, Theodore Child, who like Clemens hailed from the United States, noted that most people had sufficient resources to purchase yerba, tobacco, and manioc, which he described as the staples of their diet, and to supplement this diet by gathering "oranges, that lie in many places a foot deep on the ground."[93]

Paraguayans drank mate and smoked tobacco in public places, not only at home. In the central Plaza Independencia (Independence Square) in Asunción, for example, Child told readers, "You see the soldiers sitting with their women folk, some of them nursing their children, others drinking *maté* and all smoking cigars, both men and women alike."[94]

Other contemporary chroniclers linked this local infusion (like tobacco consumption) primarily to women. In 1877, Argentine doctor Honorario Leguizamón described rural Paraguayan woman who were able to walk 40 to 50 leguas (or 120 to 150 miles), consuming only grilled manioc root and tereré, which they could make with water they found along the way.[95] At the close of the nineteenth century, US writer Frank George Carpenter claimed that "many Paraguayan women drink from fifteen to twenty cups of it [mate] daily." He noted that its "stimulating and strengthening" properties helped stave off hunger.[96]

Before the war, the typical Paraguayan diet consisted of mate for breakfast, and for the main meal, chicken or beef *puchero* (stew) served with boiled or roasted manioc root and *chipá*, a savory roll made with ground manioc or corn flour, often mixed with cheese.[97] As the war ground on, the army received the remaining supply of beef, depleting cattle stocks.[98] After the war, "stew with meat was more the exception," according to Rivarola. As women returned home to tend their fields, they planted and harvested corn, beans, and manioc, made *chipá*, and picked oranges.[99] Locals paused to drink mate together first thing in the morning and after the midday siesta, and sometimes more often. Most drank it unsweetened through a bombilla. Some families possessed bombillas made of silver, while others made use of "the leg bone of a fowl, with a tuft of cotton wrapped at the end," as one traveler noted.[100] But unless they were very wealthy, Paraguayans did not drink coffee, which cost some five times more than yerba.[101]

While many Paraguayans and others now associate the emergence of the cold version of the infusion made with yerba, called tereré, with the Chaco War against Bolivia (1932–35), during the War of the Triple Alliance, soldiers on the Paraguayan front appear to have started drinking it in a manner consonant with current practices.[102] In his history of tereré, Paraguayan priest Derlis Benítez explains that while the Guaraní and other Indigenous groups had long consumed what they called ka'a (and the Spanish, yerba) from bowls filled with either heated water or chilled water (typically kept just below ambient temperature in large ceramic jugs), it was not until this war that soldiers began to insert a bombilla into the cold version of this infusion.[103] Why? Many have suggested that proximity to the enemy meant that lighting a fire could be dangerous. Furthermore, when water was scarce or brackish, combining it with yerba helped to quench thirst more palatably or safely while adding nutrients and a sense of normality in dire circumstances. These explanations seem apocryphal for the War of the Triple Alliance, but the scarcity of water became a significant issue some six decades later in the hot scrubland of the Chaco in the war against Bolivia, when soldiers drank both tereré and *mate cocido* when water and yerba were available.[104] More likely, in the earlier war, as supplies dried up, drinking tereré offered an easier alternative that required less yerba and made it last longer.

Survivors of the War of the Triple Alliance (and even more so, the Chaco War) brought the tradition of drinking tereré through a bombilla home with them and helped popularize it.[105] As these wars both predated refrigeration, drinking the icy version of tereré with medicinal herbs that became so popular in the late twentieth century still proved impossible for most.[106] One man recalled the intricate process he undertook to provide his boss with tereré in the early 1920s: "Early in the morning, I would gather the Pohä Ñana [wild, medicinal herbs], [and] I would crush them well and put them in the water to get as much juice as possible, until it became a deep green color. Then, to make it as cold as possible, I would put the preparation . . . in bottles . . . tie them together . . . and deposit them in the bottom of the well. And then, when the hour for tereré arrived, I would take them out of the well and serve a tasty and cool tereré to my boss."[107] While this man's boss enjoyed the labors of this servant to make a cool tereré possible each afternoon, most Paraguayans, especially those who lacked servants and access to a naturally cool water supply, did not have the resources for such a luxury.

As a result, the hot version of mate remained much more common than tereré across most of Paraguay following the War of the Triple Alliance.[108] Swiss naturalist and ethnographer Moisés Santiago Bertoni recognized that some people in Paraguay consumed yerba with cool water, especially in the Chaco region and northern Paraguay, the recently claimed Brazilian province of Mato Grosso, and northeastern Argentina.[109] He also described Indigenous groups he met in Pirapeíh in 1887 and 1888 who "drank the infusion directly from a bowl like any other tisane" with water that was cool or warm, and without a straw or a mate. Still, he concluded that most people in late nineteenth-century Paraguay shared hot mates drained through a bombilla.[110]

Served hot or cold, the local infusion sated the thirst of many locals and helped fill empty bellies, many believed. As Washburn wrote, "To Paraguayans it is the one indispensable luxury."[111] A couple of decades later, Child took this even further: "Mate sustains the poor, they live on it."[112]

Bertoni disagreed. He insisted that consuming yerba mate did not effectively placate hunger and that locals were well aware of this. Bertoni learned this painful lesson on a three-day march when his Indigenous and criollo companions stopped drinking yerba mate once their party was out of food, and he elected not to heed their warnings to do the same. As a result, he suffered "true torture." His muscles cramped up so much that he could barely walk, his heart beat irregularly, he couldn't sleep at night, and his stomach felt a "very disagreeable emptiness."[113] Based on this experience, together with his research on digestion, he explained, "It is therefore very wrong what is so insistently repeated in hundreds of publications and books, that mate sates hunger and allows one to continue working for a long time without eating; and it is false what is said in this regard of the indigenous and creole custom. On the contrary, the practical ones abstain from drinking mate when food is completely lacking."[114] Claims of people subsisting on mate alone seem to be overstated; at the same time, yerba represented a significant part of what locals consumed, including when they had some food but not much.[115]

PICTURING PARAGUAY AS A YERBA
PRODUCER AND NATION OF WOMEN

This image of hunger and yerba consumption made so evident in contemporaries' written accounts was strikingly absent from postwar photographs and postcards. The postcard makers, like postcard collectors, were mostly men from Europe who traveled to Paraguay to do business and were interested in creating a picture of this supposedly exotic country to send home.[116] Postcard buyers at the turn of the twentieth century could select from a variety of themes, especially Indigenous groups and sexualized images of Paraguayan women. Sentimental purchasers might turn to postcards featuring the colonial plazas and churches of smaller cities or communities, while more forward-looking buyers might select postcards depicting new modern buildings in Asunción and tourist attractions near Lake Ypacaraí and Iguazú Falls.[117] If senders wished to emphasize Paraguay's business potential, they might select a postcard that highlighted the country's agricultural production and exports of products, including yerba.

In contrast to contemporary photographs and postcards in the lower Platine region, the leading protagonist appearing on Paraguayan postcards was not the male figure of the gaucho but rather the Paraguayan woman. Since the end of the war, the legend of a "country of women" captivated foreigners, and their fascination with this idea persisted even after the gender gap narrowed by the turn of the twentieth century.[118] Foreign photographers never seemed to tire of showing Paraguayan woman balancing jugs on their heads in their capacity as liquor or water servers called *bolicheras*. Prolific German photographer José Fresen took numerous photographs where a Paraguayan woman appeared in an off-the-shoulder peasant dress, often with a cigar in her mouth and sometimes a child by her side. (Women also did most of the cigar making,[119] though this proved less interesting to photographers or postcard makers). Some postcards featured female laborers picking coffee and transporting oranges, making visible the major role they played in these agricultural industries. But Paraguayan women were generally absent from postcards depicting yerba production, which was revived as a male-dominated industry after the war.

When it came to yerba, postwar visuals portrayed Paraguay as a nation of production rather than consumption. Alongside Rafael Barrett's printed

Editor y Propietario: Juan Quell, Asunción.

Rancho Yerbatero.

FIGURE 3.4. Postcard, "Rancho Yerbatero," ca. 1905, ed. Juan Quell, Asunción. Courtesy of Special Collections and College Archives, Skillman Library, Lafayette College, Eaton, PA.

indictment of the yerba industry, a series of photographs produced in the 1890s allowed for an updated view of laborers and the work they performed. Around 1898, an unknown photographer showed for the first time the meager straw huts in which the yerba workers slept.[120] Unlike other photographs from this series, however, these humble sleeping quarters did not appear on post-cards for sale in Paraguay in the first decade of the twentieth century. Instead, like most earlier illustrations, postcards that included yerba highlighted the stages of work these laborers undertook to pick, cure, and chop it.

Photographs focusing on stages of work provide valuable clues about the composition of the workforce. As Barrett suggested, in the yerbales, young boys frequently worked alongside older men. Many appeared to have some Indigenous or African as well as European ancestry. Take, for example, the series of postcards published in Asunción around 1905–6 by local postcard editor and owner Juan Quell. In two images, both captioned "Rancho Yerbatero," referring to the small country houses where yerba was processed, a range of workers appears in front of a *barbacuá*, or the open, tentlike scaffolded structure on which yerba was heated and dried. In the first photograph, five laborers, at least some of whom appear to have some Indigenous ancestry, chop the previously cured yerba in large sacks (fig. 3.4). This photograph, like others produced at the time, is clearly posed; here, workers hold their *palos* (or sticks) to crush the yerba at different heights. In the second postcard, the workers perform the same task but are depicted in closer focus. While three men look intently into their bags, the fourth figure appears to be a young dark-skinned boy (perhaps of partial African descent) who is curiously well dressed and checks the grind of the yerba.

While female figures did not appear in most photographs of yerba production, one exception has made its way to us. In yet another postcard captioned "Rancho Yerbatero," the workers are all assembled and joined by a fair-skinned couple who appear to be the owners or managers.[121] The woman is seated at the forefront of the image, and the man is perched behind her in a chair that elevates his height over the rest of the standing workers. Off to the left, one worker grinds the yerba while another holds the bag. The viewer cannot see their faces, but these workers are cast as dark-skinned, in contrast to the lightened faces of the couple and some of the likely higher-ranking workers who flank them.

Postcard makers also frequently highlighted the process of moving the yerba from the yerbales to the port and downriver. Here, the emphasis was not on the people who did this work but rather on the animals and riverboats that made it possible. Juan Quell, for example, offered postcards in which a team of oxen pulled a cart full of yerba away from a *rancho yerbatero* in Caaguazú.[122] He issued another featuring a *chata* (a long, flat riverboat) loaded with bags of yerba (fig. 3.5). Quell directed the viewer's attention to the boat and the yerba it carried with the caption "Chata conduciendo Yerba" (Boat carrying yerba). In the photograph, the boat dominates the frame and the workers appear as afterthoughts. Three men cast in shadows steer the boat with long oars, and a fourth person is nearly edited out of the photograph. In this way, Quell directed the viewer's attention to the means of transporting yerba, rather than to the human laborers involved in this process.

The other main Paraguayan postcard editor, known simply as Gruter, also showcased the transportation of yerba. In the first decade of the twentieth century, Gruter released a series of hand-colored postcards. One showed ox-drawn carts transporting yerba from the yerbales, and another their arrival at the port city of Villa Concepción. A third featured *chatas* that would take this product downriver. In contrast to Quell's postcard highlighting a riverboat, Gruter's included many more workers on the boats and the shore, along with some male and female passengers catching a ride on boats used primarily for the transportation of goods like yerba.[123]

Chata conduciendo Yerba.

FIGURE 3.5. Postcard, "Chata conduciendo Yerba," ca. 1905, ed. Juan Quell, Asunción. Courtesy of Special Collections and College Archives, Skillman Library, Lafayette College, Eaton, PA.

Despite the focus on yerba production and transportation on Paraguayan postcards, people across the social classes regularly consumed yerba. In a rare moment captured on camera and highlighted on another Gruter postcard, a lace worker with a child on her lap sips from a mate. This mate likely provided her with energy but also a source of comfort and sociability during long workdays. Unlike the deliberate emphasis on mate drinking that we will see presented in contemporary Argentine and Uruguayan postcards in the next chapter, this inclusion seems peripheral to the lace work (or *ñanduti*) that is held up by the other women and a few of the girls for the viewer.

The Paraguayan thirst for mate clearly survived the war intact, and not just for lace workers. Foreign chroniclers continued to remark upon the enduring popularity of the local infusion across all echelons of Paraguayan society. In 1915, Henry Stephens called mate the "national soft drink of Paraguay." As elsewhere in southern South America, rich people in Paraguay drained silver mates while the poor drank from gourds or *guampas*.[124] Two years

Chapter Three

later, W. H. Koebel reported that "the teas, for instance of India, Ceylon, and China have not yet succeeded in making any appreciable headway against the popular yerba mate." He concluded that "it would be strange had they done so, considering that the chief source of Paraguayan tea is, after all, Paraguay."[125]

Even so, Paraguayans' consumption of *their* so-called tea was not highlighted in a new genre of visuals—the commercial postcard—that purported to represent local culture. Instead, the production of yerba and other agricultural products assumed an outsized role. Although postcards featuring Paraguayans drinking mate from this era do not appear to exist (save the seemingly unintentional example of the lace worker), other types of compositions predominated that showed how yerba was cut, cured, and chopped, as well as all the stages of how it traveled from sites of production to the port cities and downriver. In step with the early twentieth-century arrival of planted yerba stands in Paraguay, postcards frequently displayed yerba ranchos (small yerba enterprises) where yerba was being processed rather than hilly stands of native trees where workers continued to toil.[126] Taken together, photographs and postcards created around the turn of the twentieth century showed Paraguay as a place of yerba production and export rather than as a site of yerba consumption. After the war, image makers pictured a nation where locals no longer had time to sip mate all day.[127] They suggested that Paraguay was a place where its people, Paraguayans, made things with their hands, whether yerba or lace, for others to consume.

The general absence of images of mate consumption, which became so ubiquitous in neighboring nations around this time, suggests that Paraguayans lost this privilege after the war. Why?

Before the war broke out, the future of the yerba industry at the heart of the Paraguayan economy seemed promising. But after the conflict, liberal Paraguayan politicians saw little choice but to cede government control over land and profits. Brazil grew its industry and Argentina entered the game. A handful of international capitalists profited greatly while tens of thousands of laborers suffered the contractual obligations of toiling in the yerbales. Contemporaries caught rare glimpses of their suffering in a small number of illustrations and early photographs that paid attention to these conditions. More frequently, photographers and postcard makers highlighted the making and transporting of yerba instead of the people who worked to produce and move this commodity.

The story of how foreigners, with the support of liberal Paraguayan allies, privatized the yerba industry became fairly well known within Paraguay. Although less recognized, foreigners also dominated the business of taking and circulating photographs on postcards. Foreigners' feminized visions of Paraguay went hand in hand with the notion that their ability to profit depended on maintaining a cheap and vulnerable labor force.

The oppression of yerba laborers became better known because of Rafael Barrett's exposés from the first decade of the twentieth century. In the following decades, writers from the lower Platine region joined this critique. For example, Horacio Quiroga, a Uruguayan writer who moved to Argentina, famously referred to the region of Misiones as "un infierno verde" (a green hell) in a series of "jungle stories" published in 1914. In one called "*Los mensú*" (The monthly laborers), he dramatized the trap of exploitation that two monthly laborers found themselves in and from which no escape proved possible, despite their dramatic attempts to flee.[128]

While Quiroga invented names for his proletarian protagonists, the actual names and stories of the successful capitalists who profited off such laborers became the stuff of lore. For example, Frenchman Domingo Barthe, who owned large swaths of yerba land in southern Paraguay, had by 1915 reportedly "amassed a fortune in Paraguay in the river boat, live stock, and *maté* business," totaling some $19 million. He set up his residence not in Paraguay but in Posadas, the capital city of the new Argentine territory of Misiones, and also regularly traveled to Buenos Aires and Paris.[129] In Barthe's view, producing and shipping Paraguayan yerba (and cattle) for an Argentine market promised the greatest profit margin.

And yet in Buenos Aires, Barthe's elite peers were beginning to publicly turn away from their conspicuous consumption of the local infusion and toward hot drinks they considered more cosmopolitan, like coffee or tea. At the same time, image makers in Argentina and Uruguay associated these nations' mate cultures not with the urban well-to-do but with rural figures. Why did the primary association of mate drinkers in Argentina and Uruguay shift away from feminized urban elites and toward the masculinized rural poor? The next chapter explains how the gaucho became not only the iconic national symbol in these nations but also its most symbolically important mate drinker, while his female counterpart became the most famous mate server.

CHAPTER FOUR

Picturing Mate as Rural in Argentina and Uruguay, 1870s–1920s

Outside a simple adobe home, a woman heats a fire to warm the water she has carried from a distant well. She spoons dusty green yerba into a mate made from a gourd seasoned by many previous mates. When the water is hot, she pours some of the water into the vessel and takes a sip to ensure that the yerba has not clogged the straw. The first sip fills her mouth with a few stray leaves and the smoky, bitter flavor of the hot infused water. But this mate is not for her. She brings the mate and the kettle outside. There, she sees her common-law husband—who many would call a gaucho—astride his horse, preparing to depart. She infuses the mate with hot water once more and hands it to him. He takes a sip before galloping away.

In the countryside, this man and other gauchos like him spend their days rustling cattle. When they need a respite from their work, they gather together around a campfire. This being far from home, there is no woman present to make the men's mates, so the youngest man does the job. He tends the fire and heats the water in the kettle. Like the woman, he tastes the first mate to make sure the bombilla is unclogged, the water hot, and the mate ready to share. Then, he passes it to an older man, who takes a break from playing

FIGURE 4.1. Francisco Ayerza, photograph of *mate del estribo* (goodbye mate). Courtesy of Archivo General de la Nación, Buenos Aires, Argentina, original 1894, reprint.

guitar to slurp the hot infusion. Another man holds a flask of liquor to his lips. The guitar player hands the mate back to the young man, who pours the water into the mate and passes it to the man with the flask. The men continue in this way for hours.

These two idyllic scenes of rural mate drinking became increasingly familiar to people living in Argentina and Uruguay around the turn of the twentieth century. Inspired in part by earlier illustrations of rural life, Argentine photographer Dr. Francisco Ayerza first captured them on camera in the 1890s (figs. 4.1 and 4.2).

A leader in amateur photography in Argentina, Ayerza took about a dozen photographs featuring mate. In all but one, where a woman sits at a dance drinking a mate, men are pictured as mate drinkers, highlighting nostalgic associations of self-sufficiency, male friendship, and leisure on the open plains. When present, rural women are featured as rural men's mate servers—a dramatic shift from earlier compositions that showed Black and Brown mate servers attending White women or socializing over a round of

FIGURE 4.2. Francisco Ayerza, photograph, *Campaña de Buenos Aires.*
Courtesy of Archivo General de la Nación, Buenos Aires, Argentina, ca. 1891.

mate. This was part of a larger turn from a feminine and urban vision of the lower Platine region in the early nineteenth century to a masculine criollo conception by its end.[1]

How did women go from being envisioned as the preeminent mate drinkers in the colonial and early national era to either serving the mate or not being shown at all? What did this have to do with local elites' new and sometimes conflicting visions for themselves as modern, European-style actors in South America? And how did the massive arrival of immigrants from Europe help foster tighter links—now pictured as traditional—between mate, rural masculinity, and national identity?

Most sectors of South American society that enjoyed mate during the early national period continued to drink this Indigenous infusion throughout the modernizing era that stretched from the 1870s to the 1920s.[2] This included pretty much all rural dwellers across the region and even most urban elites in cities, including Asunción and Montevideo. And yet there were some dramatic disaffections. In the city of Buenos Aires, members of the upper class turned away from their conspicuous mate drinking, which, as we have seen, they had highlighted at parties and in artwork depicting them in the decades following independence. Although this ritual had a long urban history, it now became tightly connected to rural life. Following Domingo Sarmiento's influential mid-nineteenth-century division of the nation into the "barbaric interior" and "civilized city," *porteño* elites increasingly associated mate drinking with the denigrated rural side of this equation.[3] Their public shift away from the local drink and toward coffee and tea coincided not only with the increased availability of pricier alternatives but also with a successful effort to recruit European immigrants to the region.

From the 1870s to the 1920s, European immigrants streamed not only to Argentina but also to Uruguay and southern Brazil. A smaller but still significant number made their way to Paraguay. Many immigrants, like travelers before them, turned to mate drinking as a material way of assimilating into a new culture, but now on a massive scale and in a permanent way. Scientists and businessmen regularly wrote about these enthusiastic newcomers, and a few photographers even captured them in black-and-white photographs in the late nineteenth and early twentieth centuries. And yet most contemporary photographers and postcard makers generally left out immigrants, elites, and urbanites from a new, more nationalistic visual culture surrounding mate drinking. They looked to the poor and the provinces for seemingly authentic local practices around which to construct a national identity.[4]

This chapter traces the most dramatic changes with regard to the practice and representation of mate drinking in the lower Platine republics of Argentina and Uruguay from the 1870s to the 1920s. We will first explore the reasons behind *porteño* elites' move away from mate drinking in public and then shift to immigrants' interest in adopting this local ritual. In the second half of the chapter, we will witness a shift in the visual depiction of mate drinking in paintings, photographs, and especially postcards purporting to represent national culture. Tracing this visual culture over time enables us to see how and why the gaucho became the most important mate drinker on both sides of the Río de la Plata.

Because mate had long served as a symbol of the region's identity, when the gaucho replaced the White woman as the cultural embodiment of both the Argentine and Uruguayan nations, he became the mate drinker par excellence.[5] Elites' newfound love of the no longer autonomous or threatening rural figure served as a counterpoint to the growing class-conscious militancy of immigrant workers. Such militants, in turn, embraced a feistier version of the gaucho who stood up for his rights. This was not a gender-neutral project. The fetishization of the hypermasculine gaucho reinforced women's second-class status just as a small but vocal number of women advocated for greater rights.[6] But men continued to dominate politics and image production. Image makers, like Ayerza, pictured the gaucho on relatively equal ground with other men but placed him on his horse high above his female counterpart. This was part of a nineteenth-century trend in which the public performance of men's authority over women intensified in step with the formation of new male-dominated republics.[7]

Despite their constitutional separation, Argentina and Uruguay maintained a shared visual and media culture as well as physical proximity.[8] Thus, their stories, which we will follow here, often overlapped. Even so, when it came to the practices of mate drinking, elites in Buenos Aires carved a distinctive path.

ELITE DISAFFECTIONS?

In the wake of the wars of independence, elites in Buenos Aires showed off their mate consumption with aplomb. As we saw in chapter 2, they included mates in their portraits and had servants supply mate at parties. Dressed in formal suits and ball gowns, fair-skinned men and women proudly drained silver mates replenished by Black servants who ran back and forth to the kitchen for more hot water. Artists and travelers from Europe celebrated this ritual as defining local high-class culture in Buenos Aires, especially in the heady 1830s. Some four decades later, though, locals began to tell a different story. Argentine army doctor and mate enthusiast Honorario Leguizamón, who hailed from the committed mate-drinking province of Entre Ríos but lived in Buenos Aires, lamented that "the use of mate among us is being abandoned by the *primera sociedad* [top echelon of society]."[9] He was joined by others, including writer José Antonio Wilde, who remarked in 1881 that mate had fallen out favor with the Buenos Aires elite.[10] What happened to cause this shift?

Some contemporaries blamed the apparent abandonment of mate drinking by elites on the recent decline in yerba quality. As we saw in the previous chapter, the Great War disrupted the production of Paraguayan yerba, widely regarded as the highest quality and thus what elites in Buenos Aires (and elsewhere) preferred. And yet in the past, when higher-quality yerba went missing, the well-to-do consumed the inferior product.

Leguizamón argued that quality was not the problem, as most assumed; instead, it was new ideas about hygiene that precipitated the decline. In his opinion, elites turned away from mate not because the yerba was subpar but rather because of "the harmful custom of using of the same mate and the same bombilla to serve it, a custom that certainly must be encountering lots of resistance today due to hygienic recommendations that are more accessible to families."[11] In the 1860s, Frenchman Louis Pasteur and other scientists established the relationship between germs and disease. In Argentina, as Leguizamón suggested, well-educated elites with access to European scientific publications learned about these new ideas. Argentine scientists gravitated toward Lamarckian eugenics that held that biology did not fully determine people's "racial fitness" and that changes in lifestyle and diet could make significant improvements.[12] As such, new ideas about hygiene and eugenics likely shaped some elites' decisions to shy away from their conspicuous consumption of a drink that featured a communal cup and a shared straw.

Despite the contemporary popularity of explanations about quality or hygiene, elites' new ideas about consumption and status appear even more influential. As historian Leandro Losada explains, from the 1880s through the 1910s, members of the upper class distinguished themselves by publicly moving away from rustic local criollo traditions toward the patina of cosmopolitanism associated with western Europe. Contemporaries defined elite status not only by wealth but also by what people did with it. Attending the opera, going to balls, and touring Europe verified a family's elite status.[13] At home, the upper crust could do the same by serving French-style (or at least, French-sounding) dishes on individual plates. When they paused to share a caffeinated drink, they could show their refinement by drinking coffee or tea instead of mate. As Argentine nationalist writer Manuel Gálvez wrote in 1910, "Tea replaces mate, which demonstrates that we are pretty adaptable to civilization."[14] In a context in which most elites equated civilization with European-style urbanity, and barbarism with native peoples and rural customs, it makes sense that members of this sector of society stopped serving mate at their parties and began frequenting the growing number of cafés and tea rooms.[15] Similarly, when well-off Argentines posed before the camera, they refrained from including a mate in their portraits.[16]

Despite their carefully crafted appearances to the contrary, these elites did not stop drinking mate altogether. Lucio V. Mansilla remarked that he knew "families who drink it in hiding."[17] For his part, Wilde noted that elites regularly asked their servants to bring them mates in bed, especially first thing in the morning.[18] As had been the case in earlier eras, these servants were likely expected to prepare the mates, but also to try them first to make sure they were to their masters' liking. As such, neither the quality of the yerba nor the sharing of the bombilla suffices as a main explanation for elites' new feelings about mate.

Porteño elites' shift away from public mate drinking moved them closer to the image of themselves they wished to project. After living in the Argentine provinces of Córdoba and Tucuman in the 1880s and returning in 1918 to travel throughout Argentina (and Brazil and Chile) at the behest of the American Geographical Society, US scientist and businessman Mark Jefferson concluded that while the domineering city of Buenos Aires sought to project a vision of itself as European "on the surface," it was "Creole at heart." He explained, "The Porteños carry their desire to be regarded as European to the extreme of self-consciousness—most perceptibly, of course, in matters of external manners and dress."[19] But behind closed doors, they made different decisions. In Jefferson's view, elites' relationship to mate best illustrated the dichotomy between public personas and private choices. "Most Porteños would give you the impression that mate drinking is unknown in Buenos Aires," he wrote. And yet, "it is consumed in quantities. You can buy yerba and the gourds in which it is prepared everywhere, but the use is concealed and hidden by those who have any pretense to style or fashion." In contrast, members of lower classes drank their mate openly. "With them its popularity lasts and increases, as the growing consumption of yerba attests."[20]

Similarly, in 1915, Argentine scientist Alberto J. Corrado reported that the upper class, as well as some members of the middle class, which was growing in size and cultural importance with the expansion of public education, had replaced mate with coffee and tea.[21] Even so, like Wilde before him, Corrado noted that members of these privileged groups still enjoyed mate in more "intimate" moments.[22]

What changed most dramatically from the early nineteenth century to the early twentieth, then, was elites' eagerness to make this ritual private—for instance, having their mate served to them in bed or in the back kitchen by servants, rather than serving it at their parties. In the liberal, modernizing era that became known as the Belle Époque, porteño elites asserted a new vision of who they were and what they wanted their nation to be, and conspicuous consumption of a local drink with Indigenous roots ran counter to their desire to project Argentina as a modern, European-style, White nation.

Even so, most Argentines continued to drink mate, which remained firmly entrenched in the social lives of the urban popular classes and rural dwellers across the social spectrum. The Argentine Ministry of Agriculture calculated

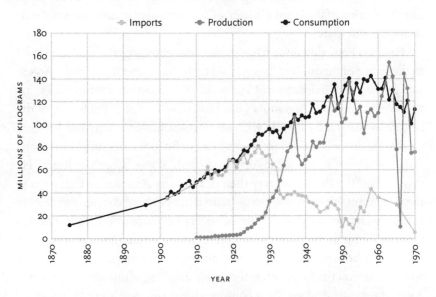

Source: Created by Paul Miller, visual resources curator at Lafayette College,
Eaton, PA, from statistics published in the sources indicated in note 24.
Figures were aggregated, converted to kilograms as required, and compared.
In cases of disparity, any instances of major deviation, lesser precision,
or obvious error were discarded. Reasonably differing figures were then
averaged together per annum to arrive at the data points rendered.

in 1902 that the average person consumed six kilos of yerba per year; ten years
later, per capita consumption grew to eight kilos per year. As of 1912, even as
urban Argentines drank more coffee than before, Argentines on the whole
consumed roughly four times as much yerba mate as they did coffee.[23] Their
consumption climbed significantly during Argentina's Belle Époque.[24]

Farther from yerba production and trade routes, yerba mate consumption
in Belle Époque Chile followed a downward trajectory, even as it remained
the most popular beverage in rural areas. Benjamin Orlove and Arnold Bauer
explain that between 1870 and 1930, per capita consumption of coffee and tea
grew significantly in Chile, while that of yerba mate modestly declined. In
this progressive era, coffee and tea acquired what Orlove and Bauer call the
"allure of the foreign." Despite the proximity of yerba and coffee estates in
Paraguay and Brazil, yerba mate became associated with local, rural culture,
while coffee became linked with Europe and new progressive values. Chilean

city dwellers began to regularly frequent cafés and serve coffee at their banquets. They also served tea in their parlors. Some Chilean miners began to receive rations of coffee rather than yerba to stimulate their work.[25] And a number of urban working-class Chileans apparently switched from mate to coffee, at least on occasion. Still, many people in Chile, including most of the rural poor, continued to drink yerba mate. Indeed, from 1870 to 1930, Chile continued to import and consume more yerba than coffee or tea, none of which it could self-provision.[26]

Consumption statistics are harder to come by for Uruguay (which, like Chile, had to import its caffeinated beverages), but mate remained at the center of local culture in both the capital and the countryside. In the 1890s, traveler Theodore Child remarked that in Montevideo, he "saw people in the summer evenings sitting on their balconies sucking *maté* and thrumming guitars." Child suggested that for the working poor across Spanish America, other options were off the table. "Laborers do not drink tea or coffee," he claimed.[27] Whether or not this was fully accurate, the majority of people in the Belle Époque Río de la Plata region found themselves among the working poor who regularly drank mate instead of the pricier alternatives.

In 1915, the Argentine scientist Corrado argued before a Pan-American conference that yerba mate in Argentina was as important as tea, coffee, coca, and kola in the regions where these were produced. "This acceptance is common not only for the native born, but also the foreigners, who at first resist drinking it, but after a short time get accustomed to using the *bombilla*, to such a point that it becomes a vice for them," he elaborated. For those lower down the social scale, mate consumption appeared less self-conscious and more functional. "It still offers much utility for those without sufficient resources" to purchase coffee and tea, Corrado noted, and such folks drank mate without sugar, "many times per day."[28] As Corrado suggested, agricultural families facing a drought in the province of Córdoba in 1902, for example, reportedly subsisted "on a diet with only bread, *mate cocido*," and, when they were lucky, a local rodent called a *vizcacha*.[29] In that context, necessity and price determined consumption more than anything else.

DRINKING IN LOCAL CULTURE

In addition to helping fill empty bellies, the mate ritual offered non-elites, including a growing number of immigrants, a quotidian practice that fueled their days, relationships, and sense of belonging in new nations. In step with contemporary elites, these immigrants incorporated a novel hot drink into their lives but also preserved their commitment to the traditional hot drinks of their homelands, especially in their own domestic space. Because so many immigrants came to the lower Platine region, they had a dramatic impact on the ideas and practices surrounding mate there.

During the late nineteenth and early twentieth century, Argentina received the second largest number of immigrants after the United States, and the largest percentage vis-à-vis the local population. Despite Argentine elites' preference for northern Europeans, most came from southern Europe, specifically Italy and Spain. Nineteenth-century Uruguay received a significant influx of immigrants with similar origins. While immigration to this smaller nation picked up sharply in the second half of the nineteenth century, it dropped around the turn of the twentieth century, in contrast to Argentina, where the number of new arrivals continued to climb. Accordingly, immigrants made up about a third of the total Argentine population of nearly 8 million residents on the 1914 census and accounted for nearly a fifth of the 1 million people in Uruguay according to the 1908 census there.[30]

The majority of newcomers to the lower Platine region settled in cities, and most seemed eager to take up locals' habit of mate drinking. This was part of a longer trend. For instance, when her family immigrated to Argentina from Spain in the early nineteenth century, a woman I interviewed, María José, shared that "*pronto* empezaron a tomar mate" (they *quickly* started to drink mate).[31] So too did early generations of Irish immigrants take up the habit. Mid-nineteenth-century Irish ranchers in Argentina drank mate and posed with it in pictures.[32] In daily life, Irish women shared rounds of mate with their neighbors, even as they continued to prepare and serve tea and scones at home as a way of maintaining their Irishness.[33] German immigrants became mate enthusiasts, even if some hygienically minded drinkers preferred to use what became known as the *mate higénico alemán* (German hygienic mate)—a mate made of glass with a stainless steel strainer that allowed each person to easily insert their own bombilla into the common mate.[34]

As the number of immigrants increased dramatically in the late nineteenth and early twentieth centuries, drinking mate in the traditional manner entered the pantheon of nativist criollo culture, which was now celebrated to differentiate Argentines of long standing from newcomers.[35] Concurrently, participating in the local mate ritual served as a critical way for this latest wave of newcomers to make a claim of local belonging. Italian immigrants, who streamed into the region in the largest numbers during this period, drank mate at the encouragement of their neighbors, fellow Italian immigrants, and even employers. Italian railway workers, for example, received mate for breakfast from the companies that employed them.[36] And Italian-language newspapers included recipes for Italian regional specialties alongside recipes for local foods like empanadas and advertisements for yerba.[37]

Because yerba cost less than the alternatives, drinking mate made economic sense for immigrants with fewer resources. And yet we have material evidence that upwardly mobile immigrants drank mate too. Accustomed to drinking coffee and tea out of porcelain cups, relatively well-off immigrants ordered thousands of hand-painted porcelain mates (called *mates de loza*) from German (and after World War I, Czechoslovakian and French) factories. Women took the lead in commissioning and drinking out of these mates, which featured flowers, animals, and angels frequently embellished with silver or gold and words or phrases like "friendship" and "love."[38]

We know the most about the manner that Jewish immigrants—some of whom likely drank out of these ceramic mates—incorporated the local infusion into their culinary traditions because of rich historical accounts of this diaspora in Argentina. Both Sephardic and Ashkenazi Jews drank mate and ate local foods while preserving culinary traditions they associated with their ancestral homelands and with Judaism. For instance, historian Adriana Brodsky shows that while some Sephardic families drank coffee at home, they also drank mate outside and even included it in family photographs—visibly marking their adoption of local customs in a new homeland.[39] The so-called Jewish gauchos, who went to rural areas like Entre Ríos to farm, quickly began drinking mate, as did their rural-dwelling female peers, who shared rounds of mates with relatives and friends, especially on the weekends.[40]

Members of the Jewish diaspora also wrote about drinking mate. In her study of Jewish immigration to Buenos Aires, historian Mollie Lewis Nouwen points to numerous examples, including Samuel Glusberg's 1924 story "Mate amargo" (Bitter mate), which features Jewish immigrant Abraham "Tío" Petacóvsky's story. She explains that this protagonist "embraced Argentina through the *alpargatas* [humble espadrilles] he wore and the [unsweetened] *mate* he drank with his non-Jewish neighbors." Despite the fact that he spoke Yiddish and they Spanish, sharing some rounds of mate helped cement new friendships. For Petacóvsky and other Jewish immigrants, partaking in this local custom allowed them to feel a sense of belonging in new nations, while maintaining a Jewish identity through other means, like language.[41] In fiction as in real life, however, this claim was not necessarily accepted by their elite contemporaries as legitimate. Lewis Nouwen concludes, "Elites saw immigrants like Petacóvsky who embraced mate and other symbols of national identity as making a mockery of Argentine culture, even though the national identity was rapidly changing because of the presence of those very immigrants."[42] As Adolfo Prieto has argued, nativist claims to local, criollo customs as authentically Argentine represented, in large part, a reaction against the perceived threat of immigration.[43]

In Uruguay, immigrants also changed ideas about national identity, and drinking mate served as a way for them to declare their relationship to local tradition. In the late 1960s, Uruguayan historian and anthropologist Fernando O. Assunçao explained in his book about mate, "Galicians, Italians, Russians, etc., all of them before learning the country's language, before knowing how to move through the unknown city or even more unknown countryside, already knew how to drink mate." Immigrants' mate consumption shifted their identity, for as Assunçao put it, "Through the native sap that begins to melt into their blood, they begin becoming Americans, sons of the new homeland."[44] Referring to Jewish immigrants in Montevideo, a group of Uruguayan historians declared that they lived between "matzoh and mate."[45]

We have little evidence that native-born Uruguayan elites publicly eschewed mate drinking like their contemporaries in Buenos Aires. Progressive president José Batlle y Ordóñez (1903–7; 1911–15) became well known for his appreciation of mate.[46] And yet some upper-class Uruguayan immigrants never took up the practice and looked down upon those who did. For example, María José noted that her Uruguayan mother-in-law's family never drank mate because her immigrant father was "un gran empresario de barcos" (a big businessman in shipping) and thought the local custom to be beneath them.[47] As this example suggests, social standing and ethnic identity worked together to influence ideas about appropriate and inappropriate markers of national identity to consume or avoid on both sides of the Río de la Plata.

Still, most immigrants to Uruguay and Argentina became mate drinkers. Yerba's lower price point compared to coffee or tea certainly played a role. At the same time, the mate ritual's unique ability to incorporate newcomers fueled their enthusiasm. Uruguayan anthropologist Daniel Vidart explains, "In all times, it was the mate that made the circle and not the circle that brought the mate."[48] Locals did not invite immigrants over and then decide what to serve them. Instead, locals invited immigrants to join a ritual where inviting outsiders to partake had long been a defining feature.

Despite immigrants' commitment both to drinking mate and to creating visual representations of it, these newcomers remained absent from postcards or other official representations of the nation. Similarly, women's previously highlighted passion for mate drinking went missing.[49] When local women appeared in this new generation of visuals, they now served the decidedly non-immigrant figure of the gaucho what became *his* mate.

PICTURING MATE AS A RURAL TRADITION

Interest in the social lives of rural dwellers became manifest in visuals from the 1840s, as we saw in chapter 2. But it was in the 1860s, in the liberal wake of Governor Rosas' 1852 demise, that the obsession with gauchos grew alongside their declining numbers due to the intensification of private property and wage labor.[50] The 1865 Rural Code outlawed the gaucho way of life by making it illegal not to have a fixed residence or an evident means of subsistence.[51] Paired with the expansion of fencing, the Rural Code facilitated the state's forcible conscription of poor rural men sent to the frontier to serve in the War of the Triple Alliance and fight Indigenous groups that continued to live autonomously on land desired by the Argentine state.

The end of a seminomadic way of life in rural areas, along with massive waves of immigrants arriving in Argentina and Uruguay, inspired greater local interest in highlighting the figure of the gaucho in plays, books, illustrations, and photographs. For elites and xenophobic nationalists, the celebration of a romanticized local figure served as an antidote to the growing number of immigrants who often made demands for better working conditions and dared to participate in national traditions like mate drinking.[52] At the same time, for the rural and urban poor, including immigrants, the embrace of the justifiably unruly gaucho allowed them to articulate a politics of resistance against the ruling class, as Ezequiel Adamovksy explains.[53] In other words, the meanings attached to the figure of the gaucho varied according to social class. While elites saw this figure as a bucolic hero, their popular counterparts celebrated him as an unruly rebel.[54] And yet across the sociopolitical divide, casting a hyper-male figure as the symbol of the nation, and literally elevating him onto a "high horse" above his female counterpart, only served to intensify men's symbolic power over women.

The gaucho's female counterpart was referred to as *la china* (la CHEE-nah), a term used to describe an Indigenous or mixed-race poor woman from the countryside.[55] In both elite and popular versions, the gaucho symbolically trotted off to become a national symbol, while the china—a figure associated with Indigenous roots and female servitude—was stuck in an underappreciated no-(wo)man's-land.[56] Elite nativist compositions (like Ayerza's in fig. 4.1) sought to invent a heterosexual domesticity that was anchored by the china's faithfulness to the orderly gaucho and their iconic rancho, or small adobe hut. More popular *criollista* accounts celebrated righteously unruly gauchos[57] but their protagonists nevertheless pined for a faithful china who stayed home. That is, when the rural woman appeared in popular discourse, her central role and productivity in rural areas tended to be overshadowed by a stereotyped vision of her as a sexual being, as the gaucho's woman, or as a domestic worker. She was there to serve men.

It was not only the china and the horseback-riding accessories but also the mate that became a defining feature of the gaucho's visual (and literary) identity in the late nineteenth century. Like the china, this infusion possessed local, Indigenous roots. Still, even as these roots have been conflated in popular culture, they belong to distinct Indigenous heritages. Whereas the china was associated with the Pampas region and the peoples of central Argentina,[58] yerba mate and the precolonial Guaraní hailed from the subtropical region to the northeast.

Today it would be easy to imagine that close links between gauchos and mate, sometimes served by the so-called chinas, have always been around, but it was only in the liberalizing late nineteenth century that this association grew. As we saw in chapter 2, starting in the late 1830s and 1840s, drawings and paintings of more popular rural scenes joined depictions of the urban environment in sometimes including a mate. Even so, for the next few decades, most visual portrayals of the gaucho did not present this local ritual. For example, in Bonafacio del Carril's reproductions of some sixty iconographic images of the gaucho from the colonial era until 1870, only a handful (or less than 10 percent) show a mate. In turn, about a quarter included a woman.[59] This female figure was often but not always pictured in scenes inside a rancho, as well as at dances. On other occasions, she rode horseback "a las ancas" (sideways behind the gaucho) or ground corn.[60]

In the late 1860s, the trend of linking official national culture in Argentina with the gaucho, china, and mate began in earnest. General Justo José de Urquiza, president of the Argentine Confederation, commissioned *The Atlas of the Argentine Confederation* in the 1860s, which appeared in 1869 with a cover illustration of a china handing a gaucho a "goodbye mate," and perhaps inspiring Francisco Ayerza a couple of decades later (fig. 4.3). At the center of the composition, French artist Charles Sauvageot pictured a woman with long braids down her back, bare feet, and a peasant blouse handing a man on horseback a mate. To her left, an Indigenous person stands with a spear, while a woman of unclear origin (likely African or mixed descent) cradles a young child. In this way, Sauvageot links but also distinguishes the modern china who provides the mate to the gaucho from the nation's Indigenous,

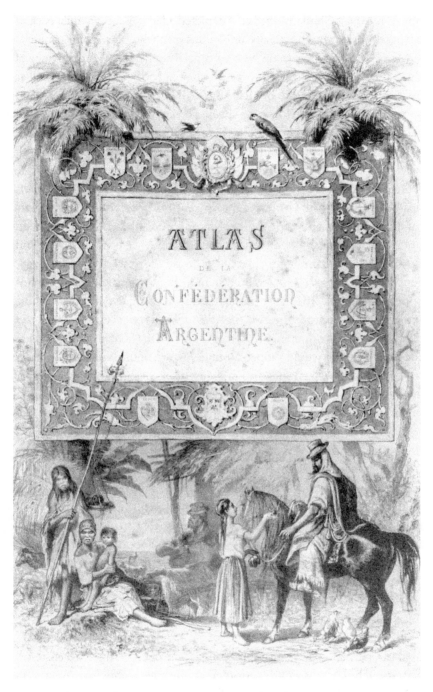

FIGURE 4.3. Charles Sauvageot, interior cover illustration of
the *Atlas de la Confédération Argentine*, ed. Jean Antoine Victor
Martin de Moussy (Paris: Firmin Didot Frères, ca. 1869).

non-White past. Similarly, the artist depicted a fair gaucho on horseback as having evolved from the racially ambiguous man who sits playing a guitar.

As part of a similar current, in 1869, official bank notes of the province of Buenos Aires began to regularly feature the figure of the gaucho (as well as political elites and classical mythical figures). In that year alone, the gaucho appeared rustling cattle, shearing sheep, playing guitar, and, in a couple of cases, serving and drinking a mate by himself. On the fifty-peso banknote, a common woman also entered the scene. Behind a wagon overflowing with wheat, she sits on the ground at the edge of a group of four men who converse around an open-air asado, the seated man on the right lifting a mate to his lips. Kettle in hand, the woman appears to be ready to infuse another mate for this group of men. While the men's faces are only partially shown and do not reveal a clear racialized identity, the woman's face is notably pale, and her hair is covered but not braided. In contrast, the much less valuable ten-cent bill from the same year featured an Indigenous woman with long braids appearing alone.[61] The figure of the mate-serving china with some visible Indigenous ancestry featured on *The Atlas of the Argentine Confederation* had not yet become the dominant vision of the *cebadora* (female mate server) in the late 1860s; this would happen around the turn of the twentieth century.

Contemporary paintings also offered visions of the White mate server and, to an even greater extent, celebrated the peaceful mate-drinking gaucho in the countryside. Ignacio Manzoni's prize-winning painting *El asado* (The barbecue) (ca. 1871) shows a gaucho explaining to fair-skinned immigrants how to grill and cut beef in the local manner while a young girl, an immigrant, hands him a mate in recompense. Some ten years later, Uruguayan painter Juan Manuel Blanes in *Los tres chripaes* offered a romanticized portrait of life on the frontier in 1881 in which a mate-drinking gaucho leans against the fence in front of his rancho and slurps his mate, presumably prepared by one of the fair women in the painting. In the Argentine province of Córdoba, Genaro Pérez, a local landowner, theologian, and politician, offered his vindication of provincial ways of life by featuring two men—one in gaucho attire and the other in modern clothing—sharing a mate and amicably conversing outdoors in an 1888 painting titled *Escena de costumbres* (Scene of customs).[62]

Beginning in the 1860s, the arrival of photography in this region contributed to a new and seemingly more realistic way of capturing local customs. Entranced by the possibilities afforded by this new technology, Ayerza, in 1889, joined with other elite men in Buenos Aires—who, like him, did not need to take photos for compensation—to form the Sociedad Fotográfica Argentina de Aficionados.[63] According to art historian Verónica Tell, this

Argentine association of amateur photographers was tightly linked with the Argentine state and served as "a kind of graphic design agency," deciding who and what was photographed and, by extension, what image of Argentina would be projected both locally and to outsiders.[64] The photographic society mostly took pictures of the newer and more polished parts of the city of Buenos Aires, publishing its work in illustrated magazines, calendars, and postcards, as well as showing it in parlors and exhibitions.[65] As the leading founding member, Ayerza was unique in signing his photographs with his own last name but also in concerning himself with rural subjects.[66]

In the mid-1890s, Ayerza took a series of photographs (including figs. 4.1 and 4.2) on the Estancia San Juan, which was owned by another member of the photographic society.[67] Ayerza posed his mostly male subjects enjoying their work or leisure with other men, or sometimes with a woman who was there to serve or dance with him. Likely inspired by previous paintings and lithographs, Ayerza's female subjects ride sidesaddle behind their men, or flirt, talk, or dance with them in front of a rancho, a water well, or a *pulpería* (country store).[68]

Ayerza hoped to publish these photographs in a deluxe Parisian edition of the popular Argentine epic poem by José Hernández, *Martín Fierro*, which bemoaned the plight of the rural man.[69] But it was not to be. Perhaps the gulf between Ayerza's elitist vision of the countryside and the more popular attitudes of Hernández and contemporary fans of *Martín Fierro* proved too wide. In contrast to Hernández's depiction of starving men absconding from the army and fighting one another, sometimes to the death, Ayerza's photographs show well-fed gauchos with plentiful access to mate and meat.[70] Ayerza's bucolic visions first appeared in magazines and later proliferated on postcards, a genre clearly intended to highlight a more romanticized rural culture than the more popular view of the righteously unruly gaucho depicted in *Martín Fierro*.[71]

Like Ayerza, some commercial photographers, including brothers Samuel and Arturo Boote, saw great value in photographing the countryside.[72] In the 1880s and 1890s, the Boote brothers captured a handful of distinct images of rural folks drinking mate in a manner less glamorous and seemingly more realistic than Ayerza's subjects.[73] In one photograph from around 1880, four gauchos drink mate in front of a rancho while one plays guitar, another sharpens his knife, and a third stands up, a long knife gleaming in his belt strap. The threat of violence is clear. In 1895, personnel from a working ranch posed in front of a building. Four men held individual mates with bombillas to their lips while a woman stands in front of a large pot with a barefoot boy in front

FIGURE 4.4. Arturo W. Boote y Cía, *Paisano y mujer*, ca. 1890,
Colección César Gotta. Reproduced in José X. Martini, ed.,
*La Argentina a fines del siglo XIX: Fotografías de Samuel y Arturo Boote
1880–1900* (Buenos Aires: Ediciones de la Antorcha, 2012).

of her. Likely, this boy is her son or a child serving as a *criado*, expected to labor for the ranch owners for free. Here, and elsewhere, the Bootes adopted a documentary photographic style toward their rural subjects and included more women and children than Ayerza did.[74]

In contrast to Ayerza's "goodbye mate," the Bootes pictured the domestic mate ritual as a humble daily routine rather than an act with extraordinary romantic flourish. For example, in *Paisano y mujer* (Countryman and woman) (ca. 1890), an older couple sit in front of their rancho, the man with a mate in his hand, the woman with her arms crossed; in between them is the kettle from which she will presumably serve the hot water to infuse the mate for both of them (fig. 4.4).[75] Unlike in Ayerza's version, the woman's posture seems more resigned than amorous, while the man's body language suggests he had nowhere else to go. Similarly, a photograph of a family in the northern province of Tucumán taken by the Bootes five years later features an older couple sitting outside their modest mud hut, with a child in the doorway and a young man (presumably their son) off to the side. The woman tips the large kettle in her hand toward a mate, which she will pass to her husband at some point. Even when the Bootes pictured the sexes on level ground sharing a mate, they, and nearly all other photographers, showed women serving men. This reflected gendered expectations and practices, as women in rural areas typically did the strenuous work of lighting and maintaining the fire and preparing mate.[76]

CIRCULATING POSTCARDS

During the first two decades of the twentieth century, postcards became incredibly popular in the Río de la Plata region, especially in the highly literate capital cities of Buenos Aires and Montevideo. While the Bootes' documentary-style photographs appeared on a small number of postcards, Ayerza's more romanticized vision of the countryside took hold, shaping the notion that the mate belonged to the gaucho.

Postcards are particularly useful historical sources for understanding the symbolic and social place of mate for two reasons. First, this genre claimed to visually represent local places and figures as well as national cultures. Second, because everyday people who lived in the region or were visiting it frequently bought postcards and wrote on them before sending to a friend or relative, their notes allow us to contemplate how contemporaries interacted with representations of mate drinking in the premier visual of the day.

The novel and inexpensive genre of the postcard enjoyed a broad audience in the lower Platine region that far surpassed the paintings and lithographs that preceded it. Two leading postcard editors in Buenos Aires, immigrants R. Rosauer y Peuser and Fumagalli, published more than 6,000 distinct postcards—with hundreds of thousands of copies each—from the 1890s to the 1920s.[77] In Montevideo, Galli, Franco & Cía and Albert Aust dominated the flourishing Uruguayan postcard industry.[78] In this case, as in so many others, recent immigrants living in Buenos Aires and Montevideo took the lead in representing local customs.[79] In turn, locals and tourists sent and voraciously collected postcards purchased at editors' offices or at photographers' studios, bookstores, or kiosks in cities across the Río de la Plata region.[80] While many foreign collectors were male, local collectors were mostly female.[81]

On both sides of the Río de la Plata, early twentieth-century postcard enthusiasts were exposed to tropes that consolidated a new and powerful vision of Argentine and Uruguayan cultures.[82] In both nations, the modernity of the capital cities was juxtaposed with the traditionalism of the countryside. While city pictures were site-specific, those of rural dwellers proved more generic and mobile, with the same photograph appearing as a representation of local culture in both Argentina and Uruguay.

Many of Ayerza's photographs traveled in this manner, acquiring different captions along the way. For example, while an Argentine postcard described his picture of three men around a campfire that opened this chapter (see fig. 4.2) as "Campaña de Buenos Aires [Buenos Aires countryside]—El mate—1891," the Uruguayan postcard captioned the very same image "Uruguay—Escenas Campestres" (Uruguay—rural scenes). Likewise, Ayerza's photograph of a rural woman handing a mate up to a gaucho (fig. 4.1) circulated on numerous postcards across the Río de la Plata in both Argentina and Uruguay during the late nineteenth and early twentieth centuries.

The china's complementary role in goodbye mate postcards represented the most common one for the rural woman to play on postcards. That is, while there were many compositions featuring gauchos (with captions that pointed to their clothing, tools, or horses) or all-male groups (rustling cattle, making an asado, playing cards, or sitting in a circle drinking mate), there were very few that featured only women. Those that did tended to domesticate the rural woman by positioning her in front of the iconic rancho or somewhere nearby grinding corn or baking bread. Sometimes women appeared farther afield to gather water, presumably with which to cook and serve mate. In one of the few postcards that depicted a china by herself, the caption read "Waiting for the gaucho."[83] This was the most extreme example in which the rural woman's presence was justified by her waiting for her man. In contrast, another contemporary but rare postcard featured two women, who were referred to in the caption as "chinas," side by side on horseback.[84] This served as a more realistic representation, since rural women did spend much of their time without men and rode horses. But unlike male friendship, rural female friendship was not a common trope in visual or literary sources of the time. Neither was female mobility.

Gauchos and romantic rural couples regularly appeared on both sides of the Río de la Plata, even if there were some notable points of divergence. Uruguayan postcard editors, unlike their Argentine counterparts, did not produce images of Indigenous people, who many believed no longer existed in their nation. While the symbolic place of people of African descent was relatively similar in both nations in the nineteenth century, by the early twentieth century this demographic remained much more visible in Uruguay.[85] There, postcard makers featured people of African descent, sometimes linking them to the national custom of mate drinking, a trend that did not occur in Argentina. An early twentieth-century series of Uruguayan postcards showcased "un baile de negros" (a Black people's dance), where an older man watching the dance subtly drinks mate, and another labeled

FIGURE 4.5. Postcard, "Costumbres del Uruguay—El Mate,"
ca. 1900, ed. A. Marchetti y Cía. Courtesy of Biblioteca Nacional
de Uruguay, Montevideo, Sala de Materiales Especiales.

"Costumbres del Uruguay—El Mate" (Uruguayan costumes: The mate), in
which Afro-Uruguayans are depicted as unmarked purveyors of a national
custom (fig. 4.5).[86] As in these examples, national image makers in Uruguay
selectively incorporated Afro-Uruguayan culture into national narratives,
either exoticizing it or presenting it as a standard part of the nation.[87] These
postcards also pointed to a slightly more urban depiction of the mate ritual
in Uruguay than in Argentina.[88]

In Argentina, Afro-Argentines, Indigenous groups, and city dwellers
were not portrayed as agents of this national custom on postcards, which
played a large role in representing the nation and its inhabitants.[89] Argentine
anthropologist Carlos Masotta explains that almost all the people featured
on Argentine postcards fell into two types, specifically "Indians" and "gauchos."[90] These were not gender-neutral categories. While both were used to
"recreate the country's 'Native image,'" there were many more female Indians
and only male gauchos. As literary scholar Mary Louise Pratt argues of Latin
America more broadly, the "subordinated woman has stood for all the Indigenous peoples conquered (feminized) and co-opted (seduced) by European

expansion."[91] On Argentine postcards, Indigenous subjects symbolized the feminized and primitive local, while hyper-masculinized and often whitened gauchos represented the national. The gaucho's female counterpart, the china, gestured toward a rooted and vaguely Indigenous past.

While both Indians and gauchos represented the country's local population on postcards, only gauchos and other rural types were shown drinking mate.[92] The Argentine postcard editor R. Rosauer published postcards from a wide variety of locales including Salinas Chicas, Mendoza, Tucumán, and the Pampas, where rural dwellers, and even a group of engineers, drank mate. And yet it appears that Rosauer did not issue postcards featuring clearly marked Indigenous people drinking this native infusion. Despite the immigrants behind this enterprise, immigrants designated as such did not appear on Rosauer's postcards or those produced by other editors.

Of course, the absence of Indigenous people, Afro-Argentines, immigrants, and urbanites on Argentine postcards did not mean that they were not drinking mate. Rather, their absence simply tells us that the producers of these postcards did not wish to highlight the full scope of their local mate culture.[93] Photographers took pictures of a Black man serving a gaucho a mate in an urban setting in 1868 and of some Mapuches in the pampas drinking mate in 1880.[94] In 1920, the popular children's magazine *Billiken* featured on the cover a young Black boy trying his first mate.[95] But these kinds of striking images presenting Black and Indigenous people participating in the mate ritual did not make their way onto Argentine postcards.

Instead, Argentine postcards pictured mate as a decidedly rural and masculine ritual, if facilitated by a rural woman at times. They juxtaposed the supposedly consistent rhythm of rural life with the dynamism of urban modernity. Uruguayan postcards emphasized the same idea while allowing for more allusions to urban mate drinking, including among Black Uruguayans.

Locals and visitors snapped up these postcards, and while intended to be ephemeral, some have survived to this day. Take for example the romantic goodbye mate postcards that Ayerza initiated. In Ayerza's composition, a man is pictured as a protagonist who drinks the mate before he trots away, while the woman is shown in a subservient and stationary role, like the mate servers who preceded her (fig. 4.1).[96] Even as we know that women also drank mate and traveled beyond the confines of their homes, postcard senders who commented directly on this tableau, in which women served men mate, tended to agree that this was the natural order of things. Despite the negative's provenance in Argentina, Uruguayan postcard editor C. Galli, Franco & Cía featured Ayerza's romantic goodbye mate photograph without attribution as part

Recuerdo
de la República
Argentina.

Deseando que
alguna yankie
acriollada, te
alcanze un
mate al estri-
bo, te saluda
desde la patria
con recuerdos
de la numerosa
prole, tu primo
El Mono

Gaucho Tomando Mate

Bs. As. 4-27-03.

FIGURE 4.6. Postcard, "Recuerdo de la República Argentina: Gaucho Tomando Mate [Souvenir from the Argentine Republic: Gaucho drinking mate]" ca. 1903, R. Rosauer; H. G. Olds, photographer.

of a series of "countryside scenes" around 1901.[97] José M. Nuñez, who sent this card, referenced a seventeenth-century quote in a passage he penned next to the photo: "Beauty without grace is like a fishhook without bait." Perhaps he chose this quote to stress the importance of a beautiful woman's generosity, embodied by her offering of a mate, after finding it in one of the phrasebooks sold with postcards.[98]

The allure of the companionship that women provided men (or men provided men) helped make goodbye mate and all-male mate postcards so enduring. The sender of another Argentine postcard featuring a colorized version of Ayerza's original photograph of the goodbye mate wrote on the back, "For my dear Aunt, so that she can invite my uncle and godfather to some mates like the ones my mom made me for my birthday."[99] As in this case, postcard senders sometimes joined postcard makers in embracing the notion, also widespread in society, that women were responsible for serving mate to their men—here, in a familial rather than a romantic fashion.

Around 1903, postcard editor R. Rosauer released another version of the goodbye mate with a different photograph and a caption that emphasized the man's leading role: "Souvenir from the Argentine Republic: Gaucho Drinking Mate" (fig. 4.6).[100] In this photograph, a couple pose in front of two thatched buildings with a dog in the foreground. The woman appears to have some Indigenous ancestry and wears a more modest dress and simpler (espadrille) shoes than the other women on postcards who serve mate. She also appears better prepared than the lighter-skinned mate servers, given that she holds a kettle with which to infuse the mate in her other hand. This vision of the goodbye mate became the most popular and well-traveled within Argentina. The original photograph, taken in the Argentine province of Entre Ríos, was reproduced on at least four different postcards and sent to far-off locales like Cuba and Italy between 1903 and 1926.[101] Unlike the other two frequently reproduced photographs of the goodbye mate, there is no evidence of it (re)appearing as an Uruguayan postcard.[102]

We also have evidence of how this particular image circulated and was interpreted by postcard senders at the time. In 1902, an Argentine man nicknamed "El mono" (The monkey) sent this postcard to his uncle aboard the *President Sarmiento* naval ship. Below the caption, he penned the following note in neat cursive lettering: "Wishing that some *yanki acriollada* [creolized female Yankee] gets you a bootstrap mate, sending you greetings from the homeland with regards from the big family."[103] Clearly, the author of this postcard understood this scene as representative of Argentina and its customs. These customs were infused not only with the grassy, bitter flavor of the yerba but also with gender expectations about who should serve whom. Such expectations, it should be pointed out, were similar to those of whom the Argentines called "yankis" in the United States, where gender norms also held that women should be the ones to serve men (and children) food and drink.[104]

Some postcard senders imagined themselves playing the role of the gaucho and the china in an exoticizing and Orientalizing fashion. For example, a French speaker in Buenos Aires bought the Rosauer postcard and sent it to Montevideo. He drew a line next to the gaucho and scribbled his name, "Armand," at the end. He labeled the woman to whom he presumably sent this postcard "Poupée," the French word for doll.[105]

Locals joined visitors in this adult game of "dress up." A photograph on a *foto postal* (less commercial photo postcard) from the late 1920s provides powerful evidence of how the visual culture of the romantic goodbye mate extended beyond the postcard industry and outsiders to influence the behavior of people with deep roots in the countryside. Taken in the northwestern Argentine province of Salta, this high-quality photograph featured a poor rural couple performing the goodbye mate for the camera (fig. 4.7). As in other commercial postcards, the female protagonist hands the mate up to the

FIGURE 4.7. Photo postcard, "El mate de la despedida," by Foto Belgrano, ca. 1925–30. Courtesy of Special Collections and College Archives, Skillman Library, Lafayette College, Easton, PA.

man on horseback. In contrast to other photographs, the woman has darker skin and appears to be of Indigenous descent. She also wears a practical, frayed overcoat rather than a fancy dress. While she looks at the camera, the man appears to have his eyes closed, making her seem the more confident subject in front of the camera. Even so, the photograph presents what had become a well-known choreography of domesticity, romance, and power, in which the man sits high above the woman serving him.

Despite the abundance of heterosexual romance and the paucity of female friendship, this did not mean that postcard senders wrote only about romance or male friendship. Indeed, while absent in the compositions, female friendship buoyed the popularity of postcards. For example, in a version of Ayerza's photograph of three men sharing a mate, a Uruguayan woman, Blanca, said nothing about the image when she penned a chatty postcard to her friend María Inés in 1905. Writing from rural Canelones, Uruguay, she noted she was "already tired of the quiet" and hoped to go horseback riding the next day. She also mentioned a wedding she attended and that she would tell her friend more about it the next time they saw each another.[106] The previous year, an Argentine woman named Matilde selected a postcard on which a woman gazes up toward her gaucho on horseback (sans mate) as an opportunity to write a note in hopes of reconnecting with her "forever friend," named Elvira, in the city of Buenos Aires.[107]

The vision of local culture promoted by Argentine and Uruguayan postcard makers clearly influenced locals' and visitors' understandings of the region and its culture. It emphasized a new hegemonic picture of mate drinking as traditionally rural and masculine. If included, women were there to serve. Many postcard senders endorsed and even extended this vision to their own lives. At the same time, some local women used this tableau to connect with female friends rather than focus on heterosexual romance. They did so even as female friendship disappeared in contemporary visual representations of mate drinking.

After spending much of the 1910s in Argentina, Chile, Paraguay, Uruguay, and southern Brazil, US visitor Henry Stephens arrived at the following conclusion: "This maté drinking habit, which is considered beneficial, is indulged in universally by everybody in Paraguay, Argentina, Uruguay, and southern Brazil."[108] As Stephens suggested, despite the considerable attention dedicated to *porteño* elites' supposed disaffection, most people across the region who drank mate in the mid-nineteenth century still did so in the early twentieth. And yet the symbolic place of this ritualized drink shifted dramatically because elite *porteños* switched their allegiance—in public anyway—from mate to coffee and tea. Their public shift toward drinks they considered more modern, more European, or whiter made sense in an era in which elites envisioned progress in Latin America as stemming from their choices to live and work like (and with) White Europeans.

In 1927, Paraguayan journalist and government official Genaro Romero worried that the "lure of the foreign" was also rearing its ugly head in his country. After the Great War, he asserted, foreigners who came to profit off Paraguay threatened local customs and challenged Paraguayan identity. In the late 1920s, he positioned yerba mate at the center of the ongoing fight: "The wealthy classes are wanting to impose the use of tea and coffee, to the economic detriment of homes of the popular sectors." Romero understood this as part of a pattern where wealthy people imagined products from abroad as superior to anything locally produced. He expressed his disgust and disputed that way of thinking: "Yerba mate is the genuine product of Paraguay and it is proven to be the cheapest, healthiest and most convenient for the popular masses, the laboring classes."[109] Despite Romero's concern, the local commitment to yerba remained strong in Paraguay across social classes, and the threat of local disaffections gathered less intensity there than in Argentina.

Even as worries grew about urban elites' public move away from mate in Argentina, most people there continued to consume yerba. On average, Argentines consumed more, not less, yerba in the late nineteenth and early twentieth centuries (see graph 4.1). "If one could declare our national drink," Argentine Dr. Ricardo Albornoz remarked in 1937, "it is mate."[110] He continued that in Argentina, immigrants (most of whom settled in urban areas) had overtaken the rural "gauchos" in their consumption of this "national drink," noting that "British and Spanish, Italian and German compete equally in their consumption of mate."[111] For these immigrants, mate drinking provided a unique way to participate in local culture and assert their belonging in a new homeland. Like others before them, they pictured themselves with mates and wrote about their enthusiasm for this local custom. Immigrants also maintained traditional hot drinks (and foods) from their homelands. Both elites and immigrants were more eager to add than subtract. As we shall see in the next chapter, immigrants also began to assume leading roles in developing the Argentine yerba industry in the province of Misiones.

In the new generation of visuals purporting to represent the nations of Argentina and Uruguay that we have seen here, neither elites nor newcomers played a visible role. Instead, political leaders and cultural producers turned toward the unique but no longer threatening figure of the gaucho as a symbol of the nation. They plastered bucolic visions of this male figure on the Argentine atlas, on money for the province of Buenos Aires, and on postcards across the Río de la Plata. Often, the gaucho stood, rode, or rested with other men or alone. In more popular visions, he also put up a good and justified fight against elites. In both elite and popular representations, when a rural woman joined him, she did so in a subordinate and servile role. The china served the gaucho his last mate before his departure, tended their home, and awaited his return. Across sociopolitical divides, the consistency of this portrayal of the rural woman fetishized the gaucho's mobility and political agency, as well as the supposed lack of her own.

The modernizing Belle Époque cemented the link between the gaucho and *his* mate, replacing previous symbolic associations with predominantly female urban elites. In addition, the written and visual culture of this era muddied awareness of the local infusion's Indigenous and regional roots in the upper Platine region. Some still called it the "herb of Paraguay" or "Paraguayan tea," but more now simply referred to "yerba mate." During the late nineteenth and early twentieth centuries, yerba mate became associated with the rough-and-tumble lifestyle of the gaucho in the lower Platine scrubland in a manner that has endured.

These figures of the gaucho and, to a lesser but still significant extent, the china would also become powerful symbols of the culture of southern Brazil, and even rural Chile, a bit later in the twentieth century.[112] Paraguay, for its part, did not adopt this iconography. After the devastation of the Great War, postcards pictured Paraguay primarily as a land of women, Indians, and agriculture, rather than one of bucolic rural men who were avid mate drinkers.

As the Argentine yerba industry began to compete with Paraguayan and Brazilian producers for consumers in the late 1920s and 1930s, regional tensions around provenance became more important, symbolically and financially. Local politicians, engineers, and scientists paired up with yerba producers to convince consumers, especially in the large Argentine market, to drink more of their yerba. How would they do this? As we shall see, they commissioned national promotional boards and scientific studies. Advertisers also recycled elements of visual culture from earlier periods and the Belle Époque and introduced new visions of place, patriotism, and modernity in their quest to promote specific brands of yerba to predominantly female consumers.

CHAPTER FIVE

Selling Yerba/Erva Mate as Modern in Argentina and Brazil, 1900s–1960s

The Roman goddess spreads her arms with authority. In one hand, she holds a wreath made of laurel leaves, which also adorn her headdress. Below her, a more diminutive woman prepares to take a sip from a mate filled with the leaves of a plant formally called *Ilex paraguariensis*. She wears a headband festooned with the Argentine colors, white and pale blue, and a scarf around her neck that suggests she is a patriotic rural woman from nineteenth-century Argentina.

In 1933, a new Argentine yerba company formed by a British and Brazilian duo paired these female figures in an advertisement in *Caras y caretas*, one of Argentina's most popular magazines (fig. 5.1).[1] Two years prior, they had trademarked the brand name "Salus," an homage to the eponymous Roman goddess of safety and protection, as a gesture toward new scientific ideas about nutrition and health that emerged in the late 1920s and 1930s.[2] Mackinnon & Coelho also trademarked its drawing of a rural woman. The company's new logo and brand name positioned its product as safe, healthy, traditional, and in the service of discerning modern consumers.

FIGURE 5.1. Salus advertisement, *Caras y caretas*, Nov. 25, 1933, 56.

Salus likely included Brazilian yerba, and yet Mackinnon & Coelho's advertising campaign touted its exclusive Argentine provenance, despite the owners not being Argentine either. The ad's tagline screams out in all capitals: "SALUS: THE FIRST YERBA THAT PROCLAIMED ITS NATIONAL ORIGIN." The copy elaborates: "Against popular and defeatist prejudice that only assigns merit to exotic things, SALUS, aware of its superiority, was the first brand of yerba, proud of being Argentine, that proclaimed its origin to the four winds." The company positioned itself and its consumers as brave and patriotic. Argentines desiring "freedom," who rejected the idea of continuing as a "tributary of the foreign," switched to Salus-brand yerba right away. The ad concludes, "Be a Patriot Too!!! Consume SALUS, tasty and enduring like a good criolla." While the sexual innuendo might be missed, the imperative to patriotic, nationalist consumption was far from subtle.

Mackinnon & Coelho's promotion of patriotic yerba consumption drew on earlier associations. As in the independence era, yerba mate signified autonomy, no longer from Spain but rather from Argentina's yerba-producing neighbors Paraguay and Brazil. Despite referring to its logo as a criolla, or a common rural woman, Salus also associated her with the more deferential, partially Indigenous, and sexualized figure of *la china*, whom we met in the previous chapter. Instead of serving mate to her gaucho alone, this china promised to serve the Argentine nation the "tasty and enduring" infusion that Argentina had only recently begun to mass-produce.

A few years after this advertisement appeared, Argentine growers surpassed Brazilians as the world's largest total yerba producers. Colonial and early national observers would have been shocked by this achievement and wondered how Argentina had managed to grow the "herb of Paraguay" in the first place. Those who lived through the War of the Triple Alliance and its aftermath would also have been perplexed. For though they witnessed Argentina's seizure of the territory of Misiones, they also saw Brazil, which established itself as the main yerba producer prior to the war, take even more yerba-growing territory and dominate the late nineteenth-century yerba industry. The arrival of Argentine-grown yerba forced Brazilian planters to face a far more powerful competitor than Paraguay. The rivalry between Argentine and Brazilian yerba interests buoyed the larger process of nation building within each country and revealed fissures between competing economic and regional interests within them.

Brazil's southernmost states stood apart from the rest of the country for their temperate climate and native yerba mate forests, as well as for their history of territorial disputes and different demographic composition. By the early twentieth century, Brazil's southernmost states possessed a sense of Whiteness linked with the arrival of European immigrants to a borderland region with Indigenous, African, and mixed roots.[3] Similarly, Argentina as a whole, and Misiones in particular, played host to a large number of Europe immigrants and similarly claimed a White identity that belied the region's diversity and enduring Indigenous presence.[4]

While Salus's advertising copy and government-produced sources might lead us to believe that the state was the most important actor in the process of ushering in commercial and scientific modernization, multinational commercial interests often led these processes when it came to yerba. This was especially the case in Argentina, which possessed a number of traditional and powerful agricultural interests (like wheat growers and exporters) that politicians supported over new yerba growers. In contrast, in Brazil, the state government of Paraná supported local producers in the face of mounting Argentine competition because so much of the state's revenue and power depended on a dominant *erva* (yerba in Portuguese) industry. As the Argentine import market shrank, commercial entities in Brazil worked to promote the consumption of mate within Brazil for the first time. Meanwhile in Argentina, local and transnational entrepreneurs initiated the modernization of yerba production and promotion while planters lobbied for government support.

We focus here on early twentieth-century competition for Argentine consumers because yerba producers from Brazil, Paraguay, and Argentina did the same. Argentina had long gobbled up the majority of yerba and now offered a booming consumer market for branded products fed by the rapid expansion of cities, industry, mass media, and per capita consumption. More than half of Argentines lived in cities by 1930, and urban dwellers became accustomed to satisfying their needs and wants at the market.[5] In 1943, people living in and around Argentina's capital bought around 60 percent of yerba milled in the country, most of it processed by mills in Buenos Aires or Rosario, regardless of its national origin.[6] Seeking to reach these modern consumers, Brazilian, Paraguayan, and Argentine yerba companies promoted their factories as modern and worked with scientists to emphasize the hygiene and nutrition of their products for more than two decades before the Argentine government became involved in the 1930s.

Yerba advertisements varied by brand but typically maintained women's status as the most symbolically important mate servers while restoring their earlier visibility as mate drinkers. This was part of a larger trend whereby women gained public recognition of their power as consumers responsible for the well-being of their families and nations prior to their acquisition of full political and voting rights.[7] Although men across the region shaped most yerba policy, production, and promotion, women in Argentina became the most important yerba consumers in the world.

As we saw in chapters 2 and 3, elite male politicians and businessmen in South America began to chase dreams of liberal economic modernity that centered on the expansion of private property and free trade in the late nineteenth century. Some responded to new scientific ideas concerning hygiene by adopting a softer approach to eugenics, suggesting that by changing how people ate and lived, the "race" could be improved.[8] This chapter explores the impact of new ideas of modernity and science, infused with a stronger sense of nationalism, on the rapidly changing yerba industry during the first half of the twentieth century.

Our journey starts with Brazil and Argentina's battles over yerba at the level of exports and policy. As we shall see, the growth of Argentine yerba production not only worried Brazilian producers and ultimately limited Brazilian exports to Argentina but also spurred promotional campaigns within Brazil. We will then shift our attention to conflicts within Argentina between northeastern planters and central millers—neither of whom felt fully satisfied with the outcome. Finally, we will turn to promotional campaigns by specific brands that ushered in a new era of directly targeting consumers, transforming the visual culture of mate drinking made visible in magazine advertisements, on store shelves, and beyond. In contrast to previous artwork, the specific people behind this new era of explicitly commercial, branded visual sources are generally unknowable, even as their output dramatically changed how people across the region saw, purchased, and thought about yerba mate.

THE FIGHT FOR CONSUMERS IN ARGENTINA AND BRAZIL

Around the turn of the twentieth century, Argentina offered the largest and most competitive destination for its neighbors' yerba, gobbling up more than half of all yerba produced in Brazil and Paraguay.[9] From 1922 to 1932, Brazil supplied almost 90 percent of Argentina's yerba while Paraguay delivered the remaining 10 percent.[10] Whereas Paraguay mainly exported yerba in need of milling, Brazil primarily exported the milled variety, generating even more revenue for Brazilians in this business than their Paraguayan counterparts.[11] When a small but vocal number of Argentines began to question their nation's dependence on yerba imports, alarm bells sounded for planters and politicians in southern Brazil.

In 1898, an Argentine reader, M. Cabral Jr., published a scathing letter to the editor in *La Nación*, the country's leading newspaper. Why, he asked, was Argentina giving away over 4 million *pesos de oro* (golden pesos) to Brazil and Paraguay by buying yerba from them rather than producing it within the country's borders? "There is nothing more national than the yerba industry. The masses of this society are soaked in the yerba-mate infusion." And yet he lamented that "its importance seems to pass by unnoticed" by those focused on limiting other less economically significant imports.[12] He concluded that if Argentina invested in locally grown yerba, it would boost national industry and benefit Argentine consumers, who could buy lower-priced yerba and, with the leftover money, other locally produced goods such as sugar. Government officials in Argentina needed to act.

A Brazilian lawyer, Francisco R. A. Macedo, responded not in a letter to the editor but in a pamphlet funded by the Centro dos Industriaes de Herva Mate do Paraná (Center of Yerba Mate Industries in the State of Paraná). He dedicated four pages to painstakingly "correcting" Cabral's mathematical calculations about what turn-of-the-twentieth-century Brazilians referred to as *herva* or *erva mate*. Macedo accused the Argentine of exaggerating Brazilian profits and underestimating Brazilian expenses. He also emphasized that this was a two-way relationship, since Brazil bought many products, including wheat, meat, and alfalfa, from Argentina. If Cabral's wishes were to come true, it would hurt the Argentine economy and Argentine consumers most of all. Macedo argued, "If yerba mate is a national *alimento* [loosely, nutritious foodstuff] and indispensable for Argentines, as Sr. Cabral recognizes, and, it is not possible, as we can see, for the country to supply itself with this commodity, then it must be agreed that, if the Argentines declarewar on our exports, it will make this primary product more expensive, which would be bad for their country, harming their own."[13] In Cabral's estimation, Brazil was not taking from Argentina but rather supplying the plant material for its national drink.

Like Cabral, most Brazilians in the yerba business continued to focus on protecting their market share in Argentina rather on than boosting internal consumption in Brazil or promoting the product outside of southern South America. Starting in the late 1890s, a handful of Brazilian and Paraguayan yerba promoters partnered with American businessmen in an effort to promote yerba mate as a healthier alternative to coffee and tea in the United States and Canada. Ultimately, they had little luck convincing North American consumers to take up the habit of sipping yerba mate through a

FIGURE 5.2. Political cartoon, "Gentilezas commerciaes,"
O malho (Rio de Janeiro), no. 227, Jan. 1907, 24.

bombilla.[14] Argentina remained the most reliable market. Argentines continued to prefer yerba from Paraguay but consumed more from Brazil, given the lower price point and greater supply.

Brazilians bristled at what they understood to be the Argentine government's preferential treatment of Paraguayan yerba. A 1907 cartoon in *O malho*, the popular satirical magazine published in Rio de Janeiro, depicted Argentina's republican lady liberty opening her arms to embrace a personified Paraguayan mate while pointing a dagger at the shrinking figure of the Brazilian mate in another (fig. 5.2). The text claimed that while the Argentine government applied "almost prohibitive duties" on Brazilian erva imports, it let in the Paraguayan product "almost free."[15] The cartoon did not communicate that due to Paraguay's weak supply chain and lack of government protection, it supplied Argentina with only a modest supply of yerba. If drawn to scale, the Paraguayan mate would have amounted to one-tenth the size of the Brazilian one.

Brazilian yerba suffered from both a political problem and an image problem in Argentina. Amid the intensifying industrialization of the food supply and worries about adulteration, Brazilian millers were reputed to have an inferior and potentially harmful drying process (called *carijo*) and to add fillers that were at worst dangerous and at best not real yerba.[16] Most turn-of-the-twentieth-century Brazilian producers continued to mill their own erva and ship Argentines the finished product, competing more on price than on Argentines' perceptions of quality. A small number of forward-looking Brazilian companies recognized the need to address negative perceptions of their product. In 1899, a Brazilian export-import company advertised that it did not use a harmful drying process to make its "Special and Pure Yerba Mate: The Only Brand without Smoke."[17]

That same year, Matte Larangeira went a step further and set up a "hygienic" mill in Buenos Aires to process its Brazilian-grown yerba closer to the consumers it coveted. Like many contemporary Brazilian yerba companies, it had previously processed its products in southern Brazil.[18] A full-page story in the Argentine magazine *Caras y caretas* showed off the company's new mill, featuring photographs of the new, mechanized presses that packaged the yerba. These presses better preserved yerba's flavor, the article emphasized, and prevented the "dirty hands" and "sweat" of the peon or a "black cigarette butt" from falling into the product.[19] Argentina's industrializing capital city housed this modern factory and played a key role in developing the technology it touted. Fontana Brothers, a Buenos Aires firm, created new machines used by yerba mills across the region to hygienically package, compact, and seal the yerba for a "demanding clientele." Such technology helped allay Argentine consumers' growing concerns about the rural conditions of yerba production, especially in Brazil.[20]

Even so, naysayers persisted. In 1913, Argentine doctor and mate enthusiast Honorario Leguizamón recognized the contrast between Brazil and Argentina: Brazilians produced a lot of yerba but barely consumed it, while Argentines consumed a lot of yerba but barely produced it. He worried about the adulteration of the Brazilian yerba that Argentines were drinking, since "it seems in Brazil that they mix together many different varieties of Holly." In the interest of enriching the national economy and improving public health, Leguizamón, like Cabral before him, suggested that the Argentine government get involved. "Our yerba industry in still in diapers," he remarked, and Argentina would benefit from nurturing its growth.[21] Leguizamón advocated for government support for founding yerba plantations in Misiones and for the establishment of tariffs to discourage the importation and milling of foreign yerba.

Leguizamón's call for the state-led revival of the plantation model piloted by the Jesuits was not initiated by the Argentine (or Brazilian) government but rather by entrepreneurial agriculturalists. Landowners cleared land to plant germinated yerba seedlings in evenly spaced rows, first in Mato Grosso, Brazil, but soon after and on a larger scale in Misiones, Argentina.[22] Argentina had formally incorporated Misiones as a national territory in 1881.[23] In the subsequent four decades, most people in Misiones, as elsewhere, harvested the still more abundant wild yerba mate groves.[24]

Around the turn of the twentieth century, however, a small number of European immigrants began establishing plantations that eventually led to the dominance of the plantation model in Argentina. While not yet a point of focus, the expansionist governments of Argentine president Julio Roca (1880–86; 1898–1904) proved eager to boost this distant territory's productivity and sense of Whiteness.[25] Toward the tail end of the nineteenth century, immigrants from Galicia (today southeastern Poland and western Ukraine) began making their way to the southern part of Misiones to start family farms there.[26] With a larger commercial model in mind, Julio Ulises Martín, a French Swiss entrepreneur who previously milled Paraguayan yerba with an old, modified flour mill, joined forces with Swiss agronomist Paul Allain at the suggestion of President Roca.[27] Martín related, "In 1903 President Roca and Minister Ezcurra sent me to the Directorate of Land run by the ex-minister Pico to facilitate my work in the desert."[28] By 1908, Martín y Cía, as they called their new company, had planted some seventy-three hectares in this so-called desert, which was actually subtropical in nature. Because yerba seedlings take ten years to mature, the harvest began in 1913.

Martín and Allain were accompanied by others who went in search of land and economic opportunity in the territory of Misiones. For example, Juan Szychowski, a Polish engineer who moved with his family to Misiones around 1900, tried his hand at planting other crops before settling on yerba and rice.[29] While Misiones produced only 2,000 tons of yerba in 1915, the first generation of planters and the yerba pickers they employed had begun preparing the ground for Argentina's entry as a major yerba producer.[30]

Worry mounted in the Brazilian state of Paraná. In the first years of the twentieth century, erva mate accounted for a whopping 98 percent of Paraná's exports, most of which went to Argentina.[31] In 1916, Paraná passed legislation that applied tariffs on exports of unground erva mate. As historian María Victoria Magán explains, this policy made unground yerba pricey in Argentina, leading to the closure of some 40 percent of Argentine mills that processed the Brazilian product and, ironically, contributing to the growth of Argentine plantations. Producers in the Brazilian state of Santa Catarina, which also possessed its own mills, followed Paraná's lead in applying a tariff on unground erva mate, while those in Mato Grosso and Rio Grande do Sul did not, since they lacked mills and had to rely on exporting the unfinished product to Argentina.[32]

In a 1920 message to Paraná's legislature, the governor urged that the "intensive yerba mate culture in the Argentine Republic should make us all apprehensive about the future of the industry in Paraná."[33] If Argentina could self-provision yerba, Paraná's economy would either be decimated or transformed. He initiated greater government oversight, imposing a limit on the harvesting of erva mate from May to October in 1920.[34]

The province of Paraná also sent an official commission headed by Lysimaco F. da Costa, a well-known scholar and yerba industry insider, to research the status of yerba plantations in Misiones in 1927. Upon his return, he delivered a speech warning of the grave danger posed by Argentine yerba production before a formal assembly of erva mate industrialists and lawmakers from Paraná. He proposed flooding the Argentine market with low-priced Brazilian erva mate so that Argentine producers could not compete. The local newspaper, *O Paraná*, quoted him: "Our mate needs, even at the cost of some sacrifice, to impose itself in the Argentine market, so that the product extracted from Misiones, expensive by nature, cannot disturb the Brazilian economy. If there is no outlet for Argentine mate, this [will be] fatal [and will lead to] the abandonment of the plantations of Misiones, and this is exactly what those who have employed large amounts of money in that region fear."[35] Just as Costa suggested, less expensive Brazilian erva mate flooded Argentine markets and made it difficult for Argentine producers to cover even just production costs in the late 1920s.[36]

Argentine production struggled but did not cease. This led some Brazilians to promote erva within Brazil and beyond South America.[37] They sent samples to exhibits in the United State and Europe and published pamphlets celebrating mate's economic and health benefits in English, German, Portuguese, and Spanish. This gesture, intended to lure US and European consumers, was neither novel nor successful.[38] In contrast, the attention paid to the long-neglected Brazilian market ushered in a new era. In 1928, the province of Paraná passed a decree that removed provincial taxes on erva sent to other provinces within Brazil for the next three years. That same year, the recently formed Instituto do Matte do Estado do Paraná (Paraná Mate Institute) began publishing a monthly magazine called *O Matte* to increase local knowledge of the industry and local consumption.

The highpoint of the Paraná Mate Institute's campaign was a new venture in the city of Curitiba: a café called the Casa do Matte (Mate House). In 1930, a regular advertisement ran in *O Matte* describing the Casa do Matte as "Curityba's [*sic*] most comfortable and distinctive 'brasserie'" (fig. 5.3).[39] At this French-styled eatery, guests could enjoy ice cream and cocktails in a new "elegant meeting spot" for what it called a special "FIVE-O'CLOCK APPERITIVE." At the center of this ritual, the Caso do Matte served "Chá de Matte do Paraná! Chimarrão amargo! Matte doce!" (Mate tea from Paraná!

Casa do Matte

A "brasserie" mais confortavel e mais distincta de Curityba.

Serviço caprichoso na distribuição e confecção de

Sorvetes

Cock=tails

Apperitivos

Ponto de reunião elegante para o "FIVE - O' CLOCK APPERITIVE"

Chá de Matte do Paraná !

Chimarrão amargo !

Matte doce !

As melhores bebidas que existem no mundo, são especialidades da

CASA DO MATTE

que é a "BOITE" mais confortavel e mais elegante de CURITYBA

FIGURE 5.3. Casa do Matte advertisement, *O Matte*, no. 6, Feb. 1930, 25.

Bitter mate! Sweet mate!). In other words, "the best drinks that exist in the world." In Curitiba, yerba interests pitched mate as a modern, high-class drink, offered at an establishment that played up its fancy French ties by dubbing itself a brasserie serving an aperitif.

During the late 1920s and 1930s, the Brazilian erva industry engaged in experiments such as this "mate brasserie" in the hopes of increasing consumption in Brazil. At the same time, some planters in Paraná began to shift their attention away from yerba and toward coffee and timber plantations.

Many hedged their bets by combining these pursuits, including Leão Junior & Co., a business that emerged in 1901 to sell yerba before diversifying into timber in the 1910s and later coffee.[40] After founder Agostinho Ermelino de Leão Jr.'s death in 1908, his wife, Maria Clara, took over as the company's director. When a 1912 fire destroyed the original mill, she moved the factory to Curitiba, where she directed the company that produced the most exported Brazilian-milled yerba in the 1920s.[41]

While dominating exports, Leão also led an effort to pay greater attention to the local market. In 1929, the company placed a large billboard in the center of Curitiba, touting its product and roaring lion logo under the brand name "Matte Leão" and the tagline "O Chá Brasileiro" (The Brazilian Tea).[42] Like Salus a few years later, Leão made a nationalist appeal to Brazilian consumers to purchase its "Brazilian tea."

Businesses dedicated to growing erva within Brazil realized they had work to do to promote their product elsewhere in the country. A February 1930 issue of O Matte lamented, "The use of mate in Brazil is not as extensive as desired. It is almost limited to Rio de Janeiro and the Southern States." The author proposed that governors in northern Brazil give it to the police brigades and offer it at other public institutions, which, it seems, never came to pass.[43]

Brazil's southern states and private commercial interests continued to push for the expansion of Brazilian erva consumption. The Leão company tried to speed up the pace of erva mate consumption in urban centers by introducing varieties of its product that did not require city dwellers to take up the traditional habit of drinking mate out of a shared cup and straw. In 1938, the company launched a new toasted version of Matte Leão in a tea bag that featured an illuminated boat in Rio and the slogan "Já vem queimado, use e abuse" (Already burned, use and abuse). In the 1950s, Leão commercialized a cold version of this infusion, to be made at home or sold on the street during the hot summer months in Rio and other cities, as "Matte Leão Gelado" (Cold Mate Leão) in hygienically sealed cups.[44] Street vendors and small shops now offered chilled mate along with coconut water, tropical fruit drinks, and sodas to city residents and visitors.

Despite the success of cold mate drinks in Brazil, by the time local producers began paying attention to their internal market, coffee had already taken hold in all but the southernmost parts of Brazil. Soda made with highly caffeinated guaraná was also becoming more and more popular across the nation.[45] Early promotional campaigns therefore proved most effective where erva mate was already a known entity. A 1948 article noted that locals in the three most southerly states of Brazil (Paraná, Santa Catarina, and Rio Grande do Sul) selected "herva-mate" as their preferred beverage.[46] In contrast, the author explained that in the large, dense urban centers of São Paulo and Rio de Janeiro, "the consumption of mate makes slow but steady progress."[47] There was no mention of northern Brazil, where mate, hot or cold, did not become a popular drink.

FIGHTING FOR PROFITS IN ARGENTINA

Argentina had a much longer history of importing and drinking mate and thus did not need to innovate to spur local consumption. Instead, Argentine growers had to build their own productive capacity, convince the government to support their interests, and persuade Argentine consumers to purchase Argentine-grown rather than imported yerba to fill their mates.

In the 1920s, a new generation of immigrants (mostly from Europe) joined the first small generation of yerba plantation owners in Misiones, hoping to find fortune by growing yerba. The Argentine national government accelerated this process in 1926, when it passed a law offering settlers free state-owned land, where they were obligated to dedicate between 25 to 50 percent to planting yerba trees in the first two years. Those wealthy enough to cover 75 percent of their land with yerbales gained exemption from the residence requirement. By 1929, yerba provided the main source of revenue for Misiones.[48]

It was not quite the California gold rush, but what might be called the "Misiones green rush" significantly increased and diversified the region's population and remade its environment in the early twentieth century.[49] Yerba became a successful "cultivo poblador" (population cultivator), drawing European immigrants up to Argentina's northeast corner, as anthropologist Leopoldo Bartolomé explains.[50] A well-off Swiss immigrant and yerba plantation owner, Eugenio Lagier, wrote in a 1927 letter to his children studying in Europe, "You cannot imagine how Misiones has changed. Everybody is planting yerba mate, even in the most remote places which could only be reached by donkey ten years ago." New roads facilitated this expansion, he added, sharing his amazement that "the raft of Yabebiry transports more than one hundred motored vehicles each day."[51] The amount of land dedicated to growing yerba increased nearly fivefold in Misiones from 1925 to 1935, and the population grew alongside it, as Víctor Rau has shown in his analysis of yerba mate production.[52]

Growers anticipated that despite the high price of establishing Argentine yerba plantations and the challenge of competing with lower-priced Brazilian production, these dynamics would soon shift in their favor. In the nation's capital, most Argentine politicians (members of the conservative and the liberal parties, the latter referred to as Radicales) prioritized the interests of more traditional agriculturists in wheat and beef production, but there were a few notable exceptions. In 1924, Lisandro de la Torre argued before Congress that the Argentine government needed to protect Argentine yerba growers against the "Curitiba Trust," a group of erva mate businessmen with major political influence in the Brazilian state of Paraná. But de la Torre fell short of convincing others to prioritize the interests of this new group of entrepreneurs in a distant national territory.[53]

The global economic crisis of 1930 changed the equation, leading governments across the Americas and Europe to reconsider the liberal "free market" model that had dominated for nearly a half century. The weakness of this model became painfully apparent in economies like South America's, where nations dependent on agricultural exports saw demand and prices shrivel up as the United States and Europe plunged into depressions. In step with other Western nations, Brazil and Argentina implemented protectionist policies in the early 1930s to prop up national producers and industries.

In 1930, Ernesto Daumas argued on behalf of the Argentine Yerba Planters Association (formed three years prior) for protection from Brazil. "The day our men of state are convinced of this truth, the problem of yerba mate will be resolved."[54] With the weight of the global economic crisis on their side, yerba growers finally swayed government officials. In March 1931, the Argentine government established quotas on Brazilian imports and implemented new hygienic standards. The new policy stated that Brazilians could export only 60,000 tons of erva mate in installments. Specifying hygienic standards and a precise level of caffeine (sometimes called mateine), which was naturally lower in Atlantic-grown yerba in the Brazilian forests of Paraná, Santa Catarina, and Rio Grande do Sul, Argentine growers thereby sought to limit Brazilian exports in another, less direct manner.[55]

For Argentine yerba producers, victory was short-lived. Brazil responded by enacting an eighteen-month ban on the import of wheat from Argentina while simultaneously publicizing a trade deal with the United States to export Brazilian coffee in return for US-grown wheat. Argentine wheat producers and their political allies became incensed since wheat, wheat flour, and flax made up some 90 percent of Argentine exports to Brazil.[56] In October 1932, Argentine president Agustín B. Justo signed a provisional treaty with Brazilian president Getúlio Vargas. They agreed not to impose any volume limits on imports, including yerba and wheat, and settled on a 10 percent tariff on imported Brazilian yerba. Despite protests by Argentine yerba growers, Argentine leaders agreed to continue to import Brazilian yerba with a relatively low tariff to maintain the market for Argentine wheat in Brazil.[57]

In May 1935, President Vargas came to Argentina to sign a bilateral treaty. Brazil agreed not to set any limits on Argentine wheat, and Argentina agreed to remove the 10 percent tariff on Brazilian erva mate as long as it was assured of "the genuine nature and purity of the product."[58] That same year, the Argentine government announced the establishment of the Comisión Reguladora de la Producción y Comercio de la Yerba Mate (Regulatory Commission of Yerba Mate Production and Commerce, or CRYM). The CRYM's charge was to "govern the entire process of mate production and sales." The minister of agriculture served as the board's president; he was joined by two representatives from major banks, three plantation owners, three yerba manufacturers, one importer, and one consumer.[59] This group set production limits, helped promote yerba consumption, gave credit, and sought to eliminate intermediaries to lower the final price. It also responded to pressures within the Argentine yerba business and sought to maintain relatively good relations with Brazil.[60]

Three years after Argentina established the CRYM, Brazil responded by creating its own "National Institute of Mate."[61] Previously, state-led organizations, such as the Curitiba Yerba Trust, led decision-making in Brazil. Now Brazil under Getúlio Vargas made erva mate a national concern.[62]

In Paraguay, which lacked government support for the industry in the postwar era, the creation of a national yerba mate institute did not occur until 2017. Some ninety years prior, in the late 1920s, Paraguayan scholar Caesar Samaniego published a book in homage to Paraguayan yerba (or ca'a, as he referred to it in Guaraní). In it, Samaniego crowed with pride for the "superior quality" of Paraguayan yerba but expressed dismay at the national government's squandering of this precious resource. Because the Paraguayan government did little to protect its workforce or its borders, he lamented that many Paraguayans fled to yerbales in Brazil and northeastern Argentina in search of slightly higher wages for their still heavily exploited labor, significantly decreasing the potential for Paraguayan production. He also charged that the government looked the other way as some Paraguayans passed off the "inferior product grown in Mato Grosso" and imported into Paraguay (without tariffs) as its own. Incensed, he argued that the Paraguayan government needed to act to defend its "national plant."[63] But the government did not heed his call. Instead, it established moderate price levels for the domestic market and levied taxes on exports, generating a stream of illegal exports both into and out of the country.[64] As a result, most twentieth-century bureaucratic wrangling over the so-called herb of Paraguay took place between South America's two giants.

By 1936, Argentina did what once seemed impossible: it overtook Brazil as the world's largest total producer of yerba. While Argentine planters and laborers in Misiones produced just over 2,000 tons in 1915, by 1937 they surpassed 100,000 tons (see graph 4.1).[65] The national government had also introduced official norms for yerba, including a standard amount of caffeine.[66] These achievements promised to solve the problems Argentine producers faced.

Because the level of Argentine production *and* imports from Brazil and Paraguay continued to outpace internal consumption, however, yerba flooded the market. In 1937, the CRYM stepped in to limit Argentine harvests for the next fifteen years. Now Argentina, like Paraguay and Brazil before, struggled to promote its product outside South America.[67] In a more saturated market than Brazil, Argentine yerba interests also plotted to boost internal consumption. The CRYM, together with a growing number of yerba companies that predated it, turned to the emerging science of nutrition to promote the health benefits of yerba mate to Argentine consumers.

In the 1920s and 1930s, scientists and governments across much of the world began to consider the impact of food on the population. In Argentina, Dr. Pedro Escudero and his colleagues successfully lobbied the government to establish the National Institute of Nutrition in the mid-1930s. As historian José Buschini explains, the Argentine government funded this new institute because it now recognized food as a key input to maintain the health of its population and productivity of its workforce. Researchers affiliated with the institute studied diseases linked to diet, identified problems with malnutrition, suggested the components of a healthy diet, and researched the impact of specific foods on the body. They paid particular attention to locally produced foods, like yerba, which promised benefits for locals' health and the national economy.[68]

Scholars, many of whom received funding from commercial entities, had studied yerba's botanical qualities since the early twentieth century. Researchers in the 1910s and 1920s focused on varieties of yerba and the plant's chemical composition and on developing a model for comparing caffeine levels. With state involvement in the 1930s, a larger, better-funded group concentrated on the biology of the plant, the impact of processing methods, the industry's economic potential, and yerba's vitamin and mineral composition.[69] As director of the National Institute of Nutrition, Escudero participated in three studies.[70] By the late 1930s, scientists concurred that yerba mate was a healthy stimulant; while the calories were negligible, it was rich in vitamin C, caffeine, and minerals, including magnesium.

With scientific authority now firmly on its side, the CRYM convinced the Ministry of Education in 1940 to serve *mate cocido*—brewed mate—instead of coffee or tea to public schoolchildren across the country.[71] Escudero reported in 1944 that children in the Andes, who lived far from the northeastern growing region or the central milling one, regularly drank brewed mate made with reconstituted milk provided by the government for lunch and as an afternoon snack. A half century later, as I conducted research for this book, I met an elderly man from a small town in southern Patagonia who recalled arriving at his one-room schoolhouse after a long, chilly walk to find his teacher preparing a pot of milky, sweetened yerba tea that he and his classmates drank first thing in the morning. In this way, students in public schools across the nation learned to think of mate as nutritious and quintessentially Argentine.

In 1942, Angélica Felisa Schnarback, the founder of a rural school in Misiones organized the first regional festival in homage to yerba mate. Two years later, locals celebrated their accomplishments growing yerba and expanding consumption on a national scale in Argentina, launching the Fiesta Nacional de la Yerba Mate (National Festival of Yerba Mate). The event took place in Posadas, the would-be capital city of Misiones, which had become Argentina's leading yerba-producing region. By calling it a "national" festival, yerba planters and local officials sought to make their progress and belonging visible at both the local and national levels.[72]

But not all Argentines celebrated. While conservatives supported industrialists (including yerba millers) over yerba growers, and the Radical Party was split, communists and anarchists began to emphasize the labor exploitation at the root of the yerba industry. Most dramatically, Argentine journalist and Communist Party member Alfredo Varela, following in the footsteps of Rafael Barrett and Horacio Quiroga, aimed to expose the exploitation of yerba peons, whose numbers had swelled in northeastern Argentina along with yerba plantations. In 1941, Varela published a series of articles in *La hora*, the official Communist Party newspaper, after traveling through Misiones, often accompanied by Marcos Kaner, a labor activist in Misiones who once worked as a yerba picker. Varela described the grueling sixteen-hour days of laborers, who in exchange received a few coins or credit that was insufficient to use at the company store. Varela also published stories on workers' resistance and crackdowns on their organizing, including the 1936 massacre of labor activists in Oberá.[73]

Varela encouraged readers across the country not to distance themselves from such exploitation and violence but to understand their intimate connection to it. He opened his 1943 novel, *El río Oscuro* (Dark river), "*¡'CHE, CEBAME UNOS MATES'!* [Hey, serve me up some mates!] How many times a day will this phrase be uttered in Argentina! Millions, perhaps. We are a mate people. We like to slurp the greenish liquid, until we get a chortle out of it, at all times. At dawn, before lunch, in the afternoon. But it never occurred to us to think that what reaches us through the warm tube is actually the sweat and blood of many generations of anonymous men with dark skin and muscular arms."[74] No matter how far from the country's northeastern corner, Argentines, Varela suggested, needed to know the stories of "men with dark skin" who suffered to harvest yerba for the benefit of major yerba companies and mate drinkers. In 1952, Peronist Hugo del Carril turned Varela's work into a highly successful movie, *Las aguas bajan turbias* (Dark river), that exposed even more Argentines to the persistent mistreatment of yerba workers.[75]

SELLING PROVENANCE IN ARGENTINE YERBA ADVERTISEMENTS (OR, PRETENDING TO BE PARAGUAYAN)

Argentine consumers may have developed a new awareness about how yerba workers' exploitation in their nation's northeastern corner facilitated their own access to an affordable, stimulating drink. But in the first three decades of the twentieth century, the most visible shift in the yerba mate landscape appeared in proliferating advertisements that encouraged citizens to purchase a particular brand of yerba.

During the colonial era and the nineteenth century, the price of yerba varied primarily by quality, which was determined by national origin and market. As in other parts of the consumer market, there was not yet significant branding, and yerba was sold in bulk.[76] Around 1900, the first yerba brands stamped brand names on their barrels and bags of yerba and published informational advertisements about how to obtain their product. Brazilian exporters sought to profit off the spirit of rising national pride in their main import markets: Argentina and Uruguay. On the topper for its yerba barrels, the brand "Gloria," for example, featured a mythical republican woman charging ahead with a blue sky and large sun behind her that echoed the Argentine flag. Brazil's "Leonor"-brand yerba, which was sent to Montevideo, employed a similar color scheme, with golden suns circling a decidedly more modern woman cradling an art deco mate.[77] Importers and shop owners served as the main audience for these early visual attempts at branding.

In the early twentieth century, agricultural interests across the Americas stepped up their promotional campaigns for everything from Brazilian coffee to Central American bananas, often directing them to coveted consumers in the United States.[78] Yerba companies across southern South America also increased their promotional efforts but focused on South American consumers. Mirroring other businesses, they began to shift their attention to swelling numbers of city dwellers. Most pitched their products to women, who they thought would pay attention to their campaigns and do the family's shopping.[79] At first, the Argentine advertising industry looked to the United States for executives and advertising strategies, but following the nationalism and increased consumption that accompanied the Peronist era (1946–55), Argentine advertisers became more proudly local.[80] Yerba companies based in Brazil and Paraguay likewise adopted Argentine tropes to appeal to Argentine consumers.[81] From the 1920s on, advertisements for yerba as well as other goods proliferated in newspapers and magazines, on the radio, and on the walls of the city. Unlike posters and radio broadcasts, more magazine and newspaper advertisements have been preserved for us to analyze.[82]

In contrast to the yerba barrel toppers that preceded them, modern print ads for yerba announced the superiority of specific brands, regions of origin, and production processes. Because it was difficult to tell yerba apart simply by looking at it, companies sought to educate consumers with the goal of convincing them to trust their particular brand. Yerba grown in Paraguay continued to enjoy a superior reputation, and up through the 1930s, many Argentine brands touted Paraguayan origins, accurately or not. With the growth of commercial-scale Argentine yerbales during this decade, a small number of brands—most visibly Salus—promoted patriotic consumption of a supposedly national product.

Despite Brazil still exporting much more of its yerba into Argentina than did Paraguay, new brands sold in Argentina—the majority of which surely included some of this Brazilian yerba—omitted any mention of Brazil in their promotional campaigns. In contrast, in neighboring Uruguay, yerba from Brazil remained highly valued, and Brazilian companies emphasized the special type of yerba without *palos* (little branches) that it produced for the Uruguayan market.[83] Because Argentine consumers assumed Brazilian yerba to be of lower quality, unhygienic, and even adulterated, only Paraguayan and eventually Argentine yerba could be effectively promoted there.

In the first decade of the twentieth century, Argentine importer Frexias, Urquijo & Cía, which sold Aguila-brand yerba purportedly grown in Paraguay, warned consumers that they needed to pay greater attention to the yerba they purchased. "No, no, no, no . . . ," chides a bespectacled male authority figure in a 1907 advertisement in the magazine *Caras y caretas*. "It has to be with Paraguayan yerba 'AGUILA' for mate to feel good for you."[84] Here, the celebration of yerba from Paraguay stands apart from unbranded yerba, which the ad implies likely came from Brazil and might be adulterated, thus making the uninformed mate drinker sick.

Campaigns like Aguila's incensed La Industrial Paraguaya (LIPSA), Paraguay's largest yerba company. Like the pioneering Brazilian company Matte Larangeira, LIP decided that the most effective way to reach the Argentine market was to establish a modern mill in Argentina. It also promoted the idea that its product offered the only reliably "pure Paraguayan yerba" on the Argentine market. And yet, even LIP may have been selling yerba produced outside of Paraguay. In the early 1930s, Paraguayan journalist Ramos Giménez charged that LIP mills in Buenos Aires and Corrientes produced yerba that was only 30 percent Paraguayan, filling the rest of their tins with the cheaper Brazilian and Argentine variety.[85]

Naming its Argentine brand "Flor de Lis," after the flowerlike symbol long associated with French royalty, LIP sought to capitalize on ideas about the superiority of the "herb of Paraguay" but also on ideas about French cultural superiority that held sway in South American cities. (Recall the mate brasserie in Curitiba.) Recognizing that it had the most at stake in distinguishing its product from others, Flor de Lis outspent other producers in advertising from the 1910s through the 1940s. Flor de Lis sought to reach as wide an audience as possible, and its advertisements appeared in a variety of magazines, from the urbane *Caras y caretas* to the rural *El campo* and the women's magazine *Maribel*, as well as in newspapers, including Argentina's highest circulation *La Razón*.

In its early advertising, La Industrial Paraguaya pioneered the use of science to promote the integrity and healthfulness of its brand. Some two decades before the CRYM or National Institute of Nutrition began funding scientific studies, Flor de Lis sponsored research by Argentine doctor Francisco P. Lavalle. In response to a 1913 crisis surrounding some adulterated Brazilian yerba that made headlines in major Argentine newspapers, Lavalle verified, in a series of advertisements that ran from 1913 to 1915, that his chemical studies of Flor de Lis's product showed that it contained only "genuine yerba" without any "extraneous elements."[86]

In other advertisements, LIPSA emphasized that the company, founded in 1886, possessed unique control over the entire commodity chain, growing yerba in Paraguay that it processed in its own mills in Buenos Aires and Corrientes. Next to a December 1913 advertisement featuring a weathered gaucho sipping a mate, the copy claims, "FLOR DE LIS is the product of 1,150 square leagues of yerbales on our property located in Paraguay. Being harvested, processed, and sold by us, we can guarantee its absolute purity." Consumers who wanted high-quality yerba were encouraged "to ask the grocer for it by its name."[87] Fearing this might not be enough, in 1914, Flor de Lis began topping its tins with aged Paraguayan cedar and advertised this detail so that consumers would not be tricked into buying an impostor.[88]

Flor de Lis continued to aggressively promote the distinctive quality of its "genuine Paraguayan yerba" in the 1920s and 1930s in the face of mounting competition from a growing number of yerba brands. In June 1927, the company addressed the "numerous yerbas that try to thrive" by pretending to be Paraguayan.[89] The following month, an advertisement pitied "that we don't all have microscopes" to tell the difference between Flor de Lis's "pure yerba" and other adulterated yerbas (unstated but implied to be from Brazil) containing "an unrelated mix of herbs" and "foreign materials, like dirt."[90] Given the hostility of this language, this campaign seemed to reflect not only the spirit of corporate competition but also a latent form of racism toward a country imagined by many Paraguayans and Argentines as Black.

As Argentine production ramped up, Flor de Lis had to distinguish itself from Brazilian and Argentine yerba as well. In response, LIP began forcefully asserting yerba's terroir. A June 1927 Flor de Lis advertisement pointed to its enduring "supremacy," due to its Paraguayan origins, like that of "tobacco from Havana" and "sparkling wine from Champagne." The advertisement concludes, "It turns out to be impossible to confer on products from other soils the virtues of the original, because that 'something' so unique that defines them comes from the climatic conditions in which they are produced."[91] As historian Kolleen Guy points out for French champagne, the invention of terroir was a nationalist project. In both Guy's case and LIPSA's, claims about terroir were made around what were (and are) essentially industrialized drinks in which the grapes and yerba come from a wide variety of locations to be processed and packaged together.[92]

Because the Flor de Lis brand was milled, packaged, and sold in Argentina, the company hoped to differentiate its Paraguayan origins without alienating Argentine consumers. Playing on the popularity of gauchesque tropes, from 1929 through 1933 it published a series of advertisements highlighting a character it called "Mateo Mate," a gaucho who sets off to rescue the feminized figure of Flor de Lis yerba and then travels the Argentine nation pitching the superiority of the Paraguayan product.[93] Another June 1936 advertisement showed Flor de Lis's logo, a mate with arms and legs embellished with a fleur-de-lis on its belly, marching "directly" from Paraguay to Argentina with a large tin of its yerba in its hand. Brazil was nowhere to be seen on the map. The copy also emphasizes the connection between Paraguay and Argentina: "Without any foreign interference from resellers or mediators, Flor de Lis yerba comes to us directly from our ancient and immense natural yerba mate plantations in Paraguay."[94]

Other advertisements urged Argentine consumers to pay more for Flor de Lis yerba because of its superior quality, owing to the way it was produced: picked only every four years from long-standing yerbales in Paraguay, aged for several months, and hygienically processed in the company's own mills in Argentina. A May 1934 advertisement showed its iconic mate with legs and arms infusing one mate after another due to the high quality of the yerba, which made it last longer than any other brand.[95]

As Flor de Lis ramped up advertising, those among the first generation of Argentine yerba companies began to make the case for their own products. Among them was Martín y Cía, the company founded by the Swiss immigrant and self-proclaimed "pioneer" in the establishment of modern plantations in the Argentine territory of Misiones, Julio Ulises Martín. In 1930, Martín y Cía launched a promotional campaign for a new yerba brand, "La Hoja" (The leaf). Did the company highlight its Argentine bona fides? No, it did not. Despite selling Argentine yerba from its own yerbales, perhaps with some less expensive Brazilian-grown yerba mixed in, the company's tagline in the early 1930s was "yerba pura Paraguaya" (pure Paraguayan yerba).

Like Matte Larangeira and Flor de Lis, La Hoja's advertisements also emphasized the company's "modern" and "hygienic" mills in Argentina, declaring the company's yerba mills "the most important ones in the world." By 1932, Martín claimed that "modesty aside," his mills in Rosario produced more yerba than anywhere else on the planet and processed 20 percent of all yerba consumed within Argentina.[96]

Like Flor de Lis, La Hoja's early advertising campaign featured illustrations of its product (lots of yerba leaves), procreating mates (showing off durability and economy), and packaging (so that people would know it was hygienically produced and how to identify it at the market) rather than illustrations of people buying or drinking La Hoja–brand yerba. When people appeared, Flor de Lis and La Hoja rather unusually highlighted more men drinking mate than women. For example, a September 1932 La Hoja advertisement pictured a scene from the epic poem *Martín Fierro* in which a gaucho sits and drinks a mate before the fire while his "china slept under the protection of his poncho." In this image, as in the visual culture of the Belle Époque, mate was presented as a man's rather than a woman's "inseparable friend."[97]

As we saw at the outset of this chapter, the figure of the china became the brand logo for Salus, a major competitor for La Hoja and Flor de Lis. Yet this was not Mackinnon & Coelho's earliest foray into the yerba market. Between 1926 and 1932, this company pitched another brand it called Ñanduty, a Guaraní term for spiderweb, as well as for the lace work done by Paraguayan women. Like Martín y Cía, the packaging defined the product as "yerba paraguaya," but this was not a point of emphasis.[98] Ñanduty's promotional campaign paid less attention than other brands to the yerba's provenance and processing and more to piquing the interest of female consumers and establishing the classiness of drinking mate with the tagline "La más cara de las yerbas" (The most expensive of yerbas). Since yerba mate was now an affordable drink primarily consumed by the middle and working classes, it clarified: "Ñanduty, the most expensive of yerbas, is [also] the most economical due to its long duration."[99]

In the late 1920s and early 1930s, Mackinnon & Coelho appealed to popular ideas about eugenics and women's maternalism, running an annual contest where "señoras" had to correctly identify the gender of ten babies pictured in an ad to be eligible for a cash prize. "Healthy baby" contests cropped up across Latin America in the 1930s, underscoring the links between a mother's milk, children's well-being, and the health of "germ plasma."[100] An early indicator of this trend, Mackinnon & Coelho's 1926 advertisements promised contestants, for two pesos, a half kilo of yerba in a Ñanduty can, an engraved mate with "a legitimate silver rim," ten coupons, and a brochure. (In contrast, Flor de Lis told consumers that it did not give away "obsequios" [free gifts] because that would necessitate lowering the quality of its yerba.) Ñanduty also reassured new urban consumers, and perhaps immigrants who did not yet have a mate of their own, that mate was "a fashionable drink" that local "patrician families" enjoyed.[101]

Mackinnon & Coelho promoted its yerba as classy—and increasingly, as criolla. In 1929, the company added the criolla figure of the china to the fourth iteration of its guess-the-gender baby contest. With her dark hair in two pleated braids, she proudly held a mate in her hand (fig. 5.4).[102]

The previous year, after Uruguay defeated Argentina in the Olympic final in men's soccer, Mackinnon & Coelho took out a huge advertisement in *La*

FIGURE 5.4. Ñanduty advertisement, *Caras y caretas*, Oct. 12, 1929, 76.

Nación, showing a rural woman in braids putting her arms around a Uruguayan and an Argentine footballer with a mate between them. "¡Hermanos en la Gloria!" (Brothers in Glory!), the tagline celebrates. "Argentines and Uruguayans, by defeating all the world teams they faced in this manly sporting competition, have eloquently demonstrated the potential of the Rioplatense race––strong, sober and intelligent, *toned from the earliest age with the help of mate.*"[103] Like others, the makers of this ad associated the healthfulness of the "Rioplatense race" with its consumption of foods that helped "tone" locals' bodies. They also linked their racial identity to a now taken-for-granted Whiteness, lightly tinged with a criollo sensibility that allowed for the symbolic contributions of figures like the rural woman and the mate at the center of the composition.[104]

In 1930, in advance of the World Cup final between Uruguay and Argentina, Ñanduty published a full-page advertisement tying the success of the Argentine national team to its yerba mate. Running the ad in *Aconcagua* magazine, it reproduced a letter signed and purportedly written by the footballers, thanking the company for supplying them with Ñanduty-brand yerba: "It is undoubtable that one of the things that most reminds us of our own homeland is the *national mate*, and your gift should serve as an encouragement to us, in anticipation of the triumph of our national colors."[105] Despite this promise, Uruguay prevailed once more, 4–2.

Mackinnon & Coelho's celebration of national and criollo pride reached a fever pitch when it launched Salus-brand yerba in 1933. The company's new brand name no longer had Guaraní provenance but rather invoked the Latin root of the Spanish term *salud*, which means health, and in practice often precedes a toast. Mackinnon & Coelho celebrated Salus's supposedly distinct Argentine origins while critiquing other companies that refused to do the same. A December 1933 advertisement declares, "Salus is the only yerba that proudly proclaims its Argentina origin."[106] Never mind that the company's previous brand did not follow this proclamation and originally described itself as "pure Paraguayan yerba," or that most of the yerba in its blend probably came from Brazil, like one of its owners.[107]

The British and Brazilian duo behind Mackinnon & Coelho bet that Argentine consumers would be drawn in by a new, more Argentine-centric logo and history in this post-crisis nationalizing era. In the new brand's first year, the company published an ad that claimed its yerbales "dated back to the time of conquest, were baptized by the Jesuits and over the years became the pride of the most typical of national industries."[108] Like early twentieth-century Brazilians who dared change the scientific name to *Ilex braziliensis*

"Si, Señora:
SALUS es muy
Rica Yerba"

Esto lo dicen los almaceneros y
lo confirman todos los que con-
sumen SALUS. Y se explica:
SALUS es una yerba de sabor
delicado; liviana, pura, de gran aguante;
de espuma abundante y compacta; de fres-
co y agradable aroma y · todavía · de
precio muy económico! Además SALUS es
criolla y por eso la prefieren los buenos
patriotas, tanto como los buenos materos.
Consúmala Vd. también. Exíjala en sus
paquetes de 1/4 a $ 0.20 y 1 kilo a $ 0.80

SALUS

MACKINNON & COELHO Ltda. S. A.
COMPANIA YERBATERA

FIGURE 5.5. Salus advertisement, *Caras y caretas*, Feb. 10, 1934, 40.

(Brazilian holly) at the height of their industry, this newly patriotic Argentine yerba company now offered its own new scientific name for yerba, coining *Ilex argentiniensis legítima* (legitimate Argentine holly) in 1933.[109] With the new year, a Mackinnon & Coelho ad encouraged Argentine consumers to make a resolution: "I invite you to be patriotic in a practical manner by supporting National Industry. In 1934, consume Yerba SALUS."[110] By 1935, taglines implored "Sea Patriota: Consuma Yerba Salus" (Be a Patriot: Regularly Consume Yerba Salus). The company accentuated its already patriotic messaging for national holidays and international sporting competitions.

As in previous campaigns with Ñanduty, Mackinnon & Coelho directed Salus advertisements to modern female consumers, seeking to educate them about the quality, economy, and healthfulness of its product to the benefit of the family. Take for example a February 1934 advertisement where a smartly dressed White woman in a short, modern haircut and jaunty cap approaches a dapper White store clerk who holds up a tin of Salus-brand yerba (fig. 5.5). "Yes, Señora: SALUS is very tasty yerba." He continues, "SALUS is a yerba with a delicate flavor; light, pure, long lasting; abundant and compact foam; fresh and pleasant aroma and—still—very economically priced."[111]

In its ads published between 1934 and 1937, Salus mentioned the price of eighty cents for a kilo, which was less than imported yerba, it pointed out.[112] Alongside its appeal to modernity and economy, Salus invoked tradition, which it personified with its ever-present criolla in its brand logo.

Like other yerba businesses, Mackinnon & Coelho promoted and helped fund scientific studies on yerba's impact on the body. In the 1930s, Mackinnon & Coelho sponsored research conducted by Dr. María Julia Otero, director of the chemistry laboratory at the University of Buenos Aires and a pioneering woman scientist. Over the course of the decade, Otero studied the vitamins found in yerba, as well as yerba's impact on the muscles and liver, how it might prevent anemia, and how it affected digestion. Salus offered Otero's scientific study on yerba's beneficial impact on muscles "free to athletic mate drinkers."[113]

Salus regularly emphasized the health benefits of its product for athletes, children, homemakers, working men, and older couples. Emphasizing the new ideas of nutritional science, Salus claimed that it provided children with the vitamins they needed to grow and men with energy to be active at work and at play. It stimulated digestion and renal activity in the elderly. It allowed women to control their nervous systems, sleep better at night, and obtain nutrients "without getting fat." A 1937 ad, featuring men taking a work break and drinking mate, explains: "Before work or during breaks, SALUS mate is a natural *alimento* . . . that refreshes, quenches the thirst and suppresses fatigue." The ad continues, "Men and women, old and young, in the city or in the countryside, at any hour of the day or night, find in SALUS a beneficial effect, pleasure, and health."[114] Reflecting contemporary health and hygiene recommendations, Salus advertisements depicted people drinking from their own mate rather than sharing the same cup and straw, an individualistic practice that few mate drinkers took up.

Not all yerba brands emphasized science, hygiene, or even a criollo aesthetic in the early 1930s, even as most (save for Salus) emphasized Paraguayan origins. Domingo Barthe, discussed in chapter 3, bought yerbales in the Alto Paraná province of Paraguay in the aftermath of the war. Like Flor de Lis, Yerba Asunción's advertisements promised "a guarantee of its purity in its genuine Paraguayan origin" and highlighted that its yerba was milled in Argentina.[115] Associating itself with the Paraguayan capital city rather than with Guaraní roots or rural Paraguay, Yerba Asunción sought to position itself as a classy Paraguayan brand. Advertisements for Barthe's Yerba Asunción appeared in the Argentine magazine *Aconcagua* signed by the artists who drew them. They adapted the popular "one-step-up approach" to advertising by showing the lives of people just above those they targeted, including well-dressed families with servants. They also featured married couples, men on camping trips, and a group at the beach. Like Salus, Yerba Asunción aimed at female consumers, in one example showing an elegantly dressed woman ordering "Asunción"-brand yerba via the modern technology of the telephone "because it's the best."[116]

Yerba Asunción's advertising campaign made clear that women were supposed to buy yerba and serve the mates. Some ads showed female servants in formal attire doing so, while others featured homemakers serving mate. In a September 1932 advertisement, two men and one woman sit talking in a well-lit living room enjoying "la grata tertulia" (a pleasant gathering) with a mate (fig. 5.6). "The mate brewed by a beautiful female hand; the warmth of the home delighting the spirit of family members; a good read," the advertisement begins. "What more could one want to be happy?"[117] Barthe promoted his yerba as classy, modern, and Paraguayan to meet the exacting standards of well-off and well-educated Argentines. The suited man sipping the mate gazes appreciatively at a Yerba Asunción advertisement.

By the late 1930s and 1940s, the reputation of yerba from Argentina improved in step with growing commercial and political desires for patriotic consumption to foster the development of national industries. Yerba companies based in Argentina moved away from the earlier strategy of highlighting

FIGURE 5.6. Yerba Asunción advertisement, *Aconcagua*, Sept. 1932, 88. Clipping courtesy of Special Collections and College Archives, Skillman Library, Lafayette College, Eaton, PA.

Paraguayan origins. Some, like La Hoja and Aguila, simply stopped claiming that their yerba was Paraguayan.[118] Other players that emerged in this era never made such a claim in the first place.

New Argentine brands of yerba (milled if not exclusively grown in Argentina) emphasized and updated traditional criollo tropes in the 1940s. At the start of this decade, the flour and oil company Molinos Río de la Plata entered the yerba market with its brand called Nobleza Gaucha (Gaucho Nobility). In one ad from this era, two gauchos sit at either end of the Argentine republic preparing to drink a mate. The advertisement promises "the same taste across the Republic! WITH ANY KIND OF WATER!"[119] Then, as now, the taste of the water affected the flavor of the yerba, and despite this claim, Nobleza Gaucha's yerba (like any other) must have tasted different depending on the hardness or salinity of the water used to infuse it.

Other companies with deeper roots appealed to an invented or embellished past. In its second decade, Salus updated its advertisements by bringing the china and the gaucho into modern contexts, like a train or a party, where they offered a contemporary mixed-sex group a mate.[120] For its part, La Hoja also appealed to the past in its 1940s and 1950s advertisements, associating its product with colonial and independence heroes. In one disturbing newspaper advertisement drawn by artist Alejandro Siria, a bearded conquistador swings an ax at a pair of crouching Indigenous people, one of whom hands him a mate with a bombilla to try to get him to stop.[121]

During the 1950s, more yerba mate companies moved away from founding myths and the gauchesque and toward modern urban domesticity, regularly featuring White upper-middle-class women serving their husbands mate in modern urban apartments. The focus on women's domestic roles intensified across the Americas during this decade following World War II. In Argentina, the Peronist government, media outlets, and advertisers encouraged women to focus on their roles as professional homemakers and savvy consumers to improve the status of their families and help modernize their nation.[122] A 1950s Nobleza Gaucha advertisement shows a smiling homemaker, a "Hebe B. de Andreasen," holding a mate out for her husband, who walks in the door with a briefcase in hand, presumably returning from work (fig. 5.7). The text explains: "Dynamic, modern homemakers stimulate the healthy ambitions of their husbands, toasting with them the active pause, the flavorful, foamy mate, made with NOBLEZA GAUCHA, that they also enjoy with true pleasure."[123] Here the homemaker was celebrated for having the wisdom to make such a flavorful mate and for sharing it with her husband after a long day of work. "Because both of us are active," as the copy attests.

FIGURE 5.7. Nobleza Gaucha advertisement, ca. 1950s.
Clipping courtesy of Special Collections and College Archives,
Skillman Library, Lafayette College, Eaton, PA.

Salus advertisements in the 1950s hit similar notes, emphasizing the White middle-class status of the "good homemaker" who served her family its brand of yerba. A 1956 ad featuring a blue-eyed young woman holding a package of yerba claimed that "SALUS is preferred by good homemakers."[124] On this occasion, the company even whitened its criolla logo by making her dark eyes light blue.

A new generation of advertisements where the serving woman did not even appear and only her hand was displayed in the illustration took the women's role as mate server to an extreme. In 1960, an advertisement for Nobleza Gaucha showed a fair woman's hand with painted red fingernails passing her husband a mate as he works on a home improvement project outside.[125] Similarly, in a contemporary Salus advertisement, a disembodied woman with bright red fingernails and pale skin prepares to hand a man in a business suit a mate.[126] In this advertisement and others, modern women served mate to their husbands in ways that updated and urbanized the rural woman's subservient role in the iconography of the goodbye mate.

Argentine yerba marketers understood and participated in the outsized role that Argentine women played in the consumer market. By the 1950s, Argentine women took charge of around 80 percent of domestic purchases, a share that was even higher in poorer families.[127] Whereas such women (and men) bought loose, unbranded yerba at the start of the twentieth century, by the century's midpoint, they could choose from an array of brands at urban markets. Yerba companies, often owned by immigrants, tried to generate interest in their brands, first by emphasizing long-standing ideas about Paraguay's superior quality and then by pushing new ideas about the patriotic consumption of Argentine yerba. Even when one of the owners was Brazilian, as was the case with Salus, promotional campaigns consistently elided the enduring place of Brazilian imports in Argentine yerba brands.

~~~~~~

During the first half of the twentieth century, Argentina and Brazil fought for supremacy in the yerba market, which, like the ritual of drinking mate, remained concentrated within the southern half of South America. A few Paraguayan and Brazilian yerba businessmen partnered with American counterparts to try to woo consumers in the United States and Canada. They founded the Yerba Mate Tea Company in Philadelphia in 1899, and a couple decades later the International Mate Company in New York City. Alongside yerba, they sold and sometimes even gifted gourds and bombillas to try to teach their northern counterparts about how to partake in this intimate South American ritual. Already committed to drinking individual cups of coffee and tea, consumers in the northern hemisphere expressed little interest. A leading member of the Argentine Association of Yerba Mate Planters articulated his concern in 1930: "When can we expect an increase in consumption? The United States and France have proven themselves impervious to all temptation." As had been the case since the colonial area, the great majority of yerba was sold within South America rather than outside of it.[128]

Within South America, Argentine planters emerged victorious when they surpassed Brazilian yerba production levels in the early 1930s, a development that would have seemed nearly impossible three decades prior. But this victory was short lived, since the Argentine yerba market was already oversaturated by the mid-1930s, not only by locally produced yerba but also by significant quantities that continued to be imported from Brazil and, to a lesser extent, Paraguay. Still, Argentina's definitive entry as a producer had already begun to change the industry and nation-specific associations with yerba mate. If, at first, yerba companies in Argentina felt that they had to emphasize their Paraguayan origins to be competitive, by the late 1930s, more joined Salus in presenting themselves as proudly Argentine.

Even after Brazil had surpassed Paraguay as the largest yerba producer and exporter, its reputation for inferior quality in Argentina, alongside the absence of nationwide consumption within Brazil, made Brazil's dominance more tenuous than it appeared. Brazil maintained a significant but eroding level of exports to the Argentine market. Meanwhile, Uruguay, which remained unable to cultivate yerba, took over as Brazil's most important client. Some Brazilian companies, most notably Leão, succeeded in growing consumption in Brazil of its erva mate tea and bottled iced drinks in major cities beyond rural zones in the southern provinces where locals preserved the mate-drinking custom.[129] In the 1940s and 1950s, most planters in southern Brazil shifted their attention to focus on coffee cultivation and pine extraction, causing erva mate exports to diminish as they became less important to the local economy.[130]

Just as in earlier times, mate operated as a powerful social symbol, but it also served as a political one that linked a new generation of regional, nationalist, and populist leaders to the masses. Despite the shift away from a focus on erva mate production in Brazil during his presidency, President Getúlio Vargas, who hailed from the southern part of the country, appeared in a photograph drinking a mate, gaucho-style, in 1943.[131] In subsequent decades, southern Brazilian identity would become tightly associated with the figure of the gaucho who drank his *chimarrão* (bitter mate) and feasted on *churrasco* (grilled beef).[132] Vargas's hometown of São Borja even recently built a statue of the former president with an overflowing mate in his hand.[133]

Like Vargas, and some earlier post-independence leaders across the region, the nationalist Argentine president Juan Domingo Perón (1946–55) leaned on mate's symbolic power. In 1952, he graced the cover of his government's widely read magazine, *Mundo Peronista* (Peronist world) in front of his collection of mates at home.[134] In this way, Perón signaled his appreciation for and participation in a popular, often domestic ritual.

The Argentine government took greater control over planning for the yerba industry, as with other areas of the economy in the 1940s and early 1950s. In 1943 and 1944, the country's interim military government began restructuring the Ministry of Agriculture so that it could exercise greater control over production without the interference of interested parties, in this case, yerba growers and millers. It replaced members of the yerba industry board with government officials on the board of the CRYM.[135]

After taking office in 1946, Juan Perón accelerated the level of state involvement in industry and agriculture, embracing a model of import substitution industrialization intended to propel Argentina forward and provide his working-class supporters with a "dignified life." By subsidizing local industries, negotiating substantial wage increases, and reducing food and housing costs, Peronist policies created tangible, everyday changes for working-class people. For example, in its first five years, the Peronist government subsidized and celebrated its expansion of access to beef. After a drought and economic downturn in 1951, however, it began to prioritize exporting Argentina's beef and wheat for profit. Because yerba was already a working-class staple and had a much smaller and less profitable foreign market, the Peronist government initially seemed less interested in it. But in 1953, the government authorized the renovation and expansion of yerba mate cultivation and made Misiones an official province in the Argentine republic. The following year, it prohibited the sale of loose yerba, following a similar measure in Buenos Aires a couple of decades prior.[136]

Despite the Peronist government's emphasis on improving working-class living standards, it did little to better conditions for those who worked harvesting yerba. The situation in Brazil and Paraguay, where photographers captured yerba laborers porting heavy sacks stuffed with yerba on their backs in the 1940s, was similar.[137] The modernization of the yerba industry, which was evident in new packing plants, brands, and ideas about nutrition, was not accompanied by enhancements of yerba pickers' labor practices or rights.

Argentina continued producing more yerba than it could consume. In 1966, the Argentine government took the dramatic step of prohibiting the harvest of any more yerba that year. For the first time, it also prohibited the importation of Brazilian yerba and introduced a quota on what could be imported from Paraguay.[138] The following year, the Brazilian National Institute of Mate ceased to exist.[139] While some Brazilian planters continued to grow and export erva mate, their numbers and political influence had diminished in the mid-twentieth century. By the 1960s, it seemed that Brazil did not intend to fight Argentina for predominance in yerba production. The twentieth-century story of yerba mate was about nation building in Argentina and literally put Misiones on the national map. But in Brazil, regionalism was at issue, as was the emergence of a distinctive southern Brazilian cultural identity that foregrounded the figure of the Whitened gaucho who enjoyed his *chimarrão*.[140]

Yerba had become Argentine, but to what end? By the 1960s, the Argentine market appeared fully saturated. Furthermore, while rural areas remained committed to slowly savoring the mate-drinking ritual, the accelerated pace of modern life in rapidly growing cities seemed to threaten its demise. Some predicted yet another disaffection, this time not by Belle Époque elites but instead by a new generation of middle-class urbanites. What would happen to the ritual of mate drinking as the region experienced the intensifying modernization and industrialization of the food industry? Furthermore, how would the dictatorial regimes that would soon seize power shape yerba mate's new political associations during their reigns of terror?

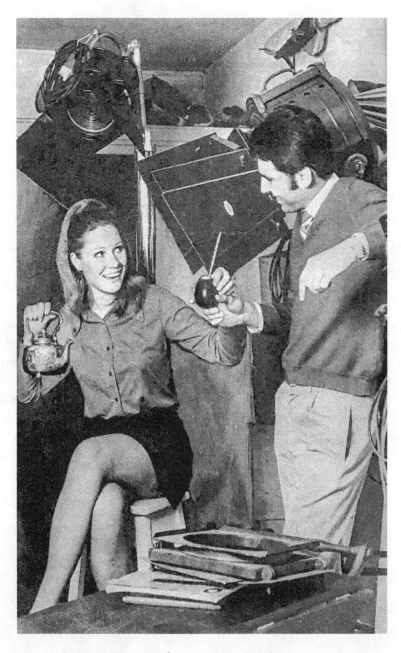

FIGURE 6.1. Photograph from promotional article "EL MATE: UNA
BEBIDA PARA LOS JOVENES JOVENES," *Gente*, Oct. 16, 1969, 80–81.

CHAPTER SIX

Conspicuously Consuming Mate in Urban Argentina and Uruguay, 1960s–2000s

In a photograph of a modern city apartment in Argentina, a young woman sporting a high ponytail and miniskirt serves a mate to a young man in side-burns and chinos. In another photograph, a woman's hands appear to tip a kettle to infuse a mate for some friends seated behind her in the living room. The magazine headline accompanying these two photographs proclaims, "EL MATE: UNA BEBIDA PARA LOS JOVENES JOVENES" (Mate: A drink for youthful youth). Published in 1969 in *Gente*, the Argentine version of *People* magazine, this two-page spread seems at first glance to be an article but is an advertisement (fig. 6.1).[1]

In the late 1960s and early 1970s, the Argentine yerba industry engaged in promotional campaigns, including this one, out of concern that its primary consumer market in Argentine cities was slipping away. Competing not only with coffee and tea but now also soda and the hustle and bustle of daily life, drinking mate seemed an uneasy fit for a new generation of Argentine city dwellers. Echoing contemporary Coca-Cola slogans, the ad in *Gente* strikes a new tone: "The maelstrom of urban life today demands this pause, this respite 'to drink life in.'"[2] Making the appeal of mate even more explicit, the text specifies that "for both sexes and any moment, mate appears today as the ideal beverage, combining tradition with modernism, the past with tomorrow, in a today full of possibilities."[3] It features testimonials from men and women of different ages and socioeconomic classes who share their appreciation of mate, from Nobel Prize winner Bernardo Houssay, who was then eighty-two, to an eighteen-year-old student, a twenty-five-year-old electrician, and a forty-two-year-old homemaker.[4]

The latent anxiety expressed in the 1969 ad about whether young people in Argentina would continue to drink mate reflected reality. A growing number of upwardly striving, middle-class Argentine consumers, who associated the drink with the rural past and contemporary poverty, moved away from mate in the mid-twentieth century, just like elites did a half century earlier. Per capita consumption in Argentina hovered between 7 and 8 kilos a year from the 1910s through the 1940s but began to dip in the 1950s and to decline more significantly in the 1960s, reaching a low point of 4.3 kilos per person in 1969 (graph 6.1).[5]

Two years prior, Argentina ended the importation of Brazilian yerba due to its own overproduction. Because Greater Buenos Aires consumed about two-thirds of all yerba produced in Argentina, the region drew the most attention from worried yerba interests.[6]

On the other side of the River Plate, Orientales, or Easterners, as they were called, became more conspicuous mate consumers in the 1960s. Spanning age and socioeconomic class, Uruguayans consistently consumed a whopping 9 kilograms of yerba per capita in 1961, more than Argentina's still relatively high 6.5 kilograms.[7] Orientales further distinguished themselves through their early adoption of the thermos and a proclivity to drink mate outside in the city. By the 1990s, Uruguayan national identity had become so tightly associated with the thermos of hot water tucked under an arm that guide-books and outsiders claimed it was possible to identify Uruguayans by this extra appendage.

In late twentieth-century Uruguay and Argentina, the place of mate was shaped by the size of each nation and its political trajectory. There were regions within Argentina, especially in the northeast and along the historic yerba trade route of the Paraná River, where per capita consumption matched that of the much smaller republic to the east, and other areas where it proved considerably lower. Furthermore, Juan Perón's radically redistributionist policies and their fallout divided an already more class-conscious Argentina more deeply in the wake of his 1955 departure. Well-to-do Argentines eager to distance themselves from Peronism seemed to associate mate with the populist government's

GRAPH 6.1. Per capita consumption of yerba in Argentina, 1900–present

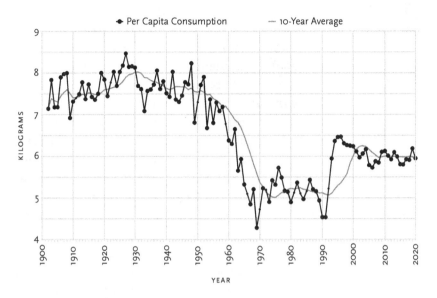

Source: Created by Paul Miller, visual resources curator at Lafayette College, Eaton, PA, from gross annual consumption statistics published in the sources indicated in note 5. Figures were aggregated, converted to kilograms as required, and compared. In cases of disparity, any instances of major deviation, lesser precision, or obvious error were discarded. Reasonably differing figures were then averaged together per annum to arrive at consensus totals, to which were then applied annual population statistics as derived from censuses and projections by Gapminder (see www.gapminder.org/data/documentation/gd003/).

working-class followers, especially migrants with rural origins.[8] Meanwhile, because Uruguayans did not experience a mid-twentieth-century populist government that regularly talked about class distinctions, Uruguay's political and socioeconomic landscape proved less fractious in the late 1950s and early 1960s. Even so, during this period, the sustainability of the Uruguayan model of development came into question as exports fell and inflation rose.[9] By the 1960s, mate consumption united Uruguayans while dividing Argentines along the fault lines of social class and urban versus rural.

This chapter tells the story of the symbolic place of mate drinking during the tumultuous decades of the 1960s through the first decade of the 2000s, when intensified political struggles accompanied a new era of modernization and urbanization. In the 1960s, many young people around the world dreamed of and fought for a more equal world order. As the Cold War heated up and the United States supported what it labeled "counterinsurgency" efforts in Latin America, right-wing military dictatorships seized power across the Southern Cone (Argentina, 1966–73, 1976–83; Brazil, 1964–85; Chile, 1973–90; Paraguay, 1954–89; and Uruguay, 1973–85). Starting in the 1970s, US-backed military dictatorships carried out a region-wide campaign of terror known as "Operation Condor" that targeted (among others) young political and labor activists.[10] With the democratic restoration of the 1980s, South Americans reclaimed their rights as citizens and reentered public spaces. In Uruguayan and Argentine cities, a growing number brought their mate and thermos with them, contributing to the trend of conspicuous consumption in Uruguay and reversing the trend of waning consumption in Argentina.

As in previous chapters, we will explore what visual culture can tell us about the social and symbolic place of yerba mate. In step with the growing number of genres in which mate appeared, we will consider artwork, photographs, and television advertisements. We will also analyze what contemporaries did or did not see in everyday life, such as the presence or absence of the thermos, which allowed late twentieth-century mate drinkers to bring their hot water and mate ritual into the city streets. This chapter focuses on the conspicuous consumption of mate in late twentieth-century Argentine and Uruguayan cities because their trajectories were more similar than those that characterized neighboring nations. While yerba consumption crossed much of Paraguay, late twentieth-century locals tended to consume mate at home and tereré—the chilled yerba drink made with wild herbs—in public, because of the warmer climate. In southern Brazil, both mate and tereré remained primarily rural drinks, as residents of large cities, such as São Paulo and Rio de Janeiro, mostly drank yerba as a premade iced beverage. Most importantly, due to the proximity of Argentina and Uruguay's rapidly growing capital cities, denizens of Buenos Aires and Montevideo frequently traveled or gazed across the muddy River Plate and compared themselves to each other.[11]

We begin this chapter in 1960s Argentina to witness how contemporary artwork and media coverage reflected and enhanced the association of mate with urban poverty and the rural past. We will then turn to 1960s Uruguay, where conspicuous public mate drinking cut across social classes and the urban-rural divide. How would the dictatorships that rocked both nations impact the place of mate? And how would the restoration of democracy matter for mate's future? As we shall see, in Uruguay's run-up to the dictatorship, members of the Uruguayan political left adopted the mate as a potent symbol of its resistance. In contrast, while leftists in Argentina drank mate, they did not embrace it as a political symbol to the same extent that their Uruguayan counterparts did. This enabled the Argentine military junta to endorse nationalist celebrations of yerba mate. In the aftermath of the Uruguayan dictatorship, mate became an even more potent signifier of Uruguayan national identity. Meanwhile, in post-dictatorial Argentina, relatively well-off urban Argentines began to shed the cosmopolitan, class-conscious shame that had built around the local drink for a century, allowing mate to become a potent symbol of Argentina's stronger ideological attachment to South America and its customs, rather than to those of Europe.

MATE'S ASSOCIATION WITH THE POOR IN 1960S ARGENTINA

Drinking mate remained an important part of most people's daily lives through the ups and downs of the mid- to late twentieth century. In rural areas of Argentina, southern Brazil, southern Chile, pockets of Bolivia, and pretty much all of Uruguay and Paraguay, most people marked the start of the day and other moments to pause and reconnect by drinking mate with friends, family members, or coworkers. In 1958, US geologist Victor Oppenheim, who spent the 1940s and 1950s in South America, wrote that people all across "the Plata region in Paraguay, Argentina, Uruguay, and parts of Southern Brazil" regularly consumed and offered visitors what he condescendingly called the "invariable yerba mate."[12]

In a more positive take, British traveler and sometime resident of Argentina Gordon Meyer shared that drinking mate and smoking cigars filled idle moments in the river region of northeastern Argentina and Paraguay in the early 1960s. Echoing earlier travel writers who had become smitten with the local drink, Meyer expressed, "Few moments [are] so enjoyable, giving one so much awareness of life, as taking maté in the early hours. . . . A stranger might think that all were awaiting some announcement of far-reaching importance, a great event, the beginning of a battle. But the group is just 'mateando'; in a little while, still before light, it will mount and ride away." As Meyer traveled from northeastern Argentina into Paraguay, he found a similar reverence for the first mate of the day that he appreciated even if he could not fully understand it. He reported that Paraguayans dedicated the first hour or two to drinking mate together, concluding, "There is about mates in the early morning something religious; not to observe the custom would show want of decorum."[13]

As the heat set in later in the day, most people in Paraguay (and their counterparts in border regions of Brazil and Argentina) drank a cool tereré rather than a hot mate. In the aftermath of the Chaco War in the 1930s and with the arrival of freezers in Paraguay in the late 1960s, consumption of an icier version of tereré took off and became more tightly associated with national identity than mate drinking.[14] Around 1968, Adolfo Friedrich took a staged photograph showing a group of rural farmhands enjoying a tereré and guitar playing in front of a wood-planked rancho.[15] In Asunción, women and girls sold tereré in the city's central plaza to locals and visitors.[16]

In contrast, in contemporary urban Argentina, relatively well-off people were not publicly drinking mate or tereré in big cities. Until the 1860s, visitors might observe *porteños* drinking a mate together on the sidewalk, but a hundred years later, this tradition was nowhere to be seen in the bustling capital city. In contrast, sidewalk mates remained popular in small cities and towns across 1960s Argentina.[17]

Of course, just because you could not see them in public did not mean that young urbanites in Greater Buenos Aires stopped drinking mate altogether. For example, in 1962, Elena, a young woman in a relatively prosperous city on the outskirts of Buenos Aires, wrote to Argentina's premier culinary expert, Doña Petrona, to settle a debate among her friends about the proper temperature to heat the water for mate. Doña Petrona responded that the "water must come to a boil."[18] (This is a point on which many disagreed, arguing that boiling water would scorch and decrease the flavor emitted by the tender yerba leaves.) She further instructed Elena to keep the kettle close to a heat source to keep it warm, making clear that she did not expect her and her friends to have or use a thermos. Elena and her friends wanted to drink mate in domestic settings but lacked the confidence to know whether they were doing so properly.

Some highly educated, middle-class young people like Elena and her friends were clearly interested in mate as advertisers hoped, but the poor and working classes were the most committed yerba mate consumers. A 1965 survey of Greater Buenos Aires (encompassing the capital city and its environs) found that residents in four of the six lowest socioeconomic groups boasted over seven kilograms of per capita consumption per year. The wealthiest sector of society consumed only around four kilograms per capita and the next best-off strata (those with university degrees or "mid-level business" people) around five kilograms per capita, some two to three kilograms less than their poorer counterparts.[19] Writer and social commentator Rodolfo Walsh issued a pessimistic diagnosis in 1966: "Argentina no longer drinks mate."[20]

Clearly, mate had an image problem among the relatively well-to-do in 1960s Argentina. Considering the plunging demand for yerba in Argentina from 1951 to 1970, Enrique de Arrechea speculated that it likely stemmed from "a cultural type of problem, since the population would associate the consumption of yerba mate with lower social levels."[21] Contemporary artwork and media coverage both reflected and enhanced the growing perception that mate did not fit with the lifestyles of upwardly striving, middle-class Argentines.

In 1964, prominent Argentine artists collaborated with journalist and mate expert Amaro Villanueva to release a beautiful, new paperback book with twenty new fine arts compositions featuring mate.[22] Intended for locals and foreigners, Villanueva recounted the history of mate and analyzed the paintings in Spanish, English, and French. He did not pronounce his art book political, but Villanueva had run for office as a member of the Communist Party in the previous decade, and the ten male artists he recruited for this venture had leftist leanings or affiliations. As opposed to the foreign background of many earlier generations of artists drawn to mate, all were born and raised in a variety of locations across Argentina, save one (Juan Batlle Planas) who emigrated from Spain with his family at two years old. Considered part of the Nuevo Realismo (New Realist) movement, participating artists, most of whom studied in Buenos Aires and also trained or exhibited their works in Europe, shared a commitment to depicting what Villanueva referred to as "the reality of our changing social atmosphere," frequently using their artwork to denounce injustice.[23]

When this new socially conscious generation of Argentine fine arts painters turned their attention to mate, they depicted poor urbanites, traditional rural elites, Indigenous people, or the figure of the gaucho as the most important mate drinkers. Artist Juan Grela stood apart in offering two works featuring contemporary young and middle-aged lovers; in contrast, the rest of the contributors pictured earlier, more rural, or poorer mate drinkers. Horacio Butler, for example, contributed two paintings of women in elaborate long dresses and men wearing traditional rural attire sharing a mate on a patio outside their family home; and Enrique Policastro depicted a humbler version of the rural tradition of the welcome mate. For his part, Héctor Balsaldúa featured two elite women from the past sharing a sidewalk mate. Other artists signaled mate's Indigenous past and present. Juan Carlos Castagnino offered an *indigenista* (Indigenous) version of the goodbye mate where a brown-skinned woman hands a mate to a noble, brownskinned man astride his horse. Antonio Berni, who had become famous for

FIGURE 6.2. Raúl Schurjin, *Mate costero*, 1963, in Amaro Villanueva, *El mate*
(Buenos Aires: Editorial El Mate, 1964). Courtesy of Daniel Schurjin.

launching the Nuevo Realismo movement in Argentina, painted a weary,
Indigenous-looking woman from the province of Santiago del Estero sol-
emnly drinking a mate alone as well as a scruffy gaucho doing the same.[24]
Highlighting urban working-class mate drinkers, Juan Batlle Planas depicted a
"tenement mate" consumed by poor immigrants, and Carlos Alonso showed
a group of contemporary construction workers sharing a mate with a thermos
during a work break.

Even more explicitly associating mate with poverty, artist Raúl Schurjin
offered an image of a shoeless boy from the river region of the province of
Santa Fe slurping out of a humble mate (fig. 6.2). Zooming in on this artist's

backstory and composition enables us to better understand his approach. Born in Mendoza in 1907, Schurjin at age twelve fled his abusive father, moving to Buenos Aires at the behest of some anarchist immigrants he met at a train station. There, he supported himself by becoming a newspaper delivery and shoeshine boy and began to pursue his interest in art, eventually studying painting at the National Academy of Art. In Santa Fe, Schurjin became well known for his sympathetic portraits of poor coastal dwellers who lived along the Paraná River.[25] He featured wide-eyed women and children, typically showing them with a mate as a tangible symbol of their poverty and fortitude. Villanueva drew readers' attention to these dynamics in evocative prose as he introduced Schurjin's painting: "The 'mate of the coast' that the poor little guy sips slowly to 'warm his guts' is roughly expressing all that inveterate social process of misery. A tin can is fished out of the garbage and yerba has to be bought. To one side, half lying on the improvised brazier, the blackened kettle denounces the usual type of fuel: branches and sticks, between green and wet, collected in passing, from the undertow. In the background, it is suggested that the humble rancho has been reduced to an abandoned dwelling by the invasion of the waters."[26] Life was materially challenging for this young boy, and for many others like him; the precarious mate he drank served as one of his few consistent comforts.

Schurjin's painting also reflected how the mate (or cup) continued to mark social status. "The mate is prepared in a small calabash, silver-mounted and elaborately ornamented in the case of the wealthy; the poorest use a tin mug," a traveler at the time noted.[27] In Schurjin's composition, the barefoot boy drinks out of a tin can that he likely scavenged from the trash, as Villanueva suggested.

Socially conscious Argentine journalists joined artists in linking mate consumption with contemporary poverty. The country's leading newspaper, *La Nación*, published a Sunday morning article featuring Villanueva's edited compilation and reproducing some of its artwork for a wider audience.[28] In another widely circulated 1965 magazine article, "Food and Argentines," journalist Ricardo Warnes contrasted urban areas where the well-to-do enjoyed a diet of beef and other rich foods with "regions where children's only food is *mate cocido*." He relayed new research in the shantytown of Lacarra in the city of Buenos Aires and in the provinces of Rioja and Misiones, where children survived on a diet of this local infusion and a basic starch.[29] Around this time, the saying "mate cocido y galletitas" (brewed mate and crackers) became a popular way to signify poor people's limited resources. This was not just empty rhetoric for the well-fed. A woman I interviewed, Stella, referred to this saying to underline her family's insufficient food in Bahía Blanca during the 1970s.[30]

While they were exceptional, not all contemporary media stories linked mate consumption with the urban poor or rural dwellers. In 1965, for example, Time Inc published a book on the River Plate republics and featured the daily life of a "typical" Buenos Aires middle-class family, the Dillons. In one photograph, the father, a high school principal, drinks a mate in his son's bedroom. Still, it is notable that his wife served their boys not mate but a mug likely filled with coffee or tea.[31]

Argentine yerba interests worked to counteract the growing association of mate with the poor and the old in the media by presenting this traditional drink as desirable to a new generation.[32] Just as in the 1969 *Gente* ad we saw at the start of the chapter, most marketers focused their attention on young, middle-class Argentines who symbolized the latest iteration of modernity. Starting in the late 1950s, contemporaries began to associate a new category of people referred to as "the youth" with the ways in which Argentina was changing, pinning their hopes and anxieties on them, as historian Valeria Manzano has explained. Argentine youth challenged social and political norms, donning blue jeans and miniskirts, listening to rock and roll, embracing premarital sex, and fighting for a new political order.[33] While marketers coveted this demographic as a new group of consumers to target, in Argentina, mate was not yet part of the youth's worldly and rebellious public image.

Young people's hopes for a different way of living and a more egalitarian political and economic system worried conservatives, including members of the military who seized power from the national government in 1966. Gen. Juan Carlos Onganía (1966–70) led a military government that sought to impose what political scientist Guillermo O'Donnell called an "authoritarian-bureaucratic state" in Argentina.[34] The neoliberal Argentine military junta froze wages, favored foreign capital, suspended the right to strike, ended university autonomy, and cracked down on political opponents. It also targeted youth, seeking to quash their political activism and countercultural initiatives.[35] Most resisted these measures peacefully, but some groups, including the Montoneros, who were associated with the revolutionary left wing of Peronism, took up arms.

As would be the case in the dictatorship that followed, Argentine advertisers did not address the political climate or repression of youth culture in their commercial messaging. Instead, yerba promoters followed up their 1969 initiatives to young people "to drink life in" with a bubbly new national campaign. Investing significant resources in their 1970 initiatives, they hired up-and-coming director Juan José Jusid to create a television advertisement with some well-known actors and a catchy tune repeating the new slogan: "What a swing mate gives me! Where there is mate, there's love." In this peppy forty-one-second ad, euphoric young couples flirt as they happily share and sip from mates in urban apartments and on balconies. "What a Swing Mate Gives Me!" appeared on matchbooks as well as in TV advertisements.[36]

In 1972, *La Nación*'s weekly magazine ran a story on the history of mate that suggested the local drink was enjoying a small resurgence. It featured three pictures of people drinking mate. One showed a marine on a boat serving himself a mate; another, an elderly man and woman sharing a mate and conversation through a window gate; and the third, a young couple sharing a mate near the river where the young man fished. The caption for the third photograph suggested that "mate appears to have set down new roots, principally for the youth, who have rediscovered it."[37] Indeed, as the piece implied, mate consumption was enjoying a modest rebound. The government of Misiones noted that due to this intense promotional campaign, per capita consumption in Argentina grew by 13 percent to over 5 kilos per capita by 1976, from its low of just over 4 kilos per capita in 1969 (see graph 6.1).[38] But yerba consumption still remained well below what it had been during the first half of the twentieth century. In 1975, food journalist Marta Beines located Argentines' preference for mate in the past, writing, "There is no doubt that it *was* the criollos' preferred infusion."[39]

Despite per capita declines and statements about mate as a thing of the past, most people in Argentina still consumed more yerba mate than coffee or tea in the 1960s and 1970s.[40] Like Elena, who worried about the temperature of the water, they tended to do so inside or near their homes where they could keep the water warm on the kitchen stove or a small burner or on a small stove or open fire outside. Perhaps the girl who gave her boyfriend a mate at the river in the 1972 photograph from *La Nación* took a thermos along with her, but it was not in the frame. Similarly, in the twenty artistic compositions featured in the 1964 art book edited by Villanueva, only Juan Battl Planas's construction workers had a thermos. Most paintings and photographs featured a kettle. A small number of Argentines I spoke with remembered their families acquiring and traveling with a thermos on car trips starting in the 1950s and 1960s, but even they associated this new technology with Uruguayans on the other side of the River Plate.[41] In urban Argentina, mate remained a primarily domestic ritual with increasing associations with the working poor.

Even as mate had slipped out of fashion in urban Argentina, it reigned supreme in 1960s Uruguay. Fernando O. Assunçao, the Uruguayan anthropologist and historian, opened his 1967 book about mate with memories of drinking it with his friends as a student, with the help of a thermos to keep the water warm: "We remember (naturally adorning the memory with the rosy and romantic light of distance and nostalgia) the early mornings on the eve of exams in which drowsiness, tedium, anguish and even the 'anger' of the beautiful summertime that was wasted in confinement was only dissipated with the help of a bitter mate. Each suck on the bombilla was a neuron that was activated; with each gulp, a concept, an idea, a piece of knowledge entered. Each thermos fully drained was an exam question conquered."[42] Drinking mate helped Assunçao and his friends get through long hours of studying. By the 1960s, Uruguayans, like Assunçao and his friends, had incorporated the thermos as a key part of their mate ritual that enabled them to keep the water warm wherever they went.

Because of their deep and public commitment to mate drinking, Uruguayans could claim mate as their national drink, Assunçao argued. While he recognized that Paraguayans and Argentines could make a similar assertion, he noted that Uruguay dominated consumption statistics and what he referred to as the drink's "vertical universality," in that people up and down the social ranks enjoyed it at least once a day.[43] The public nature and social importance of mate in Uruguay had no counterpart in other national contexts in South America: "What distinguishes Uruguayans is not that they drink mate (we have already seen that there are many others who do so) but . . . the public status they give to this 'vice.'"[44] Uruguayans, Assunçao emphasized, drank mate not only in the intimacy of the home but everywhere else too. The "exhibitionist coquetry" of the Uruguayan mate drinker, as he put it, did not appear in other national contexts.[45]

Despite Uruguay not producing yerba at any significant scale, Uruguayans' enthusiasm for public mate drinking made this practice into a powerful national symbol (a trend that persists to this day, as we will see later). It is striking that in 1967, Assunçao already claimed that "the Uruguayan is always wanting to show his mate."[46] Indeed, in the 1950s, workers home from their jobs at meat processing plants in Montevideo changed into pajamas and brought their mates out to the sidewalk to enjoy after work.[47]

FIGURE 6.3. Illustrations of mate drinking from Pierre Fossey, *Montevideo: 150 apuntes del natural* (Montevideo, Uru.: Ediciones Rex, 1962), 80–81.

Contemporary artists in Uruguay offered visions of traditional mate drinking among gauchos and rural dwellers, as in contemporary Argentina and southern Brazil, but they also showed current middle-class (rather than poor) urbanites drinking mate. For example, in 1962, artist Pierre Fossey—who was born to French painters in Paris and then moved to Montevideo in the 1930s, where he married an Uruguayan woman and lived until his death in 1976—made two illustrations of people in Montevideo drinking a mate (fig. 6.3). In his first illustration, Fossey depicted a well-dressed, fair-skinned man sitting on a bench under a grape arbor sipping his mate, the kettle at his feet suggesting this might be his garden at home. In the second, a middle-aged woman in a collared shirt is shown drinking from a mate, her thermos in the foreground.[48] The man and woman appear in separate sketches, but the tree extends over both, offering a vision of domestic mate drinking linked to the outdoors.

In contrast to these idyllic visions, domestic tranquility did not dominate 1960s or 1970s Uruguay. During this era, the political scene became more contentious—first internationally and then within national boundaries.

FIGURE 6.4. Uruguayan president Eduardo Haedo handing Ernesto "Che" Guevara a mate in Punta del Este, Uruguay, August 1961. From Mecha Gattás and Blanca Guiria, *Crónica de Punta del Este* (Montevideo: Linardi y Risso, 1987), 104; photographer unknown.

In August 1961, Uruguayan president Eduardo Haedo hosted the annual meeting of the Organization of American States in Punta del Este, Uruguay, as the Cuban government began moving toward socialism. In advance of the meeting, US president John F. Kennedy made clear that Latin American governments needed to show their loyalty to the United States or risk being associated with Cuba; there was no intermediary position in the Cold War intensifying between the United States and the Soviet Union. And yet a black-and-white photograph captured Haedo amicably sharing a mate with the Cuban representative, Argentine-born revolutionary Ernesto "Che" Guevara (fig. 6.4).

Political tension had dominated the first closed-door meeting between Haedo and Guevara, but at their second meeting, Haedo's cook, María, apparently offered her boss a thermos and mate. "Would you like a mate, my friend?" Haedo asked Guevara, who accepted with great enthusiasm. Whether or not this was exactly how it happened, the story and photograph

Chapter Six

of this mate became a potent symbol of how this ritual connected would-be political adversaries. In Uruguay, this shared mate is remembered as establishing an enduring friendship between the two men while sparking an international political crisis.[49] Uruguayans were divided between those who were inspired by or appalled by the revolutionary ethos embodied by Guevara, and those who wished for a more intermediary position.

As in many places across the globe, including Argentina in the 1960s and Uruguay in the early 1970s, students, workers, and activists banded together to work toward a more egalitarian order. In Uruguay, as wages precipitously declined, some strikers began to bring their mates and thermoses with them to the picket lines. In photos of the 1964 sugarcane workers' strike, men hold mates and thermoses as they wait to register in the lead-up to their march.[50]

The previous year, a young labor organizer named Raúl Sendic founded the National Liberation Movement–Tupamaros to improve labor conditions for impoverished sugar workers. The Tupamaros became South America's best-known urban leftist group, owing to its guerrilla-style activism. According to political scientist Patrice McSherry, members of this group initially adopted a "Robin Hood" strategy, lobbying for poor workers and seeking to embarrass the police and military. In 1967, after new president Jorge Pacheco Areco banned several political parties on the left and decreed a wage and price freeze in his first weeks in office, the Tupamaros took up arms. In response to US-backed Uruguayan death squads' disappearance and murder of political opponents, the Tupamaros kidnapped and killed various paramilitary leaders. In April 1972, paramilitary squads supported by the Uruguayan government and buoyed by US training and funding launched a brutal campaign of violence that within six months decimated the capabilities of this group to effectively resist.[51]

On March 13, 1973, the first edition of a new magazine called *Mate Amargo* (Bitter mate) appeared, launched by some of the surviving members of the National Liberation Movement–Tupamaros.[52] The editorial team not only named the magazine after the once again explicitly political local drink but also adopted the figure of a gaucho with a trident (or three-pointed spear) sipping from a mate as their logo. The editors made their intentions clear early on, specifying in the first edition, "For two decades the country has been sinking in an inexorable crisis with the increasingly violent confrontation between different sectors and the loss of our national individuality." They continued, "We want to be a bitter mate, a facilitator of relationships and fruitful exchange between Orientales."[53] As this quote suggests, the team behind *Mate Amargo* still held out hope that frank journalistic inquiry and some mate could bring Uruguayans together again. For the next two months, the editorial staff pumped out weekly editions of this magazine with brave commentaries questioning the state of national and international politics. One of the last known pre-dictatorship editions, released on May 6, 1973, featured a cover story about the CIA's campaigns against Peronist Hugo Campora in Argentina and Democratic Socialist Salvador Allende in Chile.[54]

On June 27, 1973, the Uruguayan military seized control of the executive branch in what is often referred to as the *auto-golpe* (self-inflicted coup). President Juan María Bordaberry, elected in which many considered to be a fraudulent election in 1971, dissolved parliament and suspended the constitution, forming a council that granted power to the armed forces and continuing as its figurehead. Prior to this historic day, Uruguay's constitutionalist military had not attempted a government takeover. Now the military's actions shattered the long-standing idea of Uruguay as the "Switzerland of South America," rooted in its history of social democracy and relative prosperity.[55]

For the next two weeks, workers across Uruguay participated in a national strike.[56] Photographs by Aurelio González, a former metalworker who became a documentary photographer working for the communist publication *El popular*, show still-optimistic workers occupying factories and workshops, sometimes with a thermos and mate in hand.[57] In the occupation of the PHUASA textile factory, for example, a group of eight women and two children smile for the camera (fig. 6.5). The woman in the center of the frame sips from a mate; to her right, two women make peace signs, the one closest to her holding a thermos.[58] Here, the women demonstrate the joy of solidarity and hope that their sacrifices will lead to better working conditions in Uruguay.

The brutality of the new military regime quashed any expectations for a peaceful reconciliation. Eduardo Galeano, Uruguay's celebrated writer, explains that "the guerilla threat provided the alibi for State terrorism, which set its wheels in motion to cut workers' salaries in half, crush unions, and suppress critical thought."[59] Bordaberry censored the press while the state's paramilitary death squads ramped up kidnapping, torture, and murders. After targeting the organized labor movement and purging universities and schools of leftist instructors, their campaigns of terror expanded.[60] In a country with just 3 million inhabitants at the time, some 60,000 people were detained by the military. With 1 in 50 Uruguayans illegally incarcerated over the course of the dictatorship, Uruguay claimed the unfortunate distinction of possessing the highest rate of political incarceration in the world.[61]

FIGURE 6.5. Photograph taken by Aurelio González of striking workers occupying the PHUASA textile factory, June–July 1973. Courtesy of the photographer, from published collection of photographs, *Fui testigo: Una historia en imágenes* (Montevideo, Uru.: Ediciones CMDF, 2011), 47.

Even those who avoided detention centers suffered during the dictatorship.[62] Many lost loved ones or saw them flee into exile, as some 14 percent of Uruguayans did.[63] Galeano argued that in the end, "everyone was imprisoned . . . three million prisoners even if the jails seemed to hold only a few thousand." He continued, "Invisible hoods covered the rest as well, condemned to isolation and incommunication [*sic*], even if they were spared the torture."[64]

Uruguayans recall that people brought their mates and thermoses into the streets under the dictatorship as a subtle form of rejecting military rule. Uruguayan anthropologist Daniel Vidart observed of mate that a "political sector of the Uruguayan population wielded it as social insignia, as an indicator of rebellion," bringing mate to places previously considered unacceptable. In this way, leftist mate drinkers—like independence soldiers before them—made the local drink into a potent political symbol of dissent against the ruling government.[65] At a minimum, that is how it is remembered. "Mate was a symbol of protest in Uruguay," an Argentine woman who spent time in Uruguay told me.[66] A Uruguayan historian recalled that before the dictatorship, mate was enjoyed in the "intimacy of the family," but during the dictatorship, it helped make "certain sectors of society visible." A Uruguayan librarian concurred,

"In the beginning who drank mate in the street was reserved to the left . . . and now it has become generalized."[67]

As we have seen, the public consumption of mate and its association with the political left predated the dictatorship. In 1967, Assunçao already spoke with great reverence of Uruguayans' desire to drink and show off their mates beyond the confines of the home. Photographs of President Haedo and Che Guevara sharing a mate outdoors and sugar strikers with their thermoses and mates attest to this idea. So too the publication of a new critical leftist magazine, *Mate Amargo*, in 1973 in the months prior to the dictatorship reveals an earlier association. Even so, the memory of mate as a symbol of Uruguayan protest against the dictatorship gained strength, subsuming this earlier history in the popular imagination. As a result, Uruguayans tend to remember the initiation of public mate drinking as a courageous act in response to a vicious dictatorship.[68]

ARGENTINE HORRORS, MATE EULOGIES, AND REVIVALS, 1970S–1980S

While Uruguayans preserve the memory of leftists taking to the street with their mates during the dictatorship, Argentines often associate the public urban consumption of mate with the return of democracy after the dictatorship they endured from 1976 to 1983. Unlike in Uruguay, it does not appear that members of the Argentine resistance made mate into an explicit symbol of their resistance. But that does not mean they did not drink it. Union members and leftist activists regularly shared mates with their comrades prior to, during, and after the military dictatorship.[69] And while leftist political magazines in Argentina such as *El descamisado* and *Evita Montonera* did not explicitly embrace mate as a symbol in the way their Uruguayan counterparts did, the humoristic magazine *Satiricón* regularly used the local drink as a way to offer humorous commentary on politics, social class, gender norms, sexuality, and national identity in the lead-up to the dictatorship.[70] Because mate lacked a leftist political charge in Argentina as it did in Uruguay, and because yerba was also a business in Argentina, the military junta's neoliberal economic philosophy enabled Argentine museums, media outlets, and advertisers to publicly celebrate the local drink during the dictatorship.

On March 24, 1976, the Argentine military seized power of the executive branch. While this did not represent a death knell for mate, it would for many labor activists, academics, and journalists, as well as their families, friends, and acquaintances. On the morning of the coup, a member of the state workers' union in Villa María in the province of Córdoba, Cacho Mengarelli, recalled that after being awoken at 4 a.m. with the chilling but anticipated news, a few hours later he left to buy biscuits for mate, and when he returned, he found military and police officers surrounding the union. "In the back, we had already burned the books and all the papers that probably would have compromised us," he explained. "The thing is that [one of the union members nicknamed] El Gallo [the Rooster] opens the door as calmly as possible and offers them a mate." Perhaps as a result of this classic gesture, while the military men harassed and intimidated the union members, they did not do more on this occasion, as they soon would to labor organizers and union members.[71]

To the northeast, when Eugenio Kalsaba, a member of the yerba growers' association in Oberá, Misiones, that advocated for better labor conditions (called the Movimiento Agrario de Misiones—MAM—or Agrarian Movement of Misiones), awoke on the morning of the coup, he and his father engaged in their ritual of turning on the radio and heating water for mate. Chillingly, they found every station up and down the dial to be blasting "Avenida de las camelias," the military's favorite marching band song. They understood immediately that a coup had taken place. "Papá, el golpe, el golpe" (Dad, the coup, the coup), Eugenio said. In an effort to calm his son, Eugenio's father told him, "Come, let's have a mate." As journalist Teo Ballvé, who relayed this story, suggests, "Even in the worst of times—or especially in the worst of times—drinking an infusion of yerba mate . . . is a fixture of daily life."[72] The military declared the MAM and other workers' unions illegal and began to target their leaders. In November 1976, they arrested, tortured, and killed labor MAM leader Pedro Oreste Peczak in Oberá before returning his mutilated body to his family as a macabre warning to local labor activists and those who loved them.[73]

The state's murder of Peczak was far from an isolated incident. Over the course of its self-declared "Dirty War," the Argentine military junta ushered in a new level of state-led violence, abetted by the coordinated efforts of Operation Condor. From 1976 to 1983, the Argentine military disappeared an estimated 30,000 people.[74] Members of the military savagely tortured detainees in clandestine detention centers before killing most and burying many in unmarked gravesites or dumping their bodies in the sea.[75]

In Argentina, as in Uruguay, a ruthless military government violently quashed the revolutionary dreams of young people, leftists, and their family and friends who dreamed of a more equal world. The junta combined its campaign of disappearances with an official veil of silence, formally ending the freedom of the press and making public gatherings, union organizing, and political parties illegal.[76] It also prohibited any "reference to subjects related to subversive incidents, the appearance of bodies and the deaths of subversive elements and/or members of the armed or security forces, unless these are announced by a responsible official source."[77] These measures created what sociologist Juan Corradi called a "culture of fear," in which self-censorship became vital to survival.[78]

The military junta's campaign shut down most avenues for the public expression of ideas. It clamped down on universities, the media, and the industrial workplace. After the coup, workers in the Acindar steel mill, for example, lost job security and suffered deteriorating work conditions. A former steelworker recalled that management prohibited mate drinking in an effort to suppress social bonding. While workers would have likely protested such a policy in the past, now they snuck a heater into a closet and hid out there to drink mate in short shifts of five to ten minutes. "When the boss found out, he threw the mate and everything else into the liquid steel," the worker recalled.[79]

As a result of such draconian measures, the military threatened to quash the previous commitment to sociability both inside and outside the workplace. In a sense, "only the voice of the state remained, addressing itself to an atomized collection of inhabitants," as Luis Alberto Romero has eloquently argued.[80] Yet while intellectual and political debates were silenced or pushed underground, certain types of non-state-led discourse persisted. Outside of work, it was acceptable and even encouraged to talk about presumably apolitical topics like food and drink under a military junta eager to promote criollo nationalism, culinary and otherwise.[81] Furthermore, since one of the military's primary objectives was to implement a free market "by force," as Minister of the Economy José Alfredo Martínez de Hoz put it, corporations were not only permitted but encouraged to promote their products.[82]

Yerba interests were no exception. In 1976, the six leading Argentine brands banded together to create the Asociación Promotora de Yerba Mate.[83] Soon thereafter, the association published a shiny, thirteen-page pamphlet on the history and modern process of making yerba mate. The companies celebrated that their association represented the "large industry that brings men and women together with a common goal: to provide a whole, nutritious food for all ages."[84]

The companies behind this initiative energetically promoted their brands via print and television advertisements before and during the dictatorship.[85] Las Marías, which sold the brand Taraguï, began working with an advertising agency in the early 1970s. One year into the dictatorship, the company released a handful of television advertisements touting the quality of its Taragüi-brand yerba. In one, a man reading a newspaper sips from a mate and chastises his wife for giving him a mate with yerba other than Taraguï. (Like in earlier generations of advertisements, the woman was the one expected to shop and serve the domestic mate.) In another, a well-known actor, Daniel Guerrero, pitches the convenience of Taraguï tea bags. And in a third and fourth, the company promotes its filtered yerba, which could be used in an automatic coffee maker, to brew mate.[86] Although this experiment did not take off, it reveals the extent to which companies continued to innovate and promote new products during this era.

Neoliberal policies not only spurred promotional campaigns but also imports. In Uruguay, locals continued to fill their mates with Brazilian yerba and infuse them with water from imported thermoses. In Argentina, more consumers began to adopt the thermos as an accompaniment to drink their nationally produced yerba, as prices for imported thermoses dropped with the neoliberal opening. Valeria, a fifty-year-old woman, remembered receiving her first Brazilian-made thermos for Christmas in 1977 or 1978. "It was cream-colored with an orange spout," she recalled. Her family, who lived in a small city outside the capital, did not use the thermos when they drank mate at home, only when they went out. "My father took it with him when he went fishing. We brought it when we went on a picnic or camping."[87]

In 1982, Argentine comedian and mate fan Luis Landriscina suggested that Argentines who did not like mate thought it a "waste of time." In contrast, Landriscina, who shared that he learned how to "properly" infuse a mate in Uruguay and carried a thermos with him everywhere he went, suggested that mate stimulated work, helped alleviate hunger, and served as a valuable "symbol of friendship."[88]

La Nación ran a contemporaneous piece with quotes from famous Argentine writers about their relationship to mate. While some still drank mate at home, others associated mate drinking with the past or with rural settings. Jorge Luis Borges, for example, recalled drinking a lot of mate as a child but confessed he had "lost the habit." Silvana Bullrich shared that she used to drink mate often when her family had a *tambo* (dairy farm). Ernesto Sabato explained that only high-class families with a strong connection to rural life still drank mate; he blamed urban elites' distaste on British influence.[89] For his part, Bernardo Kordon said that he enjoyed mate and drank it in Chile and Rio Grande do Sul, Brazil, concluding, "The truth is that mate is the national brew that the Argentine cultivates outside of the country, like the tango."[90]

Even as some intellectuals and elites imagined that Argentina's national drink had greater purchase beyond the nation's borders, Argentines in the provinces told different stories. Across most of the country, mate remained an everyday staple. For example, Verónica, a woman who grew up in an impoverished town in the province of Córdoba in the 1970s and early 1980s, shared that she did not know a single person who did not drink mate there, describing mate as "the only comfort" for people living in poverty. Her family purchased as much loose yerba as they could afford and augmented it with wild herbs, including peppermint, spearmint, lemongrass, or lemon balm, as was typical in this province. Her grandmother Elba, the matriarch of her family and their small community, oversaw regular rounds of mate outdoors where "romances and relationships were started and ended, and big decisions were made." At school, Verónica volunteered to distribute bread and brewed mate (served with milk in good times).[91]

As mate continued to play a central role in the daily lives of rural dwellers and the poor, it assumed a new public presence in 1980s Buenos Aires as more media outlets and museums celebrated and even eulogized Argentina's long mate history. They frequently referred to the time when elites collected and served guests elaborate mates covered in silver, or when gauchos roamed the plains and drank mate in the open air.

In June 1978, *La Nación* magazine ran a two-page story on Josefina Ruiz Falco de Pérez Fernández y Moreno, the Spanish ambassador's wife, talking with Adolfo P. Ribera, the director of the Museo de Bellas Artes, to discuss her mate collection featuring dozens of antique and elaborate silver mates. As Ribera noted, "The original mate, a simple 'cured' gourd, was not suited to the refined lifestyles of the upper classes and the process of embellishment began."[92] That year, the Buenos Aires ethnographic museum began to feature its collection of silver mates and *apartadores* (mate separators or strainers popular in the early colonial era), and the Museo Fernández Blanco showed off its collection of antique fine arts mates too.[93] In this way, the mate became fine art—an elegant decoration rather than a useful, embellished vessel from which to drink.

In 1981, the Argentine military government's Ministry of Public Works staged a free mate exhibit during the summer vacation, sponsored by the state-run oil company, Yacimiento Petroliferos Fiscales. The public oil company's showroom included a few shiny silver and porcelain mates, but the exhibit's focus was on more simple mates made from gourds or pieces of wood. Visitors saw these humble mates and listened to *ranchera* music, read about rural foods like *tortas fritas* (fried dough), and witnessed the artwork originally featured in Villanueva's 1964 art book. One Argentine gentleman who attended the exhibit remarked, "I've known all these things . . . and they're already in the museum; so, I can't have much hope."[94]

While this gentleman had lived this history, another exhibit targeting children ages five to eight sought to familiarize them with the history of mate drinking and revive interest. Founded in 1948, the Museo de Motivos Argentinos José Hernández, named in honor of the author of the epic poem about the gaucho Martín Fierro, had long celebrated rural traditions and possessed an extensive mate collection.[95] At the start of 1983, it debuted a new program conceived by the head of the Cultural Division, Graciela Taquini, to introduce children to Argentina's folkloric history through an interactive exhibit on mate. The exhibit aimed to engender in Argentine children a love of their own traditions.[96] The mate exhibit started not with the Guaraní or colonial elites but with the gaucho. Kids were encouraged to visit the museum's *pulpería*, where they bought mate supplies and moved outside to collect water in the garden and learned the art of preparing a mate around the campfire.[97]

The following year, after the dictatorship had fallen, the Museo de Motivos Argentinos, José Hernandez, hosted another mate exhibit for adults, sponsored by the new democratically elected Argentine government and Yacimiento Petroliferos Fiscales. In a pamphlet made for the exhibit, the director of the museum, Professor María Carmen Lauría, shared her hope that the exhibition's symbolism, which focused on the "fraternal criolla friendship that crosses borders . . . would serve as a vehicle for lasting union and peace."[98] With the restoration of democracy, Lauría articulated her hopes for a peaceful future in Argentina and throughout the Río de la Plata region.

Profound hopefulness accompanied the restoration of democracy of Argentina in 1983. But first there was war. In the early 1980s, the Argentine military's hold over the nation became precarious in the face of mounting economic problems and human rights protests led by the Mothers and Grandmothers of the Plaza de Mayo, which drew international pressure.[99] In March 1982, the military junta invaded the Malvinas (Falkland) Islands in an effort to buoy national pride by reclaiming these islands from the British. Overly optimistic that Britain would not respond, military leaders sent woefully underprepared and under-resourced soldiers. A telling artifact of this ultimately unsuccessful war is the *mate malvinero* (or Malvinas mate), made out of an empty combat grenade with the empty tube of a ballpoint pen used as the bombilla. As yerba mate researcher Jerónimo Lagier writes, "I can imagine how cold, empty, and anguished they must have felt, but at least they could find some comfort and balance in that safe and real mate . . . made with what was at hand, and . . . shared with someone that would watch their backs when death knocked at the door."[100]

Like the soldiers to whom Lagier refers, for many civilians, mate acted as an anchor, enabling a sense of normalcy and connection to help survive the dark period of military rule. When Argentine expat Mirta Inés Trupp visited her family in Buenos Aires and southern Argentina, they shared regular daily rounds of mate.[101] As it had for centuries, mate accompanied the rhythms of everyday life under military rule across the Río de la Plata region.

DRINKING MATE IN PUBLIC? URBAN URUGUAY
AND ARGENTINA, 1980S–1990S

The political landscape shifted dramatically as the countries of the Río de la Plata experienced a wave of youthful rebellion and left-leaning optimism in the 1960s, followed by a tsunami of right-wing oppression in the 1970s and early 1980s. In October 1983, constitutional democracy returned to Argentina. The process of democratic restoration started earlier in Uruguay with the 1980 referendum, but presidential elections were not held there until 1984, and the newly democratically elected president took office in March 1985.[102] With the revival of democracy, new governments began taking stock of the political and socioeconomic situation they inherited.

The Argentine military junta that promised to bring economic stability had accrued massive debt, and the cost of living became prohibitive. Food and drink prices skyrocketed, and people had to get by with less.[103] What did this mean for the consumption of yerba mate? As we saw earlier in this chapter, since at least the mid-twentieth century, yerba consumption increased as resources decreased in Argentina. The poorest sectors typically drank the most mate, the middle sectors the next most, and the wealthiest, the least. While coffee consumption dropped off by a third from 1965 to 1986 due to its high price, lower-priced yerba became even more desirable, accounting for 75 percent of the overall infusion category during this period. Still, deteriorating economic conditions forced poor families to restrict their consumption of yerba by 40 percent. Unlike their better-off peers, the poor had not replaced yerba with another more coveted stimulant; instead, they had to get by with less of the least expensive option. The 1987 crisis, when the yerba supply fell short and prices skyrocketed, further intensified this trend.[104]

There is scant evidence to suggest any meaningful decline in late twentieth-century Uruguayan yerba consumption or major distinctions in patterns of consumption by social class. After the fall of the dictatorship, members of the middle classes began to consume even more mate in public. Photographs from the late 1980s show Uruguayans drinking mate at central markets and fishermen doing the same, always with a thermos nearby.[105] Many in Uruguay also used the thermos to drink mate at home, including well-known writers who began to feature a mate and thermos in their photographs both before and after the dictatorship. Before, Francisco "Paco" Espínola appears in a famous photograph tipping a thermos into a mate in what looks to be his living room.[106] And after, Juan Carlos Onetti slurps mate through a bombilla in bed, with the requisite thermos next to him on the bedside table, in another well-traveled photograph.[107] If Argentine writers like Jorge Luis Borges and Silvana Bullrich had lived on the other side of the River Plate, it is far less likely that they would have stopped drinking mate.

In the aftermath of the dictatorship, Uruguayans also began to participate in large-scale, politically charged rounds of mate referred to as *mateadas*. Lucía Topolansky, a former member of the Tupamaros who went on to become a senator and the wife of fellow activist, politician, and eventual president José Mujica (2010–15), told a Spanish journalist that Raúl Sendic deserved credit for initiating this practice. With the return of democracy in 1985, this former leader of the Tupamaros and his comrades emerged from some fourteen harrowing years in prison, much of it spent in isolation. Topolansky recalled, "To reinsert themselves into political activity and reconnect with members of society, the old Tupamaros began to organize '*mateadas*' in neighborhoods and plazas. With each sip, they were shaping their self-critiques and learning to act on the 'surface.'" Tupamaros from the past not only initiated *mateadas*, a political tradition that persists in Uruguay and Argentina to this day, but also revived their magazine, *Mate Amargo*, and established an affiliated radio station and editorial press.[108]

More professional Uruguayans also began drinking mate at work in the post-dictatorial era. When historian Gustavo Laborde began working at the Uruguayan newspaper *El País* in 1988, no one in the main writers' room drank mate at work. But a couple of months later, journalists, fueled by mate, typed up their stories.[109] After moving to television in 1989, journalist Omar Gutiérrez became the first to drink mate on camera, with a thermos on set and a cigarette in hand.[110] By the 1990s, more white-collar employees in Montevideo had replaced coffee or tea with mate in the workplace.[111] In 2006, leftist members of the Uruguayan Congress began to bring their mates and thermoses with them into session.[112]

Not everyone in Uruguay thought highly of professional and public mate drinking. Some critiqued Uruguayan senators' lack of decorum for drinking mate during official business.[113] In upscale destinations in Uruguay, such as the posh beach town of Punta del Este, where South American elites mingled, drinking mate in public remained taboo. Leandro Sagastizabal recalled that when his yerba-producing family from Corrientes, Argentina, took out their mate kit in Punta del Este in the mid-1980s, they felt they were being looked down upon, perhaps due to mate's association with the poorer sectors of society or to their own self-consciousness.[114]

On the other side of the River Plate, Argentines still mostly drank mate at home. Verónica, whose grandmother oversaw rounds of mate outside her home in Corrientes, remembered that when she and her family arrived in Buenos Aires in 1986, she noticed that people drank mate inside their homes in a more "solitary and rushed manner" than the long and social outdoor rounds to which she was accustomed in the rural community where she grew up. And while members of the working class possessed a history of drinking mate or *mate cocido* at work, no one I spoke with suggested that white-collar employees had started to drink mate at work yet in Argentina, even as some recalled drinking mate (sometimes with a thermos) while studying or on vacation in the 1980s.[115]

Buenos Aires took the lead but was not the only Argentine city where public mate drinking was frowned upon in the late 1980s. In 1988, Victor Saguier left his native city of Asunción, Paraguay, and went to visit his then girlfriend, Victoria Szychowski, in the city of Corrientes. The daughter of one of the largest Argentine yerba producers, La Cachuera, and an enthusiast of this bitter green infusion, Victoria brought her mate, yerba, and thermos along for the ride. Nearly three decades later, Victor recalled, "I said to her, if you're going to make mate, let me know." But the couple decided to wait to make the mate until they left the city. For Victor (an engineer who became the president of the Yerba Mate Millers Association in Misiones), this decision stuck with him as an example of how drinking mate in the city remained distasteful up through the late 1980s.[116]

While some popular memories suggest that city-dwelling Argentines began to drink mate in the plaza with the fall of the dictatorship, the practice did not become widespread right away. Most Argentines I spoke with recalled first seeing people drink mate with a thermos in the city only in the 1990s. Two women who arrived in Buenos Aires in 1992 separately remembered being struck by the numbers of people in the plazas, some of whom drank mate.[117] A woman named Flor recalled that her father's family of British and German descent did not drink mate but instead served a British-style tea service on their ranch in the southern Patagonia region. Mate "was poorly seen" and "associated with the lower classes," she noted, when her parents were growing up in the mid-twentieth century. But in 1993, she and her siblings started drinking mate with a thermos on the beach and even convinced their parents to join them.[118]

Flor's family did not represent an isolated case. Contemporary travel books made evident the extent to which yerba mate had regained its place in Argentine culture. In the 1990s, Lonely Planet guidebook authors Wayne Bernhardson and María Massolo (both scholars with doctoral degrees: the latter an anthropologist from the province of Buenos Aires, and the former a geographer from the United States who had lived in South America) argued that mate drinking "captured the essence of *argentinidad*" (Argentine identity) and was "perhaps the only cultural practice that transcends barriers of ethnicity, class, and occupation."[119] Argentines drank four times more mate than coffee, they pointed out, often enjoying it for breakfast or with sweet pastries for an afternoon snack. The guidebook encouraged readers to not refuse an invitation to drink mate with locals but rather to appreciate it as a "sign of acceptance." They continued, "More than a simple drink like tea or coffee, mate is an elaborate ritual, shared among family, friends, and coworkers. In many ways, sharing is the point of mate."[120]

Even as Bernhardson and Massolo highlighted the connection between Argentine national identity and mate drinking in Argentina, they provided evidence that suggested it played a similar or even stronger role in neighboring nations. They pointed out that Uruguayans drank twice as much yerba per capita as their Argentine counterparts (some ten kilograms), "lugging a thermos wherever they go." They emphasized that Paraguayans preferred the "ice-cold *tereré*," mentioning that trying this local drink "can be a good introduction to Paraguay and its people."[121]

Like travelers in the past, tourists embraced mate and tereré as ways of learning about local culture. These attempts sometimes produced humorous misunderstandings. The owners of a store selling all things mate related in Buenos Aires called Kelly's Todo Mates shared an anecdote with me about a group of tourists from the United States who bought one mate and five bombillas so that they each could drink out of their own straw. They apparently missed or dismissed the point that sharing the bombilla as well as the mate remained central to the ritual.[122]

In contrast, the dramatic impact of soaring inflation and rising food prices was no laughing matter in late 1980s Argentina. Given the country's massive debt and pressures from international lending agencies with free-market philosophies, Argentines began to see the inevitability of neoliberal policies and elected a new president, Carlos Menem (1989–99), who implemented them. As historian Jennifer Adair demonstrates, this was part of a broader regional trend in which the post–World War II acceptance of state-led development and the post-dictatorial emphasis on human rights was tabled in favor of the free market.[123]

Menem's neoliberal policies and the crisis they provoked proved particularly damaging for small yerba farmers. In 1991, Menem's government dissolved the Comisión Reguladora de la Producción y Comercio de la Yerba Mate (or CRYM), which previously set limits on yerba production. Large yerba companies dramatically increased production, leading to plummeting prices that decimated the profits of smaller farmers. As in other sectors of the economy, wealth in the yerba industry became more concentrated within the largest firms that possessed the technology to process yerba on their own. The rise of major supermarket chains further decreased profit margins for producers. By the mid-1990s, the Argentine yerba sector began to feel the effects of unregulated overproduction.[124] "In a lot of ways, the 1990s were worse for the MAM than the dictatorship," Ramón Martín Enríquez, a MAM member and military detainee, told a journalist. Farmers sold their land to large yerba companies better positioned to absorb the economic shock, and the province's deforestation for large-scale yerba production and monoculture intensified.[125]

The situation exploded in 2001, when yerba farmers drove their old tractors into the center of Posadas, the capital of Misiones, where they stayed for the next couple months. Before the dissolution of the CRYM, yerba producers received twenty cents per kilo, but a decade later, at the height of the 2000–2001 crisis, they commanded only a tenth of this value (or two cents), which did not even cover production costs. The yerba farmers' protest led to the founding of the Instituto Nacional de la Yerba Mate in 2002, which had a similar charge to the previously dissolved CRYM, including setting off a biannual agreed-upon minimum price per kilo of yerba.[126]

Yerba-growing families in Oberá that belonged to the MAM decided to band together to provide a living wage for small yerba farmers and encourage more environmentally friendly ways of producing yerba in Misiones. In 2001, they launched a yerba brand called Titrayju, an abbreviation for their slogan of "tierra, trabajo, y justicia" (land, work, and justice). Their timing proved fortuitous. As the neoliberal system came crashing down, solidarity networks and alternative markets emerged across the country. Teo Ballvé explains, "The social upheaval allowed Titrayju to easily fulfill its strategy of circumventing all intermediaries and selling a value-added finished product directly to the consumer. The result was grassroots, word-of-mouth marketing. Titrayju soon became known as the *'yerba of the piqueteros,'* as Argentina's militant unemployed workers are known."[127] Titrayju yerba offered a different model for small yerba farmers that allowed them to survive and even thrive in the early 2000s.

In contrast, the most vulnerable yerba workers, or *tareferos*, employed to pick yerba on the land of others, continued to suffer the long history of exploitation and precarity at the beginning of the commodity chain.[128] A 1996 exposé published in the magazine *Viva* shared the experiences of the 12,000 or so seasonal workers in Argentina's northeastern corner who found themselves on the lowest, most precarious rung of the yerba commodity chain. Most hailed from local families and worked for the 100 industrial yerba firms or the 15,000 smaller farmers, the majority descendants of Poles, Ukrainians, and Germans, "something like the yerba middle class," the article explained. The author continued that while these settlers owned lands, animals, and homes with light and running water, the harvesters possessed none of these things. "The more fortunate live in small shacks made of corrugated iron and cardboard; the less fortunate live in the open, in other people's fields, among snakes and spiders." Children as young as five years old, who frequently joined their parents in this work, also endured these brutal conditions reminiscent of those first critiqued by Jesuit priests in the colonial era.[129]

~~~~~~

In the 1990s as previously, those with power in the yerba industry focused more on reaching consumers than on addressing the enduring exploitation of wage laborers. In 1992, the government of the province of Misiones, which produced 90 percent of Argentina's yerba and drew half of its revenue from this crop, decided to launch a three-year promotional campaign. As in the late 1960s, the plan was to highlight mate as a drink for young people and the "ideal complement to the hustle and bustle of big cities," while seeking to raise its social standing and pointing to the ways in which this infusion embodied traditional values.[130] It set out to celebrate mate as a key symbol of national identity and a regional drink: "a custom that unites" the people of Argentina, Brazil, Paraguay, and Uruguay "more than any other." The promotional campaign planned to show how "mate is consumed in Brazil (in a large gourd) and in Uruguay (in the street, at work, etc.)" to increase yerba mate consumption within Argentina.[131]

By the 1990s, the specific way in which South Americans enjoyed their yerba had become a key indicator of supposedly national traits. In a 1998 book called *Culture and Customs of Argentina*, cultural studies scholars, like local marketers and travel guide writers, drew attention to different mate drinking practices and ideas about them along national lines. "Uruguayans are much more likely to drink it on the street, carrying thermoses with them everywhere they go," the scholars observed. "This habit is disparaged by the Argentines, who feel that *mate* should be drunk in the home, the 'civilized way.'" For their part, "Paraguayans . . . often enjoy their *mate* ice cold, while Brazilians prefer to use very large gourds."[132]

Despite their promises to diminish the importance of political borders and increase prosperity, late twentieth-century neoliberal policies intensified nationalist sentiments and region-wide economic crises. In Argentina, Menem's 1990s neoliberal policy, which touted privatization, austerity measures, and dollarization (or the pegging of the value of the Argentine peso to the US dollar) as the panacea to an unstable, inflation-ridden economy, came crashing down at the start of the twenty-first century. In 2001, Menem's successor, Fernando de la Rúa (1999–2001), defaulted on foreign loans and froze bank accounts, sparking waves of protest. In early January 2002, Eduardo Duhalde (2002–3), who became Argentina's fifth president in two weeks, de-pegged the peso from the dollar, causing many middle-class Argentines to lose the bulk of their savings overnight.

For Argentine consumers, the fallout of the 2001–2 crisis was not only political and economic but also cultural. With growing poverty and economic dependency, more Argentines came to believe that they lived in a Third World Latin American country.[133] According to Victor Saguier, after the crisis, Argentines tried to "value our own, the autochthonous, our music, our customs. Mate was part of this valuing of what is ours."[134] While members of the popular sectors never lost their appreciation for mate, their more economically comfortable counterparts rejoined them. In 2005, per capita consumption of yerba in Argentina was measured at 6.4 kilograms versus just 0.9 kilograms for coffee and 0.16 for tea.[135] In some ways this was out of necessity; yerba mate was far less expensive than competing stimulants. A 2004 article stated that yerba cost only $0.25 per liter while the same amount of coffee cost $14.00 and tea $10.60.[136] But price was not the only factor. As Argentine yerba interests had long hoped, a new generation of young people took the lead in embracing the local stimulant. A 2004 survey found that 89 percent of urban Argentines drank mate, with young people buying the majority of yerba.[137]

Traversing the city of Buenos Aires in the early twenty-first century, visitors, myself included, frequently witnessed groups of (often young) people drinking mate together on a blanket in the park or bench in the plaza. Some Argentines even began to bring mate with them to their white-collar jobs, like the archivists who first introduced me to this local drink in their break room. Coca-Cola sought to capitalize on yerba's rebounding popularity by launching a new, short-lived soda called Nativa (or Native), infused with yerba extract. And a small number of bars with regional flair began to serve a mate with a thermos and a basket of bread and pastries to tourists, students, and office workers in the afternoon.[138] Still, most Argentines continued to associate the ritual of mate drinking with noncommercial settings.

Indeed, even as young urban Argentines became more enamored with mate in the early twenty-first century, their counterparts in Uruguay appeared even more so to Argentines. For instance, an Argentine colleague in Buenos Aires asked me, "Do you know how you can tell an Argentine and Uruguayan apart?" After replying that I did not, he said that you could pick out a Uruguayan by looking for someone porting a thermos with hot water to infuse their mate. Like other urban Argentines, he explained with a chuckle that Uruguayans have "tres brazos" (three arms).[139] And indeed, in the capital city of Montevideo, I saw a striking number of people walking with thermoses tucked under their arms or sitting and enjoying a mate with a friend or loved one at a plaza or along the long *rambla* that skirts the Río de la Plata.

Despite Uruguay's lack of productive capacity and because of its smaller size and late twentieth-century history of more conspicuous consumption, Uruguayan identity became even more tightly linked with this native infusion than Argentine identity around the turn of the twenty-first century. As a journalist explained in 2009, in Montevideo and other Uruguayan cities, men and women walked the streets with "their mate kit attached to their bodies." This practice, the journalist continued, "implies a posture: sustaining the thermos that keeps the water hot between the left arm and the torso, as if embracing a small child, while the other hand holds the cup or gourd."[140] This Uruguayan posture emerged in the 1960s when mate consumption in Argentina and Uruguay took different paths. In contrast to the middle-class Argentine shift away from and then back to mate, Uruguayans continued to publicly embrace it during the turbulent period spanning the 1960s to the early 2000s. As a result, it became one of the country's most potent identifying national characteristics.

Early twenty-first-century South Americans have regularly spoken about the supposedly national distinctions surrounding the local infusion. While both Argentines and Uruguayans, for example, drink mate, Uruguayans are recognized by Argentines and others for their propensity to do so with a thermos on city streets. For their part, Uruguayans describe Argentines (by which they often mean *porteños*) as less committed and knowledgeable about how to properly serve a mate. Some people in both countries express that Paraguayans like to drink a cold version of the infusion called tereré but do not drink mate. If a contemporary traveler had the good fortune to travel across the River Plate region in the early twenty-first century, as did I, they might find these supposedly national differences inaccurate. They would likely see Argentines in the yerba-producing northeastern corner of the country drinking a tereré or carrying a thermos out in the street or learn that Paraguayans often drink mate at home in the morning.[141]

For their part, the yerba-drinking and yerba-producing nations of Argentina, Brazil, and Paraguay possess a cultural but also an economic imperative to claim the local infusion as their "national patrimony." There are parallel and yet-to-be-told stories about how tereré became a symbol of national identity in Paraguay, while mate became a regional marker of the gaucho identity of southern Brazil in the period we have examined here.[142]

How would the regional food fight around yerba mate play out in the twenty-first century? Might laborers' exploitation ease? And would yerba interests finally succeed in expanding demand beyond South America to long-coveted markets such as the United States? Furthermore, how would the global COVID-19 pandemic affect this typically communal ritual? We will begin to contemplate the most recent chapter of this transnational yerba mate history in the epilogue.

EPILOGUE

A New Age for Yerba Mate?

In March 2020, the Montevideo desk of the Associated Press published a story about the impact of the COVID-19 pandemic on the practice of sharing mate and tereré in southern South America. "Mate, this infusion that in Uruguay, Argentina, and Paraguay is a gesture of welcome and an invitation to conversation has been converted into a weapon in the times of the coronavirus," declared journalist Gabriela Vaz. Disarming this "weapon" would necessitate major cultural shifts. For unfamiliar audiences, Vaz explained: "In none of the three countries is it customary to drink mate alone when in a group: doing so is considered almost rude. Sharing is not only a show of respect and cordiality: it is the genesis for these daily ceremonies."[1]

Across southern South America, officials implored citizens to practice social distancing and pause their communal practices around mate and tereré. "It is necessary to try to get used to not sharing anymore," warned Julio Mazzoleni, Paraguay's minister of health. In Uruguay, Eduardo Savio, an expert on infectious diseases, explained that such measures were needed given that "the virus is found in saliva. If you share a mate with another person, you could be sucking in saliva with the virus and . . . get infected." On the resort beaches of Punta del Este, Uruguay, a car drove around town blasting a recording imploring people to stop drinking mate together to avoid spreading the virus.

In Argentina, the National Yerba Mate Institute launched a new campaign: "Cada uno con su mate, nos cuidamos entre todos" (Everyone with their own mate, we will take care of each other).[2]

After witnessing several turning points in the long history of yerba mate over the course of this book, the early 2020s marked another significant moment. The global COVID-19 pandemic raised the possibility that the more than five-centuries-long tradition of drinking this infusion communally could become a relic of the past. Indeed, whereas scientists' attempts at the turn of the twentieth century to discourage the use of a common bombilla and cup largely fell on deaf ears, efforts to do so during the coronavirus outbreak have led to changes. "The COVID-19 pandemic dealt a severe blow to a regional custom," explained an article published on Argentina's 2021 National Mate Day. "The arguments that 'hot water kills the virus' or 'the napkin cleans the bombilla' were of no use."[3] As governments mandated stay-at-home orders and closed public spaces, more people drank mate or tereré at home. This ritualized circle, like so much of daily life, grew smaller. "It's ugly to be like this, without giving a kiss, without embracing, without sharing mate," Roberto Gervasoni, a sixty-seven-year-old blacksmith lamented, speaking to a journalist.[4]

The desire and willingness to participate in this daily, convivial ritual did not disappear. Some, like Gervasoni, stopped sharing mate in response to public health warnings, while others took to sharing mate with loved ones online, and some fought to retain the communal custom in person. For example, Ivan Vásquez, a kiosk worker in Montevideo accustomed to sharing mate with his favorite customers, said he had no intentions to stop. Given that he made this declaration in March 2020 before the pandemic accelerated in Uruguay, it is possible he later relented.[5]

In 2021, Argentine researchers took stock of the impact of COVID-19 and public health messaging on mate-related practices. They found that the Argentines they surveyed continued to drink roughly the same amount of mate as before, but fewer shared it with others due to their awareness of new health recommendations. Nearly everyone (96 percent) said they shared mate prior to the COVID-19 outbreak, but this figure dropped substantially with the epidemic. The majority of people, however, did not give up sharing mate, since almost three-quarters continued to drink mate with family members or roommates at home rather than with a wider circle of friends and colleagues as before.[6]

This epilogue poses several questions that swirl around yerba mate in the twenty-first century. What long-term impact will COVID-19 have on this communal ritual? Is yerba mate becoming a more global drink? Might it be possible to eradicate the long-standing exploitation of yerba workers? And last, why are nations and specific provinces launching formal claims to yerba mate and tereré as their own "intangible heritage," despite this drinkable plant's native origins and shared regional presence?

MAKING YERBA GLOBAL?

In the mediascape, yerba mate has never been more visible and accessible than in the last decade.[7] On social media, Pope Francis, South American actors, and even (when he was in office) President Barack Obama have appeared drinking mate.[8] South American soccer stars also served as particularly effective "yerba mate ambassadors" on the global stage. When Argentina made the semifinals of the 2022 World Cup, the *New York Times* ran a story asking whether the yerba mate that the team imbibed daily played a key role in their success. (They players said it did.) After Argentina emerged victorious, Lionel Messi appeared on Instagram in a well-traveled early-morning photograph of him in bed with a mate in one hand and the World Cup trophy in the other.[9]

In the contemporary United States, there are fewer mates like Messi's and more bottled yerba drinks. Consumers can find organic and flavor-enhanced iced yerba "teas" at most markets, health food stores, and gyms, especially in hip, urban areas.[10] As opposed to the bitter mate popular in much of South America, most of these bottled yerba drinks are sweetened to meet US consumers' taste preferences. They are also frequently associated with the Andes or Amazon regions rather than with the less well-known subtropical region from which this infusion hails.

The growing appetite for yerba mate across the globe coincides with the rise in popularity of so-called superfoods like quinoa, chia, and maca powder. As food scholar Jessica Loyer explains, superfoods are an "increasingly significant category of foods that are celebrated for their supposed extraordinary nutritional or medicinal properties, their histories of traditional use by ancient or Indigenous communities, and their 'natural' and 'authentic' qualities." Despite the fact that such food is unregulated, marketers encourage consumers in the West to seek out superfoods associated with native peoples and exotic locales as a way to become healthier and adopt more natural habits purportedly unaffected by the industrialization of the modern food supply.[11]

It is noteworthy that while Ross Jamieson understands coffee, tea, and chocolate on European tables as a visible demonstration of colonial success shaped by non-European cultural practices, and Marcy Norton sees chocolate as traveling to Europe with its Mesoamerican cultural associations and technologies largely intact, yerba mate required the contemporary interest in Indigenous cultures and categories, like superfoods, to gain a wider following outside of South America.[12] In this vein, advertisements and media promote yerba mate as a native South American superfood that will give US consumers energy, speed up their metabolism, and improve their health.[13] A 2019 *Real Simple* article, "This Superfood Tea Is an Anti-inflammatory Hero," for example, accurately described yerba mate as packed with antioxidants, vitamins B and C, zinc, potassium, and manganese. The piece argued, unrealistically given the prominence of other more familiar caffeinated drinks, that this "tea . . . [is] about to become your next healthy (caffeinated) beverage of choice."[14] Earlier promotional efforts in the United States to increase the popularity of yerba mate—for example, touting it as a healthy "tonic" in the 1920s and 1930s or as an aphrodisiac in the late 1960s (a claim that was quickly refuted)—failed. More recent campaigns and the easily accessible iced and bottled yerba drinks, however, seem to be making the drink popular today.[15] While the United States made up only 1.6 percent of Argentina's yerba exports in 2019, yerba interests and entrepreneurs see potential there. Furthermore, because the United States and other coveted markets in western Europe have gravitated toward bottled drinks instead of the original communal ritual of sharing mate, COVID has had little impact on sales.[16]

Even as consumers in the United States and western Europe long proved elusive, since the mid-twentieth century, people in Syria—and to a lesser but still significant extent, in Lebanon and Palestine—have shown an enduring commitment to importing yerba and drinking mate. In 2019, Syria imported a whopping three-quarters of all of Argentina's exports. How did this come to pass? As the third-largest immigrant group in Argentina after Italians and Spaniards, return migrants from the Levant began taking the custom back with them. As anthropologist Christine Folch explains, drinking mate became a powerful signifier of the Druze's history of transnational travel and wealth accumulation in southern South America.[17] By the 1940s, "Syrian's most appreciated gift was a barrel of 5 kilos of Cruz de Malta–brand yerba . . . and 12 La Mulata–brand bombillas tipped with a gold border," journalist Annabella Quiroga reports.[18] Yerba exports to Syria expanded dramatically in the second half of the twentieth century, surpassing a million kilos by the 1970s and, during the export boom of the 1990s, reaching some 13 million kilos by 1997. The 2011 war ushered in violence and a refugee crisis that continues today. It also led to a temporary decline in Syria's yerba imports. Even so, Syria imported a record 34.5 million kilos in 2018, and the following year the

Central Bank of Syria named yerba mate an "essential commodity," along with rice, sugar, baby formula, and medicine, highlighting its centrality to daily life there.[19]

Despite repeated attempts to promote yerba abroad, outside of the Syrian context exports have mainly gone to South American expatriate communities. The overwhelming majority of yerba is consumed within South America rather than outside it. The Paraguayan yerba industry continues to produce primarily for Paraguayans but exports relatively small amounts to expatriate communities in Spain and mate enthusiasts in neighboring Bolivia. Brazil's largest and most faithful export market is still Uruguay. Most of Argentina's production is gobbled up by fellow Argentines and, after Syria, by Chileans, whose consumption of yerba mate has recently rebounded.[20]

Members of Chilean rural communities, including Mapuches, who live in the southern part of this long, thin nation, never stopped drinking mate communally, often adding orange peel and other herbs to the yerba. In the last decade, middle- and upper-class urban dwellers in the capital city of Santiago have revived the habit, inspired in part by promotional campaigns by Argentina's Instituto Nacional de la Yerba Mate that present mate as a healthy and classy regional tradition.[21] Some urban Chileans even imbibe bottled versions of the drink, produced locally but also in Germany and the United States.[22] Bottled yerba produced across the Atlantic might have roots in mid-twentieth-century urban Brazil (as we saw in chapter 5) but does not appear to have taken off in traditional mate-drinking regions. Even as the commodification of yerba mate into highly processed products such as bottled drinks or extracts has accelerated in nontraditional markets, it has not done so nearly as much in its long-standing primary consumer market within southern South America.

A colonial or nineteenth-century observer might be surprised by the industrialization of the "herb of Paraguay" during the twentieth century or its more recent manifestations in the twenty-first, but not by how many people across South America still drink yerba mate through a bombilla or where it is produced. Consumption in the Andean region of Peru and Ecuador has not recovered, but across the rest of southern South America, most people still consume yerba on a daily basis. In the colonial and early national eras, as today, the subtropical river region, where Paraguay, southern Brazil, and northeastern Argentina meet, accounts for nearly all the world's yerba production. Despite repeated claims that it is impossible to grow this plant elsewhere, the problem is more about limited demand beyond southern South America than about agricultural viability.[23]

After Argentina seized the province of Misiones and began producing yerba at a major scale on plantations in the 1930s, overproduction for a saturated local market has usually been the problem, not the opposite. This led yerba-producing nations to focus their neoliberal export-based economies on other more coveted global crops. Despite being the original producer of *Ilex paraguariensis*, Paraguay now ships much more soy abroad, remaking its environment and destroying Indigenous lands in the process.[24] Many rural landowners in Brazil, Argentina, Bolivia, and Uruguay also have replanted their fields with the nontraditional, genetically modified crop of soy so desired abroad, causing environmental degradation.[25]

The cultivation of yerba mate also compromised environmental ecosystems in the region before soy became king. Historian María Gallero explains that the original Paraná forest had its flora and forest in balance, but the twentieth-century shift toward plantation-based yerba production disrupted this equilibrium. As native groves disappeared due to over-picking and forest clearing, early twentieth-century plantation owners began to worry about soil erosion and production levels.[26] The monocrop plantation model of yerba production nevertheless remains dominant in Argentina, even as some native groves continue to be exploited in Brazil and Paraguay. The native south Atlantic rain forest where wild yerba groves prospered once covered some 5 million square miles, but as of 2007, only 8 percent of this forest remained.[27]

MAKING YERBA PRODUCTION LESS EXPLOITATIVE?

The task of harvesting and preparing yerba for market remains a precarious one. *Tareferos*, as yerba laborers are now called, have fought for greater protections for themselves and their families but have yet to achieve significant improvements. Save for small farmers fortunate to belong to a cooperative like Titrayju in Misiones or those connected to an international fair-trade brand like Guayakí, most yerba laborers who participate in this seasonal form of employment are among the most vulnerable and exploited members of society. Workers log twelve-hour days during the harvest season, which stretches from the semitropical winter months of April to October, often ending with scratched and bloodied hands and little money to show for their efforts. They are not paid a salary but rather by the kilo for the yerba they pick. In 2016, a group of Argentine *tareferos* told a BBC reporter that they received just .75 pesos per kilo (about 5 cents) for yerba they harvested, while a bag of flour cost some 250 pesos (or $18.00), leading them to subsist on a grisly paste made of flour, oil, and salt.[28]

Workers, many with some Indigenous heritage, labor in the yerbales for farmers of European ancestry whom the Argentine government encouraged to colonize and whiten Misiones in the early twentieth century. Yerba pickers hail from Indigenous and mixed-race communities subjected to colonialism, discrimination, and violence for some five centuries.[29] As anthropologist Jennifer Bowles explains, today this primarily "brown-skinned" demographic suffers "from intense race and class discrimination, landlessness, extreme labor exploitation, and poverty."[30] Poor local children are often forced to start picking yerba at anywhere from five to thirteen years old.[31] Given the plant's native origins, it is striking that no Indigenous individuals or groups appear to own their own yerba land or brand.

In the last decade, a new generation of journalists, activists, and scholars have worked to expose southern South Americans to the exploited people who harvest the yerba they consume in their daily mate. They have created statues, murals, and festivals in the yerba-growing region that attest to the presence and dignity of the *tareferos* and their struggles for better labor conditions.[32] In 2014, after three minors were killed in an accident on their way to pick yerba, members of the nonprofit Sueño para Misiones (Dream for Misiones) launched a multipronged campaign to end child labor in the yerbales. In a petition to Congress on Change.org, the organization urged legislation that would require yerba mate producers to certify on products that their yerba is "free from child labor'"; the group also released a documentary called *Me gusta el mate sin trabajo infantil* (I like my mate without child labor). As of 2021, more than 138,000 people have signed the group's petition, and 60 million have seen the documentary, according to Sueño para Misiones. After this seven-year campaign, the House of Representatives in the province of Misiones finally began to consider legislation that would certify yerba as "child-free and without forced labor" in October 2021.[33]

As a result of such initiatives, mate drinkers across the region appear more aware of the exploitation of yerba workers than at any other point in history. Several people I spoke with in Argentina, for example, shared their concerns about child labor in the yerbales. Some mentioned that they had signed the Change.org petition and now sought out brands with fairer and more transparent labor practices. Others told me that they purchased organic-brand yerba that they understood to be better for their health and the environment. As has long been the case, most peoples' primary relationship to yerba mate beyond the red-dirt region where it is harvested revolves around consumption instead of production of the local drink.

Foodways rarely respect national boundaries. As food historians point out, this trend is particularly intense when a supposedly national dish like *jollof* rice in West Africa or *gallo pinto* (rice and beans) in the Caribbean is shared by rivalrous neighboring nations.[34] And so while many people across southern South America expect to celebrate a weekend or special occasion with an asado (outdoor barbecue) and drink mate or tereré on a daily basis, they tend to understand the particular ways in which the asado or yerba is prepared through a national lens.

In his history of the asado, Gustavo Laborde explains that Uruguayans and Argentines distinguish their barbecuing practices by pointing to the shape of the *parilla* (grill) and type of wood; specifically, Uruguayans use *leña* (cured wood), whereas Argentines typically use *carbón* (charcoal).[35] In turn, I observed that contemporary residents of the Río de la Plata region frequently distinguish their mate-related practices using even more criteria: the type of yerba; the size of the mate; the temperature of water; the use of sugar, herbs, or juices; and whether the bombilla is moved during the ritual.[36] "The Brazilians drink out of huge mates with green yerba," several Argentines and Uruguayans told me, after I mentioned my research topic. And with visible horror, some Paraguayans shared that Argentines "bastardized" their tereré by infusing it with soda or juice. And yet context matters. Outside South America, as one Argentine pointed out to me, if you see a Uruguayan drinking mate, you will feel more connected by your shared ritual than aware of the different and supposedly national ways you drink it.

People throughout the region nevertheless regularly make claims about the superior taste of the type of yerba their nation produces or consumes. Uruguayans proudly shared with me that the Brazilians made them their own special type of yerba "without *palos*," a blend that supposedly does not include the little bits of the tender branch included in Argentine blends. Argentines, including those in the yerba industry, countered that Brazilians did include the tender branches in the Uruguayan blend but ground it up so finely that no one knew they were there. Both Argentines and Uruguayans derided the Brazilian preference for uncured green yerba consumed in exorbitantly large mates. Brazilians declared that their shade-grown yerba is superior in taste to the Argentine variety, which is largely grown on plantations in the full sun.

Today, as previously, there is only one botanical variety of *Ilex paraguariensis*, and the way that the yerba is produced distinguishes the taste of the final product. The effects of the soil, humidity, latitude, and climate on taste have been overshadowed by producers' decisions about whether to smoke the yerba, the length of the aging process, the composition of the blend—which, in its basic form, consists of a combination of the leaves and stems, which are chopped up to different sizes and often pulverized into a specific amount of *polvo* (powder) that provides the mate with its foamy quality—and the decision whether to add other herbs (like mint) or flavorings (like citrus) that dramatically change the taste of the final product. The impact of provenance is mitigated, in part, because large brands typically produce yerba that they purchase from a wide variety of producers. Most people I spoke with across the region favored a particular brand of yerba less because they had compared its taste or origins to that of other brands and more because they had been introduced to it by their family or peers and trusted its quality. Furthermore, prior to the early to mid-twentieth-century branding of yerba, the product was often indistinguishable and sold in bulk. Historically, mate drinkers had little choice when it came to the yerba they consumed. They worried more about access and purity than taste.

Following the lead of those in the wine and, more recently, coffee, tea, and chocolate industries, in the twenty-first century, yerba sommeliers—some self-designated and others recently certified—encourage consumers to distinguish the different qualities of particular brands of yerba. Karla Johan Lorenzo, for example, began doing media tours and published a book in Argentina in 2009 that explained how to properly taste yerba and assessed its qualities for some twenty-four Argentine brands, many with numerous varieties. And in August 2022, the online Argentine Universidad Abierta Interamericana announced that it will add a new course to its tea curriculum to enable students for the first time to become accredited as "yerba mate sommeliers."[37]

New ideas about the importance of expert tasting abilities were preceded by popular ideas about the importance of national distinctions. Such distinctions emerged relatively recently in our story, gaining momentum only in the twentieth and twenty-first centuries. Colonial observers differentiated European descendants in South America, whether from the Viceroyalty of Peru or the Viceroyalty of the Río de La Plata, from those in the Old World by their propensity to drink mate, nearly all of it from Paraguay. With independence from Spain came the first uses of mate as an explicitly political, regional symbol that distinguished mate-drinking locals from chocolate-drinking Spaniards. First poets and painters and then, in the Belle Époque, photographers and postcard makers used mate as a mark of the *Rioplatense* culture, which they associated with the rural figure of the gaucho and sometimes his female counterpart of *la china* in both Argentina and Uruguay. In the twentieth century, marketers exploited growing nationalist sentiment in their advertisements, seeking to sell their yerba by tapping into patriotic feelings and claims about their yerba's superior terroir. While we saw this trend most clearly in the yerba-producing nations of Argentina and, to a lesser extent, Brazil, the same trend became evident in 1960s and 1970s Paraguay.[38]

It was not until the twenty-first century that nations within this region formally engaged in what scholars refer to as "gastrodiplomacy."[39] In an effort to boost national pride and profits in the international marketplace, southern Brazil, Paraguay, Argentina, and Uruguay began to compete for patrimonial rights to border-crossing local foods, including tereré and yerba mate.

Struggles over the international recognition of intellectual property rights and the national terroir of regional plants and foods took off in the Southern Cone in the 2010s but had roots in the previous decade. In 2003, UNESCO announced that countries could apply for recognition of specific food and drinks as their "intangible heritage."[40] Argentina immediately applied to have asado, empanadas (meat-filled hand pies), and dulce de leche (or milk caramel) recognized. This set off what one scholar called the "dulce de leche war" with Uruguay. Uruguay was outraged not only because it too produced these foods but also because of the money at stake in the dulce de leche export market.[41] Uruguay, backed by its South American neighbors, convinced Argentina to relent, and the proposal went forward as a joint venture between Argentina and Uruguay.[42]

In 2010, the southern Brazilian province of Mato Grosso do Sul made the first move with yerba, officially proclaiming tereré its "intangible heritage." This declaration set off a flurry of competing claims across the region. Paraguayans expressed their incredulity that Brazil had robbed something they understood to be their own creation and therefore their national patrimony. Paraguayan blogger Ruben Alvarenga, for example, voiced outrage in a post on his *Asuncion Gourmet* blog:

> Tereré, our typical drink, part of our nation, will be proclaimed patrimony of Mato Grosso do Sul. It would seem like a joke, but it isn't.
> ... One other thing, the base of tereré is yerba mate whose scientific name is Ilex Paraguayensis [*sic*]. Yes, like it sounds, PA RA GUA YEN SIS (it must have something to do with our country, right?). I always say that it is not the fault of the Brazilians or Argentines that they want to appropriate our customs (because Paraguay truly preserves theirs despite time and the internet) but it is our fault if we do not protect our patrimonies.[43]

Alvarenga touched on a few key points. First, he clearly claimed tereré as Paraguay's national drink and justified this claim using the scientific rationale that it had been classified as *Ilex paraguariensis* (or Paraguayan holly). Second, he suggested that tereré—and by extension, yerba mate—had been "appropriated" by Argentina and Brazil, which, he charged, have been less effective at maintaining their own national customs. Still, he concluded that Paraguay is to blame for insufficiently defending its patrimony. Alvarenga continued in his blog with the apocryphal and deeply nationalist tale, still supported by the national government, in which Paraguayan soldiers fighting in the Chaco War against Bolivia supposedly invented this way of drinking yerba with cold water.[44]

Similarly inaccurate but telling, others suggest that Paraguayan soldiers invented tereré during the War of the Triple Alliance to keep the smoke produced from heating the water from giving away their location. In truth, as we have seen, tereré had a much longer and likely precolonial history linked to the desire to drink something cold in a hot climate. Still, this frequent misremembering points to Paraguayans' desires to associate their national drink with their nation's history, and in particular, with two wars: one bravely fought against Brazil and Argentina that they lost, and the other against Bolivia that they won, in redeeming fashion.[45] In Paraguay, publicly claiming tereré is a way of articulating this nation's enduring sovereignty from its neighbors.

Before Rio Grande do Sul's 2010 declaration, there was no imperative in Paraguay to formally announce that a drink that locals regularly enjoyed belonged to them. Now Paraguayans responded by pushing their government to pass a decree of its own. In January 2011, the Paraguayan government formally declared tereré "the cultural patrimony and national drink of Paraguay." It mandated that the second Saturday in February would be the "National Day of Tereré," stating that this act was meant "to protect and strengthen national identity." In addition, legislators instructed the national secretary of culture to create and oversee "plans, programs, and projects to promote the protection and national and international diffusion of tereré."[46] Paraguay formally committed to asserting itself as the undisputed owner and diffuser of tereré. More than a decade earlier, in 1997, Paraguay had declared a national mate day, but despite yerba mate's long history of popularity across the region, neither Paraguayans nor Brazilians have claimed the hot version of this infusion as their national or provincial patrimony.[47] They left that to their neighbors to the south.

Two years after Paraguay, Argentina formally entered the fray when it declared yerba mate its national infusion (and wine its national beverage) in July 2013. This was not just about a claim to cultural identity but also a business win for yerba interests, since the declaration gave Argentine yerba companies the right to use the expression and logo "Mate Infusion Nacional" on their packaging "to promote the drink and its traditions."[48] Three years later, the Argentine Ministry of Agriculture accepted a proposal from yerba producers in Misiones and Corrientes to create an official stamp that identified their product as "Yerba Mate Argentina." The president of the Instituto Nacional de la Yerba Mate at the time, Luis Petro, noted that this geographical indicator of intellectual property represented a win for Argentine yerba producers at the national and, even more, the international levels. "We are looking for our new markets and we want to make it known within international trading circles that our yerba has a unique quality due to the production and processing techniques we follow."[49]

In 2015, the Argentine Senate passed another declaration, naming November 30 "National Mate Day." They selected the date to honor the birth of political leader Andrés Guacurarí y Artigas (popularly known as "Andresito," 1778–1821), a man from a Guaraní family who governed Misiones from 1815 to 1819.[50] Invoking the only known governor of Indigenous heritage, this effort reflected twin desires to claim both Guaraní heritage and land where yerba grows for the Argentine nation and its supposedly national infusion.

Because Uruguay has not produced a significant quantity of yerba, the Uruguayan government did not make a formal claim to yerba mate as its national patrimony, nor did it react with offense to Argentina's yerba-related initiatives as it had to previous patrimonial claims. Even so, in 2011, a nationalist senator from Colonia proposed that October 12 (a national holiday first celebrated as Columbus Day and now as "Día de la Raza" or the Day of the Race) be designated "Día del mate uruguayo" (Uruguayan Mate Day). Tourism sites also regularly celebrate mate as Uruguay's national drink. For example, the website viajeauruguay.com explains that while mate is a traditional regional beverage across Paraguay, Argentina, Rio Grande do Sul, and Uruguay, "in Uruguay mate is considered that national drink." Why? The site elaborates: "Uruguay, is, of the countries mentioned, the maximum consumer of mate. In no other country in the world is so much yerba mate consumed."[51] As in the late twentieth century, twenty-first-century claims to mate as the national drink of Uruguay stem not from a history of production but rather from superior levels of consumption.

In 2018, the South American free trade association MERCOSUR declared "Yerba Mate-Ka'a"—referring to both Spanish and Guaraní names—as its "cultural patrimony." Because Argentina, Brazil, Uruguay, and Paraguay are the association's leading members, this gesture signaled the enduring ways in which this (pre)colonial infusion continued to cross national borders. The commission praised Paraguay, in particular, for emphasizing Guaraní contributions and oral traditions in its proposal.[52]

Nations under MERCOSUR's neoliberal umbrella sometimes cooperate in efforts like this one but also preserve economic, political, and cultural imperatives to advance individual claims at the national level. In 2020, Paraguay's application to UNESCO for recognition of its "ancestral Guaraní drink" of tereré prepared with Pohã Ñana (medicinal herbs) as its "intangible heritage" was approved.[53] In 2022, Paraguay applied to this same body to officially recognize a "yerba mate cultural landscape" in its yerba-growing regions.[54] Currently, Argentine yerba interests and researchers are preparing a case to present to UNESCO to claim yerba mate as the country's intangible heritage.[55] Due to the Argentine yerba sector's marketing strategies, many people in the United States, ironically, have come to think of yerba mate as Argentine, despite its longer history in Paraguay, higher per capita consumption in Uruguay, and major production and consumption in southern Brazil.[56]

In claiming intellectual property rights for both the ritualized drink and the plant from which it is made, governments in Argentina, Paraguay, and Rio Grande do Sul advance claims not only against one another but also against long-standing native producers who straddle these political borders.[57] When we spoke in July 2018, the director of the Paraguayan National Archive in Asunción, Vicente Alejandro Arrúa Avalos, poignantly remarked that while South American nations fought over who got to claim yerba mate, in truth, if this plant belonged to anyone, it was to the Guaraní. While public acknowledgment of the Guaraní heritage of yerba mate (or ka'a) took off in the twenty-first century, this did not mean that contemporary Guaraní people finally gained land rights to yerbales or profits from yerba sales.

Who profits from yerba might differ in the future. The Guaraní appear particularly well positioned to advance a claim for intellectual property rights of their own, especially given recent changes in international law, which favor such a shift. The United Nations 1992 Convention on Biological Diversity and its 2010 Nagoya Protocol created a pathway for "fair benefit sharing" with Indigenous communities regarding profits made from their traditional "biological resources."[58] In March 2019, in a pathbreaking decision, Indigenous San and Khoi people in South Africa signed a profit-sharing agreement with rooibos industry representatives. Four years earlier, the Guaraní launched a similar campaign to reclaim the sweet wild herb *ka'a he'e*, now globally known and marketed as stevia. Their ongoing lawsuit against corporations, including

Coca-Cola, advances a well-evidenced argument that "modern stevia usage derives from their traditional knowledge."[59] Perhaps the Guaraní initiated their legal quest for intellectual property rights with *ka'a he'e* rather than with *ka'a* because of this sweet plant's much more recent commercialization in the twentieth century, in contrast to the commercialization of yerba mate since the colonial era. Today, scholars, journalists, and even marketers acknowledge that the Guaraní pioneered the identification, production, and consumption of the plant that became known as yerba mate.

Whether such a lawsuit prevails, the plant harvested by the Guaraní is sure to remain a central part of everyday life across much of this river-veined South American region. If anything, its local popularity seems to poised to grow rather than wane. In the largest and most fickle local market, Argentina's inflation rate is hurtling towards 100 percent, drastically decreasing locals' spending power and encouraging them to buy more yerba and less coffee and tea.[60]

Tracing the history of yerba mate gives us insight into historical patterns that range all the way from global networks of trade to the most intimate of private spheres. At the global scale, it helps us map the impact of colonialism, capitalism, nationalism, and neoliberalism on a commodity produced and consumed primarily within rather than beyond South America for the last 500 years, helping enrich locals of European descent far more than those with Indigenous origins. Even with recent labor activism and growing interest in supposedly ethically produced bottled yerba drinks abroad, it does not appear that most yerba pickers' lives (like those of other lowly paid agricultural workers) will improve anytime soon, although perhaps they have a greater chance given the egalitarian ethics that surround the product they help to make. At the other end of the commodity chain, often at the most intimate scale, a focus on yerba mate helps us to see how so many southern South Americans across ethnic and class divides have prioritized the ritual of sharing this beverage daily.

While historically, hierarchies of race and gender determined who was expected to serve whom, many in the region have abandoned these ideas, imagining mate as the most egalitarian or democratic of rituals in the region.[61] And yet, as my colleague María Julia Rossi points out, "If you think about who typically remembers to buy yerba at the store, heat the water, prepare the kit to take mate out, that work still overwhelmingly falls to women."[62] So too, the great majority of contemporary yerba brands on the market evoke female rather than male connotations.[63] Today, who infuses the mate with hot water might seem random, but who does the other work to get it ready remains more rooted in gender and racial hierarchies than what might appear at first.

As we have seen, mate is not just a South American drink; it is also a ritual and a way of thinking about and forming human relationships since the colonial era. "Behind the liturgical gesture of preparing, brewing and drinking mate, there is a conception of the world and of life," according to Uruguayan anthropologist Daniel Vidart.[64] It is a utopian worldview, one that strives—imperfectly, but to a greater extent than many other rituals—to enact egalitarian sharing and social connection over hierarchy and isolation.

Based on the history we have explored together here and recent shifts in behavior as the coronavirus starts to wane, many South Americans across this mate-drinking region appear eager to resume the long-standing, leisurely, intimate practice of sharing the mate and bombilla with people who are in but extend beyond their inner circles. With five centuries of history behind it, the persistence of yerba mate across a wide swath of southern South American society attests to the enduring desire to participate in an energizing and meaningful ritual. It is a ritual with an important, but often symbolically distant, profit motive and a clear and persistent communal ethos at its core.

ACKNOWLEDGMENTS

When sharing rounds of mate, it is customary to say "gracias" (thank you) to let the mate server know you are done. As I finish this book, it is my honor to offer thanks to some of the many people who made its creation, like the mate ritual itself, a communal experience.

Longtime friends Gabriel Taruselli and Marisa D'Amato introduced me to the intimacy of the mate ritual and, along with the Favia family, have made Argentina feel like home for some two decades. Fellow historians and dear friends Valeria Silvina Pita, Cristiana Schettini Pereira, and Inés Pérez expressed enthusiasm for this project since the outset. Gabriel, Valeria, and Inés, along with Paula Lucía Aguilar and Cecilia Tossounian, offered opportunities to share my research in progress with Argentine audiences. They together with Andrea Andújar, Dora Barrancos, María Paula Bontempo, José Buschini, Paula Caldo, Isabella Cosse, Florencia D'Uva, Mirta Zaida Lobato, Valeria Manzano, Gabriela Mitidieri, Karina Ramacciotti, Fernando Rocchi, Lisa Ubelaker Andrade, and Marcela Vignoli provided research leads and a scholarly community in Argentina.

US-based historians of Latin America also provided crucial feedback and community. Particular thanks go to historians of Argentina and the Río de la Plata region who offered helpful research suggestions, including William (Billy) Acree, Paulina Alberto, Diego Armus, Adriana Brodksy, Eric D. Carter, Oscar Chamosa, Bridget María Chesteron, Christine Ehrick, Eduardo Elena, Donna Guy, Matthew Karush, Sandra McGee Deutsch, Natalia Milanesio, Julia Sarreal, and Jeffrey Shumway. Elizabeth Hutchison, Kathy López, Nara Milanich, Jocelyn Olcott, Lara Putnam, and Heidi Tinsman, along with members of the Red de Investigadores de Trabajo del Hogar en América Latina, have inspired me with their scholarship and feminist solidarity. The example and support of pioneering Latin American food scholars Jeffrey Pilcher and Rebecca Earle and that of other members of the Red de Estudios Históricos y Sociales de la Nutrición y Alimentación en América Latina make Latin American food studies a vibrant home. In all of my scholarly undertakings, I continue to draw on the wisdom of Sueann Caulfield and Rebecca J. Scott. And I am endlessly grateful for the advice of dear friends and fellow historians of Latin America Paulina Alberto, Jesse Hoffnung-Garskof, and Tamara Walker.

I am thankful to Lafayette College and the US Department of Education Fulbright Scholar Program for funding my research in Argentina, Uruguay, Paraguay, and southern Brazil. Since this project allowed me to venture beyond Argentine archives and historiography to those of these neighboring nations, I depended on the generous guidance of scholars of other places. For Uruguay, Billy Acree, Alex Borucki, Gustavo Laborde, Christine Ehrick, Vania Markarian, Sandra McGee Deutsch, Rodolfo Porrini, Javier Ricca, and Debbie Sharnak provided incredible insight and leads. On Paraguay, Bridget Chesterton, Michael Huner, Romy Natalia Goldberg, Barbara Potthast, and Thomas Whigham did the same. For Brazil, Paulina Alberto, Sueann Caulfield, Gillian McGillivray, and Geraldo Neto helped orient me. For Chile, Elizabeth Hutchison, Nara Milanich, and Heidi Tinsman inspired me while Karen Esther Donoso Fritz and Katherine Cedillos enriched my understanding of mate there.

As historians we rely on the generosity of colleagues but also on archivists, librarians, and local interlocutors. I am particularly grateful for the hardworking staff who facilitated my research: in Argentina, at the Biblioteca Nacional, Archivo de Clarín, Archivo General de la Nación, Museo de la Ciudad, Facultad de Medicina, Archivo de Juan Carlos Romero, and Archivo de la Gobernación de Misiones; in Uruguay, at the Biblioteca Nacional and Museo Histórico del Gobierno; in Paraguay, at the Museo Etnográfico Andrés Barbero, Archivo Nacional de Asunción, and Museo de Barro; and, in southern Brazil, at the Museu Paranese, which possesses the most expansive collection of mate-related materials in the region. I offer profound thanks to all those who shared their yerba mate stories informally or via oral history interview. A special mention goes to Pau Navajas, Javier Ricca, and Victor Saguier, who shared their knowledge of the yerba mate industry and its history, and to Javier Antonio Torres for doing so with tereré and *yuyos* (wild medicinal herbs) in Paraguay.

I am grateful for the support for this project I have found at Lafayette College. Interlibrary loan staff, especially Karen Haduck, procured numerous books for me, and research librarians Ana Ramirez Luhrs and Lijuan Xu helped me navigate online databases. Archivists Diane Windham Shawn and Elaine Stomber supported my acquisition of visual sources. Charlotte Nunes and Janna Avon helped me organize my massive database, while John Clark skillfully crafted the maps. A special thanks goes to Paul Miller, who expertly designed and maintained a quantitative database and created charts of yerba production and consumption. I also had the great privilege of working with stellar undergraduate research assistants, including Geraldo Neto, Katherine Cedillos, Daniel Gonzalez, Gabrielle Tropp, Deanna Hanchuk, and Mackenzi Berner, who did everything from primary and secondary research to correcting image files, tagging metadata for images, and inputting quantitative data. My colleagues in the history department and the Women, Gender, and Sexuality Studies program provided me with consistent encouragement. Paul Barclay, in particular, inspired my interest in conducting research with visual sources; and both he and, before him, Joshua Sanborn served as supportive history department chairs. Tammy Yeakel and Rebecca Stocker made numerous photocopies.

For invitations to present my work in progress and helpful feedback, I thank colleagues at Dickinson College, Gettysburg College, SUNY-Albany, and panelists at the food history conferences sponsored by the University of Texas–Austin, Illinois Wesleyan University, and Illinois State University. So too I appreciate opportunities to present my work in Argentina from the University of Luján, the University of San Andrés, the Argentine Association of Research on Women's and Gender History, the Instituto Cultural Argentino Norteamericano, and the Asociación Argentina de Investigadores en Historia (on its *Historiar* podcast).

To make my writing a more communal practice, I sought the guidance of editors and fellow writers. At the University of North Carolina Press, Elaine Maisner believed in this project from the beginning, and our numerous conversations inspired me. Audra Wolfe helped me frame my approach, while Anne Amienne enabled me to become a more joyful writer. I took part in a wonderfully supportive writing group she organized with Jessica Brantley, Vanessa Druskat, and, Julie Pfeiffer. I am so grateful that Julie and I have continued to regularly discuss and celebrate each other's research progress after the larger group ended. Daniela Blei became my first and last reader, helping me sharpen my analysis and enliven my writing; she also created the index.

Given the multiple demands facing scholars today, it is an act of tremendous generosity to read other scholars' work in progress. Since the beginning, Sandra McGee Deutsch and I have exchanged feedback on our book chapters. So too, Paulina Alberto and Tamara Walker read and responded to the entire manuscript. All three helped improve it in innumerable ways. Thomas Whigham regaled me with his extensive knowledge about yerba mate and offered useful comments on early versions of the first three chapters. I also benefited from workshopping my analysis of visual representations of domestic work with experts Rosario Fernández, Rachel Randall, Sonia Roncador, and María Julia Rossi. Bridget Chesterton, Benjamin R. Cohen, Michael Huner, Gillian McGillivray, Fernando Rocchi, and Debbie Sharnak also provided helpful comments on specific chapters of this book. Two wonderful external reviewers helped me to focus my final revisions. I thank Bridget María Chesterton and Jeffrey Pilcher, who revealed their identities, for their sage advice.

At UNC Press, Debbie Gershenowitz graciously agreed to take over as my editor after Elaine retired. I am particularly grateful for her advice on and enthusiasm for this book. Alyssa Brown, Carol Seigler, JessieAnne D'Amico, Mary Carley Caviness, Peter L. Perez, and Lindsay Starr shepherded me through the publication process. Julie Bush copyedited the manuscript with great care.

I also wish to thank my family and friends who have shared the ups and downs of this journey. My mom, Lindalea Pite Ludwick, has been my bedrock; among other things, she has offered words of encouragement, domestic and financial support, visits to Argentina, and draft proofing services. My grandparents Sara and Edward Pite (Nanny and Poppy) helped raise me and make me into the person and scholar I have become. My dad, Dr. William J. Pite, helped inspire my wanderlust and curiosity. I was delighted that he; my sister, Jessica Pite McNamara, and her family; aunt Barbara Pite; and cousin Allison Schofield visited us in Argentina. So too visits from lifelong friends Michelle Conroy McBean, Karen and Shawn Roman, and Olivia Pennock enriched my experience. Other members of my family (both biological and adopted)—Elizabeth Abbott; Kristin Bryson; Holley Cavanna; Joshua Cohen; Erin Cooke; Betsy Feiner; Martha Gove; Brian and Laura Harrigan; Karri Ludwick; Hayley Marcous; Jennifer McFadden; Alex Pite; and Ross, Carly, and Robbie Schofield—have kept me rooted. In Easton, friends and fellow teachers and scholars Amy Kozel, Carrie Rohman, Seo-Hyun Park, Nandini Sikand, Berry Steiner, and Sue Wenze were crucial sounding boards. Seo-Hyun and her family "bubbled" with ours during the pandemic and made it so much better. Emily Musil Church provided support and useful suggestions on the introduction. And I could always count on Margaret Page for words of encouragement, laughter, and seeing me in "all the ways."

My partner in life, Christopher Eckman, and our two children, Sofia and Elijah, lived the writing of this book alongside me. Chris enthusiastically organized our family's 2015–16 yearlong residence and subsequent visits to Argentina and trips to Paraguay, Uruguay, and southern Brazil. He took pictures of people drinking mate and served as my "research assistant," as he likes to refer to himself. Sofia and Elijah helped me experience daily life in Argentina through their eyes. Together with my mom and grandparents, Chris, Sofia, and Elijah are my home no matter where I am living, and for that reason, I dedicate this book to all of them.

NOTES

INTRODUCTION

1. For more on the pronunciation of this and other related terms in Spanish and Portuguese, see "How to Pronounce Mate, Yerba Mate, Erva Mate and Chimarrão," Mate Experience, Dec. 7, 2021, https://matexperience.com/education/faq/how-to-pronounce-yerba-mate/.

2. Juan Carlos Garavaglia, *Mercado interno y economía colonial: Tres siglos de historia de la yerba mate* (1983; Rosario, Arg.: Prohistoria, 2008), 43.

3. Sometimes mate drinkers in Lebanon and Syria share the same mate and bombilla, as in Christine Folch's ethnography, but this appears to be the exception. In their contemporary study, Sulaiman et al., find that 86 percent of their informants drank out of their own cup but shared a water pot, a sugar bowl, and snacks. On the history of yerba mate production in South America and consumption in the Levant, see Christine Folch, "Stimulating Consumption: Yerba Mate Myths, Markets, and Meanings from Conquest to Present," *Comparative Studies in Society and History* 52, no. 1 (2010): 6–36. On Syrians' contemporary relationship with yerba mate, see Naji Sulaiman, Andrea Pieroni, Renata Sõukand, Cory Whitney, and Abynek Polesny, "Socio-Cultural Significance of Yerba Maté among Syrian Residents and Diaspora," *Economic Botany* 75, no. 2 (2021): 97–111, esp. 104; and Analía Llorente, "Yerba Mate: Cómo Siria se convertió en el mayor comprador de este producto en el mundo," BBC News Mundo, Feb. 20, 2020, www.bbc.com/mundo/noticias-51392066.

4. On the history of tea, see, for example, George van Driem, *The Tale of Tea: A Comprehensive History of Tea from Prehistoric Times to the Present Day* (Boston: Brill, 2019); Erika Rappaport, *A Thirst for Empire: How Tea Shaped the Modern World* (Princeton: Princeton University Press, 2017); and Markman Ellis, Richard Coulton, and Matthew Mauger, *Empire of Tea: The Asian Leaf That Conquered the World* (London: Reaktion Books, 2015). On coffee, for example, Jeanette M. Fregulia, *A Rich and Tantalizing Brew: A History of How Coffee Connected the World* (Fayetteville: University of Arkansas Press, 2019); Jonathon Morris, *Coffee: A Global History* (London: Reaktion Books, 2019); and William Roseberry et al., eds., *Coffee, Society, and Power in Latin America* (Baltimore: Johns Hopkins University Press,

1995). And, on chocolate, Sarah Moss and Alexander Badenoch, *Chocolate: A Global History* (London: Reaktion Books, 2009); Marcy Norton, *Sacred Gifts, Profane Pleasures: A History of Tobacco and Chocolate in the Atlantic World* (Ithaca, NY: Cornell University Press, 2008); and Sophie D. Coe and Michael D. Coe, *The True History of Chocolate* (London: Thames and Hudson, 2003).

5. Folch, "Stimulating Consumption."

6. There are some indications that coffee and, to a lesser extent, tea were once communal drinks. For example, Schivelbusch explains that Ausburg physician Leonhart Rauwolf, who traveled to the "Near and Middle East" in 1582, found that "Turks and Arabs" drank coffee "from earthenware and porcelain cups early in the morning . . . but they only take small sips of it and then pass these cups around, for they are seated in a circle." Meanwhile, a Japanese Buddhist monk, Eison, was well known for the large common teacup he used, even as most people drank tea in individual porcelain cups, according to George van Driem. For food and drink more broadly, archeologist Daniel Schávelzon emphasizes the use of shared cups and bowls up until the late nineteenth century in Buenos Aires. Wolfgang Schivelbusch, *Tastes of Paradise: A Social History of Spices, Stimulants, and Intoxicants* (New York: Pantheon Books, 1992); Driem, *Tale of Tea*, 167, 271; Daniel Schávelzon, *Historias del comer y del beber en Buenos Aires: Arqueología histórica de la vajilla de mesa* (Buenos Aires: Aguilar, 2000).

7. The pioneering study is Thomas Whigham, *The Politics of River Trade: Tradition and Development in the Upper Plata, 1780–1870* (Albuquerque: University of New Mexico Press, 1991). Recent books include Adam S. Dohrenwend, *Green Gold: Contested Meanings and Socio-environmental Change in Argentina Yerba Mate Cultivation* (Cham, Switz.: Springer, 2021); and Julia Sarreal, *Yerba Mate: The Drink that Shaped a Nation* (Oakland: University of California Press, 2023).

8. These books address the history of consumption within Mexico, Honduras, and Chile, but the commodities' endpoint in the United States is the principal focus. Jeffrey M. Pilcher, *Planet Taco: A Global History of Mexican Food* (New York: Oxford University Press, 2012); John Soluri, *Banana Cultures: Agriculture, Consumption, and Environmental Change in Honduras and the United States* (Austin: University of Texas Press, 2005); Heidi Tinsman, *Buying into the Regime: Grapes and Consumption in Cold War Chile and the United States* (Durham: Duke University Press, 2014).

9. Sidney W. Mintz, *Sweetness and Power: The Place of Sugar in Modern History* (New York: Viking, 1985).

10. While much of the English-language historiography on tea focuses on Great Britain and global trade (see note 4 in this chapter), some books focus on this story within Asia, including Bret Hinsch, *The Rise of Tea Culture in China: The Invention of the Individual* (Lanham, MD: Rowman and Littlefield, 2016).

11. Uruguayan journalist Eduardo Galeano and dependency theorists preceding him argued that Latin America was created to be plundered for the profit of colonial and imperial outsiders. Journalist Andy Robinson recently published an update on Galeano's classic work. Eduardo Galeano, *Open Veins of Latin America: Five Centuries of the Pillage of a Continent*, trans. Cedric Belfrage (1971; New York: Monthly Review Press, 1973); Andy Robinson, *Gold, Oil and Avocados: A Recent History of Latin America in Sixteen Commodities* (Brooklyn: Melville House, 2021).

12. Galeano, *Open Veins of Latin America*.

13. In their scholarship and a new edited volume, Jacob Blanc and Frederico Freitas have been pushing for the transnational history of this region. See, for example, Jacob Blanc and

Frederico Freitas, eds., *Big Water: The Making of the Borderlands between Brazil, Argentina and Paraguay* (Tucson: University of Arizona Press, 2018).

14. There is a rich historiography on the Río de la Plata region during the colonial era, some of which also analyzes the immediate postindependence era. Much of it has been produced in the United States by scholars who participate in the Río de la Plata Workshop convened by Fabrício Prado at the College of William and Mary. For the late twentieth century, political scientists have dominated the political history of the "Southern Cone." See, for example, Guillermo O'Donnell, *Modernization and Bureaucratic Authoritarianism: Studies in South American Politics* (Berkeley: University of California Press, 1973); and Alfred C. Stepan, *Rethinking Military Politics: Brazil and the Southern Cone* (Princeton: Princeton University Press, 1988). For more recent transnational historical scholarship focused on political and social movements around the turn of the twentieth century, see, for example, Sandra McGee Deutsch, *Las Derechas: The Extreme Right in Argentina, Brazil, and Chile, 1890–1939* (Stanford: Stanford University Press, 1999); and Asunción Lavrin, *Women, Feminism, and Social Change in Argentina, Chile, and Uruguay, 1890–1940* (Lincoln: University of Nebraska Press, 1995). For cultural histories that adopt a transnational lens, see William Garrett Acree, *Everyday Reading: Print Culture and Collective Identity in the Río de la Plata, 1780–1910* (Nashville: Vanderbilt University Press, 2011), and *Staging Frontiers: The Making of Modern Popular Culture in Argentina and Uruguay* (Albuquerque: University New Mexico Press, 2019); and Christine Ehrick, *Radio and the Gendered Soundscape: Women and Broadcasting in Argentina and Uruguay, 1930–1950* (Cambridge: Cambridge University Press, 2015).

15. Quote from *Life Magazine*, Oct. 18, 1963, 92, as cited by Sandra A. Scham and Ann E. Killebrew, "From the Editors," *Journal of Eastern Mediterranean Archaeology and Heritage Studies* 2, no. 3 (2014): iii–iv. Will Durant is often given credit for this quote, but he and his wife, Ariel Durant, regularly researched and wrote together.

16. Michel de Certeau, *The Practice of Everyday Life*, vol. 2, *Living and Cooking*, trans. Timothy J. Tomasik (1984; Minneapolis: University of Minnesota Press, 1998).

17. León Denis, *La Yerba Mate, Propaganda brasileña en Londres* (pamphlet published in response to an article in *La Razón*, Oct. 24, 1913), Nov. 28, 1913.

18. Francisco N. Scutella, *El mate: Bebida nacional Argentina* (1989; repr., Buenos Aires: Editorial Lancelot, 2006).

19. Garavaglia, *Mercado interno*; Pau Navajas, *Caá Porã: El espíritu de la yerba mate, una historia de plata* (Corrientes, Arg.: Las Marías, 2013); Javier Ricca, *El mate: Historia, secretos y otras yerbas de una pasión rioplatense* (Buenos Aires: Sudamericana, 2009). In English, Thomas Whigham, who like Garavaglia trained as an economic historian, also explores the transnational history of this commodity. Whigham, *Politics of River Trade*.

20. On taste, see, for example, Jeffrey M. Pilcher, "The Embodied Imagination in Recent Writings on Food History," *American Historical Review* 121, no. 3 (June 2016): 861–87; and Christy Spackman and Jacob Lahne, "Sensory Labor: Considering the Work of Taste in the Food System," *Food, Culture, and Society* 22, no. 2 (2019): 142–51.

21. My argument about embodiment is inspired by Jeffrey Pilcher's conception of the "culinary embodied imagination" in his article "The Embodied Imagination." Benedict Anderson, *Imagined Communities: Reflection on the Origin and Spread of Nationalism* (1983; rev. ed., New York: Verso, 2016).

22. Arjun Appadurai, "Introduction: Commodities and the Politics of Value," in *The Social Life of Things: Commodities in Cultural Perspective*, ed. Arjun Appadurai (New York: Cambridge University Press, 1986), 5.

23. Rebecca Earle, *Potato* (New York: Bloomsbury, 2019), 89.

24. While there is relatively consistent yerba production data for Argentina, Brazil, and Paraguay (see graph 3.1), as Argentina became a major yerba producer, the Argentine government became dedicated to calculating consumption statistics more regularly than its neighbors, enabling us to trace how the relationship between Argentine production and consumption (graph 4.1) and per capita consumption (graph 6.1) changed over time.

25. Peter Burke, *Eyewitnessing: The Use of Images as Historical Evidence* (London: Reaktion Books, 2001); for Huizinga quote, see 13–14.

26. I compiled as complete a corpus of mate-related images as possible by identifying and scanning images available at all of the research institutions I have visited, as well as images reproduced in scholarship on yerba mate, in art books (including books that reproduce paintings, lithographs, postcards, and photographs), and in digitized advertisements and articles in magazines (for example, *Caras y caretas*, available via the Biblioteca Nacional de España) and those found via internet searches. I purchased some sources in the field, for example, postcards, which are now held by Lafayette College Special Collections and College Archives, Easton, PA. In conjunction with my undergraduate research scholars, I used Adobe Bridge to tag each digital file's respective metadata (author, place, date, provenance, keywords, genre, etc.), Adobe Lightroom to filter the materials, and Excel spreadsheets to organize them into a usable source base that enables me to assess trends in specific historical contexts.

27. This approach is inspired by the work of Paulina Alberto and Tamara Walker. See, in particular, Paulina Alberto, *Black Legend: The Many Lives of Raúl Grigera and the Power of Racial Storytelling in Argentina* (New York: Cambridge University Press, 2022), esp. xi–xiv; and Tamara Walker, *Exquisite Slaves: Race, Clothing, and Status in Colonial Lima* (New York: Cambridge University Press, 2017).

28. Bolivia is another nation whose yerba mate history merits future study. Following my sources and the higher levels of yerba consumption in Chile, it gets more attention here.

CHAPTER ONE

1. Elite Peruvians' mates typically held a liter and a half (or just over six cups) of water and yerba, according to Federico Oberti, making them much larger than the handheld mates that were standard in the Río de la Plata region. Frézier's mate appears oversized, requiring more water than the copper pot could hold. Federico Oberti, *Historia y folklore del mate* (Buenos Aires: Fondo Nacional de las Artes, 1979), 223–26.

2. Frézier included thirty-seven copper-cut engravings in his account. Amédée François Frézier, *A Voyage to the South-Sea and along the Coasts of Chili and Peru in the Years 1712, 1713, and 1714* (London: Jonah Bowyer, 1717), preface and plate 36. On Frézier, see Luisa Vila Vilar, *El viaje de Amédée Frézier por la América Meridional* (Seville, Spain: Diputación Provincial, 1991).

3. It is unclear what happened to item F; apparently, he skipped it.

4. Some people used both the *apartador* and the bombilla, as in this illustration, while others used just one. For a detailed history of the *apartador* and the bombilla, see José M. Eguiguren Molina, Javier Eguiguren Molina, and Roberto Vega, ed., *The Mate in América*, trans. Francis Casal (Buenos Aires: La Stampa, 2004), 221–25; and Oberti, *Historia y folklore del mate*, 207–41, esp. 218 and 227.

5. Frézier, *Voyage*, 252. Italics his, here and subsequently.

6. Irving Leonard argues that travelers from across Europe came with dreams of "quick wealth, a personal El Dorado, a position of power with all its perquisites, and the hope of an early return to the homeland to enjoy the rewards acquired." He also notes that curiosity drove some travelers. Irving A. Leonard, *Colonial Travelers in Latin America* (New York: Knopf, 1972), 1 and 18–19.

7. As recent research emphasizes, viceregal cities dominated the production of documents about colonial Latin America, but Indigenous peoples still exercised considerable agency in southeastern South America. Jeffrey A. Erbig Jr. and Sergio Latini, "Across Archival Limits: Colonial Records, Changing Ethnonyms, and Geographies of Knowledge," *Ethnohistory* 66, no. 2 (Apr. 2019): 249–73.

8. Pau Navajas, "Historia del mate (*Ilex paraguariensis*): Kaingang, los primeros consumidores," *La Nación*, Jan. 28, 2020, www.lanacion.com.ar/sociedad/historia-del-mate-ilex -paraguariensis-los-kaingang-nid2323839/.

9. The Guaraní cultivated multiple varieties of manioc, corn, batata, beans, strawberries, and blue passionflower; they also smoked and chewed tobacco and grew the gourds for containers, including mates. Pau Navajas, *Caá Porã: El Espíritu de la yerba mate, una historia de plata* (Corrientes, Arg.: Las Marías, 2013), 25.

10. This word is alternatively spelled *ka'a* and *ca'a*, with the former spelling today embraced by Paraguayan botanists and Guaraní linguists. Asociación Etnobotánica Paraguaya, *Plantas medicinales del Jardín Botánico de Asunción* (Asunción, Para., Asociación Etnobotánica Paraguaya, 2009), 140.

11. Several versions of this legend recount that Tupi transformed a young woman into the tree that produces ka'a to make both her and the tree live eternally. See, for example, Eguiguren, Eguiguren, and Vega, *Mate in América*, 22.

12. Navajas, *Caá Porã*, 32–33.

13. Juan Carlos Garavaglia, *Mercado interno y economía colonial: Tres siglos de historia de la yerba mate* (1983; Rosario, Arg,: Prohistoria, 2008), 36–37.

14. Oberti, *Historia y folklore del mate*, 219; and Eguiguren, Eguiguren, and Vega, *Mate in América*, 18.

15. Ernesto Daumas, *El problema de la yerba mate* (Buenos Aires: Compañía Impresora Argentina, 1930), 4; Carlos D. Girola, *Cultivo de la yerba mate (Ilex paraguariensis)* (Buenos Aires: Imprenta Gadola, 1915), 3, as cited in Christine Folch, "Stimulating Consumption: Yerba Mate Myths, Markets, and Meanings from Conquest to Present," *Comparative Studies in Society and History* 52, no. 1 (2010): 11.

16. I am grateful to Shawn Austin for bringing this research by Orantin to my attention. Mickaël Orantin, "Remarques sur le verbe 'vendre': Dire l'échange marchand en guarani dans les missions jésuites du Paraguay (XVIIe–XVIIIe siècle)," *L'homme* 233 (2020): 75–104.

17. Julia Sarreal, *The Guaraní and Their Missions* (Stanford: Stanford University Press, 2014), 17–18.

18. Matthew Restall, *Seven Myths of the Spanish Conquest* (New York: Oxford University Press, 2003), esp. chapters 1 and 3.

19. There are different interpretations of the original meaning of "Paraguay," some of which are linked to the Payagua people and their river, but all of which are linked to their waters. "El lugar de las aguas veteadas" is the version apparently taught in Paraguayan schools. "Etimología de Paraguay," Etimologías Latín Chistes Refranes Ciudades, http://etimologias .dechile.net/?Paraguay (accessed Apr. 14, 2020).

20. They also deemed the avocado, pineapple, and other tropical fruits "delightful" and safe for Spanish bodies. Rebecca Earle, *The Body of the Conquistador: Food, Race, and the Colonial Experience in South America, 1492–1700* (Cambridge: Cambridge University Press, 2012), see esp. 127.

21. To the north, conquistadors had recently encountered cacao. Columbus and his crew were first exposed to cacao in 1502. Córtes drank it in Tenochtitlan in 1519; he brought seeds back to Spain in 1528, but the first cargo of cacao to Spain arrived only in 1585. Eguiguren, Eguiguren, and Vega, *Mate in América*, 16.

22. Some suggest these were vanquished soldiers in Asunción and others Indigenous people in canoes in the port of Buenos Aires. For the former, see Folch, "Stimulating Consumption," 7; and for the latter, Leandro Sagastizábal, *La yerba mate y misiones: Documentos vivos de nuestro pasado* (Buenos Aires: Centro Editor de América Latina, 1984), 17; Sagastizábal draws from Padre Guevara, *Historia del Paraguay, Río de la Plata y Tucumán* (Buenos Aires: Plus Ultra, 1970), 756.

23. Earle emphasizes the widespread belief in this idea among early Spanish settlers, as well as their "contradictory desires to assimilate and differentiate" the native population. Earle, *Body of the Conquistador*, 174.

24. Folch, "Stimulating Consumption," 7.

25. As cited in Navajas, *Caá Porã*, 59.

26. Alonso de la Madrid to Governor Hernandarias, Asunción, Feb. 10, 1596, as quoted in Adalberto López, "The Economics of Yerba Mate in Seventeenth-Century South America," *Agricultural History* 48, no. 4 (Oct. 1974): 497–98.

27. Raul A. Molina, "El mate: Nuevas aportaciones sobre el uso de la bombilla y del apartador," *Historia*, no. 2 (1955): 131–36.

28. Garavaglia, *Mercado interno*, 45–46.

29. Meanwhile, Christine Folch suggests that the use of the bombilla points to the "persistence of an Indian practice." Folch, "Stimulating Consumption," 25; Navajas, *Caá Porã*, 36–37.

30. See Oberti, *Historia y folklore del mate*, 220–21, where he summarizes his argument and that of Villanueva.

31. Martín Dobrizhoffer, *Historia de los abipones*, trans. Edmundo Wernicke, vol. 1 (Resistencia, Chaco: Facultad de Humanidades, Universidad Nacional del Nordeste, 1967), 99. Dobrizhoffer wrote this in Vienna between 1777 and 1782.

32. Federico Oberti points to a trial from 1615 that describes nuns' use of the bombilla to serve and drink mate and states that the first evidence of bombillas in wills is from the early 1700s. For more on the history of the bombilla, see Oberti, *Historia y folklore del mate*, 207–41, here 215–16, 230; and Eguiguren, Eguiguren, and Vega, *Mate in América*, 221–27.

33. Garavaglia suggests this export started in small waves in 1590. López points out that in the second half of the sixteenth century, sugar, wine, and tobacco were the most important exports, but by the early seventeenth century, yerba mate had eclipsed them all as an export for the rest of the colonial period. Garavaglia, *Mercado interno*, 485; López, "Economics of Yerba Mate," 496.

34. Garavaglia, *Mercado interno*, 171.

35. This was a savvy legal move that allowed the Spanish crown to demand a tribute on yerba as if it was a precious mineral. Thomas Whigham, *The Politics of River Trade: Tradition and Development in the Upper Plata, 1780–1870* (Albuquerque: University of New Mexico Press, 1991), 14; Folch, "Stimulating Consumption," 11–12.

36. López, "Economics of Yerba Mate," 494.

37. Folch, "Stimulating Consumption," 11. On Paraguayan monetary history, see Juan Bautista Rivarola Paoli, *Historia monetaria del Paraguay: Monedas, bancos, crédito público* (Asunción, Para.: n.p., 1982).

38. On dynamics of debt peonage in this sector, see Jerry W. Cooney, "North to the Yerbales," in *Contested Ground: Comparative Frontiers on the Northern and Southern Edges of Spanish Empire*, ed. Donna J. Guy and Thomas E. Sheridan (Tucson: University of Arizona Press, 1998), 135–49, esp. 139. On the changing composition of the labor force, see Garavaglia, *Mercado interno*, 371–73, 378–79; and Jan M. G. Kleinpenning, *Rural Paraguay, 1870–1963: A Geography of Progress, Plunder and Poverty*, 2 vols. (Madrid: Iberoamericana, 2009), 1:636–37.

39. Folch, "Stimulating Consumption," 11; Garavaglia, *Mercado interno*, 257; López, "Economics of Yerba Mate," 500.

40. Efraím Cardozo, *El Paraguay colonial: Las raíces de la nacionalidad* (Buenos Aires: Nizza, 1959), 29.

41. Dobrizhoffer, *Historia de los abipones*, 1:201.

42. On the history of the Jesuit missions, see Sarreal, *Guaraní and Their Missions*; this statistic is from page 34.

43. This translation is shaped in part by the one in Eguiguren, Eguiguren, and Vega, *Mate in América*, 20.

44. Diego de Torres, "Carta del jesuita Diego de Torres a la Inquisición, sobre lo que convenía redmidiarse en las provincias del Paraguay y otras," Sept. 24, 1610, as cited in Oberti, *Historia y folklore del mate*, 92–93.

45. Antonio Ruiz de Montoya, *The Spiritual Conquest, Accomplished by the Religious of the Society of Jesus in the Provinces of Paraguay, Paraná, Uruguay, and Tape: A Personal Account of the Founding and Early Years of the Jesuit Paraguay Reductions*, trans. C. J. McNaspy (1639; St. Louis: Institute of Jesuit Sources, 1993), 41.

46. López, "Economics of Yerba Mate," 506.

47. Ruiz de Montoya, *Spiritual Conquest*, 43.

48. See, for example, C. I. Heck and E. G. de Mejia, "Yerba Mate Tea (*Ilex paraguariensis*): A Comprehensive Review on Chemistry, Health Implications, and Technological Considerations," *Journal of Food Science* 72, no. 9 (2007): 138–51. A recent review of scientific studies by students Anna Gawron-Gzella, Justyna Chanaj-Kaczmarket, and Judyta Cielecka-Pionetek ("Yerba Mate-A Long but Current History," *Nutrients* 13 [2021]: 1–19) concludes that yerba mate is largely healthy, helping to stimulate more energy, promote weight loss, fight inflammation, and prevent heart disease and some types of cancers. Yet drinking it with very hot water seems to increase some cancer risks, especially of the esophagus.

49. Garavaglia, *Mercado interno*, 53–55.

50. López, "Economics of Yerba Mate," 498.

51. Garavaglia, *Mercado interno*, 35–37.

52. López, "Economics of Yerba Mate," 501–2.

53. Eguiguren, Eguiguren, and Vega, *Mate in América*, 29.

54. Cooney, "North to the Yerbales," 142.

55. On process and profit, see Ross W. Jamieson, "The Essence of Commodification: Caffeine Dependencies in the Early Modern World," *Journal of Social History* 35, no. 2 (2001): 269–94; Sarreal, *Guaraní and Their Missions*, esp. 83; and Whigham, *Politics of River Trade*.

56. Whigham, *Politics of River Trade*, 110.

57. In 1747, Jesuit father José Cardiel specified that mate makers joined carpenters, weavers, and the like in working in specific jobs on the mission. Sánchez Labrador wrote that the Guaraní and others "beautifully drew on the gourds." Oberti, *Historia y folklore del mate*, 220–22.

58. Sarreal, *Guaraní and Their Missions*.

59. Jan M. G. Kleinpenning, *Rural Paraguay, 1515–1870: A Thematic Geography of Its Development*, 2 vols. (Madrid: Vervuert, 2003) 2:1162–63.

60. Jamieson, "Essence of Commodification," 277; Whigham, *Politics of River Trade*, esp. 11, 110.

61. Leaders in Santa Fe lobbied for this policy to support a local militia against Indigenous and Portuguese attacks, increasing prices in Tucumán, Salta, Potosí, and Lima. Marta Sánchez, "Mate in Criollo Society," in Eguiguren, Eguiguren, and Vega, *Mate in América*, 54. Due to this required stop, shops in Santa Fe were stocked with yerba paraguaya, honey, sugar, and tobacco. Florian Pauke, *Hacia allá y para acá* (1944; Santa Fe: Ministerio de Innovación y Cultura de la Provincia de Santa Fe, 2010), 138.

62. On the economics of the yerba mate trade, see López, "Economics of Yerba Mate"; Garavaglia, *Mercado interno*, 161–65; and Sarreal, *Guaraní and Their Missions*.

63. Whigam, *Politics of River Trade*, 111.

64. On protests, see Whigham, 111.

65. Garavaglia calculates this percentage during the period from 1667 to 1682 for the late seventeenth century and 1700 to 1720 for the early seventeenth century. See Garavaglia, *Mercado interno*, esp. 71–78.

66. Frézier, *Voyage*, 252. Horacio Botalla writes that yerba was introduced to Potosí in the 1640s. Horacio Botalla, "Bebidas de Ocio en el Río de la Plata," *Todo es historia*, no. 380 (Mar. 1999): 64.

67. Frézier, *Voyage*, 252.

68. Frézier, 252.

69. Pauke, *Hacia allá y para acá*, 555.

70. Garavaglia, *Mercado interno*, 61. On tea being sent back to Europe, see Eguiguren, Eguiguren, and Vega, *Mate in América*, 17.

71. Frézier, *Voyage*, 252.

72. Frézier, 253.

73. On Potosí, see Kris Lane, *Potosí: The Silver City That Changed the World* (Oakland: University of California Press, 2019).

74. Antonio de Ulloa, *A Voyage to South America*, vol. 1, 4th ed., trans. John Adams (1758; London: John Stockdale, 1806), 271.

75. Ulloa, 270-71, emphasis mine. This idea of Chapitones (or European Spaniards) not drinking mate (along with a reference to Frézier's explanation of little glass pipes) was later paraphrased and reproduced in the appendix of Anthony Zachariah Helms, *Travels from Buenos Ayres by Potosi to Lima, with Notes by the Translator* (London: Richard Phillips, 1806), 179–80.

76. Antonio de Ulloa, *Relación histórica del viaje a la América meridional*, vol. 3 (Madrid: Antonio Marin, 1748), 138.

77. Ulloa, *Voyage*, 271.

78. Citrus fruits originated in the Himalayas and traveled to southeast Asia before making it to Europe through Arab traders and eventually to the Americas with Europeans. The taste for citrus and rose water followed Arab migration to Iberia before making its

way to the New World. The preference for a flowery taste also had Mesoamerican origins. Marcy Norton describes the appreciation in Mesoamerica for the "flowery world" that locals incorporated in their consumption of cacao and transmitted back to Europe. Marcy Norton, "Tasting Empire: Chocolate and the European Internalization of Mesoamerican Aesthetics," *American Historical Review* 111, no. 3 (2006): 660–91. On oranges, see Bridget Chesterton, "Between Yerba Mate and Soy: The Orange as National Food and Landscape from the Early Nineteenth to the Early Twenty-First Centuries in Paraguay," *Global Food History* 8, no. 2 (2022): 128–48.

79. Jeffrey A. Erbig Jr., "Borderline Offerings: Toldería and Mapmakers in the Eighteenth-Century Río de la Plata," *Hispanic American Historical Review* 96, no. 3 (2016): 446 and 454.

80. Racialized definitions in the colonial era were not solely determined by ancestry but also by education, culture, and customs like dress and language. See, for example, Laura Gotkowitz, ed., *Histories of Race and Racism: The Andes and Mesoamerica from Colonial Times to the Present* (Durham: Duke University Press, 2011); and Ann Twinam, *Purchasing Whiteness: Pardos, Mulattos, and the Quest for Social Mobility in the Spanish Indies* (Stanford: Stanford University Press, 2015).

81. Ulloa, *Voyage*, 174–75.

82. Oberti, *Historia y folklore del mate*, 232.

83. On the Guaraní reaction to and complex range of reasons behind Jesuit expulsion, see Sarreal, *Guaraní and Their Missions*, esp. chap. 4.

84. Leonard, "The Expulsion of the Jesuits from Paraguay as Recounted by Louise Antoine de Bougainville (1767)," in Leonard, *Colonial Travelers*, 183.

85. See, for example, Daumas, *El problema de la yerba mate*, 5–7.

86. Sarreal, *Guaraní and Their Missions*, esp. 8–10, 89, 175, 180, and 220–22.

87. Sarreal, 220–22.

88. Cooney, "North to the Yerbales," 141; Whigham, *Politics of River Trade*, 112.

89. This did not change until the late nineteenth century. Jamieson, "Essence of Commodification," 286–87.

90. Coffee first reached the Americas in 1726, according to Eguiguren, Eguiguren, and Vega, *Mate in América*, 15; and Jamieson, "Essence of Commodification," 286–87.

91. José Cardiel, "Quadernillo sobre si en el estado presente pueden dar limosas, Concepción," May 2, 1766, as cited in Sarreal, *Guaraní and Their Missions*, 223.

92. Marta Sánchez argues that the demise of Jesuit networks limited access to yerba outside the Río de la Plata region. This was exacerbated during the wars of independence, when the Royalist army closed the borders to Alto Peru. Sánchez, "Mate in Criollo Society," 61–63.

93. Smuggled yerba deliberately escaped such official record keeping.

94. I suspect that this would not have been a common trope given the everydayness of mate for locals and the ways in which foreigners new to this ritualized drink took the lead in depicting it. On artwork in colonial Latin America, see, for example, Gauvin Alexander Bailey, *Art of Colonial Latin America* (London: Phaidon, 2005); and Susan Webster, *Lettered Artists and the Languages of Empire: Painters and the Profession in Early Colonial Quito* (Austin: University of Texas Press, 2017).

95. This analysis of Peruvian *casta* paintings draws on Tamara Walker's *Exquisite Slaves: Race, Clothing and Status in Colonial Lima* (Cambridge: Cambridge University Press, 2017), 97–127. On Peruvian *casta* paintings, see also Natalia Majluf, *Los cuadros del mestizaje del Virrey Amat: La representación etnográfica en el Perú Colonial* (Lima: Museo de Arte de Lima, 1999).

96. This illustration is reproduced in Eguiguren, Eguiguren, and Vega, *Mate in América*, preface. St. Rose of Lima was a woman from Lima named Isabel Flores de Oliva (1586–1617), who was the first person born in the New World to be canonized by the Catholic Church in 1671. She became the patron saint of Peru and all of South America. "St. Rose of Lima," Encyclopedia Britannica, www.britannica.com/biography/Saint-Rose-of-Lima (accessed Oct. 6, 2020).

97. In 1777, Juan de la Cruz Cano y Omedilla initiated his depiction of different types of Spanish clothing. On this project, see Valeriano Bozal, *Juan de la Cruz Cano y Omedilla y su Colección de trajes de España: Tantos antiguos como modernos* (Madrid: Turner, 1981), esp. plate 36; and Majluf, *Los cuadros del mestizaje*, 56.

98. Garavaglia describes Asunción as a "humble settlement" and the region as largely made up of campesinos. Garavaglia, *Mercado interno*, 214–15.

99. López cites Aguirre, who says that settlers who "refounded" Buenos Aires in 1580 regularly drank mate. He also refers to a 1683 report from the governor of Buenos Aires to the viceroy of Peru that explained that much of the yerba that passed through Buenos Aires was consumed there. Aníbal Arcondo describes mate as a staple of a colonial breakfast and as a classic "prelude" to it and mentions that chocolate was also sometimes on offer. López, "Economics of Yerba Mate"; Aníbal Arcondo, *Historia de la alimentación en Argentina, desde los orígenes hasta 1920* (Córdoba, Arg.: Ferreyra Editor, 2002), 112, 119, and 326.

100. When Pauke (sometimes spelled Bauke) drew local "Indians," he featured them drinking not yerba but the fermented and intoxicating corn drink called chicha, which he actively sought to replace with the sobering infusion. In his portraits of city dwellers, Paucke showcased Spanish and creole civilians' style of dress, which were humbler than their more lavishly dressed counterparts in Lima, with nary a mate in sight. On his attempts to convert his charges from chicha to mate, see Pauke, *Hacia allá y para acá*, esp. 227–30, 659–60. For artwork, see Florian Baucke, SJ, *Iconografía colonial rioplatense, 1749–1767: Costumbres y trajes de españoles, criollos e indios* (Buenos Aires: Viau y Zona, 1935).

101. Pauke, *Hacia allá y para acá*, 227–37, 660.

102. Pauke, 231.

103. Pedro Montenegro, *Castellano arbol de la yerba: Guaraní ibira caá miri*, published in *Materia médica misionera* (1710; Buenos Aires: Imprenta de la Biblioteca Nacional, 1945), plate 1; José Sánchez Labrador, *Caá y arbol de la yerba del Paraguay o the del Sud*. For reproductions of illustrations, see Navajas, *Caá Porã*, 96–97.

104. This was later reproduced on a Chilean postcard.

105. Francisco Xarque, *Insignes misioneros de la Compañía de Jesús en la Provincia del Paraguay* (Pamplona: Julián Picón, 1747), as cited in Oberti, *Historia y folklore del mate*, 224.

106. Perhaps he was referring to the island of Chiloe, where a Spanish population lived since early colonization.

107. John Byron, *The Narrative of the Honourable John Byron (Commodore in a Late Expedition around the World) Containing an Account of the Great Distresses Suffered by Himself and His Companions on the Coast of Patagonia, from the Year 1740, till Their Arrival in England, 1746* (London: S. Baker and G. Leigh, and T. Davies, 1768), 193.

108. George Vancouver, *A Voyage of Discovery to the North Pacific Ocean and around the World*, vol. 3 (London: printed for G. G. and J. Robinson, Pasternoster-Row and J. Edwards, Pall-Mall, 1798), 414.

109. A. Carrió de la Vandera, *El lazarillo de ciegos caminantes* (Buenos Aires: Emecé, 1979), 281–82, as cited in Eguiguren, Eguiguren, and Vega, *Mate in América*, 40.

110. For a broader study of Latin America's material culture, see Arnold J. Bauer, *Goods, Power, History: Latin America's Material Culture* (New York: Cambridge University Press, 2001).

111. Pilar González Bernaldo de Quirós explains that this new viceroyalty "covered a vast territory from Alto Peru to Tierra del Fuego, or at least theoretically given that a large part of the area, particularly south of Buenos Aires, was under the control of rebellious Indians. . . . When the insurrections began, Buenos Aires had only been the capital for thirty years and was far from stamping its authority on the whole of this vast region." Pilar González Bernaldo de Quirós, *Civility and Politics in the Origins of the Argentine Nation: Sociabilities in Buenos Aires, 1829–1862* (1999 [originally in French]; Los Angeles: UCLA Latin American Center Publications, 2006), 17.

112. Julio Djendererdijan argues, "Most of the territory occupied today by the Republic of Uruguay, the Brazilian state of Rio Grande do Sul, and the Argentine provinces of Corrientes, Misiones, and Entre Ríos was once one vast frontier area of the Spanish colonial empire of the mid-eighteenth century." Julio Djendererdijan, "Roots of Revolution: Frontier Settlement Policy and the Emergence of New Spaces of Power in the Río de la Plata Borderlands, 1777–1810," *Hispanic American Historical Review* 88, no. 4 (2008): 639–68.

113. Carlos Mordo and Roberto Vega, "Guaraní, Conquerors, and Missionaries," in Eguiguren, Eguiguren, and Vega, *Mate in América*, 34n38.

114. On financing from Buenos Aires, see Whigham, *Politics of River Trade*, 112; and Nicolas Shumway, *The Invention of Argentina* (Berkeley: University of California Press, 1991), 13. On trade, more broadly, see, for example, Fabricio Prado, *Edge of Empire: Atlantic Networks and Revolution in Bourbon Río de la Plata (Berkeley: University of California Press, 1991)*; and Susan Midgen Socolow, *The Merchants of Buenos Aires, 1778–1810: Family and Commerce* (1978; Cambridge: Cambridge University Press, 2009).

115. Cardozo, *El Paraguay colonial*, 106, as cited in Cooney, "North to the Yerbales," 141.

116. Cooney, "North to the Yerbales," 142.

117. Bragueto explains that the first references to Brazil's export of erva mate to Buenos Aires and Montevideo are from 1804. The first mill was built in in Paranaguá, Paraná, in 1815. Garavaglia points to the irony that as Paraguayan exports reached their high point in the first two decades of the 1800s, Brazil began to sporadically export its yerba. Claudio Roberto Bragueto, "O processo de industrialização do Paraná até a década de 1970," *Geografia*, 8, no. 2 (1999): 149–60, esp. 149; Garvaglia, *Mercado interno*, 84–85.

118. Paraná became a separate Brazilian province in 1853 and a state in 1891.

119. *Notes on the Viceroyalty of La Plata in South America with a Sketch of the Manners and Character of the Inhabitants, Collected during a Residence in the City of Montevideo, by a Gentleman Recently Returned from It* (London: J. J. Stockdale, 1808), 35.

120. *Notes on the Viceroyalty of La Plata*, 35–36.

121. *Notes on the Viceroyalty of La Plata*, 37.

122. *Notes on the Viceroyalty of La Plata*, 38.

123. Pauke, *Hacia allá y para acá*, 659.

124. John Luccock, *Notes on Rio de Janeiro and the Southern Parts of Brazil; Taken during a Residence of Ten Years in That Country from 1808 to 1818* (London: Samuel Leigh, 1820), 154.

125. He continues that after taking this breakfast, the traveler must hurry on to the next "friendly abode at or before midday; for however welcome a stranger may be, the master of the house seldom thinks of ordering a table to be set out at any but the usual hours; nevertheless, at these, everyone present, if a *white man*, is welcomed and partakes with the family." Luccock, 217, my emphasis.

126. Notably, this coffee was served by a household slave. Luccock, 126.

127. Sánchez claims that starting in the last decades of the eighteenth century, coffee and chocolate became the preferred drinks of Lima society. Sánchez, "Mate in Criollo Society," 42.

128. Oberti, *Historia y folklore del mate*, 225.

129. Of the illustrations we have seen thus far, Gay's portrayal of the large Chilean *tertulia* is unique in including servers, though they seem to be scooping hot chocolate rather than serving mate (see fig. 1.3). While Gay situated this composition in late colonial Santiago, he did not publish it until the postindependence era. Claudio Gay, *Atlas de la historia física y política de Chile*, vol. 1 (Paris: E. Thunot, 1854), no. 30.

CHAPTER TWO

1. The Phrygian cap was even placed at the center of the Argentine coat of arms in 1813.

2. A *cielito* is a poetic form written in the popular language of the countryside with octo-syllabic quatrains that rhyme in the second and fourth lines. Uruguayan scholar Fernando Assunçao explains that this particular *cielito* was so widely recited that it became popular folklore. This painting of a *cielito* is believed to form part of Pellegrini's first (unpublished) album of images from 1831, which were dedicated to Mr. Woodbine Parish, "the General Consul and Charge d'affaires de S.M.B." In 1841, Pellegrini published an album, *Recuerdos del Río de la Plata*, in which this particular painting apparently did not appear. The full title of this 1831 work often appears in slightly different iterations; here I follow the title from C. E. Pellegrini, *Tableau pittoresque de Buenos Ayres* (Buenos Aires: Librería L'Amateur, 1958), no. 17. On the popularity of this *cielito*, see Fernando O. Assunçao, *El mate* (Montevideo, Uru.: ACRA, 1967), 68.

3. Anonymous [Bartolomé Hidalgo], "Un gaucho de la Guardia del Monte" (1820), verse 141–44. On this *cielito* see Angel Núñez, "Un cielito gaucho contra Fernando VII," *Revista de crítica literaria latinoamericana* 15, no. 30 (1989): 9–23.

4. Marcy Norton, *Sacred Gifts, Profane Pleasures: A History of Tobacco and Chocolate in the Atlantic World* (Ithaca, NY: Cornell University Press, 2008), and "Tasting Empire: Chocolate and the European Internalization of Mesoamerican Aesthetics," *American Historical Review* 111, no. 3 (2006): 660–91.

5. Michel Gobat, "The Invention of Latin America: A Transnational History of Anti-imperialism, Democracy and Race," *American Historical Review* 118, no. 5 (2013): 1345–75.

6. Nicolas Shumway, *The Invention of Argentina* (Berkeley: University of California Press, 1991), 6.

7. On the place of pre-conquest peoples in shaping elite and national identities across the region, including in the Río de la Plata during and after the independence era, see Rebecca Earle, *The Return of the Native: Indians and Myth Making in Spanish America, 1810–1930* (Durham: Duke University Press, 2007). Among the Rioplatense political elite, Shumway argues that Oriental caudillo José Artigas was relatively unique in trying to include "Indians" into the "founding myths" of the Río de la Plata and encouraging more to settle there. Notably, Hidalgo fought under Artigas and the two were likely familiar with each other's ideas. Shumway, *Invention of Argentina*, esp. 49 and 61.

8. On Hidalgo and gauchesque poetry, see Shumway, *Invention of Argentina*, esp. 67–79.

9. William Garrett Acree, *Everyday Reading: Print Culture and Collective Identity in the Río de la Plata, 1780–1910* (Nashville: Vanderbilt University Press, 2011), 57. See also Acree, "*Divisas y deberes*: Women and the Symbolic Economy of War Rhetoric in the

Río de la Plata, 1810–1910," *Journal of Latin American Cultural Studies: Travesía* 22, no. 2 (2013): 213–37.

10. Nelly Perazzo, "Carlos Enrique Pelligrini," Grove Art Online, https://doi.org/10.1093 /gao/9781884446054.article.T066090 (accessed Apr. 7, 2020). Pellegrini was lured across the Atlantic Ocean by the liberal Unitarian government of Bernardino Rivadavia (1826–27), which had contracted him as a hydraulic engineer for Buenos Aires. When he arrived in January 1828, he found the port of Buenos Aires blockaded by the Brazilian fleet and was forced to disembark in Montevideo. In Montevideo, he was hired to engineer fortifications to protect the city. During his time there, he helped build fortifications and witnessed the political compromise brokered by the British that led to the creation of the Estado Oriental de Uruguay. When he finally made it to Buenos Aires in November 1828, Rivadavia's government was out of power and the opposition Federalist Party was taking over.

11. Alejo B. González Garaño lists the most important costumbristas of this era to be Vidal, Pellegrini, Morel, Bacle, Rugendas, d'Hastrel, and Grashof. We will discuss all of them here, but Grashof, who mostly painted in Chile and did not do any illustrations with mate to my knowledge. Alejo B. González Garaño, *Pallière: Ilustrador de la Argentina, 1856–1866* (Buenos Aires: Sociedad de Historia Argentina, 1942), 5. Some of Pellegrini's work was published in London and Paris. Other pieces were published locally. On Pellegrini and other artists of French origin, see Philippe Cros and Alberto Dodero, *Aventura en las pampas: Los pintores franceses en el Río de la Plata* (Buenos Aires: Artes Gráficos Ronor, 2003), esp. 175–78.

12. See Juan Carlos Garavaglia, *Mercado interno y economía colonial: Tres siglos de historia de la yerba mate* (1983; Rosario, Arg.: Prohistoria, 2008).

13. This interpretation of Uruguayan independence is informed by Alex Borucki's synthesis of Uruguayan history. He also points out that the continued existence of Uruguay as a republic was at stake in the 1839–51 Guerra Grande. Alex Borucki, "Uruguay," Oxford Bibliographies, June 27, 2017, www.oxfordbibliographies.com/view/document/obo-9780199766581 /obo-9780199766581-0192.xml.

14. Karen Racine, "'This England and This Now': British Cultural and Intellectual Influence in the Spanish American Independence Era," *Hispanic American Historical Review* 90, no. 3 (Aug. 2010): 425.

15. In Argentina, Unitarians wished to govern from the port city of Buenos Aires and maintain exclusive control over customs revenues, whereas Federalists rejected liberal *porteños'* leadership and argued for stronger provincial rights and, sometimes, the wider disbursement of profits to the provinces.

16. Eric D. Carter, "Misiones Province, Argentina: How Borders Shape Political Identity," in *Borderlines and Borderlands: Political Oddities at the Edge of the Nation State*, ed. Alexander C. Diener and Joshua Hagen (Lanham, MD: Rowman and Littlefield, 2010), 155–73.

17. Garavaglia inspired this point in an interview with Prof. Andrés G. Freijomil on his blog *Teoría de la historia* celebrating the twenty-fifth anniversary of *Mercado interno*, hosted at this site: https://introduccionalahistoriajvg.wordpress.com/2012/08/08/%E2%9C%8D-mercado -interno-y-economia-colonial-tres-siglos-de-historia-de-la-yerba-mate-1983/ (accessed May 15, 2018).

18. Thomas Whigham, *The Politics of River Trade: Tradition and Development in the Upper Plata, 1780–1870* (Albuquerque: University of New Mexico Press, 1991), 118.

19. Francia asked them to present these "samples of the productions of Paraguay" before the House of Commons and declare his interest in "political and commercial intercourse" between the two nations. J. P. Robertson and W. P. Robertson, *Letters on Paraguay: Comprising*

an *Account of a Four Years' Residence in That Republic under the Government of the Dictator Francia*, 2 vols., 2nd ed. (Philadelphia: E. L. Carey and A. Hart, 1838), 2:181–82.

20. Christine Folch, "Stimulating Consumption: Yerba Mate Myths, Markets, and Meanings from Conquest to Present," *Comparative Studies in Society and History* 52, no. 1 (2010): 6–36.

21. Whigham, *Politics of River Trade*, esp. 120.

22. Marta Sánchez, "Mate in Criollo Society," in *The Mate in América*, by José M. Eguiguren Molina, Javier Eguiguren Molina, and Roberto Vega (ed.), trans. Francis Casal (Buenos Aires: La Stampa, 2004), 61–62.

23. Garavaglia, *Mercado interno*, 421.

24. As discussed later, in Chile, elites would turn to the more cosmopolitan beverages of tea and coffee around the 1870s. Even so, the urban working class and poor folks in rural areas were not in a position to afford more expensive imported alternates and continued to covet mate up until at least the mid-twentieth century. Within Bolivia, Santa Cruz de la Serra retained the practice of consuming yerba mate after Jesuit expulsion and independence. Benjamin Orlove and Arnold J. Bauer, "Chile in the Belle Époque: Primitive Producers, Civilized Consumers," in *The Allure of the Foreign: Imported Goods in Postcolonial Latin America*, ed. Benjamin Orlove (Ann Arbor: University of Michigan Press, 1997), 131–38; Sánchez, "Mate in Criollo Society," 45.

25. The weight equivalent is from the Real Academia Español, https://dle.rae.es/?w= arroba (accessed June 8, 2020). For pricing, Whigham, *Politics of River Trade*, 121.

26. Whigham, *Politics of River Trade*, 121–24.

27. Jan M. G. Kleinpenning, *Rural Paraguay, 1515–1870: A Thematic Geography of Its Development*, 2 vols. (Madrid: Vervuert, 2003), 1:1230–31.

28. Email correspondence with Thomas Whigam, Sept. 2, 2020.

29. Auguste de Saint-Hilaire, *Histoire des plantes les plus remarquables du Brésil et du Paraguay*, vol. 1 (Paris: Chez A. Belin, 1824).

30. Sainte-Hillaire, 16.

31. Historian Stephen Bell supports this interpretation. He describes Bonpland's identification on this island and his subsequent efforts to establish a sustainable yerbal in Santa Ana, in the disputed territory of Entre Ríos near the former Jesuit missions and the Paraguayan border. In late 1821, Bonpland, who was invited to the region by Rivadavia and worked in association with Unitarians from Buenos Aires, was taken prisoner by Francia. Stephen Bell, *A Life in the Shadow: Aimé Bonpland in Southern South America* (Stanford: Stanford University Press, 2010), 39; Pau Navajas, *Caá Porã: El espíritu de la yerba mate, una historia de plata* (Corrientes, Arg.: Las Marías, 2013), 148–50.

32. See, for example, T. A. Joyce, "Yerba Mate, the Tea of South America," *Pan American Magazine*, Nov.–Dec. 1921, 307–8.

33. For a biography on Emeric Essex Vidal, see Alejo B. Garaño, *Iconografía argentina, anterior a 1820* (Buenos Aires: Emecé, 1947), 37–76. Vidal also illustrated gauchos without mates and two Pampean Indians, one of whom was smoking but neither of whom had a mate.

34. Emeric E. Vidal, *Picturesque Illustrations of Buenos Aires and Montevideo* (London: R. Ackermann, 1820), 108.

35. Vidal, 109.

36. For now, such a traveler was offered this mate by a male peer; as we shall see in the next chapter, it would later be offered by a rural woman. I trace the travels of this image in Rebekah E. Pite, "The Rural Woman Enters the Frame: A Visual History of Gender, Nation,

and the Goodbye Mate in the Postcolonial Río de la Plata," *Journal of Social History* 54, no. 4 (Summer 2021): 1120–59.

37. Vidal, *Picturesque Illustrations*, 77.

38. Alexander Gillespie, *Gleanings and Remarks Collected during Many Months of Residence at Buenos Ayres, and within the Upper Country* (Leeds: B. Dewhirst, 1818), 85, 157–58.

39. Alexander Gillespie, *Buenos Aires y El Interior* (Buenos Aires: Hyspamérica, 1986), 123, as cited in Horacio Botalla, "Bebidas del Ocio en el Río de la Plata," *Todo es Historia*, no. 380 (Mar. 1999): 66 and 70.

40. John Miers, *Travels in Chile and La Plata, Including Accounts respecting the Geography, Geology, Statistic, Government, Finances, Agriculture, Manners and Customs, and the Mining Operations in Chile*, vol 1. (London: Baldwin, Cradock, and Joy, 1826), 41–42.

41. Miers, 42–43.

42. Miers, 43–44.

43. Miers, 44 and 77. On the regular imperial and ecclesiastical provision of yerba mate, tobacco, and other goods to native *tolderías* in the colonial era, see Jeffrey Alan Erbig Jr., *Where Caciques and Mapmakers Met: Border Making in Eighteenth-Century South America* (Chapel Hill: University of North Carolina Press, 2020), esp. 1, 21, 30–34, 84–86.

44. William MacCann, *Two Thousand Miles' Ride through the Argentine Provinces* (London: Smith, Elder, and Co., 1853). On shepherds and herdsmen, see 25, and on privates, 62.

45. Miers, *Travels in Chile and La Plata*, vol. 1, 70.

46. More female travel writers published their work in the late nineteenth century. On Graham in particular and women travelers more broadly, see June E. Hahner, *Women through Women's Eyes: Latin American Women in Nineteenth-Century Travel Accounts* (1998; Oxford: Rowman and Littlefield, 2005). Graham spelled the local infusion both as "matte" and "matee." Maria Graham, *Journal of a Residence in Chile during the Year 1822* (London: Longman, Hurst, Rees, Orme, Brown, Green and J. Murray, 1824), 119.

47. Graham, *Journal of a Residence in Chile*, 119.

48. Sánchez, "Mate in Criollo Society," 79.

49. Graham, *Journal of a Residence in Chile*, 119.

50. Graham, 119.

51. After several rounds of mate, the group enjoyed "sugar-biscuits" and cold water before departing. Graham, 152.

52. She mentioned drinking it with friends before going to the theater (217), having it served at a party with milk and tea (224), and drinking it in a more casual manner (236) and noted that it was "more refreshing still than tea after a day's journey" (228) in her *Journal of a Residence in Chile*.

53. Of course, they could have been saying this to be polite. According to someone who traveled with San Martín, he preferred *un mate de café*, or a mate infused with coffee rather than with water. Manuel de Olazábal, *Memoria y episodios de la guerra de la independencia, Gualeguaychú, 1864*, as cited in Botalla, "Bebidas de Ocio," 68. For quote, Graham, *Journal of a Residence in Chile*, 282.

54. Graham, *Journal of a Residence in Chile*, 228.

55. Graham, 249.

56. Graham, 212.

57. See, for example, Elizabeth Anne Kuznesof, "Domestic Service and Urbanization in Latin America from Nineteenth Century to Present," in *Proletarian and Gendered Mass Migrations: A Global Perspective on Continuities and Discontinuities from the 19th to the 21st*

Centuries, ed. Dirk Hoerder and Amarjit Kaur (Leiden: Brill Publishing, 2013), 85–102; and Nara Milanich, "Women, Children, and the Social Organization of Domestic Labor in Chile," *Hispanic American Historical Review* 91, no. 1 (2011): 29–62.

58. José Gabriel Jeffs Munizaga, "Chile en el macrocircuito de la yerba mate: Auge y caída de un producto típico del Cono Sur americano," *RIVAR* 4, no. 11 (May 2017): 148–70, esp. 153, 158–63.

59. Peter Schmidtmeyer, *Travels into Chile over the Andes in the Years 1820 and 1821: With Some Sketches of the Productions and Agriculture* (London: Longman, Hurst, Orme, Brown, and Green, 1824), 216.

60. Schmidtmeyer, *Travels into Chile*, 246, plate 13.

61. Schmidtmeyer says he was in the Valle de Guasco, while Trostiné suggests this house was actually in the Argentine province of Cuyo. Schmidtmeyer, 266; Rodolfo Trostiné, *La pintura en las provincias argentinas* (Santa Fe: Universidad Nacional del Literal, 1950), 7.

62. On the composition and historiography of this region, see Juan Carlos Garavaglia and Jorge D. Gelman, "Rural History of the Río de la Plata, 1600–1850: Results of a Historiographical Renaissance," *Latin American Research Review* 30, no. 3 (1995): 75–105.

63. Narcisco Parchappe, *Diario de la expedición fundadora del fuerte 25 de mayo en Cruz Guerra*, as cited in Sánchez, "Mate in Criollo Society," 72.

64. The servants who appeared in Gay's mid-nineteenth-century vision of a colonial *tertulia* were shown serving hot chocolate rather than mate (see fig. 1.3).

65. On this trend in colonial artwork, see, for example, Tamara Walker, *Exquisite Slaves: Race, Clothing, and Status in Colonial Lima* (Cambridge: Cambridge University Press, 2017).

66. While we do not know the precise order in which Pellegrini painted them, as María de Lourdes Ghidoli has suggested, the servant's movement could provide some clues. María de Lourdes Ghidoli, *Estereotipos en negro: Representaciones y autorrepresentaciones visuales de afroporteños en el siglo XX* (Rosario, Arg.: Prohistoria, 2015), 70–75.

67. Regina A. Root, *Couture and Consensus: Fashion and Politics in Postcolonial Argentina* (Minneapolis: University of Minnesota Press, 2010).

68. For a fresh take and review of historiography on Rosas in English, see Jeffrey M. Shumway, *A Woman, a Man, a Nation: Mariquita Sánchez, Juan Manuel de Rosas, and the Beginnings of Argentina* (Albuquerque: University of New Mexico Press, 2019).

69. This painting is analyzed in a microhistory of the Villarino family in Chivilcoy, in the province of Buenos Aires. María Amanda Caggiano et al., "Antropolgía y parentesco: Aportes para una historiografía regional," *Boletín de historia de la ciencia*, no. 43 (2003): 1–39. See also Ghidoli, *Estereotipos en negro*, 75.

70. José Antonio Wilde (1813–85) was born in Buenos Aires to British immigrant parents and went on to become the director of Argentina's national library. José Antonio Wilde, *Buenos Aires desde setenta años atrás*, 2nd ed. (Buenos Aires: Imprenta y Librería de Mayo de C. Casavalle, 1881), 139.

71. Arsène Isabelle, *Viaje a Argentina, Uruguay y Brazil* (Buenos Aires: Ed. Americana, 1830; Buenos Aires: Emecé, 2001), 133. Isabell set this scene in a Buenos Aires *tertulia*.

72. Isabelle (2001), 133.

73. Paraguay only passed the "Freedom of the Womb Law" in 1842 and emancipation in 1869. On the repeated, ineffectual attempts to prohibit the slave trade and continuity of unfree labor in Buenos Aires, see Paulina Alberto, "*Liberta* by Trade: Negotiating the Terms of Unfree Labor in Gradual Abolition Buenos Aires (1820s–1830s)," *Journal of Social History* 52, no. 3 (2019): 619–51; and Ghidoli, *Estereotipos en negro*. On the slave trade to South America,

see Alex Borucki et al., "Atlantic History and the Slave Trade to Spanish America," *American Historical Review* 120, no. 2 (Apr. 2015): 433–61. For a comparative analysis of abolition and its aftermath for people of African descent in Latin America, see George Reid Andrews, *Afro-Latin America: Black Lives, 1600–2000* (Cambridge, MA: Harvard University Press, 2016).

74. At this point, census takers estimated the port city was home to some 45,000 people. Pilar González Bernaldo de Quirós, *Civility and Politics in the Origins of the Argentine Nation: Sociabilities in Buenos Aires, 1829–1862* (1999 [originally in French]; Los Angeles: UCLA Latin American Center Publications, 2006), 29.

75. An 1833 edict drafted male *libertos*, legally due to earn their freedom, into the army. Ghidoli, *Estereotipos en negro*, 67.

76. *Damas de Buenos Ayres*, lithograph by August Borget, ca. 1830–40, courtesy of Biblioteca Nacional de Uruguay; another version of this same composition, often titled *Señora Porteña. Por la mañana* and colored differently, appeared in *Trages y costumbres de la provincia de Buenos Aires*, no. 1 (Buenos Aires: Bacle y Cía, Impresores litográficos del Estado, c. 1833–35), this lithograph is reproduced on Museo Marc Facebook page; and in Ghidoli, *Estereotipos en negro*, 66.

77. Bonafacio del Carril, *Monumenta iconographica: Paisajes, tipos, usos y costumbres en la Argentina, 1536–1860* (Buenos Aires: Emecé, 1964), 57.

78. Ghidoli points out that this marginal positioning typifies the portrayal of people of African descent in nineteenth-century artwork from Buenos Aires. Ghidoli, *Esteriotipos en negro*.

79. This version of *Señoras por la mañana* (Buenos Aires, 1833) is available at Research Gate, www.researchgate.net/figure/Litografia-Bacle-Moulin-Senoras-por-la-manana-Buenos -Aires-1833_fig3_287395499 (accessed Apr. 15, 2022).

80. On the definition and "softer, more ambiguous term" of *criado/a* and the legal status of the *liberto/a* as well as the complex experiences and negotiations of a specific family of Afrodescendant women over three generations, see Alberto, "*Liberta* by Trade," esp. 626.

81. Ghidoli, *Esteriotipos en negro*, 68.

82. On Artigas, see N. Shumway, *Invention of Argentina*, esp. chap. 3. The nickname "Ansina" refers not only to Joaquín Lenzina but also to Manuel Antonio Ledesma and is also sometimes used to refer to other Afrodescendants who fought with Artigas, including Martínez, according to Alejandro Belvis Gortázar, "Ansina ¿Un heróe Afro-Uruguayo? Los héroes fundadores," *Perspectivas desde el silgo*, vol. 21, Carlos Demasi and Eduardo Piazza, comp. (Montevideo: CIEU, 2006). On Afro-Uruguayans' efforts to recognize Ansina's contributions, see Hernán Rodríguez, "Memoria e identidad en el relato histórico de los intelectuales afrouruguayos del Centenario (1925–1930)," *Claves. Revista de Historia* 5, no. 9 (July–Dec. 2019): 145–73.

83. This well-known painting is displayed at the Museo Histórico del Gobierno in Montevideo and was issued as a stamp in 1930 and 1950. In 1967, the figure of "Ansina" appeared on a stamp alone with a mate with the caption "fiel servidor del Grl. José Artigas" (faithful server of General José Artigas), and in 2019 he appeared alone in front of an Afro-Uruguayan militia. The previous year, in 2018, a national decree declared Joaquín Lenzina "Ansina" as "Comandante de las Milicias Artiguistas de Libertos" (Commander of Artiguas' Liberto Militia), enabling him to emerge as an active historical protagonist. Artigas and "Ansina" also appeared together in a televised advertisement by the Brazilian yerba brand Canarias called *Homenaje* (Homage). For analysis, see Lourdes Beatriz Zetune Ingold, "La publicidad como sistema mitopráctico: Un estudio de los mitos de la nación uruguaya en la comunicación

publicitaria de la marca de yerba mate Canarias" (master's thesis, University De la República Uruguay, 2020), esp. 39–45, 64, 114, 308–9. For stamps, see Ingold, 45, and for an online version of the painting, see Arte Activo, museos.gub.uy/arteactivo/item/blanes-viale-pedro.html (accessed Apr. 15, 2022).

84. Thomas J. Page, *La Plata, the Argentine Confederation and Paraguay, Being a Narrative of the Exploration of the Tributaries of the River La Plata and Adjacent Countries during the Years 1853, '54, '55, and '56, under the Orders of the United States Government* (New York: Harper and Brothers, 1859), 49.

85. John Parish Robertson arrived in the River Plate in 1806 and returned in 1810; in 1811 he went to Paraguay, where he was joined by his brother William Parish Robertson a few years later. After declaring bankruptcy and returning to England in the 1830s, the Robertson brothers published three volumes that covered their travels in South America called *Letters on Paraguay*, and later republished as *Four Years in Paraguay*. On the Robertson brothers, see John Hoyt Williams, "Woodbine Parish and the 'Opening' of Paraguay," *Proceedings of the American Philosophical Society* 116, no. 4 (Aug. 1972): 343–49; S. Samuel Trifilo, "A Bibliography of British Travel Books in Argentina: 1810–1860," *The Americas* 16, no. 2 (Oct. 1959): 133–43, 142; and Miguel Ángel Gauto Bejarano, ed., *Cartas sobre Paraguay por John Parish Robertson y William Parish Robertson* (1838; Asunción, Para.: Arandurã, 2019).

86. Robertson and Robertson, *Letters on Paraguay*, 2:126.

87. Robertson and Robertson, *Letters on Paraguay*, 1:172.

88. Robertson and Robertson, *Letters on Paraguay*, 1:218.

89. Johann Rengger, *The Reign of Doctor Joseph Gaspard Roderick de Francia, in Paraguay* (London: Thomas Hurst, Edward Chance and Co., 1827), 199–200.

90. Robertson and Robertson, *Letters on Paraguay*, 1:218.

91. Robertson and Robertson, *Letters on Paraguay*, 2:198.

92. This illustration originally appeared in the first edition. It is now held by the Museo del Barro in Asunción, Paraguay.

93. Milda Rivarola et al., "Republic of Paraguay," Oxford Art Online, 2003, https://doi .org/10.1093/gao/9781884446054.article.T065292.

94. The long list of subscribers published in these volumes included both male and female names.

95. Robertson and Robertson, *Letters on Paraguay*, 2:91–101.

96. Navajas makes the point that this system is depicted incorrectly by the artist, as the tunnel below was built precisely to avoid the smoke getting out of control in the first place. Navajas, *Caá Porã*, 165.

97. Dessin de Fuchs, *Récolte du mate sur les bords du Parana, au Paraguay*, from Alfred Demersay, "Fragments d'un voyage au Paraguay," in *Le Tour du monde* (Paris: Hachette, 1865); "Curing Yerba," in Page, *La Plata, the Argentine Confederation, and Paraguay*, 137. Both images are reproduced and cited in Milda Rivarola, *Paraguay ilustrado: El grabado europeo del siglo XIX* (Asunción, Para.: Editorial Servilibro, 2016), 243–44.

98. Robertson and Robertson, *Letters on Paraguay*, 2:91–101.

99. Erbig, *Caciques and Mapmakers*, esp. 29–30, 34.

100. For analysis of the narrative construction of this and other seminal moments in the construction of Uruguay as a "neo-Europe" without Indigenous people, see Vannina Sztainbok, "From Salsipuedes to Tabaré: Race, Space, and the Uruguayan Subject," *Thamyris/ Intersecting* 20 (2010): 175–92, esp. 178.

101. Sztainbok, 178.

102. The monument, which reinforced the notion that there were no longer Indigenous people in Uruguay, was inaugurated in 1938 at the Prado de Montevideo. Ingold, "La publicidad como sistema mitopráctico," 64–66; Sztainbok, "From Salsipuedes to Tabaré."

103. Sztainbok suggests Fructuoso Rivera led the troops, while Ingold suggests it was his son-in-law, Bernabé Rivera. Sztainbok, "From Salsipuedes to Tabaré," 178; Ingold, "La publicidad como sistema mitopráctico," 66n47.

104. Rosas brought thirteen-year-old Eugenia, whose father had worked as one of Rosas's ranch hands and for whom he became an official legal guardian after her father's death, into his home to care for his ill wife, Encarnación. On the relationship between Rosas and Castro, as well as Rosas's relationship to mate, see J. Shumway, *A Woman, a Man, a Nation*, esp. 223.

105. Domingo Faustino Sarmiento, *Facundo: Civilización y barbarie*, 4th ed. (1845; New York, D. Appleton y Compañía, 1868), 118.

106. Monvoisin spent just a short time in Buenos Aires due to Rosas. Cros explains that this painting and one of a Federalist gaucho (without mate) and a *porteña* at church were commissioned by a local, Baron Picole d'Hermillon. Cros, *Aventura en las pampas*, 74; for image, see 81. To see this painting, see Biblioteca Virtual Miguel Cervantes, www.cervantesvirtual .com/portales/jose_marmol/imagenes_contexto/imagen/imagenes_contexto_08_quinsac _soldado_de_rosas/ (accessed Apr. 1, 2021).

107. The presence of Rosas's portrait echoed that of the conquistadors included in Frèzier's depiction of the elite Chilean women drinking mate inside, over a century earlier. Descalzi arrived in the Río de la Plata region in 1823; he is best known for his portrait of Rosas. His mother was married to fellow artist Carlos Morel from 1830 to 1838. Wikipedia, https:// en.wikipedia.org/wiki/Cayetano_Descalzi; painting at Wikimedia, https://commons .wikimedia.org/wiki/File:Boudoir_federal.jpg (accessed Apr. 15, 2023).

108. Philippe Cros and Alberto Dodero, *Aventura en las pampas: Los pintores franceses en el Río de la Plata* (Buenos Aires: self-published, 2003), 86.

109. He published this series with the Litografía de las Artes de Luis Aldao. This analysis is drawn from an online newspaper article by Nanu Zalazar, "Carlos Morel: Un verdadero pionero del arte argentino," *Gaceta mercantil*, June 4, 2016, www.gacetamercantil.com/notas /102387/.

110. Nelly Perazzo, "Carlos Morel," Grove Art Online, https://doi.org/10.1093/gao /9781884446054.article.T059558 (accessed Apr. 7, 2020).

111. For a reproduction and analysis of *Una hora antes de partir*, see Bellas Artes, www .bellasartes.gob.ar/coleccion/obra/5222/. In his rendering of an elite urban home, Morel made a different choice. In 1844, he painted a White woman sipping a mate with a Black servant standing behind her with her arms crossed, which appears on the cover of Root, *Couture and Consensus*.

112. *Parada para hacer noche, Cabildo y piramide*, and *Baile Criollo*, reproduced in Johann Moritz Rugendas, *Costumbres sudamericanas: Argentina, Chile, Uruguay: 25 agudas* (Buenos Aires: Pardo-Emecé, 1959).

113. Juan Camaña, untitled painting of "Soldados de Rosas jugando a las cartas," 1852, available at https://artedelaargentina.com/disciplinas/artista/pintura/juan-camana (accessed Jan. 17, 2023); and W. Baldino, *La tarde en el campo* (1860), reproduced in Véra Stedile Zattera, *Gaúcho: Iconografia, séculos XIX e XX* (Porto Alegre: Pallotti, 1995).

114. I make this claim based on my review of seventy-three images that include a mate that I have been able to identify from 1820 to 1869.

115. Jean León Pallière was born in 1823 to French parents and brought back to France at age seven. He began studying art in Paris at age thirteen and first traveled to Buenos Aires in 1848, settling there in 1856 but continuing to travel throughout Latin America and Europe. Leon Pallière, Miguel Solá, and Ricardo Gutiérrez, *Diario de viaje por la América del Sud* (Buenos Aires: Ediciones Peuser, 1945), 16–32.

116. Sztainbok, "From Salsipuedes to Tabaré," 178.

117. It is not clear whether the servant, who has straight dark hair, was intended to be of African descent or of mixed or Indigenous descent.

118. This piece of art appeared in nearly every collection of Argentine art I reviewed, including Fundación Konex, *100 obras maestras, 100 pintores argentinos* (Buenos Aires: Museo Nacional de Bellas Artes, 1994).

119. *La tribuna* (Buenos Aires), Aug. 7, 1861 as cited in Roberto Amigo, *Un alto en el campo*, Bellas Artes, www.bellasartes.gob.ar/coleccion/obra/3187/ (accessed Apr. 30, 2020).

120. Amigo, *Un alto en el campo*.

121. Silvia Glocer explains that the lyrics were written by Estanislao del Campo. Silvia Glocer, "La Lira Argentina, de José Amat," *Archivo histórico de revistas Argentina* (2019): 1, accessible via www.ahira.com.ar. See also Ricardo Horvath, *Esos malditos tangos: Apuntes para la otra historia* (Buenos Aires: Editorial Biblos, 2006), esp. 31.

122. On the history of café culture, sociability, and revolutionary politics, see Botalla, "Bebidas del Ocio," 69; Sandra Gayol, *Sociabilidad en Buenos Aires: Hombres, honor y cafés, 1862–1910* (Buenos Aires: Ediciones del Signo, 2000); and González, *Civility and Politics*.

123. MacCann, *Two Thousand Miles' Ride*, 92.

124. MacCann, 78.

125. This point about Mansfield's unique lack of commercial interest is made by S. Samuel Triflilo in "A Bibliography of British Travel Books: 1810–1860," *The Americas* 16, no. 2 (Oct. 1959): 143. For poem, see Charles Blachford Mansfield, *Paraguay, Brazil, and the Plate, Letters Written 1852–2* (Cambridge: Macmillan, 1856), appendix.

126. For many of d'Hastrel's works, including his self-portrait and a portrait of his wife, see the Museo de Bellas Artes digital collection, specifically at www.bellasartes.gob.ar/coleccion/buscar/?autor=153#resultados (accessed Apr. 15, 2022).

127. I have found evidence that these two female types were included in the exhibit. In contrast, the illustration of the woman from Lima in the exhibit *Tapada de Saya*, published by Ancienne Maison Aubert in 1850, did not include a mate. In contrast to darker-hued mate servers in other compositions, d'Hastrel's fair *cebadora* was not actively serving anyone (beyond the viewer) in her composition. Her downward glance suggests a coquettish nature that would become a defining feature of mate servers in the second half of the nineteenth century (as we shall see in chapter 4). See Maps-Prints.com, https://maps-prints.com/antique-prints-fashion-costumes/8050-antique-print-of-a-woman-from-lima-by-aubert-1850.html (accessed Apr. 28, 2020).

128. Thomas Woodbine Hinchliff, *South American Sketches; or a Visit to Rio de Janeiro, the Organ Mountains, La Plata and the Paraná* (London: Longman, Hurst, Rees, Orme, and Brown, 1863), 165.

129. Hinchliff, vii and 165–66.

130. On the workforce and volume of yerba production in Paraguay, see Vera Blinn Reber, "Commerce and Industry in Nineteenth-Century Paraguay: The Example of Yerba Mate," *The Americas* 42, no. 1 (1985): 29–53; and Whigham, *Politics of River Trade*, esp. 124–25.

131. Whigham, *Politics of River Trade*, 124–25.

132. Whigham, 125–26.

133. On Rosas's drinking mate in exile, see J. Shumway, *A Woman, a Man, a Nation*, 245.

134. Whigham, *Politics of River Trade*, 124–29.

CHAPTER THREE

1. As discussed later, this boy's family and other contemporary Paraguayans would have likely considered themselves to be White as well, given the derogatory meanings associated with Indigenous or African descent. It was only in the twentieth century that Paraguayans proudly claimed a mestizo (or mixed) identity. Up until the twentieth century, a clearly marked Indigenous identity was contrasted with being Paraguayan. See, for example, Michael Kenneth Huner, "Toikove Ñane Retá! Republican Nationalism at the Battlefield Crossings of Print and Speech in Wartime Paraguay, 1867–1868," in *Building Nineteenth-Century Latin America: Re-rooted Cultures, Identities, and Nations*, ed. William G. Acree Jr. and Juan Carlos González Espitia (Nashville: Vanderbilt University Press, 2009), 79–97; Bridget María Chesterton, *The Grandchildren of Solano López: Frontier and Nation in Paraguay, 1904–1936* (Albuquerque: University of New Mexico Press, 2013); and Barbara Potthast, "Mestizaje and Convivality in Paraguay," Mecila Working Paper Series, no. 22, São Paulo, 2020, 1–16.

2. I am grateful to Alberto del Pino Menck for helping me identify the specific status of the cavalry caption as well as the original provenance of this photograph in the Biblioteca Nacional do Brazil, *Álbum escursao ao Paraguay*, photo 23.

3. It was common for Paraguayan peasants, especially women and children, not to wear shoes.

4. Miguel Angel Cuarterolo, *Soldados de la memoria: Imagenes y hombres de la Guerra del Paraguay* (Buenos Aires: Planeta, 2000), 32. Cuarterolo points to Carlos César as the main photographer of the Brazilian offensive against Humaitá in 1968 and therefore possibly the photographer of this image. Miguel Angel Cuarterolo, "Images of War: Photographers and Sketch Artists of the Triple Alliance Conflict," from *I Die with My Country*, ed. Hendrik Kraay and Thomas L. Whigham (Lincoln: University of Nebraska Press, 2005), 154–78.

5. The recent adoption of the wet plate instead of the daguerreotype allowed photographers more flexibility and speed, even if taking photographs required posing and time. Cuarterolo, *Soldados de la memoria*, 11–13.

6. Charles Washburn, *The History of Paraguay with Notes of Personal Observations and Reminiscences of Diplomacy under Difficulties*, vol. 1 (Boston: Lee and Shepard, 1871), 3–4.

7. Vitor Izecksohn, "State Formation and Identity: Historiographical Trends Concerning South America's War of the Triple Alliance," *History Compass* 17, no. 9 (2010): 4.

8. Thomas J. Page, *La Plata, the Argentine Confederation, and Paraguay, Being a Narrative of the Exploration of the Tributaries of the River La Plata and Adjacent Countries during the Years 1853, '54, '55, and '56, under the Orders of the United States Government* (New York: Harper and Brothers, 1859), 221.

9. Washburn, for instance, observed that in early 1860s Paraguay, "with oranges, a little yerba maté, a bit of *asado*, or broiled beef, or of boiled mandioca root, a Paraguayan would be perfectly contented; and if permitted to lie for three quarters of the time in his hammock and thrum his guitar, he would regard himself at the height of earthly bliss." Washburn, *History of Paraguay*, 434.

10. George Frederick Masterman, *Seven Eventful Years in Paraguay* (London: Sampson, Low and Marston, 1869), 65.

11. Page, *La Plata, the Argentine Confederation, and Paraguay*, 227. My emphasis.

12. Masterman, *Seven Eventful Years in Paraguay*, 65–66.

13. Huner, "Toikove Ñane Retá!," 85.

14. Thomas Woodbine Hinchliff, *South American Sketches; or a Visit to Rio de Janeiro, the Organ Mountains, La Plata and the Paraná* (London: Longman, Hurst, Rees, Orme, and Brown, 1863), 165–66.

15. Thomas Whigham, *The Paraguayan War: Causes and Early Conduct*, 2nd ed. (Calgary: University of Calgary Press, 2018); Michael Huner, "Liberal Youth, Modern Exuberance, and Calamity: Aspirations for Modern Nationhood in Paraguay, 1858–1870," *Contra corriente* 12, no. 2 (2015): 140–77; Izecksohn, "State Formation and Identity," 5.

16. Yerba as a percentage of export trade from 1816 to 1863 averaged 50.5 percent, according to Vera Blinn Reber, "Commerce and Industry in Nineteenth-Century Paraguay: The Example of Yerba Mate," *The Americas* 42, no. 1 (1985): 29–53, esp. 47, table 5. Whigham calculates that yerba accounted for around 70 percent of exports in the 1810s, 50 percent in 1838–39, and 40 percent in the 1860s. Thomas Whigham, *The Politics of River Trade: Tradition and Development in the Upper Plata, 1780–1870* (Albuquerque: University of New Mexico Press, 1991), 120–30.

17. Whigham, *Politics of River Trade*, 124–29; Folch, "Stimulating Consumption," 16.

18. William Scully, *Brazil: Its Provinces and Chief Cities* (London: Murray and Co., 1866), 234.

19. Please consult graph 3.1.

20. Alfred Demersay visited the region in the 1840s, as quoted in T. A. Joyce, "Yerba Mate, the Tea of South America," *Pan American Magazine*, Nov.–Dec. 1921, 315.

21. Alfred Demersay, *Étude économique sur le maté ou thé du Paraguay* (*Ilex Paraguariensis*) (Paris: Imprimerie et librarie d'agriculture et d' horticulture, 1867).

22. Demersay's account also included a detailed botanical drawing of a yerba tree branch in bloom with the wooden saber used to remove it from the tree and a mate and bombilla. These illustrations seem to have been produced in the 1840s but were first published in the 1860s.

23. Thomas Whigham shared that the brand's name refers to one of the minor spirit-beings of Guaraní mythology.

24. An illustration by Desin de H. Rousseau of a "Guerrier payaguàs" holding a mate in one hand and a pole or spear in the other was included in Alfred Demersay "Fragments d'un voyage au Paraguay," in *Le Tour de monde* (Paris: Hachette, 1865). This and a wealth of other contemporary illustrations are reproduced in Milda Rivarola, *Paraguay ilustrado: El grabado europeo del siglo XIX* (Asunción, Para.: Editorial Servilibro, 2016), here 69.

25. Barbara J. Ganson, "Following Their Children into Battle: Women at War in Paraguay," *The Americas* 46, no. 3 (Jan. 1990): 335–71, specifically 348.

26. Pau Navajas, *Caá Porã: El espíritu de la yerba mate, una historia de plata* (Corrientes, Arg.: Las Marías, 2013), 163.

27. Barbara Potthast-Jukeit, "The Ass of a Mare and Other Scandals: Marriage and Extramarital Relations in Nineteenth-Century Paraguay," *Journal of Family History* 16, no. 3 (1991): 215–39.

28. Potthast-Jukeit, "Ass of a Mare"; and Barbara Potthast, "Entre lo invisible y lo pintoresco: Las mujeres paraguayas en la economía campesina (siglo XIX)," *Jahrbuch für Geschichte Lateinamerikas* 40 (Jan. 2003): 203–20.

29. Potthast-Jukeit, "Ass of a Mare," esp. 231–32.

30. Potthast, "Entre lo visible," 13.

31. Whigham, *Paraguayan War*; Francisco Doratioto, *Maldita guerra: Nova história da Guerra do Paragui* (São Paolo: Cía de Letras, 2002).

32. Izecksohn, "State Formation and Identity," 5.

33. Peter Lambert and Andrew Nickson, eds., *The Paraguay Reader: History, Culture, Politics* (Durham: Duke University Press, 2012), 54, for analysis, and 76–81, for a translation of this document.

34. For a synthesis of this argument, see Thomas Whigham, "I Die with My Country," in Lambert and Nickson, *Paraguay Reader*, 82–89.

35. Whigham, *Paraguayan War*, xiv.

36. Michael K. Huner, "Sacred Cause, Divine Republic: A History of Nationhood, Religion, and War in Nineteenth-Century Paraguay, 1850–70" (PhD diss., University of North Carolina, 2011).

37. Huner, "Toikove Ñane Retá!"; and Thomas Whigham, "Building the Nation While Destroying the Land: Paraguayan Journalism during the Triple Alliance War, 1864–1870," *Jahrbuch für Geschichte Lateinamerikas* 49, no. 1 (2012): 157–80.

38. Barbara Potthast, "Algo más que heroínas," *Diálogos* 10, no. 1 (2006): 89–104.

39. Barbara Potthast, ¿*"Paraíso de Mahoma" o "País de Mujeres"*? El rol de la familia en la Sociedad Paraguaya del siglo XIX, 2nd ed. (Asunción: Fausto Ediciones, 2011), 311.

40. On women's roles during the war as providers, camp followers, and political victims, see Potthast, "Algo más que heroínas."

41. Ganson, "Following Their Children into Battle," 357.

42. Dionísio Cerqueira, *Reminiscências da Campanha do Paraguai, 1865–1870* (Tours, France: E. Arrault, 1910), 112; on being denied preferred "sweet mate," 52; on Bahia, 129.

43. Juan Crisóstomo Centurión, *Memorias del coronel Juan Crisóstomo Centurión ó sea reminiscencias históricas sobre la guerra del Paraguay*, 4 vols. (Buenos Aires: Imprenta de Obras de J. A. Berra, 1894); on trade, see vol. 2 (1894), 404; on drinking mate with generals, see vol. 2 (1894), 224–25, and vol. 3 (1897), 221; on soldiers collecting yerba and hunger, see vol. 4 (1901), 99.

44. Thomas Whigham, email correspondence, May 18, 2018.

45. Potthast, "Algo más que heroínas," esp. 92–94.

46. Reber, "Commerce and Industry in Nineteenth-Century Paraguay," 45, 50–51.

47. Potthast, "Algo más que heroínas," 93.

48. Potthast, 94.

49. Thomas Whigham and Barbara Potthast, "The Paraguayan Rosetta Stone: New Insights into the Demographics of the Paraguayan War, 1864–70," *Latin American Research Review* 34, no. 1 (1999): 174–86; Ignacio Telesca, "Antes y después: Del amor al espanto. Construcciones históricas y historiográficas del Paraguay del siglo XIX," in *A 150 años de la Guerra de la Triple Alianza contra el Paraguay*, ed. Juan Carlos Garavaglia and Raúl Fradkin (Buenos Aires: Promoteo, 2016), 171–200.

50. Whigham and Potthast, "Paraguayan Rosetta Stone," 185.

51. Potthast, "Algo más que heroínas," esp. 99 (for quote).

52. Lambert and Nickson, "A Slow Recovery," in *Paraguay Reader*, 129–30.

53. It would become an Argentine province only in 1953. Lisandro Rodríguez, *Yerba mate y cooperativismo en la Argentina: Sujetos sociales y acción colectiva* (Bernal, Arg.: Universidad Nacional de Quilmes, 2018), 31–32.

54. The data for late nineteenth-century Paraguay leave "much to be desired," as Jan Kleinpenning points out, as returns are missing from some years and data are unreliable due to

extensive illegal trade. Jan M. G. Kleinpenning, *Rural Paraguay, 1870–1963: A Geography of Progress, Plunder and Poverty*, 2 vols. (Madrid: Iberoamericana, 2009), 1:670. Graph 3.1 draws from data published (in chronological order) in Scully, *Brazil*; Macedo Soares, *O mate do Paraná* (Rio de Janeiro: Imperial Instituto Artístico, 1875); G. M. Mulhall and E. T. Mulhall, *Handbook of Brazil* (Buenos Aires: The Standard, 1877); G. M. Mulhall and E. T. Mulhall, *Handbook of the River Plate: Comprising the Argentine Republic, Uruguay and Paraguay* (London: Trübner and Co., 1885); Guimarães & Co., *Breve noticia sobre a herva mate pura sem fumaça* (Cuytiba, Brazil: Typographia de Livraria Economica, 1899); Sebastião Lino de Christo, "Do mate" (PhD diss., Facultad de Medicina do Rio de Janeiro, 1909); Reginald Lloyd, *Impressoes do Brasil no seculo vinte* (London: Greater Britain Publishing, 1913); Carlos D. Girola, *La yerba mate en la República Argentina* (Ilex paraguariensis) (Buenos Aires: La Facultad de Agronomia y Veterinaria, 1929); Ernesto Daumas, *El problema de la yerba mate* (Buenos Aires: Compañía Impresora Argentina, 1930); Cámara de Comercio Argentina-Brasileña, *La yerba mate: El problema económico y fiscal* (Buenos Aires: Futura, 1933); *Brazil yerba mate pamphlet* (Rio de Janeiro: Pimento di Mello y Cía, 1938); Abel Sanchez Diaz, *Consideraciones bromotológicas e industriales sobre la yerba mate* (Buenos Aires: Anales de la Academica Nacional de Ciencias Exactas, 1939); CRYM, *Memoria: Correspondiente al ejercicio de 1939* (Buenos Aires: Ministerio de Agricultura de la Nación, 1940); CRYM, *Memoria: Correspondiente al ejercicio de 1940* (Buenos Aires: Ministerio de Agricultura de la Nación, 1941); Martín y Cía, *Que es la yerba mate* (Buenos Aires: E. Fenner, 1942); Carlos Reussi, "Los alimentos de origen vegetal: La yerba mate," *El día médico*, Sept. 27, 1942; Juan J. Billard, "Economía de la industria yerbatera argentina," *Instituto de economía y legislación rural*, vol. 5, no. 3 (Buenos Aires: Imprenta de la Universidad de Buenos Aires, 1944); Temístocles Linhares, *História econômica do mate* (Rio de Janeiro: Livraria J. Olympio, 1969); Comité de Propaganda del Consumo de la Yerba Mate, *La yerba mate* (Buenos Aires: Ministerio del Interior: Talleres gráficos de la Dirección Nacional del Registro Oficial, 1971); Marisa Correia de Oliveira, "Estudo da erva mate no Paraná: 1939–1967" (master's thesis, Universidade Federal do Paraná, 1974); Aida M. Frankel, *La yerba mate: Producción, industrialización, comercio* (Buenos Aires: Editorial Albatros, 1983); Reber, "Commerce and Industry in Nineteenth-Century Paraguay"; Víctor Rau, "La yerba mate en misiones (Argentina): Estructura y significados de una producción localizada," *Agrolimentaria*, no. 28 (Jan.–June 2009): 49–58; and Jerónimo Lagier, *The Adventures of the Yerba Mate: Over Four Centuries of History* (Posadas, Arg.: Tambú, 2014).

55. Kleinpenning, *Rural Paraguay, 1870–1963*, 1:667–68.

56. Kregg Hetherington, *The Government of Beans: Regulating Life in the Age of Monocrops* (Durham: Duke University Press, 2020), 47.

57. Chesterton, *Grandchildren of Solano López*, 9.

58. Meanwhile Barthes claimed nearly 800,000 hectares in Paraguay and more land in Argentina and Brazil, and Matte Larangeira, another 800,000 hectares. On the establishment of LIPSA, see Kleinpenning, *Rural Paraguay, 1870–1963*, 1:630–41, and on landownership, 629, 641, 644.

59. Kleinpenning specifies that the original founders of the company included Luigi Patri, "the wealthiest man in Paraguay"; Guillermo de los Ríos; Juan Bautista Gaona; and ex–vice president Adolfo Saguier. President General Bernardino Caballero was the company's managing director, and his minister of finance, Augustín Cañete, also served on the board. Englishman Rodney B. Croskey, "who had come to Paraguay to represent the Council of Foreign Bondholders, was the only prominent foreigner on the board." Kleinpenning, 631.

60. Kleinpenning, 634, 637.

61. Kleinpenning, 633–34.

62. Milda Rivarola, *Obreros, utopías y revoluciones: Formaciones de las clases trabajadores en el Paraguay liberal (1870–1931)* (Asunción, Para.: Centro de Documentación y Estudios, 1993), 12.

63. Eva Maria Luiz Ferreira and Antonio Brand, "Os Guarani e a erva nate," *Fronteiras revista de história* 11, no. 19 (2009): 107–26, esp. 108.

64. Ferreira and Brand, 108.

65. Ferreira and Brand, 108.

66. Henry Stephens, *Journeys and Experiences in Argentina, Paraguay, and Chile Including a Side Trip to the Sources of the Paraguay River in the State of Matto Grosso, Brazil, and a Journey across the Andes to the Río Tambo in Brazil* (New York: Knickerbocker Press, 1920), 223, 509–11.

67. Whigham, *Politics of River Trade*, 131.

68. Washburn, *History of Paraguay*, 449.

69. See Rivarola, *Obreros, utopías y revoluciones*, 44. Mihanovich later took over this company until the 1930s.

70. Rivarola, *Obreros, utopías y revoluciones*, 42 and 185; Javier Gortari, comp., *De la tierra sin mal al tractorazo: Hacia una economía política de la yerba mate* (Posadas, Arg.: Universidad Nacional de Misiones, 2007), esp. 17.

71. Editorial de *La reforma* (Asunción), Oct. 24, 1881, as cited in Rivarola, *Obreros, utopías y revoluciones*, 49–50.

72. From June 15 to June 27, 1908, Barrett published a series of articles in *El diario* (Paraguay), reproduced in Eduardo Campo, "Rafael Barrett denuncia la esclavitud en 'Lo que son los yerbales' (1908), Fronterad, www.fronterad.com/rafael-barrett-denuncia-la-esclavitud-en -lo-que-son-los-yerbales-1908/.

73. Campo; Rafael Barrett, *El dolor paraguayo: Lo que son los yerbales* (Buenos Aires: Editorial "La Protesta," 1909), 165; and *Lo que son los yerbales* (Montevideo, Uru.: O. M. Bertani, 1910). For translation of an excerpt into English, see Rafael Barrett, "What It Is Like to Work in the Yerba Plantations," in Lambert and Nickson, *Paraguay Reader*, 146–59.

74. Barrett, "What It Is Like to Work in the Yerba Plantations," 148.

75. Barrett, 159.

76. Barrett, 151.

77. Rivarola, *Obreros, utopías y revoluciones*, 108.

78. Michael Huner, "How Pedro Quiñonez Lost His Soul: Suicide, Violence, and State Formation in Nineteenth-Century Paraguay," *Journal of Social History* 54, no. 1 (Fall 2019): 237–59, esp. 246–48.

79. Rivarola, *Obreros, utopías y revoluciones*, 51; Kleinpenning, *Rural Paraguay, 1870–1963*, 1:651–52.

80. Kleinpenning, *Rural Paraguay, 1870–1963*, 1:653.

81. Rivarola, *Obreros, utopías y revoluciones*, 51–52.

82. Huner, "How Pedro Quiñonez Lost His Soul," 240–46.

83. The illustration included in Demersay's account echoed and foreshadowed this description, which was a subject for photographers in the 1940s. Barrett, "What It Is Like to Work in the Yerba Plantations," 150; and for photograph, Lambert and Nickson, *Paraguay Reader*, 147.

84. The motivation to carry such heavy loads stemmed from the fact that workers' wages depended on how much yerba they brought in. Kleinpenning, *Rural Paraguay, 1870–1963*, 1:624.

85. Barrett, "What It Is Like to Work in the Yerba Plantations," 152.

86. On the use of this discourse in North America, see Gunther Peck, *Reinventing Free Labor: Padrones and Immigrant Workers in the North American West, 1880–1930* (New York: Cambridge University Press, 2000). One particularly infamous demographic in this South American context was women purportedly forced across the Atlantic and into prostitution in Atlantic cities. For a pioneering work on this topic, see Donna J. Guy, *White Slavery and Mothers Alive and Dead: The Troubled Meeting of Sex, Public Health, and Progress in Latin America* (Lincoln: University of Nebraska Press, 2000).

87. Clemens apparently did not visit the yerbales and cited Washburn's detailed account of the process of producing yerba there. Washburn's account emphasized the stages of this process rather than the oppression of the laborers. E. J. M. Clemens, *La Plata Countries of South America* (New York: J. B. Lipincott Co., 1886), 468–71, on peon, 43.

88. Washburn, *History of Paraguay*, 458–59, 461.

89. Up through the early twentieth century, fellow chroniclers described men who toiled in the hills as being of Indigenous descent. See, for example, Frank George Carpenter, *South America: Social, Industrial and Political; A Twenty-Five-Thousand-Mile Journey in Search of Information* (Akron, OH: Saalfield Publishing Co., 1903), 425. Carpenter was in this region in 1898. Stephens reported the same in 1915, calling laborers "natives." Stephens, *Journeys and Experiences*, 351.

90. Clemens, *La Plata Countries of South America*, 43.

91. Clemens, 473.

92. Kleinpenning, *Rural Paraguay, 1870–1963*, 1:685.

93. On oranges in Paraguay, see Bridget Chesterton, "Between Yerba Mate and Soy: The Orange as National Food and Landscape from the Early Nineteenth to the Early Twenty-First Centuries in Paraguay," *Global Food History* 8, no. 2 (2022): 128–48; and Theodore Child, *The Spanish-American Republics* (New York: Harper, 1891), 401.

94. Child, *Spanish-American Republics*, 393.

95. Honorio Leguizamón, "Yerba-mate: Observaciones sobre su cultivo i sus usos" (PhD diss., Facultad de Ciencias Médicas, Universidad de Buenos Aires, 1877), 54.

96. Carpenter, *South America*, 425.

97. Elites' diets were distinguished by the additional beef they ate not only in stews but also grilled and roasted. Washburn, *History of Paraguay*, 434, 447.

98. Rivarola, *Obreros, utopías y revoluciones*, 42.

99. Rivarola, 48.

100. Masterman, *Seven Eventful Years in Paraguay*, 66.

101. In 1888, 10 kg. of coffee cost 12,50 and an arroba of yerba mate 2,50 to 2,60 (in pesos fuertes). See Rivarola, *Obreros, utopías y revoluciones*, 73.

102. On the relationship between these two wars and early twentieth-century Paraguayan nationalism, see Chesterton, *Grandchildren of Solano López*.

103. Derlis Benítez, *El tereré: Algo más que una bebida en Paraguay* (Asunción, Para.: El Lector, 1997).

104. Paraguayan and Bolivian troops consumed yerba, while Aymara and Quechua soldiers on the Bolivian side also prized Andean coca. See Esther Breithoff, "The 'White Death': Thirst and Water in the Chaco War," in *Modern Conflict and the Senses*, ed. N. J. Saunders and P. Cornish. (Abingdon, UK: Routledge, 2017), 213–28, esp. 223–25.

105. Benítez, *El tereré*, 71.

106. Bridget Chesterton shared with me that commercial ice first appeared in 1920s Paraguay but became somewhat widespread only after the opening of Acaray Dam and the arrival of domestic freezers in 1968. For more, see her forthcoming book, *Hotel Guaraní*.

107. Benítez, *El tereré*, 57.

108. Benítez, 58–59.

109. Moisés S. Bertoni, "La civilización Guaraní: Descripción física, económica y social del Paraguay," *La higiene Guaraní: La medicina Guaraní*, 476, as cited in Benítez, *El tereré*, 62.

110. Bertoni, "La civilización Guaraní," 117, as cited in Benítez, *El tereré*, 59.

111. Washburn, *History of Paraguay*, 460.

112. Child, *Spanish-American Republics*, 401.

113. Moisés Bertoni, *De la medicina Guaraní: Etnografía sobre plantas medicinales* (1927; Córdoba, Arg.: Buena Vista Editores, 2008), 237, 245.

114. Bertoni, 237.

115. Bertoni suggested that mate sweetened with sugar or infused with milk provided more substantial sustenance. Bertoni, 237.

116. Most of the postcards I have found were sent back to Germany by German visitors.

117. Correspondence with Javier Yubi and Thomas Whigham, Sept. 2020.

118. Potthast, "Algo más que heroínas," 100–101.

119. Rivarola, *Obreros, utopías y revoluciones*, 42.

120. Javier Yubi, *Bicentenario de Paraguay: Álbum fotográfico siglos XIX y XX* (Asunción, Para.: Servilibro, 2011), 60.

121. Rivarola reproduced this photograph, taken by MacDonald in 1911, in *Obreros, utopías y revoluciones*, illus. insert before p. 145. The image was featured on a postcard also called "Rancho Yerbatero." It and the previously described postcard with the same title are held at Lafayette College Special Collections and College Archives, Easton, PA.

122. Postcard, Juan Quell, "Caaguazú, Rancho Yerbatero," ca. 1900–1906, courtesy of Lafayette College Special Collections and College Archives.

123. I found seven postcards featuring the transport of yerba mate that are now held by Lafayette College Special Collections and College Archives.

124. Henry B. Stephens, *South American Travels* (New York: Knickerbocker Press, 1915), 403, 351–52.

125. W. H. Koebel, *Paraguay* (London: T. F. Unwin, 1917), 213. Koebel included photographs of workers porting large bales of yerba and packing yerba.

126. Most yerba was still harvested from wild stands of trees in the 1910s. Kleinpenning, *Rural Paraguay, 1870–1963*, 1:663.

127. I make this claim based on my review of hundreds of Paraguayan postcards collected and reproduced in books by Javier Yubi; held by the South America postcard collector Marcelo Loeb, whose shop I visited in Buenos Aires; acquired by Lafayette College; and available online.

128. While the exploitation was similar, Quiroga's story focused on monthly laborers working in the lumber rather than the yerba industry, likely because the Argentine yerba industry had yet to develop at this point. Horacio Quiroga, *"Los Mensú,"* in *Cuentos*, ed. Horacio Quiroga, Emir Rodríguez Monegal, and Alberto F. Oreggioni (Caracas, Ven.: Biblioteca Ayacucho, 1981); Bridgette Gunnels, "The Consequences of Capitalism: Horacio Quiroga Writes the Proletariat," *Revista de estudios hispánicos* 45, no. 1 (Mar. 2011): 67–88.

129. Stephens, *South American Travels*, on Barthe, 351 and 377.

1. Carlos Masotta, "Representación e iconografía de dos tipos nacionales: El caso de las postales etnográficas en Argentina, 1900–1930," in *Arte y antropología en la Argentina*, ed. Marta Penhos and Marina Baron Supervielle (Buenos Aires: Fundación Espigas: 2005), 69–114.

2. On new patterns of consumption during this period, see Benjamin Orlove and Arnold Bauer, "Giving Importance to Imports," in *The Allure of the Foreign: Imported Goods in Postcolonial Latin America*, ed. Benjamin Orlove (Ann Arbor: University of Michigan Press, 1997), 1–29.

3. Sarmiento served as president of Argentina from 1868 to 1974. Domingo Faustino Sarmiento, *Facundo: Civilización y barbarie*, 4th ed. (1845; New York, D. Appleton y Compañía, 1868).

4. On building national identity on rural tropes, see Oscar Chamosa, *The Argentine Folklore Movement: Sugar Elites, Criollo Workers, and the Politics of Cultural Nationalism, 1900–1955* (Tucson: University of Arizona Press, 2010); and Matthew B. Karush, *Culture of Class: Radio and Cinema in the Making of a Divided Argentina* (Durham: Duke University Press, 2012).

5. On the gaucho in Argentina, where historiography is most developed, see, for example, William Acree, *Staging Frontiers: The Making of Modern Popular Culture in Argentina and Uruguay* (Albuquerque: University of New Mexico Press, 2019); Ezequiel Adamovsky, *El gaucho indómito: De Martín Fierro a Perón, el emblema imposible de una nación desgarrada* (Buenos Aires: Siglo Veintiuno Editores, 2019); Matías Emiliano Casas, *La metamorfosis del gaucho: Circos criollos, tradicionalists y política en la provincial de Buenos Aires (1930–1960)* (Buenos Aires: Promoteo Libros 2017); Ariel De la Fuente, *Children of Facundo: Caudillo and Gaucho Insurgency during the Argentine State-Formation Process (La Rioja, 1853–1870)* (Durham: Duke University Press, 2000); Judith Freidenberg, *The Invention of the Jewish Gaucho: Villa Clara and the Construction of Argentine Identity* (Austin: University of Texas Press, 2009); Ariana Huberman, *Gauchos and Foreigners: Glossing Culture and Identity in the Argentine Countryside* (Lanham, MD: Lexington Books, 2011); and Richard W. Slatta, *Gauchos and the Vanishing Frontier* (Lincoln: University of Nebraska Press, 1983). For an early comparative study, see Emilio A. Coni, *El gaucho: Argentina, Brasil, Uruguay* (Buenos Aires: Editorial Sudamericana, 1945).

6. On women's political activism, see, for example, Asunción Lavrin, *Women, Feminism, and Social Change in Argentina, Chile, and Uruguay, 1890–1940* (Lincoln: University of Nebraska Press, 1995); and Silvana Palermo, *Los derechos políticos de la mujer: Los proyectos y debates parlamentarios 1916–1955* (Provincia de Buenos Aires: Ediciones UNGS, 2012).

7. On the endurance of patriarchy, see, for example, Susan K. Besse, *Restructuring Patriarchy: The Modernization of Gender Inequality in Brazil, 1914–1940* (Chapel Hill: University of North Carolina Press, 1998); and Sueann Caulfield, Sarah C. Chambers, and Lara Putnam, eds., *Honor, Status and Law in Modern Latin America* (Durham: Duke University Press, 2005).

8. Some provinces in southern Brazil would eventually become enamored with the mate-drinking gaucho, but this was largely a twentieth-century phenomenon. On the formation of the gaucho identity in Brazil, see Ruben Oliven, *Tradition Matters: Modern Gaúcho Identity in Brazil* (New York: Columbia University Press, 1996).

9. Honorio Leguizamón, "Yerba-mate: Observaciones sobre su cultivo i sus usos" (PhD diss., Facultad de Ciencias Médicas, Universidad de Buenos Aires, 1877), 25.

10. José Antonio Wilde as cited in Pau Navajas, *Caá Porã: El espíritu de la yerba mate, una historia de plata* (Corrientes, Arg.: Las Marías, 2013), 251.

11. Leguizamón, "Yerba-mate," 25.

12. Nancy Leys Stepan, *"The Hour of Eugenics": Race, Gender, and Nation in Latin America* (Ithaca, NY: Cornell University Press, 1991).

13. Leandro Losada, *La alta sociedad en La Buenos Aires de la Belle Époque: Sociabilidad, estilos de vida e identidades* (Buenos Aires: Siglo XIX, 2008), esp. xxiii–xxv and chaps. 4 and 5.

14. Interestingly, Gálvez originally hailed from the northeastern part of the country where yerba consumption was high and production was getting underway. Manuel Gálvez, *El diario de Gabriel Quiroga* (Buenos Aires: Arnoldo Moen and Hermanos, 1910), 101–2.

15. While elites' access to alternative stimulating drinks certainly ramped up around the turn of the twentieth century, it was not new. At home during the mid-nineteenth century, some elites like Mariquita Sánchez already breakfasted not with mate but with chocolate or coffee with milk to accompany buttered toast or biscuits. Partygoers enjoyed mate as well as hot chocolate. Specialty shops sold tea, but mostly to local Brits in the region. Mariquita Sánchez, *Recuerdos del Buenos Aires virreyanal* (Buenos Aires: ENE Editorial, 1953), 26–27; Horacio Botalla, "Bebidas del Ocio en el Río de la Plata," *Todo es Historia*, no. 380 (Mar. 1999): 67. For more on Mariquita Sánchez, see Jeffrey M. Shumway, *A Woman, a Man, a Nation: Mariquita Sánchez, Juan Manuel de Rosas, and the Beginnings of Argentina* (Albuquerque: University of New Mexico Press, 2019).

16. This claim draws from my review of the extensive photographic collection from this period held at the Archivo General de la Nación in Argentina. One exceptional photo of an elite family with a mate from this period (taken in 1901) features a large extended family on a patio outside their home being attended to by a servant who appears to be of Indigenous descent and who holds a mate in her hand. It was originally found in the Archivo Gráfico Nacional and reproduced in Leonor Slavsky and Gladis Ceresole, "Historia de yerba y mate," *La vida de nuestro pueblo: Una historia de hombres, cosas, trabajos, lugares*, no. 17 (Buenos Aires: Centro Editor de America Latina, 1982), 10–11.

17. Lucio V. Mansilla, *Mis memorias* (Buenos Aires: El Ateneo Editorial, 1978), 137–38, as cited in Botalla, "Bebidas del Ocio," 69.

18. José Antonio Wilde, *Buenos Aires desde setenta años atrás*, 2nd ed. (Buenos Aires: Imprenta y Librería de Mayo de C. Casavalle, 1881), 212.

19. Jefferson explained that his 1918 trip was meant "to study modern European colonization in Chile, the Argentine Republic, and Brazil." He had previously spent 1884–89 in the Argentine Republic, the first three years in Córdoba as a "computer" and "astronomer," and last three in Tucumán managing and keeping the books for a sugar mill. Mark Jefferson, *Peopling the Argentine Pampa* (New York: American Geographical Society, 1926), preface; for in-text quote, 7–8.

20. Jefferson was among those who thought that the shared bombilla was part of the issue. He writes, "In better Creole families the promiscuous use of the same *bombilla* (tube) is doubtless avoided. . . . Among the lower classes the promiscuous use of the same gourd and *bombilla* is not objected to." Jefferson, 7–8.

21. On the relationship between the upper and middle class in Argentina, see Roy Hora and Leandro Losada, "Clases altas y medias en La Argentina, 1880–1930: Notas para una agenda de investigación," *Desarrollo económico* 50, no. 200 (Jan.–Mar. 2011): 611–30. Hora and Losada argue that the middle sectors sought to distinguish themselves by adopting some cultural patterns embraced by elites in the late nineteenth century. By the 1920s, they contend, the emergent middle class had overtaken (increasingly maligned) elites as the primary social influencers.

22. Alberto J. Corrado, "Contribución al estudio de la yerba mate," Paper presented at the Fourth Scientific Conference (First Pan American) in Santiago de Chile, 2nd ed. (Buenos Aires: Casa Jacobo Peuser, 1915), 7.

23. Dr. Victor Garin, *Contribución al estudio del cultivo e industria de la yerba mate* (Buenos Aires: Talleres Gráficos de Ministerio Agricultura de la Nación, 1916), 10–11.

24. Graph 4.1 draws from data published (in chronological order) in Garin, "Contribución al estudio del cultivo e industria de la yerba mate"; Carlos D. Girola, *La yerba mate en la República Argentina* (Ilex paraguariensis) (Buenos Aires: La Facultad de Agronomia y Veterinaria, 1929); Ernesto Daumas, *El problema de la yerba mate* (Buenos Aires: Compañía Impresora Argentina, 1930); Cámara de Comercio Argentina-Brasileña, *La yerba mate: El problema económico y fiscal* (Buenos Aires: Futura, 1933); CRYM, *1938 Memoria: Mar. 10, 1936–Dec. 31, 1937* (Buenos Aires: Ministerio de Agricultura, Argentina, 1938); CRYM, *Boletín Informativo, Memoria Correspondiente a 1937* (Buenos Aires: Ministerio de Agricultura, 1938); Abel Sanchez Diaz, *Consideraciones bromotológicas e industriales sobre la yerba mate* (Buenos Aires: Anales de la Academica Nacional de Ciencias Exactas, 1939); CRYM, *Memoria: Correspondiente al Ejercicio de 1939* (Buenos Aires: Ministerio de Agricultura de la Nación, 1940); CRYM, *Memoria: Correspondiente al Ejercicio de 1940* (Buenos Aires: Ministerio de Agricultura de la Nación, 1941); CRYM, *Memoria: Correspondiente al Ejercicio de 1941* (Buenos Aires: Ministerio de Agricultura de la Nación, 1942); Martín y Cía, *Que es la yerba mate* (Buenos Aires: E. Fenner, 1942); Carlos Reussi, "Los alimentos de origen vegetal: La yerba mate," *El día medico*, Sept. 27, 1942; CRYM, *Memoria: Correspondiente al Ejercicio de 1942* (Buenos Aires: Ministerio de Agricultura de la Nación, 1943); Juan J. Billard, "Economía de la industria yerbatera argentina," *Instituto de Economía y Legislación Rural* 5, no. 3 (Buenos Aires: Imprenta de la Universidad de Buenos Aires, 1944); Temístocles Linhares, *História econômica do mate* (Rio de Janeiro: Livraria J. Olympio, 1969); Comité de propaganda del consumo de la yerba mate, *La yerba mate* (Ministerio del Interior: Talleres gráficos de la Dirección Nacional del Registro Oficial, 1971); Aida M. Frankel, *La yerba mate: Producción, industrialización, comercio* (Buenos Aires: Editorial Albatros, 1983); Víctor Rau, "La yerba mate en misiones (Argentina): Estructura y significados de una producción localizada," *Agrolimentaria*, no. 28 (Jan.–June 2009): 49–58; and Jerónimo Lagier, *The Adventures of the Yerba Mate: Over Four Centuries of History* (Posadas, Arg.: Tambú, 2014).

25. Theodore Child, *The Spanish-American Republics* (New York: Harper, 1891), 144 and 233.

26. Benjamin Orlove and Arnold J. Bauer, "Chile in the Belle Époque: Primitive Producers, Civilized Consumers," in Orlove, *Allure of the Foreign*, esp. 131–36.

27. Child, *Spanish-American Republics*, 421 and 401.

28. Corrado, "Contribución al estudio de la yerba mate," 7.

29. *La libertad*, Córdoba, Jan. 24, 1902, as cited in Fernando Remedi, "Los pobres y sus estrategias alimentarias de supervivencia en Córdoba, 1870–1920," *Población and sociedad*, nos. 12–13 (2005): 165–201, esp. 174.

30. William Garrett Acree, *Everyday Reading: Print Culture and Collective Identity in the Río de la Plata, 1780–1910* (Nashville: Vanderbilt University Press, 2011), 197n6; Juan José Arteaga and Ernesto Puiggrós, "Inmigración y estadística en el Uruguay 1830–1940," in *Inmigración y estadísticas en el Cono Sur de América*, ed. Hernán Asdrúbal Silva et al., Serie Inmigración, vol. 6 (Montevideo, Uru.: Organización de los Estados Americanos, Instituto Panamericano de Geografía e Historia, 1990), 268–69, 371.

31. Informal interview with María José B., Buenos Aires, Sept. 29, 2015.

32. The Archivo General de la Nación (hereafter AGN) preserves a copy of a photograph of men labeled as "Estancieros Irlandeses, ca. 1860," one of whom holds a simple mate and bombilla out for the camera to see.

33. Sarah O'Brien, *Linguistic Diasporas, Narrative and Performance: The Irish in Argentina* (Cham, Switz.: Palgrave Macmillan, 2017). On gauchos and the adoption of mate, see 59–60. On tea and scones, see 119, 180.

34. Navajas includes an illustration of this "strange" contraption. Navajas, *Caá porã*, 264–65.

35. Brian Bockelman, "Between the Gaucho and the Tango: Popular Songs and the Shifting Landscape of Modern Argentine Identity, 1895–1915," *American Historical Review* 116, no. 3 (2011): 577–601; Adolfo Prieto, *El discurso criollista en la formación de la Argentina moderna* (1988; repr., Buenos Aires: Siglo XXI Editores Argentina, 2006).

36. Edwin Clark, *A Visit to South America* (London: Dean and Son, 1878), 129.

37. Elizabeth Zanoni, *Migrant Marketplaces: Foods and Italians in North and South America* (Urbana: University of Illinois Press, 2018), 178.

38. In May 2016, I visited an exhibit of ceramic mates in Rosario, Argentina, with Mary Ester Galera. This exhibit drew from the collection of Hugo Bonnet, which contained some 1,600 mates. My analysis also draws from the article by Graciela Frega, "Historia bien cebada," from the Juan Carlos Romero Archive in Buenos Aires, about the collection of Pedro Naón Argerich. Argerich reports having a picture of immigrants drinking out of a *mate de loza* on the patio of a *conventillo*, suggesting this custom went beyond the most successful immigrants. The Museo de la Ciudad in Buenos Aires also housed a 2014 exhibit featuring ceramic (and other types of) mates. On the art of the porcelain mate in Buenos Aires, most from Germany and others from Czechoslovakia, see Guiomar de Urgell, "Porcelain Mates," in *The Mate in América*, by José M. Eguiguren Molina, Javier Eguiguren Molina, and Roberto Vega (ed.), trans. Francis Casal (Buenos Aires: La Stampa, 2004), 231–39.

39. Adriana M. Brodsky, *Sephardi, Jewish, Argentine: Community and National Identity* (Bloomington: Indiana University Press, 2016), cover photograph, 168.

40. Freidenberg, *Invention of the Jewish Gaucho*, esp. 146–47; and Sandra McGee Deutsch, *Crossing Borders, Claiming a Nation: A History of Argentine Jewish Women, 1880–1955* (Durham: Duke University Press, 2010), 31.

41. Mollie Lewis Nouwen, *Oy, My Buenos Aires: Jewish Immigration and the Creating of Argentine National Identity* (Santa Fe: University of New Mexico Press, 2013), 56.

42. Nouwen, 42–43.

43. Prieto, *El discurso criollista*.

44. Fernando O. Assunção, *El mate* (Montevideo, Uru.: ACRA, 1967), 8.

45. On the Jewish consumption of mate in Uruguay, see also Teresa Porzecanski, "Private Life and Identity Construction: Memories of Immigrant Jews in Uruguay," *Latin American and Caribbean Ethnic Studies* 4, no. 1 (2009): 73–91, esp. 87–88; and Daniela Bouret, Alvaro Martinez, and David Telias, *Entre la matzá y el mate: La inmigración judía al Uruguay; Una historia en construcción* (Montevideo, Uru.: Ediciones de la Banda Oriental, 1997).

46. Assunçao, *El mate*, 10.

47. Informal interview with María José B.

48. Daniel Vidart, "Filosofía del mate armago," *Bitacora* (blog), www.bitacora.com.uy /auc.aspx?4246 (accessed May 5, 2021).

49. I have surveyed hundreds of postcards, including all those available in the photograph section of the AGN related to rural traditions; those reproduced in Masotta's, Loeb's,

and Silva's books; those available in Loeb's collection or via the Mercado Libre website; and those accessible online via databases or Google searches. I also consulted the place of rural figures on currency at Museo Banco Provincia, http://museobancoprovincia.com /colecciones/monedas-y-billetes/billetes/. Carlos Masotta, *Gauchos en las primeras postales fotográficas argentinas del s. xx* (Buenos Aires: La Marca, 2007), and *Indios en las primeras postales fotográficas argentinas del s. xx* (Buenos Aires: La Marca Editora, 2007); Marcelo Loeb, *Ensayo de catálogo: Las tarjetas postales de C. Galli Fraco y Cío incluyendo también las postales editadas por Albert Aust-Hamburgo* (Buenos Aires: self-published, 2003); Guillermo José Silva, *Costumbres campestres de la República Argentina en las postales y fotos del siglo XIX y XX* (Buenos Aires: Editorial Dunken, 2016).

50. Slatta, *Gauchos and the Vanishing Frontier*, 2.

51. Rural Code of 1865, article 289.

52. On xenophobia and gauchos, in addition to Slatta, *Gauchos and the Vanishing Frontier*, see Prieto, *El discurso criollista*. On class conflict and the gaucho, see Adamovsky, *El gaucho indómito*; Casas, *La metamorfosis del gaucho*; Sandra McGee Deutsch, "The Visible and Invisible Liga Patriotica Argentina, 1919–28: Gender Roles and the Right Wing," *Hispanic American Historical Review* 64, no. 2 (May 1984): 233–58; and Bockelman, "Between the Gaucho and the Tango."

53. Adamovsky, *El gaucho indómito*; Ezequiel Adamovsky, "Criollismo, experiencia popular y política: El gaucho como emblema subversivo," *Anuario del Instituto de Historia Argentina* 18, no. 1 (June 2018): 1–20.

54. Adamovsky, *El gaucho indómito*; on elites dressing up as gauchos, Acree, *Staging Frontiers*, esp. chap. 5; Casas, *La metamorfosis del gaucho*; and Masotta, *Gauchos*.

55. The rural woman was referred to most commonly as *la china*, a term in Spanish that can mean Chinese but in this South American context primarily draws from the precolonial Quechua word *c'ina*. During the colonial era, the Spanish extended this Indigenous term for a female animal to the supposedly "uncivilized," non-Christian Indigenous woman. As Diana Marre explains, this decidedly female label of *china* acquired new meanings but stuck to rural women (especially those from the Pampas or other frontier regions) in a largely pejorative way. Marre concludes that *la china* has come to refer to "an Indigenous or mixed-race (*mestiza*) woman, or a woman of similar appearance, considered ordinary, from the lower classes," who is often defined by her condition of servitude and a supposedly "dubious sexual morality." For analysis of the historical construction of the figure of the *china*, see Diana Marre, *Mujeres argentinas: Las chinas; Representación, territorio, género y nación* (Barcelona: Universitat de Barcelona, 2003), esp. 29 and 107–19; and Rebekah E. Pite, "The Rural Woman Enters the Frame: A Visual History of Gender, Nation, and the Goodbye Mate in the Postcolonial Río de la Plata," *Journal of Social History* 54, no. 4 (Summer 2021): 1120–59.

56. Indeed, only one book, Marre, *Mujeres argentinas*, and my aforementioned article from the *Journal of Social History* center the figure of the *china*.

57. Adamovsky, *El gaucho indómito* and "Criollismo, experiencia popular y política."

58. Marre, *Mujeres argentinas*, 115.

59. Bonafacio del Carril, *El gaucho a tráves de la iconografía* (Buenos Aires: Banco de la Provincia de Buenos Aires, 1978), 154.

60. See, for example, León Pallière, *Paseo del domingo*, oil painting, 1865; León Pallière, *Enamorando II*, 1865, watercolor; and Carlos Pellegrini, *Payada en el rancho*, lithograph, 1841; as reproduced in Carril, *El gaucho*, 156, 158, 170.

61. Digital versions of this currency are available at Museo Banco Provincia, http://museobancoprovincia.com/colecciones/monedas-y-billetes/billetes/ (accessed Jan. 8, 2020).

62. For access to digital versions of these paintings and more information about them, see Mazoni at Bellas Artes, www.bellasartes.gob.ar/coleccion/obra/2890/; Blanes at Arte Activo, http://museos.gub.uy/arteactivo/item/blanes-juan-manuel.html; and Pérez, at Bellas Artes, www.bellasartes.gob.ar/coleccion/obra/7553/ (accessed Apr. 15, 2022).

63. Verónica Tell, "Gentlemen, gauchos y modernización: Una lectura del proyecto de la Sociedad Fotográfica Argentina de Aficionados," *Revista de Historia del Arte y Cultura Visual del Centro Argentino de Investigadores de Arte*, no. 3 (2013): 1–19, esp. 10.

64. Tell, esp. 3.

65. Approximately three-quarters of the group's photos featured Argentina's capital city. Tell, "Gentlemen, gauchos y modernización," 1–2.

66. Ayerza inherited his last name from his Basque father, a physician who immigrated to Argentina in 1845. Ayerza sometimes signed his photographs using the pseudonym Pacovich, according to Tell, "Gentlemen, gauchos y modernización," 6.

67. Tell, 6.

68. Ayerza's photography shoot was published in its entirety (and with other photographs included) in Academia Nacional de Bellas Artes, *Escenas del campo argentino 1885–1900: Fotografías del Doctor Francisco Ayerza con una introducción de Eduardo Gonzalez Lanuza* (Buenos Aires: Academia Nacional de Bellas Artes, 1968). Women are included only in about one-tenth of the photographs.

69. Francisco de Ayerza, photograph, AGN, Colección 1699, s. 2, 1894, inventory number 16445. The note on the back of the photograph says, "Taken to illustrate an edition of Martín Fierro and then it did not happen."

70. The modern technology of the photograph may also have seemed inappropriate to illustrate this nostalgic epic poem, which has been almost exclusively accompanied by hand-drawn illustrations since 1878. A couple of decades after Ayerza's own death, a unique 1919 edition of *Martín Fierro* published in Buenos Aires finally featured seven of his photographs of an older gaucho at work or alone. Save one photograph in front of the *pulpería*, none of Ayerza's photographs featuring leisure activities appeared. *Catalogue of the Martín Fierro Materials in the University of Texas Library*, ed. Nettie Lee Benson (Austin: Institute of Latin American Studies, 1973), x. For edition with photographs, see *Martín Fierro por José Hernández* (Buenos Aires: Biblioteca Argentina, Publicación Mensual de los Mejores Libros Nacionales, no. 19, Librería La Facultad de Juan Roldán, 1919).

71. Ayerza's photographs first appeared in 1898 in the Argentine publication *Almanaque Peuser* and in a weekly arts magazine published in Barcelona called *La ilustración artística* that circulated both in Spain and Latin America.

72. While these brothers (raised in Argentina by British parents) did their own work, Abel Alexander and Luis Priamo make a compelling case to treat them together given doubts about authorship and sharing of negatives. José X. Martini, ed., *La Argentina a fines del siglo XIX: Fotografías de Samuel y Arturo Boote 1880–1900* (Buenos Aires: Ediciones de la Antorcha, 2012), 150. Samuel Rimathé was another contemporary commercial photographer who took many pictures of the countryside.

73. Some of these show men on *estancias*. In one, they drink mate in a field of cow carcasses, and in another, called *Personal de una estancia*, eight men, one woman, and one barefoot child pose stone-faced in front of a brick building; notably, four of the men

hold a mate. Samuel Boote, *Una Estancia*, ca. 1900, as reproduced in Robert M. Levine, *Images of History: Nineteenth and Early Twentieth Century Latin American Photographs as Documents* (Durham: Duke University Press, 1989), 106; and Martini, *La Argentina a fines del siglo XIX*, 93.

74. For these and other photographs, see Martini, *La Argentina a fines del siglo XIX*.

75. It is noteworthy that he called the man a "paisano" or countryman rather than a gaucho, and the woman "mujer," which can mean either wife or woman, rather than *china*. Arturo W. Boote y Cía, *Paisano y mujer*, ca. 1890, Colección César Gotta, reproduced in Martini, *La Argentina a fines del siglo XIX*, 100.

76. As Marre points out, the lack of comestible wood and rocks in the pampas required that women be skilled in starting and maintaining a fire with animal skulls or subpar wood to cook beef and warm the water for mate. Marre, *Mujeres argentinas*, 155–57.

77. Graciela Silvestri, "El viaje de las Señoritas," *Revista todaVIA* 4 (2003): 1–14, esp. 1–2.

78. Loeb, *Ensayo de catálogo*.

79. Hinnerk Onken, "Visiones y visualizaciones: La nación en tarjetas postales sudamericanas a fines del siglo xix y comienzos del siglo xx," *Iberoamericana* 14, no. 56 (2014): 60.

80. Onken, 51.

81. Hinnerk Onken, who has done considerable research with foreign collectors of Argentine postcards (especially in Germany), emphasizes the masculine nature of collecting, while Carlos Masotta, who has focused on Argentine postcards within Argentina, suggests this as a more feminized practice. Onken, "Visiones y visualizaciones"; Masotta, "Representación e iconografía," 70–71.

82. Masotta, "Representación e iconografía," 67.

83. Silva reproduces two similar postcards, one in which a woman waits for a man and the other in which she says goodbye without him in the frame. Silva, *Costumbres campestres*, 26–27.

84. Silva, *Costumbres campestres*, 24.

85. On the contributions of Afro-Rioplatenses and the visibility of blackness in Argentina and Uruguay during this era, see, for example, Paulina Alberto, *Black Legend: The Many Lives of Raúl Grigera and the Power of Racial Storytelling in Argentina* (New York: Cambridge University Press, 2022); Alex Borucki, *From Shipmate to Soldiers: Emerging Black Identities in the Río de la Plata* (Albuquerque: University of New Mexico Press, 2015); and George Reid Andrews, *The Afro-Argentines of Buenos Aires* (Madison: University of Wisconsin Press, 1980), *Blackness in the White Nation: A History of Afro-Uruguay* (Chapel Hill: University of North Carolina Press, 2010), and *Afro-Latin America: Black Lives 1600–2000* (Cambridge, MA: Harvard University Press, 2016).

86. In the mate postcard (fig. 4.5), contemporaries might have recognized the guitar player on the roof as White.

87. Alex Borucki makes this point in his research as well as in his comments on an earlier version of this chapter. Some Brazilian yerba mate sold in Uruguay also employed this trope. For instance, in 1983, the company São Mateaus was formed, which still markets a brand of mate in Uruguay sold under the name "La Mulata" with an image of a woman of African descent; see the Ervateira São Mateus website, http://ervateirasm.com.br/ (accessed Mar. 9, 2017).

88. I have found other examples of urban mate drinkers in Uruguayan postcards and paintings. And while I have seen photographs of people in urban Argentina drinking mate, I have yet to find postcards or paintings that depict them doing so.

89. For a broader analysis of public visual culture, see Sergio Caggiano, *El sentido común visual: Disputas en torno a género, raza y clase en imágenes de circulación pública* (Buenos Aires: Mino y Davila, 2012).

90. Masotta, *Gauchos*, 113.

91. Mary Louise Pratt, "Women, Literature, and National Brotherhood," *Kristische Berichte*, Mar. 1997, 13.

92. I found a similar trend in my review of the rural and urban photograph collections at the AGN, with rural people much more likely to be depicted with mate than their urban counterparts (though there were some urbanites imbibing, as opposed to the apparent lack of "indios" doing so both in postcards and in this collection). Masotta included at least five postcards that included mate in his book on gauchos and none in his book on Indians. Masotta, *Indios*; Masotta, *Gauchos*.

93. Masotta, *Indios*, 7–14; Masotta, "Representación e inconografía."

94. Esteban Gonnet, [*Tomando mate*], ca. 1866, *Album de vistas y costumbres de la provincia de Buenos Aires, 1844–1878*, The Getty Research Institute, Los Angeles, Accession no. 2016.R.39, leaf 37R; title from Luis Priamo, ed., *Buenos Aires, ciudad y campaña 1860–1870* (Buenos Aires: Fundación Antorchas, 2000), 73; and Anonymous, "*Mapuches tomando mate en la pampa*," 1880, AGN, Documento Fotográfico, Inventario 303579, available online at Facebook, https://esla.facebook.com/ArchivoGeneraldelaNacionArgentina/photos /mapuches-tomando-mate-en-la-pampa-mientras-se-asa-la-carne-c1890documento-fotogr /1052138358144713/.

95. Cover, *Billiken*, Oct. 11, 1920. I thank Paula Bontempo for sharing this unique cover and her interpretation of it, which appears to be the only cover featuring mate but not the only one highlighting a caricatured Black figure. For more on *Billiken*, see Paula Bontempo, "Los niños de *Billiken*: Las infancias en Buenos Aires en las primeras décadas de siglo XX," *Anuario del Centro de Estudios Históricos*, no. 12 (2012): 205–21.

96. Pite, "Rural Woman Enters the Frame."

97. At UCSD's digital repository, there is what appears to be an earlier postcard with the same series title featuring a romantic couple off the horse and about to kiss, which is postmarked June 28, 1901; this was accessed Mar. 28, 2018, at Digital USD, http://digital .sandiego.edu/pcsouthamerica/311/.

98. Masotta, "Representación e inconografía."

99. Postcard, Ed. Fumagilli, N. 145, "República Argentina. Campestre Alcanzando un mate," ca. 1911, courtesy of Lafayette College Special Collections and College Archives, Easton, PA (hereafter LCSC).

100. Postcard, H. G. Olde, "Recuerdo de la República Argentina: Gaucho Tomando Mate," ca. 1903, courtesy of LCSC.

101. I have found four distinct versions of this postcard, one of which I found two distinct copies of on www.todocolleción.com: one sent in 1905 and the other, a colorized version from 1908, sent to Cuba (accessed Nov. 4, 2019).

102. While it is unclear why this postcard did not cross the River Plate, perhaps it was due to the woman's more Indigenous appearance and the endurance of the popular notion that "Indians" no longer lived in Uruguay. Ariadna Islas and Ana Frega, "Identidades uruguayas: Del mito de la sociedad homogénea al reconocimiento de la pluralidad," in *Historias del Uruguay en el siglo XX (1890–2005)*, 3rd ed. (Montevideo, Uru.: EBO, 2010); Vannina Sztainbok, "From Salsipuedes to Tabaré: Race, Space, and the Uruguayan Subject," *Thamyrs/Intersecting* 20 (2010): 175–92.

103. Postcard, H. G. Olde, "Gaucho Tomando Mate."

104. On gender norms and practices in Argentina, see, for example, my first book, *Creating a Common Table in Twentieth-Century Argentina: Doña Petrona, Women, and Food* (Chapel Hill: University of North Carolina Press, 2013); for the United States, see, for example, Jessamyn Neuhaus, *Manly Meals and Mom's Home Cooking: Cookbooks and Gender in Modern America* (Baltimore: Johns Hopkins University Press, 2003).

105. Postcard, "R. Argentina—Costumbres Campestres—Tomando Mate," courtesy of LCSC.

106. Postcard, "Uruguay—Escenas Campestres," ed. C. Galli, Montevideo, courtesy of LCSC.

107. Postcard, "Costumbres de Campo en la Rep. Argentina: Será Verdad?," ed. Rosauer, courtesy of LCSC.

108. It is interesting that he didn't include Chile on this list, perhaps because he spent more time in Santiago. Henry B. Stephens, *Journeys and Experiences in Argentina, Paraguay, and Chile Including a Side Trip to the Sources of the Paraguay River in the State of Matto Grosso, Brazil, and a Journey across the Andes to the Rio Tambo in Brazil* (New York: Knickerbocker Press, 1920), 510.

109. Genaro Romero, "Anuario de Gobiero," 1927, as cited in Margarita Miró Ibars, *Tembi'u Rehuega—Reivindicaicón de la cultura guaranari y paraguaya* (Carapeuga, Para.: Estudio Ediciones, 1994), 41–42.

110. Dr. Ricardo Albornoz, "El mate bebida nacional," *Viva cien años*, Feb. 1937, 332.

111. Albornoz, 332–33.

112. A heterosexual goodbye mate was on the cover of a Chilean domestic workers' magazine, *Surge: Escrito por empleadas para las empleadas* (Santiago, 1959) from the Archivo de la Asociación Nacional de Empleadas de Casa Particular, 1959, courtesy of Elizabeth Hutchison. It also appeared on a late twentieth-century postcard from Rio Grande do Sul, "Gaúcho com prenda tomando chimarrão" (Gaucho in typical dress drinking mate), as part of a series called "Brasil Folclore." Mercado livre, https://produto.mercadolivre.com.br/MLB-968204910-rs -17168-postal-rio-grande-do-sul-pampa-gaucho-_JM (accessed June 13, 2019).

CHAPTER FIVE

1. Salus advertisement, *Caras y caretas*, Nov. 25, 1933, 56.

2. José Buschini, "La alimentación como problema científico y objeto de políticas públicas en la Argentina: Pedro Escudero y el Instituto Nacional de la Nutrición," *Apuntes* 79 (2016): 129–56.

3. On the history of regionalism and race in Brazil, see Barbara Weinstein, *The Color of Modernity: São Paulo and the Making of Race and Nation in Brazil* (Durham: Duke University Press, 2015); on region, race, and food, see Glen Goodman, "Consuming the *Café Colonial*: German Ethnicity and Tourist Migrant Marketplaces in Southern Brazil," *Global Food History* 4, no. 1 (2018): 40–58, esp. 42.

4. On histories of race in Argentina, see Paulina Alberto and Eduardo Elena, eds., *Rethinking Race in Modern Argentina* (New York: Cambridge University Press, 2016); and on Misiones and the yerba industry, Jennifer Bowles, "Making *Tarefero* Pride: The Collaborative Construction of Portable Photomurals for Farmworker Empowerment in Misiones, Argentina," *Journal of Community Practice*, Sept. 25, 2018, 1–20; Víctor Rau, *Cosechando yerba mate: Estructuras sociales de un mercado laboral agrario en el nordeste argentino* (Buenos Aires: Ciccus,

2012); and Javier Gortari, comp. *De la tierra sin mal al tractorazo: Hacia una economía política de la yerba mate* (Posadas, Arg.: Editorial Universitaria de Misiones, 2007).

5. On advertising and consumption in this era, see Fernando Rocchi, "A la vanguardia de la modernización: La incipiente formación de un campo publicitario en la Argentina durante la década de 1920," *Estudios interdisciplinarios de América Latina y el Caribe* 27 (Jan. 1, 2016): 47–76, esp. 51–52; and Fernando Rocchi, "Inventando la soberanía del consumidor: Publicidad, privacidad y revolución del mercado en Argentina, 1860–1940," in *Historia de la vida privada en la Argentina*, vol. 3, ed. Fernando Devoto and Marta Madero (Buenos Aires: Taurus, 1999), 301–21.

6. *Misiones: Oro verde* (Buenos Aires: Astro, 1945), 94–96.

7. I analyze this trend in Rebekah E. Pite, *Creating a Common Table in Twentieth-Century Argentina: Doña Petrona, Women, and Food* (Chapel Hill: University of North Carolina Press, 2013), esp. chap. 2.

8. Nancy Leys Stepan, *"The Hour of Eugenics": Race, Gender and Nation in Latin America* (Ithaca, NY: Cornell University Press, 1991).

9. In 1905, for example, Argentina imported some 40,500 tons of yerba from Brazil and Paraguay, according to Garin. In 1941, a consumer study by an Argentine yerba company found that Argentina consumed a whopping 62 percent of the total yerba. Brazil and Uruguay followed at 13–14 percent, with Paraguay and Chile following behind at 5 percent, and all other nations making up only .5 percent. Dr. Victor Garin, *Contribución al estudio del cultivo e industria de la yerba mate* (Buenos Aires: Talleres Gráficos del Ministerio de Agricultura de la Nación, 1916); and Martín y Cía, *Que es la yerba mate* (Buenos Aires: E. Fenner, 1942).

10. Cámara de Comercio Argentina-Brasileña, *La yerba mate: El problema económico y fiscal* (Buenos Aires: Futura, 1933).

11. In 1912, Paraguay exported 2.5 million pounds of unmilled yerba and 200,000 pounds of the milled variety, according to W. H. Koebel, *Paraguay* (London: T. F. Unwin, 1917), 315.

12. F. R. de Azevedo Macedo, *Commercio de herva-matte: Resposta a um artigo de "La Nación" de B. Ayres* (Curityba, Brazil: Annibal, Rocha and C., 1899), 19.

13. Macedo, *Commercio de herva-matte*, 15.

14. In 1899, Alfonso Arnoldo Rutis, an agent for Mate Larangeira, and William Mill Butler, entrepreneurial American writer and diplomat, formed the Yerba Mate Tea Company. According to Herib Caballero Campos, they did so because of the high tariffs Argentina began placing on milled yerba, which made them eager to enter North American markets. They pitched yerba mate primarily to women in the United States and Canada as an energizing but less irritating product than coffee or tea. Herib Caballero Campos, "¡Beba té de yerba mate y sea feliz! La promoción de la yerba mate en Los Estados Unidos de América a fines del siglo XIX," *Revista Latino-Americana de Historia* 6, no. 17 (June–July 2017): 80–95.

15. This disparity led the traders of Paraná to write to liberal Brazilian president Dr. Affonso Penna (1906–9) to request that he intervene. Political cartoon, "Gentilezas commerciaes," *O malho* (Rio de Janeiro), no. 227, Jan. 1907, 24. I am grateful to Bridget Chesterton for sharing this source with me.

16. For a study of the history of adulteration and industrialization of the food supply in the United States, see Benjamin R. Cohen, *Pure Adulteration: Cheating on Nature in the Age of Manufactured Food* (Chicago: University of Chicago Press, 2020).

17. Guimarães & Co., *Breve noticia* (Estado do Paraná: Typographia da Livraria Economica, 1899).

18. Fernando Rocchi, *Chimneys in the Desert: Industrialization in Argentina during the Export Boom Years, 1870–1930* (Stanford: Stanford University Press, 2006), 149.

19. "Companhia Matte Larangeira," *Caras y caretas*, Mar. 18, 1893, 6.

20. Rocchi, *Chimneys in the Desert*, 102, 149.

21. Honorio Leguizamón, "La yerba-mate: Cuestión económico-social," *Anales de la Sociedad Científica Argentina* (Buenos Aires: Imprenta de Coni Hermanos, 1913), 24–25.

22. Ross W. Jamieson, "The Essence of Commodification: Caffeine Dependencies in the Early Modern World," *Journal of Social History* 35, no. 2 (2001): 279.

23. Corrientes fought to preserve its control over the region and, before transferring what became the province of Misiones back to the national government, sold off huge tracts of land to local elites. On this process, see Eric D. Carter, "Misiones Province, Argentina: How Borders Shape Political Identity," in *Borderlines and Borderlands: Political Oddities at the Edge of the Nation State*, ed. Alexander C. Diener and Joshua Hagen (Lanham, MD: Rowman and Littlefield, 2010), 162n3; and Graciela Sturm, *Yerba buena y yerba mala: Medio siglo de historia de la producción y el trabajo en los yerbales misioneros (1890–1942)* (Buenos Aires: Ediciones Cooperativas, 2006).

24. This practice was prohibited in 1930. Rau, *Cosechando yerba mate*, 40.

25. During General Roca's so-called Conquest of the Desert (1878–85), federal troops sought to assert authority over and vanquish sovereign Indigenous groups to claim the territory for the Argentine republic and to Whiten it. For recent scholarship on this process, see Carolyn R. Larson, ed., *The Conquest of the Desert: Argentina's Indigenous Peoples and the Battle for History* (Albuquerque: University of New Mexico Press, 2020).

26. Leopoldo Bartolomé, "Colonos, plantadores y agroindustrias," *Desarrollo económico* 58, no. 15 (1975): 240–64.

27. Jerónimo Lagier, *The Adventures of the Yerba Mate: Over Four Centuries of History* (Posadas, Arg.: Tambú, 2014), 132–33.

28. "Nuestra visita al gran establecimiento industrial de yerba-mate de la sociedad anónima MARTIN y Cía. Ltda., de Rosario," *Caras y caretas*, Dec. 17, 1932, 89–92; quotes on 91–92.

29. I learned about this history firsthand during a 2015 visit to the Museo Histórico Juan Szychowski in Apóstoles, Misiones. For a published family memoir, see Juan Alfredo "Pancho" Szychowski, *Historias de mi familia* (Buenos Aires: Aracuaria, 2015).

30. Rau describes a major increase in production from Misiones from 2,169 tons in 1915 to 106,330 tons by 1937. Víctor Rau, "La yerba mate en misiones (Argentina): Estructura y significados de una producción localizada," *Agrolimentaria*, no. 28 (Jan.–June 2009): 49–58, for specific reference, 53.

31. These statistics refer to fiscal year 1901/2. By fiscal year 1916/17, Paraná exported nearly 29 million kilograms of yerba to Argentina and about a third of that (or 9.4 million kilograms) to Uruguay. In contrast, the much larger region of southern Brazil consumed less than half of the figure for Uruguay (some 4.2 million kilograms), and northern Brazil contributed a scant tenth of that amount (just over 400 thousand kilograms). Claudio Roberto Bragueto, "O proceso de industrialização do Paraná até a década de 1970," *Geografia* 8, no. 2 (1999): 149–60, esp. 150.

32. María Victoria Magán, "El intercambio entre Brasil y Argentina y los tratados de comercio de 1933 y 1935," *II Jornadas de historia regional comparada* (Second Comparative Regional History Workshop), Porto Alegre, Brazil, 2005, 4.

33. Marisa Correia de Oliveira, "Estudo da erva mate no Paraná: 1939–1967" (master's thesis, Universidade Federal do Paraná, 1974), 25.

34. Oliveira, 21–23, table 9.

35. Magán, "El intercambio," 4.

36. Pau Navajas, *Caá Porã: El espíritu de la yerba mate, una historia de plata* (Corrientes, Arg.: Las Marías, 2013), 332.

37. Oliveira, "Estudo da erva mate no Paraná."

38. In the late nineteenth century, Brazilians exhibited their erva in Europe and published pamphlets in multiple languages directed to Europeans. They used pamphlets to argue that mate was more economical and healthier than coffee or tea, such as one for free distribution at the International Exposition in Philadelphia by Macedo Soares, *O mate do Paraná* (Rio de Janeiro: Imperial Instituto Artístico, 1875), which claimed mate stimulated without creating sleeplessness and would satiate the poor masses in Europe who could not afford coffee or tea.

39. Caso do Mate advertisement, *O Matte*, no. 6, Feb. 1930, 25.

40. The company's 1929 pamphlet (written in Portuguese, Spanish, and English) emphasized its leading role in milling and exports. The photos show both men and women harvesting and preparing mate. The company started milling wood in 1912. *Leão Junior & Cia: Productores, fábricas, exportadores de herva-mate, madeiras y café* (Curityba, Brazil: Empeza Editora Olivero, 1929), 35.

41. "Matte Leão," *Mundo das marcas* (blog), July 27, 2006, https://mundodasmarcas .blogspot.com/2006/07/mate-leo-o-original.html.

42. *Leão Junior & Cia*, 35.

43. Dr. Victor do Amaral, "A propaganda do matte," *O Matte*, no. 6, Feb. 1930, 13.

44. "Matte Leão." Further innovations included a concentrate in 1969 and then flavored and instant mate, and so on.

45. On the history of the highly caffeinated Amazonian plant called *guaraná*, see Seth Garfield, *A Taste of Brazil: The History of Guaraná* (Chapel Hill: University of North Carolina Press, 2022).

46. "A herva-mate," *Logos: Orgão oficial do Centro Acadêmico da Faculdade de Filosofia, Ciências e Letras da Universidade do Paraná*, no. 7 (1948): 21.

47. "A herva-mate," 21.

48. On land policies and yerba revenue, see Rau, "La yerba mate en misiones," 52n8; Navajas, *Caá Porã*, 332; and Bartolomé, "Colonos, plantadores y agroindustrias."

49. Magán, "El intercambio"; on environment, see María Cecila Gallero, "La yerba mate en el prisma de la historia ambiental, Misones (Argentina)," in *História ambiental e migrações: Diálogos*, ed. M. Gerhardt, E. S. Nodari, and S. P. Moretto (São Leopoldo: Oikos, 2017), 193–214.

50. Bartolomé, "Colonos, plantadores y agroindustrias," 247.

51. On Lagier and other Swiss immigrants to Misiones, see Laura Mabel Zang, "Poblar la frontera: Misiones y la presencia de suizos en el Territorio Nacional, 1881–1920," *Revista Pilquen* 20, no. 4 (2017): 71–81. This letter is quoted from and reproduced in part in Lagier, *Adventures of the Yerba Mate*, 145.

52. Rau, "La yerba mate en misiones," esp. 52–53.

53. Lisandro de la Torre was a member of the Radical Party early in his career but switched to head the Partido Demócrata Progresista founded in 1919; he attacked Yrigoyen's decision to end the 30 percent reduction in Brazilian imports established in 1924. On de la Torre's defense of Argentine yerba planters' interests, see Navajas, *Caá Porã*, 338; and Lagier, *Adventures of the Yerba Mate*, 143.

54. Ernesto Daumas, *El problema de la yerba mate* (Buenos Aires: Compañía Impresora Argentina, 1930).

55. María Victoria Magán, "La Dirección de Yerba Mate y la Comisión Reguladora (CRYM): El sector yerbatero argentino y el intervencionismo estatal, entre 1947 y 1957," Universidad Nacional de Tres de Febrero, *XXI Jornadas de historia económica* (Twenty-First Economic History Workshop), Buenos Aires, Sept. 23–26, 2008.

56. Magán, "El intercambio," 5.

57. Magán, 7; Navajas, *Caá Porã*, 359–60.

58. Magán, "El intercambio," 9.

59. Magán, "La Dirección de Yerba Mate," 3.

60. Magán, "El intercambio."

61. This institute ceased to exist in 1966–67. Marlus Iasbeck Paes, "Instituto Nacional do Mate e Instituto Nacional do Pinho: Estudo institucional comparado" (thesis for title of Forestry Engineer, Universidade Federal Rural do Rio de Janeiro, 2010), esp. 1.

62. As Joel Wolfe argues, despite the textbook portrayal of Vargas as the national consolidator and champion of workers' rights, Brazil remained "highly federated" and workers frustrated. In the wake of the Great Depression, development-oriented Vargas focused his attention on supporting the coffee industry and established the Departamento Nacional do Café in 1931. For more on Vargas's approach and the numerous state-led organizations established in Brazil during this period, for coffee and sugar, cotton, and manioc, see Joel Wolfe, "Change with Continuity: Brazil from 1930 to 1945," in *The Great Depression in Latin America*, ed. Paulo Drinot and Alan Knight (Durham: Duke University Press, 2014), 81–99; and Fiona Gordon-Ashworth, "Agricultural Commodity Control under Vargas in Brazil, 1930–1945," *Journal of Latin American Studies* 12, no. 1 (May 1980): 87–105.

63. Cesar C. Samaniego, *Ilex paraguayensis: Yerba mate ca'a* (República del Paraguay: Imprenta Nacional, 1927), esp. 11 and 20.

64. Jan M. G. Kleinpenning, *Rural Paraguay, 1870–1963: A Geography of Progress, Plunder and Poverty*, 2 vols. (Madrid: Iberoamericana, 2009), 1:680.

65. Rau, "La yerba mate en misiones," 53. By this point, Argentina imported only 45 percent of Brazil's smaller 65,519 tons (down from 75 percent of Brazil's 91,902 tons a decade prior). Heron S. M. Begnis, "A economia da erva mate: Uma breve perspectiva," *Redes: Desenvolvimento regional* 5, no. 3 (Sept.–Dec. 2000): 25–44. For more on Larangeira, see Caballero Campos, "¡Beba té de yerba mate y sea feliz!," esp. 82.

66. Magán, "El intercambio," 5.

67. On earlier Paraguayan and Brazilian efforts as well as Argentina's participation in the Yerba Mate Tea Company, see Caballero Campos, "*¡Beba Té de Yerba Mate y Sea Feliz!*," 80–94.

68. Buschini, "La alimentación como problema."

69. In my research at the Facultad de Medicina and Biblioteca Nacional de Argentina, I found twenty-six studies from the 1930s, compared with two from the first decade of the 1900s, seven from the 1910s and 1920s, and eleven from the 1940s.

70. Escudero's studies focused on the vitamins, minerals, and calories present in yerba mate. For example, Pedro Escudero, "Valor mineral y vitaminico de la yerba mate (*Ilex paraguayensis*)," *Farmacia y quimica* (Lima: Organo de la Federación Nacional de Farmacéuticos, 1945).

71. Comisión Reguladora de la Producción y Comercio de la Yerba Mate, *Memoria*, Jan.–Mar. 1940.

72. Some thirty years passed before it became an annual event. I consulted the "Anteced-entes. Fiesta Nacional de la Yerba Mate" at the Archivo General de la Gobernación de Mis-iones in Posadas. One of the few scholars to trace the history of this festival is María Florencia Banacor Tuzinkievicz, "La Fiesta Nacional de la Yerba Mate ¿festival cargado de valor sim-bólico o producto de industrias culturales?" (Thesis de licenciatura, Universidad de Misiones, Posadas, 2014), esp. 37–39. On Schnarback, see Gloria Beatriz Torres, *Escuela N° 97 a los 100 años, Picada Sueca, Misiones* (Oberá: Editorial Ediciones Misioneras, 2021).

73. Kaner was previously an anarchist but had become a communist leader by this time. For more on Kaner, see Sandra McGee Deutsch, *Gendering Antifascism: Women's Activism in Argentina and the World, 1918–1947* (Pittsburgh: University of Pittsburgh Press, forthcom-ing 2023). For Varela, see Alfredo Varela, *¡También en la Argentina hay esclavos blancos!*, ed. Javier Trímboli and Guillermo Korn (Buenos Aires: Omnívora Editora, 2020); and Nicolá G. Recoaro, "Afredo Varela y el canto triste del pobre mensú," *Tiempo argentino*, Dec. 16, 2020, www.tiempoar.com.ar/nota/alfredo-varela-y-el-canto-triste-del-pobre-mensu.

74. Varela, *¡También en la Argentina hay esclavos blancos!*, 55.

75. On connections, see Cristina Mateu, "Encuentros y desencuentros entre dos grades obras: *El río Oscuro* y *Las aguas bajan turbias (Argentina, 1943/1952)*," *Nuevo mundo mundos nuevos*, 2012, doi.org/10.4000/nuevomundo.63148.

76. On branding in general, see Rocchi, "Inventando la soberanía del consumidor."

77. For an analysis and reproduction of several of these labels, see José Humberto Bog-zuswski, "Uma história cultural da erva-mate: O alimento e suas representações" (master's thesis, Universidade Federal do Paraná, 2007). This seems indicative of a larger trend as consumers in Uruguay were offered more modern and urban visuals of would-be consumers than the more historical and rural associations offered to Argentines.

78. On banana promotion, see Marcelo Bucheli and Ian Read, "Banana Boats and Baby Food: The Banana in U.S. History," in *From Silver to Cocaine: Latin American Commodity Chains and the Building of the World Economy*, ed. Steven Topik, Carlos Marichal, and Zephyr Frank (Durham: Duke University Press, 2006), 204–27; and on Brazilian coffee promotion, see Micol Siegel, *Uneven Encounters: Making Race and Nation in Brazil and the United States* (Durham: Duke University Press, 2009), 13–66.

79. Rocchi, "A la vanguardia de la modernización."

80. Natalia Milanesio, *Workers Go Shopping in Argentina: The Rise of Popular Consumer Culture* (Albuquerque: University of New Mexico Press, 2013), 83–122.

81. This trend was also evident in Mexico, where as Julio Moreno points out, successful US-based companies and politicians needed to "embrace Mexican culture" to effectively reach Mexican consumers. Julio Moreno, *Yankee Don't Go Home! Mexican Nationalism, American Business Culture, and the Shaping of Modern Mexico, 1920–1950* (Chapel Hill: University of North Carolina Press, 2003).

82. In researching this chapter, I surveyed advertisements available in the magazines, newspapers, and mate-related sources I consulted at various archives and libraries. I also found a wealth of advertisements online, via the Mercado Libre website and accessible in digitalized databases, especially *Caras y caretas*. I organized my collection of hundreds of advertisements by brand and by date and highlight examples that reveal prominent trends.

83. This sentiment was expressed by nearly all the Uruguayan consumers I spoke with, including Uruguayan mate expert Javier Ricca.

84. These ads shared the page with the company's other imports. Aguila advertisement, *Caras y caretas*, Oct. 12, 1907, 74.

85. Ultimately, Giménez blamed the Paraguayan government for not intervening to get LIP to stop tampering with the quality. Kleinpenning, *Rural Paraguay, 1870–1963*, 1:679–80.

86. See, for example, Flor de Lis advertisements, *Caras y caretas*, Sep. 27, 1913, 14; Oct. 11, 1913, 31; and Jan. 3, 1913, 27.

87. Flor de Lis advertisement, *Caras y caretas*, Dec. 6, 1913, 51. While gauchos and "men of science" (such as Lavalle) predominated in Flor de Lis early advertising campaigns, in *Caras y caretas* LIP also featured at least one ad with an Indigenous man on Feb. 26, 1916, 65; another with a Paraguayan woman on Dec. 20, 1913, 31; and another with a suited blond man blindfolded and able to distinguish the superiority of its yerba on June 5, 1915, 75.

88. Flor de Lis advertisement, *Caras y caretas*, Nov. 7, 1914, 17; and Jan. 1, 1915, 141.

89. Flor de Lis advertisement, *Caras y caretas*, June 18, 1927, 23.

90. Flor de Lis advertisement, *Caras y caretas*, July 30, 1927, 33.

91. Flor de Lis advertisement, *Caras y caretas*, June 11, 1927, 135.

92. Kolleen M. Guy, *When Champagne Became French* (Baltimore: Johns Hopkins University Press, 2003).

93. Flor de Lis advertisements, *El campo*, Dec. 1929–Feb. 1933.

94. Flor de Lis advertisement, *Caras y caretas*, June 17, 1936, 45.

95. Flor de Lis advertisement, *Caras y caretas*, May 26, 1934, 30.

96. "Nuestra visita al gran establecimiento industrial de yerba-mate," 89–92.

97. La Hoja advertisement, Caras y Caretas, Sept. 17, 1932, 21.

98. See, for example, Ñanduty advertisement, *Caras y caretas*, May 1, 1926, 41.

99. "Ñanduty la más cara de las yerbas es la más económica por su larga duración," Ñanduty advertisement, *Caras y caretas*, Oct. 30, 1926, 47.

100. On ideas about racial fitness and the "germ plasma" in Argentina, see Paulina L. Alberto, *Black Legend: The Many Lives of Raúl Grigera and the Power of Racial Storytelling in Argentina* (New York: Cambridge University Press, 2022), esp. chap. 6. On healthy baby contests in Mexico, see Alexandra Minna Stern, "'The Hour of Eugenics' in Veracruz, Mexico: Radical Politics, Public Health, and Latin America's Only Sterilization Law," *Hispanic American Historical Review* 91, no. 3 (2011): 431–43, esp. 436.

101. Ñanduty advertisement, *Caras y caretas*, Oct. 30, 1926, 47.

102. Ñanduty advertisement, *Caras y caretas*, Oct. 12, 1929, 76. In 1932, this figure in braids reappeared in a servant's outfit and pointed upward toward the babies, encouraging women to take part in the baby contest and to allow her to serve them Ñanduty-brand yerba.

103. Ñanduty advertisement, "Hermanos en la Gloria," *La Nación*, 1928. I thank Diego Armus for sharing this clipping with me.

104. On dominant ideas about race in this era, see Alberto and Elena, *Rethinking Race in Modern Argentina*.

105. Ñanduty advertisement, *Aconcagua*, Aug. 1930, clipping courtesy of LCSC.

106. Salus advertisement, *Caras y caretas*, Dec. 8, 1933, 117.

107. Conversation with Pau Navajas, Jan. 26, 2021. Ñanduty yerba is still sold today and has the same tagline but is directed to a Lebanese consumer market, not a South American one.

108. Salus advertisement, *Caras y caretas*, Oct. 28, 1933, 38.

109. Salus advertisement, *Caras y caretas*, Nov. 11, 1933, 108. In 1899, a decade after Brazil transitioned from a monarchy to a republic, a Brazilian company called Guimarães & Co. referred to the product it shipped as *Ilex mate* (*lex Braziliensis*), the holly to make mate, or

specifically, "Brazilian holly." In 1909, Sebastião Lino de Christo presented a thesis to the medical school in Rio de Janeiro in which he asserted that the holly leaves used to make mate should be called *Ilex braziliensis,* or perhaps *Ilex matogrensensis,* or holly from Mato Grosso del Sur, the province from which the author also hailed. He failed to mention that just over three decades prior, his province's yerbales had been Paraguayan. Guimarães & Co., *Breve noticia,* 1; and Sebastião Lino de Christo, "Do mate" (PhD diss., Facultad de Medicina do Rio de Janeiro, 1909), 7, 11.

110. Salus advertisement, *Caras y caretas,* Jan. 27, 1934, 49.

111. Salus advertisement, *Caras y caretas,* Feb. 10, 1934, 40.

112. The company tried out a new tagline, "Better and less expensive than imported yerbas," in *Caras y caretas,* Sept. 29, 1934, 138.

113. "Gratis para los materos deportistas," clipping, ca. 1935, courtesy of LCSC. Otero worked in Mackinnon & Coelho's labs in 1932 and published a study on this topic in 1935.

114. Salus advertimiento, *Caras y caretas,* Mar. 13, 1937, 35.

115. Barthes's company milled its yerba in Rosario and Buenos Aires, as highlighted in Yerba Asunción advertisement, *Aconcagua,* Apr. 1934, 104.

116. Yerba Asunción advertisement, *Aconcagua,* July 1931, 92.

117. Yerba Asunción advertisement, *Aconcagua,* Sept. 1932, 88.

118. By 1941, La Hoja had stopped including the phrase "yerba paraguaya" (Paraguayan herb) on its advertisements and replaced it with "Ojala que sea la Hoja" (I pray it is La Hoja). Aguila did a series of mid-twentieth-century advertisements with the popular political humorist known as Landru, in which there was no longer any reference to Paraguay.

119. Nobleza Gaucha advertisement, ca. 1940s, courtesy of Lafayette College Special Collections and College Archives, Easton, PA.

120. See, for example, a Yerba Salus ad from 1948 featuring a *china* figure handing a mate to a woman on a train. Salus advertisement, 1948, Pinterest, https://in.pinterest.com/pin/358247345352784628/ (accessed Dec. 16, 2020).

121. La Hoja advertisement, drawn by Alejandro Sirio, 1944, found on Mercado Libre website, https://articulo.mercadolibre.com.ar/MLA-668196772-alejandro-sirio-yerba-la-hojapublicidadoriginal_JM#position=12&search_layout=grid&type=item&tracking_id=1ae9927a-43ee-4cec-aebf-8192732d1632 (accessed Dec. 16, 2020).

122. I analyze these trends in Pite, *Creating a Common Table,* esp. chaps. 3 and 4.

123. Nobleza Gaucha advertisement, ca. 1950s, courtesy of Lafayette College Special Collections and College Archives, Easton, PA.

124. Salus advertisement, 1956, Pinterest, https://ar.pinterest.com/pin/358247345353057910/ (accessed Feb. 6. 2023). "SALUS es la preferida por las buenas amas de casa."

125. Nobleza Gaucha advertisement, 1960, Pinterest, https://ar.pinterest.com/pin/384283780688837396/ (accessed Feb. 6. 2023).

126. Salus advertisement, ca. 1962, courtesy of Lafayette College Special Collections and College Archives, Easton, PA.

127. Milanesio, *Workers Go Shopping,* 71.

128. On the Yerba Mate Tea Company, see Caballero Campos, "*¡Beba Té de Yerba Mate y Sea Feliz!*"; and for a primary source related to the International Mate Company, which eventually branded its product as Joyz Mate, see, "Yerba Mate in the United States," *Wileman's Brazilian Review* 20, no. 27 (July 4, 1929): 709–10. For 1930 quote, see Ernesto Daumas, *El problema de la yerba mate* (Buenos Aires: Compañía Impresora Argentina, 1930), 31, as cited in Folch, "Stimulating Consumption," 16.

129. Making the mate brasserie model more accessible and widespread, mom-and-pop shops and a popular chain called Rei do Mate (founded in the 1970s and franchised in the 1990s) began to offer a variety of mate drinks across Brazil in the late twentieth century. Reidomate website, www.reidomate.com.br/sobre (accessed Jan. 1, 2022).

130. In Paraná, for example, coffee became the most important exported product. The state's population doubled between 1940 and 1950 as the coffee industry rapidly expanded—a trend that lasted in Paraná until the 1960s. Meanwhile, production of erva mate in Brazil declined due to the expanding extraction of wood in southern Brazil. Sonia Mar dos Santos Migliorini, "Indústria Paranaense: Formação, transformação econômica a partir da década de 1960 e distribuição espacial da indústria no início do século XXI," *Revista Eletrônica Geografar* 1, no. 1 (2006): 62–80, esp. 65.

131. Other Brazilian leaders also appeared in this publication enjoying "mate gelado" (iced mate). Dr. Hemilode Cunha Cesar, *Lennda da herva mate sapecada* (Rio de Janeiro: Grafica Olimpica, 1943), before preface (Vargas), 46–49 (other politicians).

132. Goodman, "Consuming the *Café Colonial*," esp. 43, 48.

133. "Nova estátua do Getúlio Vargas em São Borja," Reddit, www.reddit.com/r/brasil /comments/phcxut/nova_est%C3%A1tua_do_get%C3%BAlio_vargas_em_s%C3%A3o _borja/ (accessed Jan. 20, 2022).

134. Cover, *Mundo Peronista*, Apr. 15, 1952.

135. Magán, "La Dirección de Yerba Mate," 12.

136. On Peronist food policy, see Eduardo Elena, *Dignifying Argentina: Peronism, Citizenship, and Mass Consumption* (Pittsburgh: University of Pittsburgh Press, 2011); Natalia Milanesio, "Food Politics and Consumption in Peronist Argentina," *Hispanic American Historical Review* 90, no. 1 (2010): 75–108; and Pite, *Creating a Common Table*, chap. 4. On regulations, see Lagier, *Adventures of the Yerba Mate*, 150.

137. In Paraguay, Adolfo María Friedrich published a series of photographs that also circulated as postcards around 1940, highlighting the heavy labor undertaken by *mensúes*, including the ways in which they carried huge bales of yerba on their backs. Several of these *foto-postales* are reproduced in Javier Yubi, *Bicententario del Paraguay: Álbum fotográfico siglos XIX y XX* (Asunción, Para.: Servilibro, 2011), 164–69.

138. Comisión Reguladora de la Producción y Comercio de la Yerba Mate, Comité de propaganda del consumo de la yerba mate, *La yerba mate* (Ministerio del Interior: Talleres gráficos de la Dirección Nacional del Registro Oficial, 1971), 38.

139. Paes, "Instituto Nacional do Mate, 7.

140. On the formation of the gaucho identity in Brazil, see Ruben Oliven, *Tradition Matters: Modern Gaúcho Identity in Brazil* (New York: Columbia University Press, 1996). On race and region in Brazil more broadly, see Weinstein, *Color of Modernity*.

CHAPTER SIX

1. "EL MATE: UNA BEBIDA PARA LOS JOVENES JOVENES," *Gente*, Oct. 16, 1969, 80–81. The small text in the upper left corner specifies that it is an "anuncio" (advertisement). I thank Valeria Mazano for sharing this clipping with me.

2. "EL MATE," 81

3. "EL MATE," 81.

4. "EL MATE," 80–82.

5. Graph 6.1 draws from data published (in chronological order) in Dr. Victor Garin, *Contribución al estudio del cultivo e industria de la yerba mate* (Buenos Aires: Talleres Gráficos del Ministerio Agricultura de la Nación, 1916); Carlos D. Girola, *La yerba mate en la República Argentina (Ilex paraguariensis)* (Buenos Aires: La Facultad de Agronomia y Veterinaria, 1929); Ernesto Daumas, *El problema de la yerba mate* (Buenos Aires: Asociación Argentina de Plantadores de Yerba Mate, 1930); Cámara de Comercio Argentina-Brasileña, *La yerba mate: El problema económico y fiscal* (Buenos Aires: Futura, 1933); CRYM, *1938 Memoria: Mar. 10, 1936–Dec. 31, 1937* (Buenos Aires: Ministerio de Agricultura, Argentina, 1938); CRYM, *Boletín Informativo, Memoria Correspondiente a 1937* (Buenos Aires: Ministerio de Agricultura, 1938); Abel Sanchez Diaz, *Consideraciones bromotológicas e industriales sobre la yerba mate* (Buenos Aires: Anales de la Academica Nacional de Ciencias Exactas, 1939); CRYM, *Memoria: Correspondiente al Ejercicio de 1939* (Buenos Aires: Ministerio de Agricultura de la Nación, 1940); CRYM, *Memoria: Correspondiente al Ejercicio de 1940* (Buenos Aires: Ministerio de Agricultura de la Nación, 1941); CRYM, *Memoria: Correspondiente al Ejercicio de 1941* (Buenos Aires: Ministerio de Agricultura de la Nación, 1942); Martín y Cía, *Que es la yerba mate* (Buenos Aires: E. Fenner, 1942); Carlos Reussi, "Los alimentos de origen vegetal: La yerba mate," *El día medico*, Sept. 27, 1942; CRYM, *Memoria: Correspondiente al Ejercicio de 1942* (Buenos Aires: Ministerio de Agricultura de la Nación, 1943); Juan J. Billard, "Economía de la industria yerbatera argentina," *Instituto de Economía y Legislación Rural* 5, no. 3 (Buenos Aires: Imprenta de la Universidad de Buenos Aires, 1944); Comité de propaganda del consumo de la yerba mate, *La yerba mate* (Ministerio del Interior: Talleres gráficos de la Dirección Nacional del Registro Oficial, 1971); Aida M. Frankel, *La yerba mate: Producción, industrialización, comercio* (Buenos Aires: Editorial Albatros, 1983); Carlos A. Bas, "La actividad yerbatera en la Provincia de Misiones," preliminary report (Buenos Aires: Consejo Federal de Inversiones Dirección de Estudios Básicos y Desarrollo Económico, Aug. 1990); María Victoria Magán, "Once años sin regulación: La evolución del sector yerbatero argentino desde 1991 a 2002," *IV Jornadas de Estudios Agrarios y Agroindustriales* (Fourth Workshop of Agricultural and Agro-Industrial Studies), Facultad de Ciencias Económica de la Universidad de Buenos Aires (University of Buenos Aires, Economic Sciences Division), Nov. 2005; Instituto Nacional de la Yerba Mate, "Informe del Sector Yerbatero," online reports from 2011 to 2020; Jerónimo Lagier, *The Adventures of the Yerba Mate: Over Four Centuries of History* (Posadas, Arg.: Tambú, 2014); and Adam S. Dohrenwend, *Green Gold: Contested Meanings and Socio-environmental Change in Argentina Yerba Mate Cultivation* (Cham, Switz.: Springer, 2021).

6. Specifically, 65 percent of nationally produced yerba, according to "Una estadística deprimente: El mate, en retirada," *El Clarín*, ca. 1983, 25, clipping courtesy of Juan Carlos Romero Archive, Buenos Aires, Argentina (hereafter JCR).

7. Fernando O. Assunçao, *El mate* (Montevideo, Uru.: ACRA, 1967), 12.

8. This was an association that at least one yerba brand tried to promote. During Perón's presidency, Santa Teresita launched a brand that it advertised with the motto "La yerba de los descamisados" (The yerba of the shirtless ones, as Perón's followers were known). Natalia Milanesio, *Workers Go Shopping in Argentina: The Rise of Popular Consumer Culture* (Albuquerque: University of New Mexico, 2013), 89.

9. On mid-twentieth-century Uruguay, see, for example, Ximena Espeche, *La paradoja uruguaya: Intelectuales, latinoamericanismo y nación a mediados del siglo XX* (Bernal: Universidad Nacional de Quilmes, 2016); and Silvia Duténit Bielous and Gonzalo Varela Petito,

"El sistema politico entre dos épocas: Represión estatal y democracia tradicional," *European Review of Latin American and Caribbean Studies*, no. 60 (June 1996): 71–85.

10. While I include it here, Paraguay, which endured three decades of dictatorship under General Alfredo Stoessner (1954–89), is often studied separately from the other nations. J. Patrice McSherry, *Predatory States: Operation Condor and Covert War in Latin America* (Lanham, MD: Rowman and Littlefield, 2005).

11. Most Argentines and Uruguayans lived in cities in this period. According to the World Bank, in 1960, some 73 percent of Argentines lived in locations that were home to at least 2,000 people or more, while by the year 2000, 89 percent did. The figures were similar in Uruguay, where 80 percent of the population already resided in urban areas of this size in 1960, a figure that grew to 92 percent by 2000. On the historic connections between Argentina and Uruguay's capital cities, see, for example, William Acree, *Staging Frontiers: The Making of Modern Popular Culture in Argentina and Uruguay* (Albuquerque: University of New Mexico Press, 2019); Christine Ehrick, *Radio and the Gendered Soundscape: Women and Broadcasting in Argentina and Uruguay, 1930–1950* (Cambridge: Cambridge University Press, 2015); and Mirta Zaida Lobato, *La prensa obrera: Buenos Aires y Montevideo, 1890–1958* (Buenos Aires: Edhasa, 2009). For the statistics, see the World Bank website https://data.worldbank.org /indicator (accessed Nov. 18, 2021).

12. Victor Oppenheim, *Explorations East of the High Andes* (New York: Pageant Press, 1958), 41–42.

13. Gordon Meyer, *The River and Its People* (London: Cox and Wyman, 1965), 153, 212.

14. On tereré, see chapter 3 and Derlis Benítez, *El tereré: Algo más que una bebida en Paraguay* (Asunción, Para.: El Lector, 1997). Bridget Chesterton's forthcoming research in *Hotel Guaraní* discusses (among many other things) how the opening of the Acaray Dam in 1968 changed Paraguayans' access to new technologies to make and conserve ice.

15. Friedrich, who also took prior photos of *mensúes*, hailed from Austria but spent considerable time living and taking photographs in Paraguay. Adolfo María Friedrich and Cirilo Zayas, "Horas de Descanso con guitarra and tereré," *Paraguay: Una obra con fotografías en colores* (Asunción, Para.: Dirección General de Turismo, 1968).

16. Meyer, *River and Its People*, 105.

17. Amaro Villanueva, *El mate: Alonso, Basladua, Battle Planas, Berni, Butler, Castagnino, Grela, González, Policastro, Schurjin* (Buenos Aires: Editorial El Mate, 1964).

18. Letter from Petrona C. de Gandulfo to Elena T., Buenos Aires, Dec. 26, 1962, courtesy of Elena T.

19. Cintia Russo and Daniel Diaz, "La situación alimentaria en Argentina: Una aproximación desde la perspectiva del consumo," unpublished report, Oct. 1989, 51, courtesy of Instituto Nacional de Estadística y Censos, Argentina.

20. Rodolfo Walsh, "La Argentina ya no toma mate," *Revista Panorama*, no. 43 (Buenos Aires, 1966), as reproduced in Javier Gortari, comp., *De la tierra sin mal al tractorazo: Hacia una economía política de la yerba mate* (Posadas, Arg.: Editorial Universitaria de Misiones, 2007), 155–61.

21. Enrique de Arrechea, "Consideraciones sobre la demanda de yerba mate en la República Argentina: Período 1951–1970," as reproduced in Gortari, *De la tierra sin mal al tractorazo*, 163.

22. Villanueva was the first to write a book about the technique and art of serving mate before he compiled this mate art book, published as *El mate: Alonso*. For his previous publications, see Amaro Villanueva, *Mate: Exposción de la ténica de cebar* (Buenos Aires: Ediciones

Argentina, 1938), reissued as *El mate: Arte de cebar* (Buenos Aires: Compañía General Fabril Editora, 1960).

23. In keeping with the process of urbanization described in this chapter, these artists all appear to have died in the city of Buenos Aires. Villanueva, *El mate: Alonso*, 7.

24. On Berni and Nuevo Realismo, see Roberto Amigo, "Antonio Berni: Denuncia y sentimiento," *Malba diario*, Aug. 7, 2020, www.malba.org.ar/tag/antonio-berni/?v=diario.

25. For an excellent documentary that traces Schurjin's grandson's journey to understand his grandfather's place in the Argentine art world, see Martín Vaisman, dir., *Schurjin, el pintor*, Buenos Aires: #mdoc, 2019, 72 min.

26. Schurjin also offers a line drawing of two young people sharing a mate, the girl eagerly awaiting her turn. This translation is a mash-up of the one offered by Villanueva and my own.

27. Meyer, *River and Its People*, 153.

28. "El mate en la pintura," *La Nación*, Feb. 9, 1964, courtesy of JCR.

29. Ricardo Warnes, based on research by Alberto Agostinelli and Pablo Anania, "La comida y los argentinos," *Revista 7 Días* or *La Razón* (writing unclear), Oct. 13, 1965, unpaginated.

30. Interview with Stella M. D., Puerto Ingeniero White, May 19, 2004.

31. John Ferguson, *The River Plate Republics* (New York: Time, 1965), 72–73. In this same book, a poor rural Paraguayan family is shown with a mate while laborers are shown porting heavy sacks of yerba on their backs.

32. I have consulted four extensive folders at *El Clarín* with regard to yerba mate, which includes but extends beyond *El Clarín*'s coverage. I have also reviewed and cataloged the extensive collection of clippings about yerba mate, most of which date to this era, in JCR.

33. Valeria Manzano, *The Age of Youth in Argentina: Culture, Politics, and Sexuality from Perón to Videla* (Chapel Hill: University of North Carolina Press, 2014).

34. Guillermo O'Donnell, *Bureaucratic Authoritarianism: Argentina 1966–1973 in Comparative Perspective* (Berkeley: University of California Press, 1988).

35. Manzano, *Age of Youth*.

36. Television advertisement, "Que swing me da el mate," on YouTube, www.youtube.com/watch?v=2s41S8koDcQ (accessed Oct. 19, 2021). The first (blond) man who appears seems to have an American accent, perhaps suggesting a desire to portray mate as cosmopolitan. Matchbook, "Que Swing me Da el Mate!," courtesy of JCR.

37. Raúl A. Díaz Castelli, photographs by Norberto Mosteirín, "Los argentinos y el mate," *Revista la Nación* (Buenos Aires), Apr. 2, 1972, 4.

38. Provincia de Misiones Gobernación, "Fundamentos para el programa de promoción de consumo de yerba mate," 1992, courtesy of *El Clarín*'s newspaper archive, Buenos Aires.

39. Marta Beines, "Tertulias de antaño: El mate," *La Nación*, May 25, 1975, no page, clipping courtesy of JCR.

40. Russo and Diaz, "La situación alimentaria en Argentina," 65, 131–32.

41. María Jose B., interview by author, Buenos Aires, July 12, 2017; and Pelusa Molina, interview by author, Buenos Aires, July 26, 2017.

42. Assunçao, *El mate*, 7. At the end of the quote, the author refers to the "bolilla" or lottery machine used to select the question chosen for the exam. As in this case, many people in Uruguay and Argentina drank mate while studying.

43. Assunçao, 12. Neither he nor other contemporary writers I have read pointed to an elite or middle class that wished to distance itself from mate (like contemporaries did vis-à-vis Buenos Aires) even if, surely, small numbers of such people existed, especially in the capital.

44. Assunçao, 9.

45. Assunçao, 10.

46. Assunçao, 11.

47. Javier Ricca, conversation in Montevideo, Uru., Nov. 30, 2015.

48. Pierre Fossey, *Montevideo: 150 apuntes del natural* (Montevideo, Uru.: Ediciones Rex, 1962), 80–81.

49. "Una foto y una mateada que generó crisis política," *El País*, Jan. 25, 2015, www.elpais.com.uy/informacion/foto-mateada-genero-crisis-politica.html#.

50. Aurelio González, *Fui testigo: Una historia en imágenes* (Montevideo, Uru.: Ediciones CMDF, 2011), 186–88.

51. J. Patrice McSherry, "Death Squads as Parallel Forces: Uruguay, Operation Condor, and the United States," *Journal of Third World Studies* 24, no. 1 (2007): 20, 29.

52. The human rights "Sitios de Memoria Uruguay" project states that members of the Tupamaros were responsible for the editions prior to the dictatorship, as well as those they publicly claimed after it: https://sitiosdememoria.uy/prensa/mate-amargo (accessed Oct. 28, 2021). Aldo Marchesi also links this magazine with this group. Aldo Marchesi, *Latin America's Radical Left*, trans. Laura Pérez Carrara (New York: Cambridge University Press, 2018), 212. See also Mate Amargo, on which a digitized version of this magazine is now published: www.mateamargo.org.uy/ (accessed Dec. 15, 2021).

53. *Mate Amargo*, Mar. 13, 1973, opening note.

54. *Mate Amargo*, May 6, 1973, cover and 12–13.

55. McSherry, "Death Squads," 20.

56. Carlos Demasi et al., *La caida de la democracia: Cronología comparada de la historia reciente del Uruguay, 1976–1973* (Montevideo, Uru.: Fundación de Cultural Universitaria, 1996).

57. Aurelio González's story is remarkable. Born to Spanish parents in 1932, he fled to Uruguay as a stowaway in 1952. In Montevideo, he eventually became a documentary photographer interested in chronicling resistance movements and military repression, publishing many of his photographs in the communist-affiliated publication *El Popular*. After the 1973 coup, he proposed to his colleagues that they head to the factories to document the workers' resistance. After being interrogated by the military, he hid the publication's 57,000 negatives before fleeing into exile, only to find them missing when he returned in 1986. In 2006, they were found, and in 2011, he published some of his photographs in his book *Fui testigo*. For more on González, see his book and Samuel Blixen, "Aurelio González, testigo y fotógrafo de la historia reciente," donde-estan.com, Nov. 19, 2021, https://donde-estan.com/2021/11/19/aurelio-gonzalez-testigo-y-fotografo-de-la-historia-reciente/.

58. González, *Fui testigo*, 74.

59. Eduardo Galeano, "The Dictatorship and Its Aftermath: The Secret Wounds," *Contemporary Marxism* 14 (Fall 1986): 16, trans. Mark Fried.

60. Sharnak emphasizes the targeting of Blacks, Jews, and members of the gay community under the dictatorship as well. Debbie Sharnak, chap. 2, "Uruguay and the Rise of the Transnational Human Rights Movement," in her forthcoming book, *Of Light and Struggle: International Human Rights and Justice in Uruguay* (Philadelphia: University of Pennsylvania Press, forthcoming, 2023).

61. Sharnak, ms. p. 75.

62. Sharnak, ms. p. 76.

63. Magdalena Schelotto, "La dictadura cívico-militar uruguaya (1973–1985): La construcción de la noción de víctima y la figura del exiliado en el Uruguay post-dictatorial," *Nuevo Mundo Mundos Nuevos*, 2015, note 6.

64. Galeano, "Dictatorship and Its Aftermath," 16.

65. Daniel Vidart, "Mate e identidad nacional," *Bitacora* (blog), www.bitacora.com.uy /auc.aspx?5031,7 (accessed Feb. 8, 2023).

66. Conversation with María N., Buenos Aires, June 14, 2016.

67. Conversation with Alicia F. and Victoria, Biblioteca Nacional de Uruguay, Mar. 9, 2016.

68. My approach to oral history and memory-making is inspired by Alessandro Portelli, *The Death of Luigi Trastulli and Other Stories* (Albany: State University of New York Press, 1991).

69. In testimonies gathered from members of the Asociación Trabajadores del Estado, many mention mates shared with other militants; see Marcel Paredes, *Un cauce: Orígenes de Anusate* (Buenos Aires: CTA Ediciones, 2014), esp. 66, 87, 107–8, 256. A review of the leftist press of the early 1970s, including *El Descamisado*, occasionally showed members of the Peronist Youth Party drinking mate together. See, for example, "Si los diputados aprueban las leyes represivas votaran: Lena para el pueblo," *El Descamisado*, Jan. 1974. And in 1973, Argentines who went to Ezeiza airport to await General Juan Perón's return, some of whom were members of the People's Revolutionary Army, brought mates and thermoses as well as sandwiches, empanadas, and soccer balls with them. Matilde Herrera, *José* (Buenos Aires: Editorial Contrapunto, 1987), 173–76.

70. The Montoneros publication *Evita Montonera* only included one photograph of a man, referred to as "Ongaro hijo," drinking mate, who it alleged was assassinated by the Argentine Anticommunist Alliance. "Crónica de resistencia," *Evita Montonera*, June 1975. The magazine's comic strip *Camote* showed the protagonists drinking *mate amargo*, as the family housing Camote could not afford sugar, Aug. 1975. From 1972 through 1974, cartoonists who worked for *Satiricón* offered many more images of politicians, gauchos, married couples, and even children drinking mate. They pictured mate as a masculine symbol of national identity served by women whenever they were present. For example, in a July 1973 comic about parents teaching their children to be masculine nationalists, a mother offers her child a mate, while the father tells her the bombilla should be very hot to toughen up the boy. In the lead-up to the dictatorship in February 1976, before the magazine was shut down by the military dictatorship, just one composition showed a family at a pool with a mate and thermos in tow. In contrast, prior compositions featured a kettle and, often, more domestic scenes.

71. Mengarelli also belonged to Argentina's umbrella workers' union, referred to as the CGT, and mentioned the military visit to CGT headquarters later that day. Paredes, *Un cauce*, esp. 54.

72. Teo Ballvé, "Mate on the Market: Fair Trade and the Gaucho's 'Liquid Vegetable,'" *NACLA Report on the Americas*, Sept.–Oct. 2007, 10–13.

73. Ballvé, 10; Eduardo Enrique Torres, *Cosechas de injusticias: Historias de vida, lucha, horror y muerte* (Posadas, Arg.: Piramide Centro Graf, 2006); Mario Pernigotti, "Desaparecidos, siempre en el corazón: La historia de Pedro Peczak," Periodismo Misionero, Mar. 23, 2022, www.periodismomisionero.com.ar/2022/03/23/desaparecidos-siempre-en-el-corazon -la-historia-de-pedro-peczak/.

74. About 80 percent of the "disappeared" were between the ages of sixteen and thirty-five. Roughly 70 percent were male and 30 percent female. Comisión Nacional sobre Desaparición de Personas, *Nunca más* (Buenos Aires: EDUEBA, 1984), esp. 294.

75. Marguerite Feitlowitz, *A Lexicon of Terror: Argentina and the Legacies of Torture* (New York: Oxford University Press, 1998; updated 2011).

76. Gabriela Nouzeilles and Graciela Montaldo, "Revolutionary Dreams," *The Argentina Reader: History, Culture, Politics* (Durham: Duke University Press, 2002), 341–44.

77. Amnesty International, *Extracts from the Report of an Amnesty International Mission to Argentina 6–15 November 1976* (London: Amnesty International Publications, 1977), 15, available at amnesty.org, amnesty.org/en/documents/amr13/083/1977/en/.

78. This term was coined in Juan E. Corradi, *The Fitful Republic* (Boulder, CO: Westview Press, 1985).

79. Victoria Basualdo references this episode in her doctoral thesis and explains the repressive role of corporations under and after the dictatorship in subsequent publications. Victoria Basualdo, "Labor and Structural Change: Shop-Floor Organization and Militancy in Argentine Industrial Factories (1943–1983)" (PhD thesis, Columbia University, 2010), 396. She draws this example from Marcela Jabbaz, *Modernización social o flexibilidad salarial: Impacto selectivo de un cambio organizacional en una empresa siderúrgica Argentina* (Buenos Aires: CEAL, 1996), 106. I thank Gabriela Mitideri for introducing me to this reference.

80. Luis Alberto Romero, *A History of Argentina in the Twentieth Century* (Philadelphia: Penn State University Press, 2002), 219–20.

81. I write more about this in Pite, *Creating a Common Table*, chap. 6, and "¿Solo se trata de cocinar? Repensando las tareas domésticas de las mujeres argentinas con Doña Petrona," in *De minifaldas, militancias y revoluciones: Exploraciones sobre los 70 en la Argentina*, ed. Andrea Andújar et al. (Buenos Aires: Luxemburg, 2009), 187–205.

82. Romero, *History of Argentina*, 232.

83. The yerba companies included Mate Larangeira Mendes, Las Marías, Flor de Lis, J. A. Blanco y Cía, Martín y Cía, and Molinos Río de la Plata.

84. Asociación Promotora de Yerba Mate, *La yerba mate le cuenta su historia*, ca. late 1970s, courtesy of JCR.

85. On the history of Argentine television, see Mirta Varela, *La television criolla: Desde sus inicios hasta la llegada del hombre a la Luna, 1951–1969* (Buenos Aires: Edhasa, 2005).

86. I am grateful to María Navajas and her colleagues at Las Marías for allowing me to watch a loop of their advertising from 1971 to 1999, some of which is also accessible via YouTube.

87. Conversation with Valeria P. via Zoom, Sept. 30, 2021.

88. Luis Landriscina, "El mate es símbolo de amistad," *El Clarín*, July 22, 1982, special supplement, 4; "Landriscina dice cómo se ceba un buen mate," *El Clarín*, Ollas y Sartenes (Pots and pans section), p. 8, no date, both clippings courtesy of JCR.

89. M. E. V., "Instántaneas," *La Nación*, ca. 1981, courtesy of JCR.

90. M. E. V., "Instántaneas."

91. Interview with Verónica A., Buenos Aires, July 13, 2017.

92. "El mate, tradición y artesanía," *Revista la Nación*, June 18, 1978, 28–29, courtesy of JCR.

93. Agustín Zapata Gollán, "Del bernegal y el apartador al mate y la bombilla," *La Nación*, May 14, 1978, clipping courtesy of JCR.

94. "Del mate como pasión que se niega a morir: Original muestra en el salón YPF," 1981, clipping from JCR.

95. Matías Emiliano Casas, "El criollismo en la gestación del museo de motivos populares José Hernández (1939–1949)," *Cuadernos de la Facultad de Humanidades y Ciencias Sociales* (Universidad Nacional de Jujuy), no. 53 (2018): 39–52.

96. Taquini had recently returned from an internship in the United States at the Smithsonian Museum and said she was partly inspired by "Please Touch" museums in the United States. Graciela Taquini, "Mateando en el fogón," exhibit report for the Museo de Motivos Argentinos José Hernández, p. 2, courtesy of JCR.

97. Taquini, 3–4.

98. Pamphlet, Yacimiento Petroliferos Fiscales, Museo de Motivos Argentinos "José Hernandez," Mar.–Apr. 1984, Municipalidad de la Ciudad de Buenos Aires, Secretaria de Cultura, courtesy of JCR.

99. Dissent among different factions of the leadership was exposed through leaks about the controversy surrounding General Roberto Viola's replacement of his boss Gen. Jorge Rafael Videla in March 1981, followed by Gen. Leopoldo Galtieri's replacement of Viola later that year.

100. This mate is held at Francisco Scutella Mate Museum in Paraná and reproduced in his book. Francisco N. Scutella, *El mate: Bebida nacional Argentina* (1989; repr., Buenos Aires: Editorial Lancelot, 2006), 173. For quote, Lagier, *Adventures of the Yerba Mate*, 169.

101. Mirta Inés Trupp, *With Love, the Argentina Family: Memories of Tango and Kugel, Mate with Knishes* (Middletown, DE: self-published, 2012).

102. In the 1980 promotion for the referendum, politicians were shown with coffee, not mate, as Debbie Sharnak shared with me.

103. On daily struggles for food and rights in the 1980s, see Jennifer Adair, *In Search of the Lost Decade: Everyday Rights in Post-Dictatorship Argentina* (Berkeley: University of California Press, 2019).

104. Russo and Diaz, "La situación alimentaria en Argentina," 132.

105. See, for example, photographs from Rodolfo Muniz, *Uruguay en imágenes* (Montevideo, Uru.: Barreiro y Ramos Editores, 1988), 46 and 51.

106. Espínola joined the Communist Party in 1971 and died the night of the military coup. Photograph, *Francisco (Paco) Espínola. Escritor*, without date or author, courtesy of Archivo Chelle/Semanario Brecha, Centro de Fotografía de Montevideo, https://cdf.montevideo .gub.uy/foto/17-1 (accessed Nov. 16, 2021).

107. Fernando Aínsa, "Onetti, la muerte tan temida," ca. 1989, article with photographs available at Centro Virtual Cervantes, https://cvc.cervantes.es/literatura/escritores/onetti /acerca/ainsa.htm (accessed Nov. 9. 2021).

108. Marchesi, *Latin America's Radical Left*, 211–12; "El mate es lo contrario al jaque," *El periódico* Nov. 13, 2009, www.elperiodico.com/es/internacional/20091113/mate-contrario -jaque-94418.

109. I thank Gustavo Laborde for sharing this anecdote with me in a conversation on Feb. 29, 2016.

110. Javier Ricca shared this anecdote about Gutiérrez, who adapted an informally "neighborly" style on air, calling everyone "vecino" or "vecina" (neighbor).

111. Conversation with Victoria, Montevideo, Uru., Mar. 2016.

112. Email correspondence with Javier Ricca, Nov. 18, 2021.

113. Opinion, "Uruguay: El 'protocolo' del termo y el mate," Iberoamérica Central de Noticias, Jan. 3, 2016, www.icndiario.com/2016/01/uruguay-el-protocolo-del-termo-y-el -mate/. According to Javier Ricca, who shared this story with me, such critiques are no longer common.

114. Conversation with Leandro Sagastizabal, Buenos Aires, Dec. 2015.

115. Workers at the Maprico juice factory, for example, sometimes pooled their money together to make *mate cocido*, according to a 1974 article in *El descamisado* called "240 traba-jadores de la alimentación tomaron la fábrica de Maprico luchando por sus derechos, desde el primer día del año." Pelusa Molina interview; Fernando C., interview with author, Buenos Aires, July 26, 2017; interview with Verónica A., Buenos Aires, July 13, 2017.

116. I originally spoke with both Victoria Szychowski and Victor Saguier about this story at the Fiesta Nacional e Internacional de la Yerba Mate in Apostoles, Misiones, on Oct. 2, 2015. I confirmed it in an interview with Victor Saguier in Buenos Aires in Dec. 2015.

117. María José B., interview with author, Buenos Aires, July 12, 2017; and Ana C., interview with author, Buenos Aires, July 13, 2017.

118. Flor T., interview with author, Buenos Aires, July 13, 2017.

119. Wayne Bernhardson and María Massolo, *Argentina, Uruguay and Paraguay: A Lonely Planet Travel Survival Kit* (1992; Australia: Lonely Planet Publications, 1996), 90.

120. Bernhardson and Massolo, 90–91.

121. Bernhardson and Massolo, important ritual, 46; *mate con facturas*, 89; per capita consumption, 90–91; Uruguayans' thermos, 615; tereré in Paraguay, 687.

122. Conversation with owners of Kelly's Todo Mates, Buenos Aires, Oct. 28, 2015.

123. Adair, *In Search of the Lost Decade*, introduction.

124. Javier Gortari, "El instituto nacional de la yerba mate (INYM) como dispositivo político de economía social," *De la tierra sin mal al tractorazo*, 401–24.

125. As Janet Lawson details, in the post–World War II era, more land in Misiones was converted to commercial yerba plantations. In keeping with the paradigm of the green revolution, farmers were encouraged to plant more crops closer together and in a neater manner, leading to their reliance on pesticides and herbicides, especially since the 1980s, which cut labor costs. More yerba plantations relied on tractors, compromising the quality of the soil and the roots of the yerba plants. She concludes, "Without mulch, shade, and the incorporation of organic matter into the system, yerba mate agriculture suffered from soil erosion, nutrient loss, and decreasing yields." For Enríquez quote and more, see Ballvé, "Mate on the Market," 10–11; and Janet Lawson, "Cultivating Green Gold: A Political Ecology of Land Use Changes for Small Yerba Mate Farmers in Misiones, Argentina" (master's thesis, Yale University, 2009), esp. 28–29.

126. Javier Gortari, "Introducción" and "La lección de la economía: Economía política del tractorazo" (the latter originally in *El territorio*, June 14, 2001), as reprinted in *De la tierra sin mal al tractorazo*, esp. 20–21 and 247.

127. Ballvé, "Mate on the Market," 11.

128. On the conditions of the *tareferos*, see Víctor Rau, *Cosechando yerba mate: Estructuras sociales de un mercado laboral agrario en el nordeste argentino* (Buenos Aires: Ciccus, 2012); and Daniel Re, *Tareferos: Vida y trabajo en los yerbales* (Posadas, Arg.: Editorial Universitaria, Universidad Nacional de Misiones, 2017).

129. Miguel Frías, "Yerba buena," *Viva*, July 28, 1996, 56–64.

130. Provincia de Misiones Gobernación, "Fundamentos para el programa."

131. Provincia de Misiones Gobernación, "Fundamentos para el programa."

132. David William Foster, Melissa Fitch Lockhart, Darrell B. Lockhart, *Culture and Customs of Argentina* (Westport, CT: Greenwood Press, 1998), 41–42.

133. Sergio E. Visacovsky, "The Days Argentina Stood Still: History, Nation and Imaginable Futures in the Public Interpretations of the Argentine Crisis at the Beginning of the Twenty-First Century," *Espaço aberto*, no. 54 (2018): 311–41.

134. Victor Saguier interview.

135. "Los argentinos lo prefieren por sobre infusiones como té y café," *El Clarín*, Feb. 7, 2006, 18, clipping courtesy of *El Clarín*'s newspaper archive.

136. AC Nielsen, "Más gente elige la yerba mate," *La Nación,* courtesy of *El Clarín*'s newspaper archive (admitted to archive Oct. 3, 2004).

137. "Los argentinos lo prefieren."

138. Natasha Niebieskikwiat, "Con gaseosas y bares temáticos, la yerba busca salir de su crisis," *El Clarín*, Aug. 13, 2003, courtesy of *El Clarín*'s newspaper archive.

139. Conversation with Juan Suriano, Universidad Nacional de San Martin, Sept. 3, 2015. I was also told this story by people I met in Rosario and Mar del Plata.

140. "El mate es lo contrario al jaque."

141. For example, as early as 1996, journalist Miguel Frías explained that in Posadas, the capital of Misiones, "people of all social classes drink mate in the street, at businesses, at schools, on buses. With their enormous thermoses of warm water set up at any business." Frías, "Yerba buena."

142. On Brazil, see Ruben Oliven, *Tradition Matters: Modern Gaúcho Identity in Brazil* (New York: Columbia University Press, 1996); and Glen Goodman, "Consuming the *Café Colonial*: German Ethnicity and Tourist Migrant Marketplaces in Southern Brazil," *Global Food History* 4, no. 1 (2018): 40–58; and on Paraguay, Benítez, *El tereré*.

EPILOGUE

1. Gabriela Vaz, "Mate, tereré y Covid-19: Cuando compartir es peligroso," Montevideo AFP, Mar. 17, 2020, available at *La Nación* (Paraguay) website, www.lanacion.com.py /tendencias/2020/03/17/mate-terere-y-covid-19-cuando-compartir-es-peligroso/.

2. Julio Mazzoleni and Eduardo Savio as quoted in Vaz, "Mate"; on Uruguay, Lola Mendez, "How Coronavirus Is Changing Mateando Culture in the Southern Cone," Culture Trip, https://theculturetrip.com/south-america/uruguay/articles/how-coronavirus-is-changing -mateando-culture-in-the-southern-cone/ (accessed Jan. 13, 2022); and, on Argentina, Victoria Arrabal, "Una sola ronda con varios mates: Investigadores de la Universidades de Rosario y Entre Ríos estudian cómo cambió el uso y la circulación de la infusión a raíz de la pandemia que obligó adaptar una costumbre arraigada," Universidad Nacional de Rosario website, Oct. 17, 2021, https://unr.edu.ar/una-sola-ronda-con-varios-mates/.

3. "Día Nacional de Mate 2021," Veronese producciones, Nov. 30, 2021, https:// veroneseproducciones.com/dia-nacional-del-mate-2021/.

4. Almudena Calatrava, "Efecto coronavirus: Sudamericanos ya no comparten el mate," *Chicago Tribune* (Associated Press Spanish), Mar. 20, 2020, www.chicagotribune.com/espanol /sns-es-coronavirus-ya-no-se-comparte-el-mate-20200320-zlbrln3ievgb3dolplnbxjjhr4-story .html.

5. Calatrava, "Efecto coronavirus."

6. Specifically, 66 percent reported their awareness of new health recommendations, and 71 percent continued to share mate with a family member or roommate. Arrabal, "Una sola ronda."

7. Guayakí began marketing its product in the United States in 1998. By 2005, some journalists were claiming that yerba mate had moved from fad to mainstream drink. See, for example, Claudia Feldman, "Yerba Mate Moves into American Mainstream," *Houston Chronicle*, Sept. 18, 2005, www.chron.com/life/article/Yerba-Mate-moves-into-American-mainstream-1919456.php.

8. See, for example, "10 Celebs That Drink Yerba Mate," Native Leaf, www.nativeleaf.co.uk/10-celebrity-yerba-mate-drinkers/ (accessed Jan. 26, 2022). This website, like many others, is a promotional effort for yerba.

9. For article and quote about soccer players as ambassadors, see James Wagner, "What's Powering Argentina at the World Cup?: 1,100 Pounds of Yerba Mate," *New York Times*, Dec. 13, 2022, https://www.nytimes.com/2022/12/13/sports/soccer/argentina-yerba-mate.html. The photograph of Lionel Messi cradling the World Cup trophy in one hand and a mate in the other hand appeared on his personal Instagram account on December 20, 2022. For the photograph and a sense of how it went viral on social media, see "La nueva bombilla para el mate de Messi que es furor," TyC Sports, Jan. 10, 2023, www.tycsports.com/seleccion-argentina/la-nueva-bombilla-para-el-mate-de-messi-que-es-furor-tres-estrellas-y-la-copa-del-mundo-id486129.html.

10. The production of organic yerba was originally generated for the export market, especially to meet EU standards. Firms with certified organic yerba brands peaked at thirty-nine in 2007 but dropped to nineteen by 2016. On this history, see Pablo Forni and Camila Lorenzo, "Entre sellos y porotos sable: La conformación y los límites de la red sociotécnica de producción de yerba mate con certificación orgánica en la Argentina," *Redes* (Bernal) 24, no. 46 (June 2018): 55–86.

11. As we learned in chapter 5, yerba producers were keen on modernizing yerba production; for example, by industrializing the packaging process. Jessica Loyer, "Superfoods," *Encyclopedia of Food and Agriculture Ethics*, 2nd ed., ed. David M. Kaplan (Dordrecht, Netherlands: Springer, 2019), 2269–75; quote on 2270.

12. Ross W. Jamieson, "The Essence of Commodification: Caffeine Dependencies in the Early Modern World," *Journal of Social History* 35, no. 2 (2001): 269–94, esp. 280, 287; Marcy Norton, *Sacred Gifts, Profane Pleasures: A History of Tobacco and Chocolate in the Atlantic World* (Ithaca, NY: Cornell University Press, 2008).

13. See, for example, Carly Graf, "Is Yerba Mate the New 'It' Superfood?," *Shape*, Apr. 27, 2015, www.shape.com/healthy-eating/healthy-drinks/yerba-mate-new-it-superfood.

14. Betty Gold, "This Superfood Tea Is an Anti-inflammatory Hero," *Real Simple*, July 30, 2019, www.realsimple.com/food-recipes/recipe-collections-favorites/popular-ingredients/yerba-mate (updated July 20, 2022; orginal article no longer available).

15. For research and reproductions of the 1920s JOYZ campaign, see historian Pablo Pryluka's informative Twitter post on July 16, 2019, in which he shares early advertisements and the story of how a German company bought the rights to the logo and initiated a successful bottled drink called "Club Mate" popular not only in Germany and neighboring France but also in Chile: https://twitter.com/ppryluka/status/1151136600086073345?s=20. On initiatives to sell yerba as an aphrodisiac, see Virogain Products, Inc., "Yerba de los Gauchos," 1969 ad clipping courtesy of Juan Carlos Romero Archive, Buenos Aires. For refutations of these claims, see "Tea for Woo: Trouble Brewing," *Daily News*, Feb. 7, 1973, 277; and "Tea for Two or More? 'Sex Brew' Stirs Tempest over Its Potency," *Philadelphia Inquirer*, Feb. 8, 1973, 51.

16. "Yerba Mate Market Size," Market Watch, Nov. 25, 2021, for example, predicts that yerba mate market revenue will continue to grow. See www.marketwatch.com/press-release /yerba-mate-market-size—growth-statistics-2022-latest-industry-scope-global-business -share-regional-segmentation-revenue-expectations-and-covid-19-impact-on-industry-till -2025-2021-11-25 (accessed Dec. 15, 2021).

17. Sulaiman et al. found that yerba mate's popularity in Syria and its diaspora stemmed from "social and cultural reasons" (for 49 percent of respondents) and "perceived pleasure" for the next largest group (25 percent), as it helps them spend time with others "in a joyful manner and with happiness." Naji Sulaiman, Andrea Pieroni, Renata Sõukand, Cory Whitney, and Abynek Polesny, "Socio-Cultural Significance of Yerba Maté among Syrian Residents and Diaspora," *Economic Botany* 75, no. 2 (2021): 97–111, esp. 101. Christine Folch, "Stimulating Consumption: Yerba Mate Myths, Markets, and Meanings from Conquest to Present," *Comparative Studies in Society and History* 52, no. 1 (2010): 6–36.

18. Gift-givers brought so many bombillas because many Syrians prefer to participate in this communal ceremony by sharing the hot water but drinking from individual glass cups. Annabella Quiroga, "Para la yerba mate, la meca queda en Siria," *El Clarín*, Mar. 29, 1999, Economy sec., 26.

19. On trade statistics, see Analía Llorete, "Yerba mate: Cómo Siria se convirtió en el mayor comprador de este producto en el mundo," BBC News, Feb. 20, 2020, www.bbc.com /mundo/noticias-51392066; on the Central Bank's policy, see Sulaiman, Pieroni, Sõukand, Whitney, and Polesny, "Socio-Cultural Significance of Yerba Maté," 98.

20. In 2018, Chile imported $12.2 million of yerba primarily from Argentina, whereas in 2013 it had imported only half that amount. Still, its high of $18.8 million of imports in 2015 declined in 2016–18. "Imports of Yerba Mate in Chile from 2013 to 2018," Statista, www.statista .com/statistics/1061455/chile-yerba-mate-import-value/ (accessed Dec. 15, 2021).

21. On regional and class-based distinctions in mate consumption practices, see Martina Cayul and Daniela Pessoa, "El mate en Chile: Entre lo comunitario y la individualización del gusto," *Maguaré* 34, no. 2 (July–Dec. 2020): 85–112; "El mate conquista a los jóvenes chilenos," Yerba Mate Argentina, Dec. 14, 2017, https://yerbamateargentina.org.ar/es/noticias/nuevos -mercados/79146-el-mate-conquista-a-los-jovenes-chilenos.html; and Instituto Nacional de Yerba Mate, "Todo está en el mate" promotional website, www.todoestaenelmate.cl/ (accessed Dec. 16, 2021).

22. Cayul and Pessoa, in "El mate en Chile," describe the consumption of Caá Yari Mate made in Chile, Club Mate produced in Germany, and (Organic) Marley Coffee Yerba Mate made in the United Sates.

23. This became apparent when the Pennsylvanian farmer who sells kombucha at the Easton (PA) Farmers' Market told me in 2017 that he grows in his greenhouse the yerba he adds to the brew.

24. "Paraguay Violated Indigenous Rights, UN Committee Rules in Landmark Decision," UN News, Oct. 13, 2021, https://news.un.org/en/story/2021/10/1102922.

25. According to Hugo Javier Aguinaga, in Paraguay, the reduction in the number of yerba plantations stems from the advance in the monoculture of soy, which has often directly replaced the former as a monocrop. Hugo Javier Aguinaga, "Trayectoria histórica y context actual de la yerba mate en Paraguay: Destino de la producción campesina en el distrito de Dr. Juan Manuel Frutos, Caaguazú" (bachelor thesis, Universidade Federal da Integraçao Latino-Americana Foz do Iguaçu, 2017), 23. On the dynamics of soy in Paraguay

and Argentina, see Craig Heatherton, *The Government of Beans: Regulating Life in the Age of Monocrops* (Durham: Duke University Press, 2020); and Amalia Leguizamón, *Seeds of Power: Environmental Injustice and Genetically Modified Soybeans in Argentina* (Durham: Duke University Press, 2020).

26. María Cecila Gallero, "La yerba mate en el prisma de la historia ambiental, Misiones (Argentina)," in *História ambiental e migrações: Diálogos*, ed. M. Gerhardt, E. S. Nodari, and S. P. Moretto (São Leopoldo: Oikos, 2017), 193–214, esp. 206.

27. Teo Ballvé, "Mate on the Market: Fair Trade and the Gaucho's 'Liquid Vegetable,'" *NACLA Report on the Americas*, Sept.–Oct. 2007, 11–12.

28. Catalina Oquendo B., "Trabajo infantil: El trago amargo del mate, la bebida nacional argentina," BBC Mundo, Argentina, July 12, 2016, www.bbc.com/mundo/noticias -internacional-36644713.

29. Javier Gortari, comp., *De la tierra sin mal al tractorazo: Hacia una economía política de la yerba mate* (Misiones: Editorial Universitaria de Misiones, 2007); Víctor Rau, *Cosechando yerba mate: Estructuras sociales de un mercado laboral agrario en el nordeste argentino* (Buenos Aires: Ciccus, 2012); Daniel Re, *Tareferos: Vida y trabajo en los yerbales* (Posadas, Arg.: Editorial Universitaria, Universidad Nacional de Misiones, 2017); Jennifer Bowles, "Making *Tarefero* Pride: The Collaborative Construction of Portable Photomurals for Farmworker Empowerment in Misiones, Argentina," *Journal of Community Practice*, Sept. 25, 2018, 1–20.

30. Bowles, "Making *Tarefero* Pride," 2.

31. Guido Lautaro Padin, "¿Le molesta al campo hablar de trabajo infantil?," *Revista Inter-Nos*, Aug. 13, 2021, www.revistainternos.com.ar/2021/08/le-molesta-al-campo-hablar-de -trabajo-infantil/.

32. Bowles, "Making *Tarefero* Pride." Bowles did ethnographic fieldwork in Montecarlo in collaboration with rural teacher and organizer Rubén Ortiz, who migrated from Paraguay to Argentina as a child. In 2008, the Argentine national government passed a "Día del Tarefero" to be celebrated on November 9 every year in the city of Concepción de Sierra, Misiones. Cámara de Diputados de la Nación, Regular Sessions, Agenda no. 888.

33. "Presentan un proyecto de ley para certificar la producción de yerba mate sin trabajo infantil," *Revista InterNos*, Oct. 20, 2021, www.revistainternos.com.ar/2021/10/presentan-un -proyecto-de-ley-para-certificar-la-produccion-de-yerba-mate-sin-trabajo-infantil/.

34. See, for example, Brandi Simpson Miller, *Food and Identity in Nineteenth and Twentieth Century Ghana: Food, Fights, and Regionalism* (Cham, Switz.: Springer International, 2022), esp. chap. 7; and Patricia Vega Jiménez, "El Gallo Pinto: Afro-Caribbean Rice and Beans Conquer the Costa Rican National Cuisine," *Food, Culture and Society* 15, no. 2 (2012): 223–40.

35. Gustavo Laborde, *El asado: Origen, historia, ritual* (Montevideo, Uru.: Ediciones de la Banda Oriental, 2013).

36. This conclusion is drawn from my conversations with people across the region and my ethnographic notes. It is also echoed by numerous media stories online (and in print). For example, see Daniela Gutierrez, "Día nacional del mate: Las diferencias entre el argentino y el uruguayo," Clarín.com, Nov. 29, 2018, www.clarin.com/sociedad/dia-nacional-mate -diferencias-argentino-uruguayo_0_yxz3mU3zF.html.

37. Karla Johan Lorenzo, *El libro de yerba mate* (Buenos Aires: Grupo Editorial del Nuevo Extremo, 2013); "Sommelier de Yerba Mate—Nivel 1," Escuela Argentina de Té, www .escueladete.org/curso.php?id=MTE0 (accessed July 14, 2022).

38. For example, yerba brands like Tres Estrellas pitched their product as "tierra adentro." Advertisement, *ABC en color*, May 1, 1979, 47. I thank Bridget Chesterton for sharing this and other contemporary advertisements from Paraguay.

39. See, for example, Raúl Matta, "Gastro-diplomatie: Un soft power," *Essachess* 12, no. 1 (2019): 99–120.

40. In 2003, the "Representative List" was created to "encourage dialogue which respects cultural diversity" and "safeguard[s] such heritage." "Convention for the Safeguarding of Intangible Cultural Heritage," UNESCO, Oct. 17, 2013, https://ich.unesco.org/en/convention. For an example of how this process played out in Peru, see Raúl Matta, "Food Incursions into Global Heritage: Peruvian Cuisine's Slippery Road to UNESCO," *Social Anthropology* 24, no. 3 (Aug. 2016): 338–52.

41. According to Olveira Ramos, France makes some twenty billion euros per year on products to which they have exclusive naming rights, like champagne. Armando Olveira Ramos, "La guerra del dulce de leche: Como en el siglo XIX, bombas y cañones agitaron nuevamente las aguas bravas del Río de la Plata," *Ábaco* 2, no. 37/38 (2003): 141.

42. UNESCO apparently did not approve this request. Olveira Ramos, 137–47.

43. Ruben Alvarenga, *Asunción Gourmet* (blog), Aug. 6, 2010, https://asunciongourmet.blogspot.com/2010/08/terere-sera-patrimonio-de-mato-grosso.html.

44. "Día Nacional del tereré: Jatererepy en modo COVID-19," Paraguayan Ministry of Public Health Press Release, Feb. 27, 2021, www.mspbs.gov.py/portal/22698/dia-nacional-del-terere-jatererepy-en-modo-covid-19.html.

45. On Paraguayan political memory and national identity formation, see Bridget María Chesterton, *The Grandchildren of Solano López: Frontier and Nation in Paraguay, 1904–1936* (Albuquerque: University of New Mexico Press, 2013).

46. "Ley Nº 4261 DECLARA PATRIMONIO CULTURAL Y BEBIDA NACIONAL DEL PARAGUAY AL TERERE," Jan. 2011, available at Biblioteca y Archivo Central del Congreso Nacional, www.bacn.gov.py/leyes-paraguayas/2899/ley-n-4261-declara-patrimonio-cultural-y-bebida-nacional-del-paraguay-al-terere.

47. Decree 15.528 declared October 11 "Yerba Mate Day" in 1997 at the request of the Ministerio de Agricultura y Ganadería, the Municipalidad de Bella Vista (Itapúa), and the Centro Yerbatero de Paraguay. "Día de la Yerba Mate: Producción y tradición paraguayas pujantes que transcienden las fronteras," abc.com.py, Oct. 11, 2021, www.abc.com.py/empresariales/2021/10/11/dia-de-la-yerba-mate-produccion-y-tradicion-paraguayas-pujantes-que-trascienden-las-fronteras/.

48. Law 26.871, July 30, 2013, available at Argentina Presidencia, www.boletinoficial.gov.ar/. The law also stated that this logo should be present in official social, cultural, or sporting events.

49. Ernesto Azarkevich, "La yerba mate, cada vez más argentina y con sello propio," Clarín.com, Mar. 16, 2016, www.clarin.com/sociedad/yerba-mate-argentina-sello-propio_o_NJIkoYZax.html.

50. Daniela Gutierrez, "30 de noviembre: Día nacional del mate: Las diferencias entre el argentino y el uruguayo," Clarín.com, Nov. 29, 2018, www.clarin.com/sociedad/dia-nacional-mate-diferencias-argentino-uruguayo_o_yxz3mU3zF.html.

51. "El mate uruguayo," viajeauruguay.com, www.viajeauruguay.com/gastronomia/el-mate-uruguayo.php (accessed Aug. 19, 2022).

52. "La yerba mate fue declarada Patrimonio Cultural del Mercosur," Economis.com.ar, Nov. 3, 2018, https://economis.com.ar/la-yerba-mate-fue-declarada-patrimonio-cultural -del-mercosur/.

53. "Practices and Traditional Knowledge of Terere in the Culture of Pohã Ñana, Guaraní Ancestral Drink in Paraguay," UNESCO, https://ich.unesco.org/en/RL/practices-and -traditional-knowledge-of-terere-in-the-culture-of-poh-ana-guaran-ancestral-drink-in -paraguay-01603 (accessed Dec. 7, 2021).

54. "Yerba Mate: Cultural Landscape," UNESCO, https://whc.unesco.org/en /tentativelists/6612/(accessed June 2, 2022).

55. Arrabal, "Una sola ronda."

56. Indeed, when I tell people in the United States about my research, many respond, "Oh, yerba mate, that's from Argentina, right?"

57. Ana Fochesatto, "Yerba Mate: National Project to Emerging Superfood," (master's thesis, Illinois State University, 2019), 5.

58. Doris Schroeder et al., "The Rooibos Benefit Sharing Agreement—Breaking New Ground with Respect, Honesty, Fairness, and Care," *Camb Q Healthcare Ethics* 29, no. 2 (Nov. 5, 2019): 285–301.

59. On the Guaraní and global history of *ka'a he'e* and how Paraguayan politicians and businessmen sought to "unsuccessfully . . . (re)claim stevia as their own," see Bridget María Chesterton and Timothy Yang, "The Global Origins of a 'Paraguayan' Sweetener: Ka'a He'e and Stevia in the Twentieth Century," *Journal of World History* 27, no. 2 (June 2016): 255–79. On the battle against Coca-Cola, see Eric J. Wallace, "The Indigenous Tribes Fighting to Reclaim Stevia from Coca-Cola," Gastro Obscura, July 12, 2019, www.atlasobscura.com /articles/where-is-stevia-from.

60. Rodrigo Campos and Belen Liotti, "In Hangover of World Cup Fiesta, Argentina's Economic Reality Bites," Reuters, Dec. 21, 2022. https://www.reuters.com/world/americas /hangover-world-cup-fiesta-argentinas-economic-reality-bites-2022-12-21/.

61. For example, in the late 1990s, a group of cultural studies scholars explained that "to drink mate is to engage in the most democratic of Argentine traditions, one that blurs all socioeconomic distinctions and ethnic groups." Uruguayan scholar Daniel Vidart expressed, "Mate, in its way, makes the social classes equal because it belongs to everyone." David William Foster, Melissa Fitch Lockhart, and Darrell B. Lockhart, *Culture and Customs of Argentina* (Westport, CT: Greenwood Press, 1998), 41; Daniel Vidart, "Filosofía del mate amargo," *Bitacora* (blog), www.bitacora.com.uy/auc.aspx?4246 (accessed May 5, 2021).

62. María Julia Rossi, comment in response to my presentation at virtual RITHAL conference, Mar. 28, 2022.

63. Pau Navajas shared with me in 2015 that in a recent Argentine marketing study, consumers imagined only Taraguï as having a male "personality," with the rest of the brands conceived of as female. This suggests the continuity of the ideological association of yerba with a feminized (and often Indigenous) servility, emphasized in visual culture since the late nineteenth century.

64. Vidart, "Filosofía del mate armago."

INDEX

advertising, 151, 160, 169, 259n5; and Aguila, 152; and Casa do Matte, 142–43; and Flor de Lis, 153–54, 264n87; La Hoja, 154–55, 162; and La Industrial Paraguaya, 152; and Las Marías, 188; and MacKinnon & Coelho, 133, 135, 155, 159; and Ñanduty, 156–57; in newspapers, 115, 151–52, 263n82; and Nobleza Gaucha, 162–64; on radio, 151; and Salus, 134–35, 136, 157–58, 164; on television, 172, 179, 188–89, 193; and women, 159–60, 162, 164; and Yerba Asunción, 160–61. *See also* magazines

Afro-Argentines, 125–26

Afro-Uruguayans, 62, 125

Aguila, 152, 162

alcohol, 34, 36. *See also* wine

Allain, Paul, 141

Allende, Salvador, 184

Alonso, Carlos, 176

Alto Paraná, 93, 160

Alvarenga, Ruben, 210–11

anarchists, 93, 177

Andes, 17, 24, 30–31, 46, 52, 56, 149, 203

Apa River, 30

apartador (separator), 14, 190, 226n4

Archivo General de la Nación (Argentina), 1, 106–7, 218, 251n16

Areco, Jorge Pacheco, 183

Arequipa, 36

Argentina, 1, 103, 213; and Afro-Argentines, 125; and artists, 176–77; and Brazil, 137–41, 146– 47, 150–52, 164–65, 167; and capital city, 10, 36, 172, 174, 189; and china figure, 118, 135, 209; and consumption of yerba, 106, 111, 136–37, 145, 166, 171, 192, 197–98; and COVID-19, 201; and declining demand for yerba, 174–75, 179; and elites, 30, 108, 110–11, 131; and emergence of republic, 81; and European immigrants, 91, 108, 114–17, 131, 136; and European travelers, 59, 81, 98, 173; and gaucho figure, 44, 118, 131, 181; and immigrants from Middle East, 204; and inflation, 195; and "intangible heritage," 210; and Jews, 115; and labor exploitation, 149–50, 207; and leftists, 173, 186–87; and *mateadas*, 193; and mate as symbol of national identity, 195, 197–98; and military dictatorship, 172; Ministry of Agriculture, 111, 166, 212; Ministry of Education, 149; Ministry of Public Works, 190; and Misiones, 48, 82, 88, 104, 136, 140, 167, 206; and modernization, 123, 126, 132, 169, 178; and National Academy of Art, 177; and National Institute of Nutrition, 148, 152; and nationalism, 160, 162, 210; and

in colonial South America, 40; and Rio de Janeiro, 40, 54; and sommeliers, 209; and Uruguayans, 193; and young people, 169

Cold War, 172, 182

colonialism, 11, 28, 31, 33, 37, 41–42, 58, 207, 214. *See also* Portugal; Spain

Colorado Party, 48, 95

Comisión Reguladora de la Producción y Comercio de la Yerba Mate (CRYM, Regulatory Commission of Yerba Mate Production and Commerce), 147–49, 152, 166, 196

commodity chain, 4–5, 75, 153, 197, 214

Communist Party, 149, 175, 184

Concepción, 18, 25, 101

conquistadors, 14, 18–20, 33, 228n21

copper, 13–14, 53, 69

Córdoba (province), 111, 113, 120, 187, 190

corn, 85, 87, 97, 118, 124, 227n9, 232n100. *See also* maize

Corradi, Juan, 188

Corrado, Alberto J., 111, 113

Corrientes, 16, 23, 25–26, 49, 63, 194, 233n112, 260n23; and indentured laborers, 75; and native yerba forests, 65; and "Yerba Mate Argentina," 212; and yerba mills, 91, 152–53

Costa, Lysimaco F. da, 142

costumbristas, 46, 235n11

COVID-19, 200–202, 204, 220

creoles, 9, 28, 31, 33, 47, 98, 111

criollos/as, 110; and colonial rule, 33; definition of, 31; and depictions of women, 31–33, 74, 135; and masculinity, 107; and mate drinkers, 41, 98, 179; and military dictatorship in Argentina, 188; and race, 157; and xenophobia/nativism, 72, 114, 116; and yerba brands, 135, 155, 157, 159–60, 162, 164

Cruz Cano y Olmedilla, Juan de la, 31–32

Cruz de Malta, 204

Cuba, 128, 153, 182

Curitiba, 50, 144, 152; and Casa do Matte café, 142–43

Curitiba Yerba Trust, 146–47

Cuzco, 26, 36, 42

daily life, 15, 36, 41, 114, 169, 178, 187, 214; and COVID-19, 202; and dictatorship, 192; history of, 6; and racial hierarchies, 47, 74–75; and tereré, 2; and thermoses, 172; travelers' and artists' depictions of, 33, 85, 96; and yerba consumption in Syria, 205

Daumas, Ernesto, 146

de la Rúa, Fernando, 198

de la Torre, Lisandro, 146, 261n53

del Carril, Hugo, 150

Demersay, Alfred, 82–83

Denis, León, 6

Descalzi, Cayetano, 67

de Ulloa, Antonio, 27–28

d'Hastrel, Adolphe, 73–74, 83–85, 235n11

dictatorships, 173, 178, 184–86, 188–89, 191–94, 196, 268n10, 271n70

Dirty War, 187

Dobrizhoffer, Martin, 20–21

domesticity, 117, 129, 162, 166. *See also* domestic work/labor; men; sexuality; women

domestic work/labor, 38, 57, 85. *See also* servants

Doña Petrona, 174

Druze, 204

Duhalde, Eduardo, 198

dulce de leche, 210

Dupuy, José María, 69

Ecuador, 10, 46, 49, 205

elites/upper classes, 36, 49, 61, 92, 107–8, 167, 170, 190; and artists/artwork, 34, 41–42, 51, 57–58, 67, 69–70, 75; in Buenos Aires, 47, 104, 108–9, 111, 120, 130; in Chile, 51, 54; and coffee, 4, 30, 40; colonial, 28, 57, 191; as creole, 9; as criollo, 41, 72; and entrepreneurs, 7; and gaucho figure, 117, 120, 131; and hygiene, 110; and immigrants, 113–15, 117; and leisure, 41; and Paraguayan yerba, 92; and Punta del Este, 194; and race, 9, 57, 59, 67, 70, 72, 74–75, 130; rural, 175; and servants, 42, 57, 60, 95; urban, 15, 51, 104, 107–9, 131, 189; Uruguayan, 116, 131; and Viceroyalty of Peru, 14, 30–31, 34,

elites/upper classes (*continued*)
40–41, 47; and Viceroyalty of Río de la
Plata, 51; and War of the Triple Alliance,
88; as White, 28, 57, 67, 70, 75; women,
33, 41, 47, 51, 57, 59, 70; and yerba mate,
4; and yerba quality, 30, 40, 49, 109, 111
El País, 193
encomenderos, 20
Entre Ríos, 62, 109, 115, 128, 233n112
erva mate. *See* yerba mate
Escudero, Pedro, 148–49
Espínola, Francisco "Paco," 193
Estado Oriental de Uruguay, 48, 235n10. *See
also* Uruguay
eugenics, 110, 137, 155
everyday life. *See* daily life

Federalist Party/Federalists, 45, 48, 58–59,
67–69, 74, 86
Fernando VII, 43
Fiesta Nacional de la Yerba Mate, 149
Flor de Lis, 152–55, 160
folklore, 20, 191
Fontana Brothers, 140
food history, 208, 218–19
foodways, 208
Fossey, Pierre, 181
France, 26, 29, 73, 92, 110, 115, 152, 165; and
Aimé Bonpland, 50; and costumbristas,
46; and "last Charrúas," 66; and Charles
Henri Pellegrini, 43; and Auguste de
Saint-Hilaire, 50
Francia, José Gaspar Rodríguez de, 48,
63–65, 75, 80
Francis (pope), 203
Frexias, Urquijo & Cía, 15
Frézier, Amédée François, 12–15, 26–27
Friedrich, Adolfo, 174, 266n137

Galeano, Eduardo, 5, 184–85, 224n11
Galli, Franco & Cía, 123, 126. *See also*
postcards
Gálvez, Manuel, 110
Garavaglia, Juan Carlos, 3, 7, 20, 26, 49
gastrodiplomacy, 210
The Gaucho of Buenos Aires, 72

gaucho figure, 43, 53, 105, 123–28, 131–32; on
banknotes, 120; and Brazil, 132, 165–67,
200, 250n8; and china figure, 118, 126,
128, 132, 135; and gender and sexuality,
109, 117–18, 124–26, 130–31, 135; as iconic
mate drinker, 9, 45, 104, 108, 117–18,
120, 131, 190–91, 209; and immigration,
118, 120, 131; as Jewish, 115; and *Martín
Fierro*, 155, 191; and Carlos Morel, 69;
and National Liberation Movement–
Tupamaros, 183; as national symbol,
44, 126, 131; and Nuevo Realismo (New
Realism), 175–76; and Paraguay, 80,
99; and postcards, 80, 99, 123–30; and
romanticized rural life, 120–21, 126; and
Juan Manuel de Rosas, 45, 67, 117; and
Uruguay, 124, 181; and yerba brands,
153–55, 162
gauchos: and bombilla, 20; declining
numbers of, 117; and European
travelers, 73–74; and Rural Code, 117
Gay, Claudio, 56
gender, 9, 155, 186, 219; and Argentine
postcards, 125, 128; and division of
labor, 85, 123; and gaucho figure, 109;
hierarchies of, 47, 75, 214–15; and
mate service/servers, 69, 74, 128; and
Paraguay, 88, 99; and race, 75, 214–15;
in United States, 128; and War of the
Triple Alliance, 88. *See also* men;
women
Germany, 114–15, 205, 256n81
Gillespie, Alexander, 52
globalization, 5, 214
Gloria, 150
Glusberg, Samuel, 115
González, Aurelio, 184–85, 270n57
gourds, 1–2, 14, 19, 40, 81, 102, 105, 111;
and Brazil, 197; and elites, 190; and
International Mate Company, 164; and
Uruguay, 199
Graham, Maria, 54–55, 237n46
Great Britain, 5, 48, 91, 224n10
Greater Buenos Aires, 171, 174
Grela, Juan, 175
Gruter, 101–2. *See also* postcards

Movimiento Agrario de Misiones (MAM, Agrarian Movement of Misiones), 187, 196

Movimiento Promoteo (Promise Movement), 96

Mujica, José, 193

Museo de Bellas Artes, 71, 190

Museo de Motivos Argentinos José Hernández, 191

Museo Fernández Blanco, 190

Ñanduty, 155–57, 159

National Institute of Mate (Brazil), 147, 167

National Institute of Nutrition (Argentina), 148, 152

nationalism, 8, 108, 137, 151, 188, 214

National Liberation Movement– Tupamaros, 183, 193

National Mate Day (Argentina), 202, 212

Nativa, 199

Navajas, Pau, 7, 17, 20, 50, 64, 218

neoliberalism, 178, 186, 189, 195–96, 198, 206, 213

New Spain, 31

newspapers, 115, 151–52, 263n82; *El País*, 193; *La Nación*, 138, 177, 179, 189–90; *La Razón*, 152

Nobleza Gaucha, 162–64

Nuevo Realismo, 175–76

nutrition, 133, 136, 148, 152, 166, 203

Obama, Barack, 203

Oberá, 149; and Movimiento Agrario de Misiones, 187, 196. *See also* labor activists

Oberti, Federico, 20

Onetti, Juan Carlos, 193

Ongañía, Juan Carlos, 178

O Paraná (newspaper), 142

Operation Condor, 172, 187

Oppenheim, Victor, 173

Organization of American States, 182

Otero, María Julia, 159

Page, Thomas Jefferson, 62, 80–81

Palestine, 204

Pallière, Jean León, 70

Pampas (people), 65

Pampas (region), 53, 56, 73, 118, 126

Paraguay, 2, 33–37, 130–31, 135, 209–10, 212, 218; and Argentina, 86, 88, 138–39, 148, 152–54, 160, 167, 197; and artwork/ artists, 12–14, 26–27, 64–65, 74, 83–85; and Asunción, 2, 96, 194, 218; and Brazil, 49–50, 79, 85–86, 88, 135, 137, 165; and Chaco War, 97, 174, 211; and Chile, 112; and COVID-19, 201; and European immigration, 108; and foreign travelers, 27, 54, 63, 80, 95–96, 98, 102, 130, 173; and José Gaspar Rodríguez de Francia, 48–49, 63–65, 75; and Guaraní, 65, 213; and *Ilex paraguariensis*, 50–51, 82, 206; and indentured laborers, 75; and independence, 47; and Jesuits, 29, 35, 37, 50; and La Industrial Paraguaya (LIPSA), 90–91, 93–94, 152–53; and Carlos Antonio López, 75; and mate as "national patrimony," 200, 210–11; and MERCOSUR, 212–13; and military dictatorship, 172; and national identity, 130, 174, 200, 211; and place of origin of ka'a, 40; and postcards, 99–103; and privatization of yerba industry, 80, 90–92, 103–4; and race, 27, 95; and Río de la Plata estuary, 10; and soy, 206; and Spanish crown, 24, 48; and tereré, 97–98, 174, 195, 200, 211; and Treaty of the Triple Alliance, 86; and Viceroyalty of the Río de la Plata, 48–49; and War of the Triple Alliance, 4, 48, 77–80, 86–87, 92, 97–98, 103, 130, 132, 211; and women, 80, 85–86, 88, 96, 99, 104, 132; and yerba brands/companies, 91, 136, 151; and yerba consumption, 22, 80, 99, 103, 172–73; and yerba exportation, 4, 37, 75, 103, 137, 165, 205–6; and yerba production, 3, 10, 82, 87–91, 99, 103, 132, 137, 147, 205–6; and yerbales, 75, 80, 82, 85, 88, 90, 92–96, 100, 154; yerba quality/perceptions of, 82, 92, 147, 151–54, 160, 164; and yerba workers, 21, 65, 75, 92–94, 103, 166

Paraguayan National Archive, 213

Paraguayan War. *See* War of the Triple Alliance

and yerba mate production, 46. *See also* Brazil

Southern Cone, 5, 172, 210

Spain, 28, 51, 72, 80, 88, 175; and chocolate, 44; and expatriates, 205; and immigration to Argentina, 114; and independence, 42–43, 46–47, 57, 60, 135, 209; and New Spain, 31; and Old Spain, 38

Spanish America, 18, 29, 39–40, 44, 113

Stephens, Henry, 102, 130

stevia, 213–14

strikes, 34, 169, 178, 183–84, 186

Sueño para Misiones, 207

sugar, 13–14, 27–28, 54, 67, 113, 138, 205, 208; and elites, 49, 51; histories of, 5; and Indigenous laborers, 20; and labor exploitation, 5, 75, 183; as luxury, 35, 40; and mate cocido, 2; and strikers, 186; and War of the Triple Alliance, 87

superfoods, 203–4

Switzerland, 55, 91, 184

Syria, 3, 204–5, 223n3

Szychowski, Juan, 141

tango, 72, 189

Taquini, Graciela, 191

Taragüi, 188–89, 283n63

tareferos, 197, 206–7

tariffs, 140–41, 146–47

taxes, 24, 30, 37, 75, 142, 147

tea, 2–3, 23, 50, 73, 82, 103, 131, 165; access to, 38, 52, 55; in Chile, 112–13; and colonialism, 203; comparisons of to yerba, 14–15, 34–35, 54–55, 138, 195; competition of, with yerba, 169, 178; consumption of, 179, 198; as cosmopolitan or "civilized," 104, 108, 110; and elites, 4; as global hot drink, 3; histories of, 5; and immigrants to Argentina, 114–16; and labor exploitation, 75; price of, 113, 116, 214; and schoolchildren in Argentina, 149; shift from mate to, 108, 110–11, 130, 193; sommeliers, 205; and *té Jesuita* (Jesuit tea), 26; and working poor, 113

television, 172, 179, 188–89, 193

tereré, 2, 4, 8, 96, 208; across region, 200; and COVID-19, 201–2; and "intangible heritage," 203, 210, 213; origin and history of, 97–98, 211; and Paraguayan national identity, 174, 195, 200, 211; persistence of, 172; and tourists/tourism, 195; and *yuyos* (wild medicinal herbs), 2, 172, 218

terroir, 153, 210

tertulia, 34–35, 55–56, 58–59, 160

textiles, 24, 184–85

theobromine, 4

thermoses, 1–2, 174, 189, 200; and Argentines, 179, 193–95, 199–200; and artists in Argentina, 176; and artists in Uruguay, 181; and restoration of democracy in Argentina and Uruguay, 172; and Uruguayans, 171, 180, 184, 193, 199–200

Tierra del Fuego, 70

Titrayju, 196–97, 206

tobacco, 35–36, 54; and Europeans, 23; and José Gaspar Rodríguez de Francia, 48–49, 63; and Indigenous laborers, 20–21; and Jesuit missions, 28; as offered by colonial authorities, 28; and Paraguayans, 96; spiritual mythology and purpose of, 23; and terroir, 153; and War of the Triple Alliance, 87; and women, 87

Topolansky, Lucía, 193

Torres, Diego de, 22

trade, 41, 137, 146, 214; and Britain, 48; and Buenos Aires, 36; and France, 13; and Guaraní, 18, 21; and Jesuits, 24, 29–30; and ka'a, 18; and MERCOSUR, 212; and Paraguay, 49, 65, 75, 82, 87, 92; slave, 60, 238–39n73; and Spanish, 21; and wars of independence, 49, 55; of yerba, 8, 10, 23, 25, 29–30, 37, 112, 171

travelers, 37, 46, 63, 65, 81, 97, 109, 177; as artists, 15, 30, 33; as mate drinkers, 3, 51, 53–55, 73, 108, 195; as women, 54–55; as writers, 8, 30, 35, 38, 41, 96, 113, 173

travel guides, 195, 198

Treaty of the Triple Alliance, 86

Tucumán, 22, 111, 122, 126

UNESCO, 210, 213
Unitarian Party, 46, 67–68
United Nations, 213
United Provinces of the River Plate, 48
United States, 95–96, 128, 195; and
    advertising industry, 151; and bottled
    yerba drinks, 3, 203, 205; and Brazil,
    146; and Cold War, 172, 182; and
    "counterinsurgency" efforts, 172; and
    Great Depression, 146; immigration to,
    114; and yerba mate, 3, 138, 164–65, 200,
    204, 213
University of Buenos Aires, 159
urban dwellers, 108, 112, 136, 144, 155; in
    Argentina, 125–26, 167, 169, 173–75, 189,
    198–99; in Chile, 113, 205; and elites, 15,
    51, 104, 107, 131, 189; in Uruguay, 181
Urquiza, General Justo José, 62–63, 118
Uruguay, 2, 37, 52, 65–68, 85, 169, 171,
    218; and Afro-Uruguayans, 125; and
    Argentina, 109, 155, 157, 210; and
    Brazilian yerba, 150–51, 165, 189, 205–6;
    and china figure, 209; and consumption
    of yerba, 113; and COVID-19, 201, 202;
    and democratic restoration, 192; and
    Estado Oriental de Uruguay, 48, 81,
    235n10; and European immigrants,
    108, 114–17; formation of, 48; and
    gastrodiplomacy, 210, 212; and gaucho
    figure, 44; and Eduardo Haedo, 182–83;
    and mate as rural, 104, 106, 124, 173, 181,
    105; and mate as symbol of national
    identity, 197, 212; and mate as symbol
    of protest, 185–85; and MERCOSUR,
    212–13; and military dictatorship, 172,
    184–85, 187; and Montevideo, 10; and
    neoliberalism, 189; and Organization
    of American States, 182; and postcards,
    123–25, 129; and public mate drinking,
    172, 180, 193, 199; and Punta del Este,
    182, 194; and Río de la Plata estuary, 10;
    and soccer, 155, 157; and strikes, 183–84;
    as "Switzerland of South America," 184;
    and thermoses, 172, 183, 189, 193, 199;
    travelers' accounts of, 33, 59, 81, 95, 130;
    and Treaty of the Triple Alliance, 86;
    and Tupamaros, 193; and visual culture,

109, 131; and War of the Triple Alliance,
    77, 79; and yerba brands/companies, 155
Uruguay River, 50

Valle de Guasco, 56
Valparaíso, 36, 54
Vancouver, George, 36
Varela, Alfredo, 149–50
Vargas, Getúlio, 146–47, 165–66
Viale, Pedro Blanes, 62
Viceroyalty of Peru, 10, 14–15, 22, 34–35,
    40, 49, 209; and criollas, 31, 33; and elite
    women, 33, 41, 47
Viceroyalty of the Río de la Plata, 15, 36–39,
    44, 46–48, 53, 209
Vidal, Emeric E., 51–52, 62
Vidart, Daniel, 116, 185, 215
Viero, Theodorum, 33
Villa Concepción, 101
Villanueva, Amaro, 20, 175–77, 179, 191
visual culture, 47, 80, 83, 108, 128, 131–32,
    137, 155, 172. *See also* advertising; artists;
    photographs/photography; postcards
vitamins, 148–49, 159, 204

Walsh, Rodolfo, 174
Warnes, Ricardo, 177
War of the Triple Alliance, 77, 79, 86, 89, 94,
    117, 135; and mate, 98–99; and Misiones,
    48; and political instability in Paraguay,
    88; and tereré, 97, 211
wars of independence, 7, 42, 44, 48, 55, 109
Washburn, Charles Ames, 79, 92, 95, 98
wheat, 19, 120, 136, 138, 146–47, 166
White elites, 67, 70
Whiteness, 95, 136, 141, 157
White women, 45, 47, 57, 60, 70, 75, 106
Wilde, José Antonio, 59, 109–11
wine, 19–20, 27, 35, 74, 209, 211
women, 2, 13–15, 19, 188, 194, 214, 219; in
    artwork, 13–14, 38, 41, 56–59, 69–70,
    83, 85, 120, 175, 177; and china figure,
    117, 124; as consumers, 137, 151, 164; as
    criollas, 31, 41; as elites, 14, 31, 33, 41, 47,
    57, 59, 70, 109; and foreign visitors, 41,
    55, 59; and gaucho figure, 69, 109, 116–17,
    120; Guaraní, 85; and immigrants,

yerba mate (*continued*)
industry, 92, 218; as intangible heritage, 213; intimacy of, 3, 214; and Jesuits, 29; and MERCOSUR, 212; and Millers Association, 194; and national institutes, 147–48, 196, 201, 205, 212; and Paraguay, 75, 80, 87, 95, 130, 147, 165, 211, 213; and patrimonial rights to, 210–11; plantations, 91, 154; and poverty, 173–75; production, 7, 37, 145, 207; recent popularity of, 203–4; and regionalism, 7; and Río de la Plata region, 10; as ritual, 6–7, 42; and schools, 149; sommeliers, 209; as South American, 3, 5, 9, 37, 205, 214–15; as stimulant, 149; as symbol of autonomy, 135; and Syria, 205; and taxes, 75; and tea, 103, 138; Tea Company, 164; trade, 29; transport, 37; and Uruguay, 212; and visual culture, 7–8, 64, 137, 172; and War of the Triple Alliance, 98. *See also* mate; yerba; yerbales

Yerba Mate Millers Association, 194

Yerba Mate Tea Company, 164

youth, 2, 169–70, 172, 174, 178–79, 187, 192, 197–99

Ypané River, 30

yuyos (wild medicinal herbs), 2, 218

Zenteno, General José Ignacio, 55